The Church
in Colonial
Latin America

Jaguar Books on Latin America

Series Editors

WILLIAM H. BEEZLEY, Professor of History, University of Arizona
COLIN M. MACLACHLAN, John Christy Barr Distinguished Professor of History, Tulane University

Volumes Published

John E. Kicza, ed., *The Indian in Latin American History: Resistance, Resilience, and Acculturation* (1993; rev. ed., 2000).
Cloth ISBN 0-8420-2822-6 Paper ISBN 0-8420-2823-4

Susan E. Place, ed., *Tropical Rainforests: Latin American Nature and Society in Transition* (1993). Cloth ISBN 0-8420-2423-9
Paper ISBN 0-8420-2427-1

Paul W. Drake, ed., *Money Doctors, Foreign Debts, and Economic Reforms in Latin America from the 1890s to the Present* (1994).
Cloth ISBN 0-8420-2434-4 Paper ISBN 0-8420-2435-2

John A. Britton, ed., *Molding the Hearts and Minds: Education, Communications, and Social Change in Latin America* (1994).
Cloth ISBN 0-8420-2489-1 Paper ISBN 0-8420-2490-5

David J. Weber and Jane M. Rausch, eds., *Where Cultures Meet: Frontiers in Latin American History* (1994). Cloth ISBN 0-8420-2477-8
Paper ISBN 0-8420-2478-6

Gertrude M. Yeager, ed., *Confronting Change, Challenging Tradition: Women in Latin American History* (1994). Cloth ISBN 0-8420-2479-4
Paper ISBN 0-8420-2480-8

Linda Alexander Rodríguez, ed., *Rank and Privilege: The Military and Society in Latin America* (1994). Cloth ISBN 0-8420-2432-8
Paper ISBN 0-8420-2433-6

Darién J. Davis, ed., *Slavery and Beyond: The African Impact on Latin America and the Caribbean* (1995). Cloth ISBN 0-8420-2484-0
Paper ISBN 0-8420-2485-9

Gilbert M. Joseph and Mark D. Szuchman, eds., *I Saw a City Invincible: Urban Portraits of Latin America* (1996). Cloth ISBN 0-8420-2495-6
Paper ISBN 0-8420-2496-4

Roderic Ai Camp, ed., *Democracy in Latin America: Patterns and Cycles* (1996). Cloth ISBN 0-8420-2512-X   Paper ISBN 0-8420-2513-8

Oscar J. Martínez, ed., *U.S.-Mexico Borderlands: Historical and Contemporary Perspectives* (1996). Cloth ISBN 0-8420-2446-8 Paper ISBN 0-8420-2447-6

William O. Walker III, ed., *Drugs in the Western Hemisphere: An Odyssey of Cultures in Conflict* (1996). Cloth ISBN 0-8420-2422-0 Paper ISBN 0-8420-2426-3

Richard R. Cole, ed., *Communication in Latin America: Journalism, Mass Media, and Society* (1996). Cloth ISBN 0-8420-2558-8 Paper ISBN 0-8420-2559-6

David G. Gutiérrez, ed., *Between Two Worlds: Mexican Immigrants in the United States* (1996). Cloth ISBN 0-8420-2473-5 Paper ISBN 0-8420-2474-3

Lynne Phillips, ed., *The Third Wave of Modernization in Latin America: Cultural Perspectives on Neoliberalism* (1998). Cloth ISBN 0-8420-2606-1   Paper ISBN 0-8420-2608-8

Daniel Castro, ed., *Revolution and Revolutionaries: Guerrilla Movements in Latin America* (1999). Cloth ISBN 0-8420-2625-8 Paper ISBN 0-8420-2626-6

Virginia Garrard-Burnett, ed., *On Earth as It Is in Heaven: Religion in Modern Latin America* (2000). Cloth ISBN 0-8420-2584-7 Paper ISBN 0-8420-2585-5

Carlos A. Aguirre and Robert Buffington, eds., *Reconstructing Criminality in Latin America* (2000). Cloth ISBN 0-8420-2620-7 Paper ISBN 0-8420-2621-5

Christon I. Archer, ed., *The Wars of Independence in Spanish America* (2000). Cloth ISBN 0-8420-2468-9   Paper ISBN 0-8420-2469-7

John F. Schwaller, ed., *The Church in Colonial Latin America* (2000). Cloth ISBN 0-8420-2703-3   Paper ISBN 0-8420-2704-1

Ingrid E. Fey and Karen Racine, eds., *Strange Pilgrimages: Exile, Travel, and National Identity in Latin America, 1800–1990s* (2000). Cloth ISBN 0-8420-2693-2   Paper ISBN 0-8420-2694-0

The Church
in Colonial
Latin America

John F. Schwaller
Editor

Jaguar Books on Latin America
Number 21

A Scholarly Resources Inc. Imprint
Wilmington, Delaware

Scholarly Resources Inc.
104 Greenhill Avenue
Wilmington, DE 19805-1897
www.scholarly.com

Library of Congress Cataloging-in-Publication Data

The church in colonial Latin America / John F. Schwaller, editor.
   p. cm. — (Jaguar books on Latin America ; no. 21)
   Includes bibliographical references.
   ISBN 0-8420-2703-3 (cloth : alk. paper) — ISBN 0-8420-2704-1
(paper : alk. paper)
   1. Catholic Church—Latin America—History—16th century.
2. Latin America—Church history—16th century. 3. Catholic
Church—Latin America—History—17th century. 4. Latin America
—Church history—17th century. 5. Catholic Church—Latin
America—History—18th century. 6. Latin America—Church history
—18th century. I. Schwaller, John Frederick. II. Series.
BX1426.2.C487 2000
282'.8'0903—dc21   99-057986

About the Editor

John F. Schwaller, associate provost and vice president for academic affairs and professor of history at the University of Montana, also serves as director of the Academy of American Franciscan History. His publications include several books dealing with the history of the Catholic Church in colonial Mexico, works on Nahuatl, the Aztec language, and numerous articles on both colonial history and Nahuatl manuscripts. He sits on several editorial boards, including that of *The Americas*. Professor Schwaller's current long-term research project is a biography of don Luis de Velasco, who served twice as viceroy of Mexico and once as viceroy of Peru, ending his career as president of the Council of the Indies.

Contents

Introduction

John F. Schwaller

One of the more unique features of the Spanish colonization of the New World was the inclusion of Catholic clergy both in the conquering expeditions and in the wave of settlers that followed the pacification. Additionally, the Church came to be one of the two most central institutions in the colonial world, second only to the Crown itself.[1] The Church played a crucial role in the establishment of Spanish culture in the Americas. Its institutions were central to the life cycle of most persons and influenced even the most mundane aspects of daily culture. Moreover, the institutions established in the colonial period would continue to play a decisive role in the nations of Latin America upon Independence. Consequently, in order to understand the historical development of Latin America in the colonial period as well as trends in the modern era, it is of central importance to understand the role of the Catholic Church.

Writing earlier in this century, the French historian, Robert Ricard, characterized clerical participation in the discovery and settlement of the New World as "the spiritual conquest."[2] Although the participation of the clergy cannot be denied, whether their actions truly constituted a spiritual conquest is open to some discussion. In fact, recent investigation, such as that of Sarah Cline in Chapter 4, indicates that the evangelization of the native peoples of the New World was neither as rapid nor as thorough as Ricard had imagined. The spiritual conquest might well be considered a spiritual accommodation.

To better understand the dynamics of the Christian evangelization of the New World by the Spanish missionaries, we need to consider the nature of the Church hierarchy and divisions within the Catholic clergy in the early sixteenth century. Although it seemed to be a monolithic institution, the Catholic Church actually consisted of several different, and sometimes antagonistic, factions. The central division of the Church related to the clergy itself. Those priests, friars, and monks who served in the forefront of the American evangelization—Franciscans, Dominicans, Augustinians, Mercedarians, and Jesuits—took special vows above and beyond those of the priesthood and pledged to live according to a special rule of life, called a *regula* in Latin. As a result, members of the religious orders were known as the "regular" clergy. The pattern in Europe was that regular clerics usually lived in monasteries and friaries, isolated from the world, although they might engage in preaching, teaching, or other missionary activity outside the cloister. The other major faction within the clergy was the secular clerics. These priests, neither members of religious orders nor cloistered, instead lived out in the world and served as parish priests under the supervision of a local bishop or archbishop. The term "secular" derives from the Latin word *saeculum,* meaning "the world."

The hierarchical organization of the two groups of clergy also differed from one another. As noted, the secular clergy served under the direction of the local bishop or archbishop. The regular clergy participated in the life of a religious order and were governed on a local level by a prior or abbot, within the local monastery or friary. The monasteries were divided into geographical regions known as provinces, over which a "provincial" ruled. The provinces, in turn, reported to authorities in Rome designated as "generals." Each of these officials, known collectively as prelates, were elected by their constituencies: friars elected their prior, priors elected the provincial, provincials elected the general. Likewise at each level there were advisory councils that were also elected to assist the prelate in the exercise of his duties. Both of the hierarchies, secular and regular, eventually fell under the authority of the pope.

As a result of these structural differences, regular clergy were in many ways better suited to evangelization in newly discovered regions. Traveling as a group, they carried with them the internal structure needed to organize themselves. In the Europe of the Middle Ages the orders emerged as a response to the Church hierarchy, which was seen as having lost the apostolic fervor of the early Church. Saint Francis, founder of the Franciscans, sought to change public morals by emulating apostolic poverty and thus teach by example. Saint Dominic likewise felt called to reinvigorate the Church through the ministry of preaching. The Dominican order, which he founded, placed great emphasis on the preaching of the Word of God as sufficient to cause a moral change in the listener. Both orders had become active in Europe in establishing the hegemony of the Catholic Church of Rome over local variants, which were perceived as heretical. In seeking to spread the Gospel they also had active missions among non-Christians. Due to internal organization and historic mission the regular clergy were well poised to carry out the evangelization of the New World.

The secular clergy, on the other hand, were not well suited to missionary activity. The hierarchical structure would have required the appointment of a bishop as well as clergy to accompany him, in order to spread out into a new region. While there were bishops appointed to the New World almost immediately on the heels of the Conquest, they initially exercised very little local authority due to the tremendous distances and difficulty of communication. In fact, in recognition of the hardships of travel and communication, the pope granted full authority to Franciscans and, by extension, to regular clerics who served in regions beyond a two-day ride of a bishop. Certain Church sacraments—for example, Confirmation—were reserved to bishops. The papal grant known as the *Omnímoda* gave these powers to the regulars where necessary.[3]

In the early sixteenth century the secular clerics were perceived by the populace as more venal than the regulars and certainly not as well trained. Because the regulars generally practiced apostolic poverty or some variation thereof, the public thought of them as further removed from mundane concerns. The seculars, on the other hand, did not reject private wealth. In fact, except for their vows of celibacy and obedience and the requirement that they dress in clerical garb, the secular priests were essentially undifferentiated from the rest of society.

While there was not a priest on board on Columbus' first voyage, the clerical presence quickly became common on subsequent ones. On the second voyage several priests joined the expedition: four Franciscans and a Jeronymite, Fr. Ramón Pané. The leader of the Franciscans was Fr. Buil, whose origins are unclear, although he was probably a Catalan. Fr. Buil is credited with saying the first Mass in the Americas, on the Feast of the Epiphany, on January 6, 1494.[4] While Buil returned to Spain within a year, by 1500 there were several clerical establishments on Española (Hispaniola). More Franciscans arrived before 1500; in about 1500 the first Dominicans were sent to the island. Thus, the Crown justified its conquest and settlement of the New World in religious terms, to extend the benefits of Christianity to hitherto unknown populations.

Spain's earliest claims to dominion over the New World were based on papal bulls and subsequent documents. Upon the return of Columbus to Spain in 1493, the Spanish monarchs sent dispatches to Rome informing the newly elected pope, Alexander VI, of the event. The monarchs petitioned the pope to provide some confirmation of the discovery and subsequent possession. In May 1493, Alexander issued his bull, *Inter caetera divinae*, which recognized the Spanish accomplishment and divided the world into two spheres of influence: the western half fell to Spain, while the eastern half went to Portugal. The bull provided for an imaginary line drawn through the poles, one hundred leagues west of the Azores and Cape Verde Islands. Interestingly, Alexander claimed that this novel division of the world was his own idea and not merely granted at the insistence of the Spaniards.[5] He further detailed the legal extent of the Spanish dominion in a follow-up bull, *Dudum siquidem*, on September 26, 1493.

This unilateral action of the pope was followed quickly by a bilateral treaty between the Spaniards and the Portuguese. Ambassadors from the two kingdoms met in the Spanish town of Tordesillas where they molded the papal grant into a treaty that would govern their two states. The Treaty of Tordesillas, dated June 7, 1494, basically accepted the provisions of the papal bull but pushed the line of demarcation from one hundred leagues west of the Cape Verde Islands to 370 leagues.

Many legal thinkers questioned the authority of the papal bulls to grant dominion to the Spaniards. Not accepting papal justification, they then turned to natural law. In the fifteenth and sixteenth centuries there was little notion of international law. While each European state had its own regulations and statutes, there was no law that could serve to amicably resolve disputes between nations. With overseas exploration and the expansion of Europe into the surrounding world, it became very important to develop a system of international law. This international law would govern two types of activities: relations between foreign nations and European states, and conflicts among European states themselves. The two sides of the international law had different ends and different means.

A Dominican, Fr. Melchor Cano, posited that the cornerstone of Spain's claims was the *ius predicandi*, or the law of preaching.[6] Basing himself in natural law, it became clear to him that a nation could establish hegemony over a non-Christian power for the purpose of spreading the Gospel. The heathens and heretics could be subjected to foreign rule, specifically for Christianization. Spain relied on the *ius predicandi* as one of the legal bases upon which it held the New World, along with the primacy of the papal grants. The Spanish justification for its interests in the New World, by the early years of the sixteenth century, became closely related to the Patronato Real, or royal patronage over the Church. Under this concept, the Crown promised to financially support missionary activity in return for administrative control over the Church—nominally, the appointment of bishops, archbishops, and parish priests. In order to establish a firm legal claim on the New World with the *ius predicandi*, the Crown had to send out missionaries. It was not sufficient merely to promise to Christianize; concrete action had to be taken.

At the same time that Europeans developed rules of international law, there also emerged widely accepted rules about what constituted a just war. Force could only be used under the specific conditions that defined the just war. Again, scholars extrapolated their position from canon, civil, and natural law. All of these sources agreed that if one nation were attacked, a response was allowed. But under what circumstances could a nation attack another? The scholars studying the just war concluded that if a foreign people openly rejected Christianity, then war might be waged to subdue them, in order to spread the Gospel. Based on the concept of the *ius predicandi*, conquest could not occur before the Gospel had been peaceably preached. If the Gospel was rejected violently, then war was possible. But again, war had as its end the pacification and the Christianization of the people.

To have Spanish expeditions comply with these restrictions, a rather curious document was drafted, which we know as the Requerimiento, or Requirement, a statement of Christian dogma and an explanation of Spanish royal authority. It was the notification to the natives of the intentions of the Spaniards, and was an attempt, in a very legalistic way, to bring the natives into submission peaceably. Obviously there were difficulties with the system. In all likelihood the Requirement was not read to the natives in their own language. Even if the Spaniards complied with all the details, seldom did the reaction of the natives represent an informed response. The existence and occasional use of the Requirement indicate that the Spaniards seriously thought about their legal claim on the New World—a legal claim intimately related to the Christianizing mission. The Requirement called on the natives to first acknowledge the Christian Church, the pope, and the Spanish monarchs as their superiors and lords and then to allow the Gospel to be preached. If another European power could demonstrate, or at least use propaganda to show, that the Spaniards were not dutifully Christianizing the natives, then claims on the New World could be made against Spain.

As the Spaniards settled on the island of Española, they brought with them European diseases as well as the expectation that the natives would provide labor for the colonists' needs. These two factors brought about a dramatic decline in the native population. Many Spanish clerics accused the colonists of responsibility for the mortality rate due to ill treatment. A major controversy erupted on the Fourth Sunday in Advent, just before Christmas, in 1511, when the Dominican friar Antón de Montesinos delivered a scathing attack on the labor system that consigned native populations to Spanish colonists and on the Spaniards who profited from it. His sermon was based on John 1:23 where, in answer to the Pharisees, John the Baptist replies, "I am the voice of one crying in the wilderness, make straight the way of the Lord."[7] Montesinos lambasted the colonists for their mistreatment of the natives. The sermon caused a furor among the elite Spanish population of Santo Domingo. When the local citizens complained to the Dominican superior, Fr. Pedro de Córdoba, he indicated that he would do nothing to stop Montesinos from preaching again. On the subsequent Sunday, Montesinos continued his blast against Spanish exploitation, this time using as his text Job 36:2: "Bear with me a little, and I will show you, for I have yet something to say on God's behalf."[8]

Among those in the congregation on those Sundays was a parish priest who had served in the conquest of Cuba and who had himself received a grant of Indian labor. In 1512, while preparing a sermon to be delivered on Pentecost Sunday, the priest had a moral conversion. In considering the text appointed for that day, Ecclesiasticus 34:18–19, he came to the opinion that the Spanish exploitation of the New World was not lawful, according to divine law.[9] He returned to Spain where he joined the Dominican Order. Fray Bartolomé de las Casas became the most outspoken critic of Spanish policy toward the New World Indians. He spent the rest of his life seeking protection for the natives. The theology and plan of action of Las Casas are placed in their larger context in Chapter 1 by Luis Rivera.

As the Spaniards expanded out of the Antilles, each of the conquering bands contained at least one cleric. Major expeditions, such as those of Cortés and Pizarro, included several priests: one served as the private chaplain to the expedition leader, another ministered to the members of the company. In both of the major expeditions there were secular and regular priests. The Peruvian example illustrates the practical differences between them. In the conquest of Peru the defining event was the taking of Atahualpa, the Inca emperor, as prisoner. The Spaniards distributed the ransom among themselves on the basis of their participation in the expedition. The priest who was present at the event, Fr. Vicente Valverde, did not receive a share of the booty because he was a regular cleric. On the other hand, the secular priest, Juan de Sosa, who was not even present when Atahualpa was captured, was allotted a share.[10]

In the case of Mesoamerica, the two most important priests involved in the Cortés expedition were Frs. Bartolomé de Olmedo and Juan Díaz. Olmedo was a Mercedarian who functioned as the official chaplain of the expedition, and particularly as Cortés's personal chaplain. Díaz, a secular priest, served simply as a member of the company and functioned informally as the chaplain to the troops. Each played an important role in the Conquest. Olmedo said Mass and went about his sacramental duties in a very visible fashion, for the spiritual support of the troops and the enlightenment of the natives. Díaz tended to work more in the background as just another member of the expedition, although he did take center stage in the conversion of the four rulers of Tlaxcala. Díaz officiated at their baptism, their symbolic incorporation into the Spanish cause. A fairly unknown priest, Pedro de Villagrán, claimed to have been the first to celebrate Mass in Mexico/Tenochtitlan.

Upon the conclusion of the Conquest, Cortés requested that the monarch send Franciscan friars to be the first missionaries to Mexico. Although there were several secular priests in the newly conquered land within the first two years or so, the overwhelming majority of clerics were drawn from the religious orders. In 1524 the first expedition of Franciscans arrived, followed in 1533 by Augustinians and in 1538 by Dominicans. As a result of this imbalance between seculars and regulars, the latter came to serve as parish priests in most regions of the Spanish Indies where there was a Church presence. These assignments served in rather stark contrast to Europe, where most parishes fell under the jurisdiction of the seculars while regulars, more generally confined to monasteries and friaries, were active in preaching and other ministries.

As the regular clergy began their missionary efforts, they tended to focus on certain defined regions. The Franciscans, as the first order, concentrated around the major population centers of Mexico City, Tlaxcala, and Michoacán. They also became the most important order on the Yucatán peninsula, although this effort occurred slightly later than the first ones in central Mexico. The Dominicans became more localized in the south-central region of Oaxaca and the far southern province of Chiapas. The Augustinians, as the last major order, were somewhat restricted to those areas, largely to the immediate north of Mexico City and in parts of Michoacán, not already under the jurisdiction of the others. In the case of Peru, the Mercedarians were the first order to establish a monastery, in San Miguel Piura, even before the end of the Conquest, yet Franciscans and others were not far behind. Franciscans, for example, dominated the region that is today Ecuador, while Dominicans had a powerful presence in Cusco, the ancient Inca capital.

As the missionary effort evolved, the secular clergy tended to concentrate in the Spanish cities, the mining districts, the port cities, and other areas with a concentration of Spaniards. Nevertheless, they also established rural parishes in regions with large native populations, usually at the invitation of local officials or in the absence of the regular clergy. Similarly, the religious orders also had a presence in the major cities since they tended to have large establishments there, for the training of new religious and for the ministry to natives in the urban areas.

One of the most distinct features of the Spanish missionary activity in the New World was the financial support that it received. As noted, resulting from a series of papal bulls and royal decrees, the Crown claimed rights of patronage over the New World church. According to the medieval notion of patronage, the person or institution responsible for the financial support of a church, chapel, or other ecclesiastical institution had the right to appoint the cleric who served that institution. Patrons named chaplains, parish priests, and many other offices, subject to the approval of and recognition by the local bishop or other prelate. In the case of the New World, the Crown promised to support the whole Church in return for the power to appoint local ecclesiastical officials. As a result, the Crown paid the salaries of the parish priests, provided for the construction and maintenance of the cathedrals and other churches, and supported the regular clergy. In return the Crown reserved to itself the right to appoint bishops, archbishops, parish priests, and many other church functionaries.

Encomenderos, or Spaniards who held grants of labor or tribute from local Indian populations, were also responsible for paying the salary of the priests who provided religious services to those natives by virtue of an early royal decision. The Crown was itself the single largest encomendero, since natives paid tribute to the Crown in lieu of any other encomendero. Consequently, either regular or secular clergy who served in rural parishes drew their salary from the tribute revenues.

In 1574 the Crown promulgated a set of decrees known as the Ordenanza del Patronazgo, which clearly articulated the control that it believed it exercised over the clergy. One of the major goals of the legislation was to bring all appointments to parishes under the direct administration of the Crown. At roughly the same time the Catholic Church began implementation of the reforms of the Council of Trent, which had concluded in 1564; among these reforms was a call to improve the quality of the clergy. These two forces led to an inexorable movement of the regular clergy in two directions: out of the rural parishes and into more urban settings, and into new frontier regions. At the same time the secular clergy slowly expanded in the rural parishes. Robert Padden, in Chapter 2, describes the political maneuvering in Spain that brought about the development of the Ordenanza del Patronazgo. Then, in Chapter 3, I analyze the details of the implementation of that code in Mexico with its repercussions.

The parish priest, whether secular or regular, had two main obligations: to indoctrinate the natives into the Christian faith, and to administer the sacraments—Baptism, Marriage, Penance, Eucharist, and Unction. (The sacraments of Ordination and Confirmation were reserved to the bishops.) In order to administer the sacraments and evangelize the natives, the priests either had to teach the natives Spanish or learn the native languages themselves. For the friars the second option was clearly superior. Thanks to that decision, modern scholars have a fairly large corpus of materials written in the native languages using European characters. With the introduction of the printing press to Mexico in the early 1530s the clergy began to publish books in the native tongues. Within the sixteenth century there appeared works in Nahuatl, Tarascan, Timucuan, and Otomí, to name a few. Needless to say, most of these works were didactic pieces intended for the Christianization of the natives.

The various religious orders and the secular clergy each differed in their approach to the administration of the sacraments. Baptism was widely recognized as the gateway to the others; in fact, it was improper to administer any other sacrament to an unbaptized person. The Franciscans, in particular, believed that Baptism was critically important. Because of millenarian thinking among the early Franciscans in Mexico, mass Baptism was practiced. Indeed, some of the missionary accounts tell of hundreds of thousands of people being baptized. To some Franciscans, the discovery and settlement of the New World was a clear sign that the end of time was near and that Christ's return to Earth was imminent. For the Dominicans and many Augustinians, while Baptism was crucial, it should only be administered after the neophyte had been sufficiently indoctrinated to understand the tenets of the faith and make the necessary free-will decision to accept Christianity. For example, one Franciscan reported that by 1540 over six million had received the sacrament.[11] Nevertheless, there were significant numbers of natives who had not been baptized, nor married according to the rites of the Catholic Church. In Chapter 4, Sarah Cline analyzes the census records of several communities in central Mexico that date from the 1540s, thus indicating the limited reach of the "spiritual conquest."[12]

Marriage was considered an important sacrament within the context of the spiritual conquest and early missionary activity, principally because native practices did not follow European norms. Polygamy was not uncommon in native societies, but monogamy, an essential part of Christian thinking, presented a major obstacle to the conversion of the natives, especially among the nobility, where polygamy was more commonplace. Missionary techniques developed from the Middle Ages in Europe tended to focus efforts on the local rulers, consonant with the thinking that the people will tend to follow the religious orientation of their leaders. Consequently, priests frequently challenged native leaders to give up their successive wives in favor of the first wife. Cline indicates that Christian marriage had not made a significant impact on the native populations reported in the censuses. Moreover, relaxed attitudes about sexual behavior, including homosexuality, prenuptial sexual relations, and other practices, caused more than a little concern among the missionaries as they attempted to impose Christian sexual norms on the native peoples.

The picture that we see of the spiritual conquest of the sixteenth century changes according to the source of information. Most scholars have based their studies on the missionaries' accounts. Recently, they have begun to look into the reaction of the native peoples to the missionary activity, and other scholars have discovered census data for a few towns and villages that reveal the effect of such activity. The version of the evangelization provided by the friars would lead us to believe that by 1540, or over fifteen years after the Conquest, most natives had been converted. Nevertheless, the records analyzed by Cline—a series of censuses from the Cuernavaca Valley—posit a far different state of affairs. The six communities demonstrate a wide range of the imposition of Christianity. The least Christianized had only 4 percent of its population baptized, while the highest level of evangelization was seen in a village with 84 percent baptized. Likewise, at the same time that many natives had entered into Christian marriage, several of the rulers still kept concubines and several others had not bothered to have their marriages sanctioned by the Church. These data indicate that the imposition of Christianity was a far more long-term process than the enthusiastic missionaries had first thought.

Another significant problem concerning evangelization was the translation of Christian concepts into the native languages. Even the term for "God" posed difficulties: the friars did not want the Christian God confused with the many gods of the native pantheon. On the other hand, the native peoples did not grasp many Christian moral concepts, such as a sin of intent, nor did they understand why extramarital sex was forbidden. And what about Christian notions that thoughts and intentions in and of themselves could be sinful, even if not acted upon? One scholar has described this "moral dialogue" whereby the missionaries attempted to explain Christian concepts in a manner that would resonate with the natives.[13]

The sacrament of Penance was a key feature of Christianity that the missionaries wished to apply to the newly converted natives as a method to evaluate the progress of Christianization. While some native societies had similar practices, they tended to be a once-in-a-lifetime event rather than a regular examination of conscience. For other societies, Penance was completely alien. It is no wonder that there was a proliferation of confessional guides written in native languages to assist the parish priests in the administration of the sacrament. The language barrier was only one aspect of the difficulty; the cultural barrier was equally formidable. Serge Gruzinski, in Chapter 5, looks at the problems with confession among the Nahua.

When the priests preached about the soul or the Devil, there were no simple ways to translate these words into the native languages. Among the Nahua, for example, there were three rather different concepts of the soul.[14] Likewise, the Devil, as a representation of pure evil, was an alien concept. Eventually the missionaries came upon the *tlacatecolotl,* or horned owl-man, as a pre-Columbian notion (a shape-changing evil shaman) that could serve their purpose. These examples are indicative of the difficulty encountered in translating Christian concepts into native languages.

In keeping with the notion that the common people will follow the religious practices of their leaders, the early friars established schools in which to train the sons of the nobility in Christian thought and practice. The most famous was the Colegio de Santa Cruz, founded by the Franciscans in the Mexico City neighborhood of Tlatelolco.[15] These efforts raised considerable protest among the native peoples, who were fearful of having their children taken away from them. Nevertheless, the experiment at Tlatelolco created a well-trained cadre of native youths who could return to their people thoroughly indoctrinated in the new religion. Some scholars have posited that this experiment had as its goal the creation of a native clergy, but no indigenous person was ordained to the priesthood in Mexico in the sixteenth century.

A distinct shift seems to have occurred in the late sixteenth century within the Church in most of Mesoamerica. The early missionary fervor had begun to die out with the realization that the evangelization was neither as complete nor as thorough as the early missionaries had believed.

Natives, while embracing Christianity, still retained many of their earlier beliefs, only modified to fit into the new theology. Some early missionaries had anticipated the end of the world with the preaching of the Gospel to the last corners of the Earth. It did not happen, and instead the daily routine of missionary activity presented many frustrations. In addition, political shifts took place, mostly in conjunction with the expansion of royal power over the Church. With the promulgation of the Ordenanza del Patronazgo in 1574 the parish clergy, both secular and regular, came more completely under royal control. Subsequently, in the core areas of Hispanic America, the regular clergy slowly divested themselves of rural parishes in favor of the secular priests. The transition from regular to secular clergy was by no means an easy one, and conflicts among the different religious orders also created complications in the secularization process. Writing about colonial Ecuador, Karen Powers, in Chapter 6, details the many different aspects of the complex process.

In the seventeenth century several institutions emerged that would play an important role in parish life. The most important was the religious sodality, or *cofradía*. These lay associations organized parishioners around the veneration of a saint or sacrament, provided a mutual support mechanism for the laity, and frequently served as a burial society. Members paid dues in return for Masses celebrated for the collective good, and full Christian burial was arranged at death. Some of these sodalities became wealthy and were able to invest their capital in local real estate. Tensions arose between the sodalities and the parish priest, who anticipated some income from these investments but over which he had little control.

Even in rural parishes, well-off individuals were able to endow chantries—investments whose proceeds provided an income to the priest, usually for the purpose of celebrating Masses to benefit the souls of the founder and his family. These investments became important in the limited milieu of the local parish. For the Church as a whole they constituted a significant source of capital, but a capital that was generally administered by the laity under the guidance of ecclesiastical officials.

The issue of local finances became a major bone of contention between priests and their parishioners as the colonial period wore on. In the sixteenth century the natives were not expected to pay for church services but supported the clerical establishment indirectly through their tribute. The encomenderos who received the tribute were required to pay the salaries of the parish priests. Nevertheless, even in the sixteenth century, many parish priests expected free-will offerings from their parishioners, in the form of food, fuel, and labor. Although the courts routinely ruled that these offerings needed to be truly free-will and that the natives could not be coerced, the shady practices continued. By the seventeenth century, schedules of fees for services became routine in many areas.

In Peru, more than in Mesoamerica, there arose serious concerns over the incomplete evangelization by the end of the sixteenth century. In Mexico there had been an early effort to place the native peoples under the jurisdiction of the Holy Office of the Inquisition. While it monitored religious beliefs and actions and had many clergy on its staff, the Inquisition was not directly an ecclesiastical institution. Each local bishop was allowed to exercise the power of inquisitor. Nevertheless, with the formal establishment of the Holy Office by the Crown with papal authority, the local bishop ceded that power to the institution of the Inquisition. In the early years of the evangelization, Bishop Juan de Zumárraga of Mexico initiated an inquisitorial proceeding against don Carlos, the local native lord of Texcoco.[16] The case ended with the execution of don Carlos for apostasy. This incident so shocked both laity and clergy that in the aftermath the Crown withdrew all native peoples from the jurisdiction of the Inquisition.

By the end of the sixteenth century, priests noticed that many natives maintained their pre-Columbian rituals, which they modified only slightly to conform to the new religion. They feared that the natives had merely hidden away their idols and were practicing the old religion in secret. In Mexico, numerous treatises were written on the need to uncover this idolatry, but no organized response was mounted by the Church.[17] In contrast, there arose in Peru an effort known to modern scholars as the Extirpation, which sought to eliminate all traces of the old Inca religion. The Extirpation had many of the hallmarks of the Inquisition, including drastic actions and dramatic punishments, but it was institutionally and legally quite different. The Extirpation in Peru forms the major topic for Kenneth Mills in Chapter 7.

The Catholic Church held sway not only within the religious culture of colonial Latin America but in the popular culture as well. The public celebration of religious holidays, the veneration of saints, and the cult of the Virgin all had important social ramifications in the colonial world. Linda Curcio-Nagy's account of the Virgin of Remedies and Stafford Poole's history of the Virgin of Guadalupe in Chapters 8 and 9 outline the rise and flower of these two important cults in colonial Mexico. While many of the features of Christianity were troubling for native peoples to understand, given the vast differences between Christian notions of belief and native systems, the cult of the saints and the veneration of the Virgin were quickly accepted and incorporated into local popular religion.

The evangelization of the New World posed many difficulties for the priests and friars. Differences within the clergy and the political context within which the missionaries operated also influenced some of the results. The clergy were not so thorough or so successful as they might have wished. In fact, the development of Christianity in the Americas has been characterized by syncretism, the differential acceptance of the new theology while maintaining certain aspects of the old. While these missionaries spread the Gospel throughout the Americas, they were not equally successful in every area. The institutions that they did create, however, form an essential basis for understanding later periods and the region today.

Notes

1. All references to the Church pertain to the Roman Catholic Church. In the colonial period the Catholic Church was the only legal religious sect, and other denominations were all but nonexistent.

2. Robert Ricard, *La "conquête spirituelle" de Mexique: Essai sur l'apostolat et les méthodes missionaires des ordres mendicants en Nouvelle Espagne de 1523–24 à 1572* (Paris: Université de Paris, 1933), translated by Lesley B. Simpson and published in English as *The Spiritual Conquest of Mexico* (Berkeley: University of California Press, 1966).

3. This bull, also known as *Exponi nobis fecisti*, can be found in W. Eugene Shiels, *King and Church: The Rise and Fall of the Patronato Real* (Chicago: Loyola University Press, 1961), 211–15.

4. Samuel Eliot Morison, *Admiral of the Ocean Sea* (Boston: Brown, Little and Co., 1959), 397, 432, 484.

5. Shiels, *King and Church*, 77–81.

6. Anthony Pagden, *Spanish Imperialism and the Political Imagination* (New Haven: Yale University Press, 1990), 22–24.

7. The passage originally came from Isaiah 40:3, "A voice cries: 'In the wilderness prepare the way for the Lord.'" It appears in all the Gospels to describe the ministry of John the Baptist: Matthew 3:3, Mark 1:3, Luke 3:4, and John 1:23.

8. Lewis Hanke, *The Spanish Struggle for Justice in the Conquest of America* (Philadelphia: University of Pennsylvania Press, 1949), 17–19.

9. Ecclesiasticus 34:18–19, "If one sacrifices from what has been wrongfully obtained, the offering is blemished; the gifts of the lawless are not acceptable. The Most High is not pleased with the offerings of the ungodly; and He is not propitiated for sins by a multitude of sacrifices."

10. James Lockhart, *The Men of Cajamarca* (Austin: University of Texas Press, 1972), 201–7, 465–68.

11. Juan de Torquemada, *Monarquía Indiana*, 7 vols. (México: Universidad Nacional Autónoma de México, 1975–1983), 5:237–38.

12. S. L. Cline, *The Book of Tributes: Early Sixteenth-Century Nahuatl Censuses from Morelos* (Los Angeles: UCLA Latin American Center, 1993), 41–58.

13. Louise M. Burkhart, *The Slippery Earth: Nahua-Christian Moral Dialogue in Sixteenth-Century Mexico* (Tucson: University of Arizona Press, 1989), 3–7.

14. Jill Leslie McKeever Furst, *The Natural History of the Soul in Ancient Mexico* (New Haven: Yale University Press, 1995), 14–16.

15. W. Michael Mathes, *Santa Cruz de Tlatelolco: La primera biblioteca académica de las Américas* (México: Secretaría de Relaciones Exteriores, 1982).

16. Richard E. Greenleaf, *Zumárraga and the Mexican Inquisition, 1536–1543* (Washington, DC: Academy of American Franciscan History, 1961), 69–73.

17. For an example see Hernando Ruiz de Alarcón, *Treatise on the Heathen Superstitions* (Norman: University of Oklahoma Press, 1984), translated and edited by J. Richard Andrews and Ross Hassig.

I

Policy Issues

1

The Theological Juridical Debate

Luis N. Rivera

The conquest of the New World by the Spaniards was accompanied by a debate in Madrid as to its legal nature and to claims to possession in the New World. Since much of the Spanish legal justification for their American colonies was based upon papal grants and the role of the state in spreading Christianity to the natives of the New World, what could have been a purely political debate also had an extremely important theological overtone. Luis Rivera discusses the relationship between politics and theology with regard to Spanish claims in the New World.

By far the most outspoken critic of Spanish imperial policy in the New World, especially concerning the treatment of the natives, was the Dominican friar, Bartolomé de las Casas. Much of the data with the theologians in Spain that was brought to bear on the issue was provided by Las Casas in his many writings. Moreover, political critics of the Spanish state also found ample evidence for their charges in the writings of the friar. Spain in the early modern period, and especially in the middle decades of the sixteenth century, was a hotbed of social and political debate as well as the crucible for what would become the discipline of international law. The debates about Spain's claims to the New World eventually evolved into a larger argument about the rights of nations and their interactions with one another on a world scale.

Luis Rivera is professor of humanities at the University of Puerto Rico, Rio Pedras. He is the author of several studies on the theology and law of the Conquest era.

Theory and Reality

Spanish domination over the "islands and mainland of the Ocean sea" caused fiery questioning and ardent debates in respect to the justice

From *A Violent Evangelism: The Political and Religious Conquest of the Americas* (Louisville, KY: Westminster/John Knox Press, 1992), 200–16, 310–13. © 1992 by Westminster/John Knox Press. Reprinted by permission of Westminster/John Knox Press.

of the armed conquest and Christianization of its inhabitants. Lively and intense discussions continued throughout the sixteenth century among Spanish theologians and jurists, who debated the issues passionately and creatively.

The questions were many. Do the Europeans have the right to take possession of and conquer the lands and inhabitants of the New World? Are the wars against the indigenous nations that do not accept Spain's temporal and spiritual sovereignty just? Can the colonists force the indigenous peoples to work in the extraction of mineral resources? Are the differences in the cultural life of Spaniards and American natives relative and historically conditioned, or do they express an essential inequality "almost as those between humans and beasts"? (Ginés de Sepúlveda 1951, 38)

Are the natives free or servants by nature? Are they noble savages or vicious idolaters? Do they have culture or are they uncivilized? Do they or do they not have a right to their lands and possessions? Should the Christian faith be preached to them peacefully, respecting their right to reject it, or should it be imposed on them, forcing them to be baptized? Does conversion precede colonization, or vice versa?

The theological-juridical debate was exemplary and took on an exceptional intellectual and emotional intensity. If the denunciatory writings of Bartolomé de las Casas have provided abundant ammunition to the infamous "black legend," it is also true that the cordial and attentive reception that they received from the royal court and the Council of the Indies reflects their interest in combining political and material expansion with the spiritual well-being of both Europeans and American natives. The North American Sauer (1984, 10) rightly asserts that "the Spaniards were the most severe and insistent critics of the sad state of their own colonies." While the critical scourges that were the treatises of Las Casas were printed and widely distributed, the main anti-Indian writing of his rival Sepúlveda was only published four centuries after it was penned.[1] It is difficult to deny the conclusive affirmation of the North American historian Hanke (1967, 15):

> The Spanish conquest of the Americas was more than an extraordinary military and political feat . . . ; it was also one of the greatest attempts the world has seen to make Christian principles prevail in the relations between peoples. This attempt became basically a fiery defense of the rights of the Indians, which rested on two of the basic presuppositions that a Christian can make, namely: that all men are equal before God, and that a Christian is responsible for the well-being of his brothers, no matter how alien or humble they may be.

The markedly confessional character of the Spanish state, which converted the conquest into missionary activity, and the subordination of the Church to the Crown, which in turn made a state venture of the propagation of the faith, conferred on the intense debates a unique character, unequaled in history. *Every theological dispute about the New World and its inhabitants took on a political character and vice versa; every political disagreement over the relationship of Spain to the natives became a theological debate.* This phenomenon explains the public preeminence of all the writings and expositions of such theologians as Las Casas, Sepúlveda, and Vitoria, and the religious tones given to many political decrees from the Council of the Indies.

The theoretical debates, from a particular time and space, touched perennial problems deeply: Is humanity one or diverse? Are some human beings superior in intelligence and prudence, and do they therefore have a right to special privileges and unique responsibilities? Is the domination of some nations by others justified because of natural or historical inequalities? Do valuable mineral resources belong to the inhabitants of the territory where they are, or to whoever can invest in their development?

From those questions, with Francisco de Vitoria's help, modern international law was born. It is important to clarify, however, that it is an international law conceived from the perspective of the conquerors, which ultimately served to legitimize armed conquest. Many times we forget the markedly bellicose character of the law of nations in Vitoria. It is no accident that his two lectures on the Indians gravitate toward the legitimacy of the objective and methods of the wars against the "barbarians of the New World." There is a serious historical contradiction between the theoretical promulgation of the human dignity of the American natives and their displacement, oppression, and decimation. This perspective of imperial power is what gives an abstract character to the theoretical equality of sovereign nations propounded by Vitoria.[2] It does not reveal the profound inequality in economic, social, and military power between the empire and the occupied territory, which shatters the theoretical schema of equality and reciprocity. In general, it would not be untrue to assert that the promoters of the human rights of the American natives win at the level of theory but are defeated in the historical practice of conquest.

Pope Paul III's bull *Sublimis Deus*, June 2, 1537, asserts the humanity, rationality, and freedom of the natives. The papal decree, in contrast to the opinion promoted by "the enemy of the human race itself," asserts that "the Indians are true men . . . and can in no way be deprived of their freedom." The New Laws of 1542 recognized the individual autonomy of the natives and officially and formally declared the benevolent will of the empire: "Because our main intention and will has always been and is the preservation and increase of the Indians and that they be treated as free persons . . ."

Well and good, but their concrete predominant experience is defeat, suffering, decimation, and subjugation. Juan Friede (1976, 59) has made the same judgment more emphatically:

> At a distance of several thousand miles from central power . . . no royal
> decision was capable of abolishing as if by magic the self-interest that
> was leading to the "destruction" of the native population. America lived
> its own life almost, it could be said, on the fringes of legal dispositions.
> . . . It structured its society by the facts, not the laws.

This does not deprive of merit the titanic efforts of Las Casas and
other jurists and religious to promote just and humane legislation for the
natives of the New World. These efforts reflect an important idea that
Bataillon (1976, 41) captures well: "Throughout the constant lack of compliance for the Laws of the Indies the *need for legal justice* persisted."
The aspiration for the creation of a just and reasonable system of law
comes through in such works as *De indis*, by Vitoria, and *Los Tesoros del
Perú*, by Las Casas. The latter surprisingly suggests that there is only one
remedy for the cruel exploitation to which the natives are subjected: to
promote the juridical nullity of all the events. "There is no other solution
nor can we think of another one outside this one; namely, that all the
actions that have taken place, in reference to and against the natives, be
taken as null by law [*nulla de iure*]" (Las Casas 1958, 337–41). Many
pages of Las Casas reflect that juridical conscience, deeply humanistic
and at the same time idealist and utopian.

Zavala (1984, 96–97) is right in affirming that those intense theoretical debates were not "academic boasting nor juridical frills; rather, they
provided the spiritual base for an administrative regime which, faced with
the facts, would have its virtues and limitations tested daily." But it is a
non sequitur to deduce from that correct assessment the strange thesis
that "the historical reality, though dominated by avarice, remained subject to the attraction of superior principles of human dignity."[3] There is no
doubt that the battle between avarice and dignity constitutes an extraordinary struggle. In the case of the American natives and the African blacks,
it also carried with it an exceptionally high human cost.

Juan Manzano (1948, 62), too, errs in his excessive theoretical and
legalistic enthusiasm by saying that the collective effort of a great number of friars on behalf of the natives "was to see itself crowned with the
most complete success," above all thanks to the legislative actions of 1542.[4]
If that had been true, the American natives would not have seen themselves marginalized from the structures of power in their own lands, nor
would the writings of Las Casas in his final two decades have had the
bitter and denunciatory tone that characterizes them.

> Since the laws were published . . . those in charge . . . have not wished
> to comply with the laws . . . because they do not like to abandon the
> usurped haciendas they have, or grant freedom to the Indians they hold
> in perpetual captivity. Where they have ceased to kill them quickly with
> swords, they kill them little by little with personal services and other
> unjust and intolerable demands. And up to now the king is not powerful
> enough to stop it. (Las Casas 1989, 197–99)

Later, Manzano (1948, 191) admits that "this success attributed to the theologians of the Order of Saint Dominic, although considerable, was not absolute or complete."[5] The problem is that both affirmations, besides being mutually incompatible, gravitate to the level of theological and juridical abstraction. For Las Casas the primary and crucial matter was not theoretical diatribe but historical action: the concrete life of the inhabitants of the New World.

Venancio Carro (1944, 2:309, 317, 321), in his important work on Spanish juridical theology of the sixteenth century, confuses the prevalent theories in theological schools, especially Salamanca, with the historical reality of the conquest and colonization. He affirms that his extensive work of more than nine hundred pages is dedicated to "examining the conquest and colonization of the New World as it was in reality." It is a promise to which, to be truthful, he does not dedicate a single page. He analyzes an impressive number of peninsular writers, above all the Dominicans, based on the theoretical premise that the "true defense of human freedoms and rights is possible only within the principles of Christian theological-juridical science." He arrives at the impressive and triumphalistic conclusion that "the conquest and colonization of the Hispano-American world was the most humane and Christian that has occurred in the history of all the nations." In all that voluminous account of "the conquest and colonization of the New World as it was in reality," there is not one single dead, hungry, or maltreated Indian. A word of thanks here to Francisco de Vitoria, Domingo de Soto, and Domingo Bañez!

In a similar triumphalistic line, Antonio Ybot León (1948), in a study of the theological counseling committees of the Spanish Crown, concludes that starting from "the purest principles of the law of nations according to the divine origin of man," they produced "an entire body of normative and operative doctrine" and "binding norms of government" that imprinted the Spanish regime in the Indies with "its singular and exclusive distinguishing style in the history of all empires." Ybot León calls this style "a deliberate attempt to govern according to the precepts of justice and Christian law, of which the theologians were the natural definers." The relationship seems simple and direct: theological principles on the human dignity of the Indians→humanist legislation→benevolent government. Ybot León is not inclined, however, to study the possible empirical relationship between "the theory that maintained the great Spanish task in a missionary stance" and the reality of the way of the cross of the natives.

The contradiction between the legal decrees and the experience of illegal applications and the sense of powerlessness on the part of the Iberian authorities is clearly evident in a communique that on July 3, 1549, was sent to the emperor by the Council of the Indies affirming its frustration:

> . . . because those who go on these conquests do not carry with them people who would refrain from doing as they please nor anyone who

will accuse them of the evil they have done. For such is the greed of those who go on these conquests and so humble and fearful are the people they go to that we have no assurance that any instruction given to them [the Conquerors and colonists] will be observed. (in Jaime González Rodríguez in Ramos et al. 1984, 216)

Something not much different had been stated by a Dr. Montano in 1547, who said that in spite of the benevolent legislation for the Indies approved by the Castilian court, "everything is done under cover in such a way that the Indians continue in the same condition of servitude as before" (in Milhou 1975–76, 30). Anglería (1964–65, 2.7.4:607) presents a similar testimony when, after stressing the conscientious job accomplished by the Council of the Indies in the enactment of beneficial legislation of the Indies, he bitterly concludes:

But, what is happening? Our people, transported across an ocean to such strange, changing, and distant worlds, . . . and far from the authorities, allowed themselves to be carried away by the blind greed of gold, and those who leave here meeker than lambs, change as soon as they arrive there into wild wolves, forgetting all the royal commands.[6]

From their profound solidarity with the oppressed Antillean natives, the Dominican friars in Española accuse the Spanish colonists of making "fun of the provisions that in this matter [the good treatment of the natives] are provided by the Council." They recognize that they cannot "tame the rabid and disorderly greed of five hundred or a thousand men who come not knowing once there any subjection to God, even less to Your Majesty, . . . in order to come back loaded with gold" (in Pacheco et al. 1864–1884, 2:245). In the same way Las Casas, in his letter to the Council of the Indies of 1531, denounces the corruption that quickly afflicts the royal officials who go to the New World with the specific task of enforcing the laws:

Those who come here to give orders become daring and lose their fear of God and faith in their king and fidelity to him and respect for the people, and then they make a pact with the devil, to whom they give their souls so they can rob . . . for they see that the king and his Council are far away. (in Fabié [1879] 1966, 70:482)[7]

The strange contradiction between the abundant decrees and laws that the Crown and the Council of the Indies approved for the benefit and protection of the Indians and the blatant and intense injustice that they suffered was eloquently noted by Alonso de Zorita (in Pacheco et al. 1864–1884, 2:117–18; emphasis added), who in passing pointed out the saying that in the course of time became famous: "acato pero no cumplo" (I obey but do not comply).

The will of [Your Majesty] and of your Royal Council is clearly known, and it is known and understood by means of the daily instructions sent on behalf of those poor natural inhabitants, and for their increase and preservation. But they are *obeyed without being complied with*, and therefore they continue to be lost sight of, nor is there anyone who exactly knows what Y. M. has ordered. What instructions, decrees, letters are sent by the Emperor our Lord [Carlos V], already in heaven! And how many and how necessary the ones sent daily by Y. M. [Felipe II] and how little they prevail. . . . I am certain that what a philosopher used to say is very fitting: just as where there are many doctors and medicines, health is absent, and where there are many laws, justice is lacking.

Mendieta ([1596] 1980, 1.16:66), at the end of the same century, would issue the same complaint, censuring the colossal discrepancy between legislative justice and socioeconomic abuse, while at the same time pointing out the "temporary advantages" that serve as hermeneutical key for understanding the divorce between them:

Seeing that our Catholic Monarchs in Spain provided innumerable decrees, orders, and commands for and on behalf of the Indians, . . . it is a marvel that not even one of those who have governed in your royal name in the Indies was in any way inclined or interested principally in that duty . . . but only in that with which he could burden the hands of the poor ones who can do little or do not know how to or dare speak or act for themselves, and they (the royal representatives) behave in this way out of respect for their own interests and temporal benefit.

According to this Franciscan friar, in America "there is no other law nor right nor statute, except what will benefit the Spaniard justly or unjustly, and make the Indian suffer and grieve" (ibid., 4.46:561).

The historian José María Ots Capdequí (1986, 14) points out that, on the part of a government official in the Indies, the act of "obeying but not complying" reached the point of being formalized as a brief ceremony. "Upon receipt of a Royal Decree, whose fulfillment was not considered pertinent, the viceroy, president, or governor would place it solemnly on his head as sign of compliance and reverence, at the same time declaring that its fulfillment was placed in abeyance."

The theological-juridical debates were exceptionally intense in the Spain of the Golden Age. They were initiated by missionaries and theologians and eventually ended by them. If Montesinos, Las Casas, and Vitoria reflect the freshness and vigor of a debate in its fiery beginnings, Acosta by the end of the century already reflects the fatigue and exhaustion in the polemical impulse. The opportunistic pragmatism prevails, shielded by a pious evangelistic intention.

Granted that dominion of the Indies has been usurped unjustly, it is still better to believe and proclaim . . . that by law and right it is inappropriate to doubt the right of Christian princes to govern the Indies, which besides is very useful for the eternal salvation of the natives.

Acosta (1952, 2.11:186–87) promotes a policy of a strong hand against those who question the justice of the conquest. "If . . . they are not repressed with a strong hand, one cannot tell the evils and universal ruin that will follow, and the very serious disturbance and disorder in all things." The time for debate and lively polemics, stimulating to the juridical and theological mentality, has been left behind. Under the severe scrutiny of the Inquisition and of bureaucracy, the clash of ideas is avoided and the publication of divergent opinions is made difficult.[8]

The Cross and the Sword

In the entire process of conquest and evangelization of the Americas the relationship between the cross and the sword was problematic and complex. The sword, superior military technology, determined the outcome. The cross represented the final objective that the Spanish protagonists accepted, at least in juridical and theological theory. Paradoxically, the sword had religious and spiritual objectives, while the cross was invested with political and temporal characteristics.

It is significant that before Sepúlveda wrote his apologia for the Spanish wars against the Indians in *Demócrates segundo*, against the initial pacifism of some Protestant reformers he wrote a treatise—*Demócrates primo* (1525)—theologically defending war as a possible just action for Christians (i.e., against the Turks). In the same way, Vitoria immediately after his theological lectures on the justice of the Spanish domination of the New World—*De indis* (1538)—delivers others on just war—*De iure belli* (1539). The link between the cross and the sword is expressed again in the Augustinian clothing of the holy war, cultivated during centuries of crusades against the infidels.

The connection between the two is quite evident in the account that the Chontal Maya made about the execution of Cuauhtémoc (Léon Portilla 1987, 93–95). The Spaniards are convinced that his subjection is a fake and that he is planning an armed revolt. They decide, therefore, to kill him. But first they take precautionary religious steps and baptize the Aztec monarch. In this way, the Christian sacrament is linked to the conquering violence. The body of the chief is killed while at the same time an attempt is made to redeem his soul.

The Inka king Atahualpa also is baptized before his execution. In his case, the sacrament serves as amelioration of his execution, which was by hanging and burning. After his execution he is buried as a Christian, with the appropriate liturgical ceremonies ("the Governor, with the other Spaniards, took him very solemnly, with all possible honors, to be buried in the church") (Jerez 1947, 344–45). Baptism serves as an ironic exchange: eternal salvation of the soul in exchange for the temporal death of the body. In the case of Atahualpa, it is linked to the adoration of Mammon: as a useless ransom for his life the indigenous monarch gives Francisco

Pizarro an enormous amount of gold, a tragic forecast of the riches that the Spaniards could acquire if they overcame and subjected the natives.[9]

Atahualpa and his attendants were surprised and trapped. Pizarro had invited Atahualpa to Caxamarca to explain to him the purpose of the Spaniards' arrival. After the king refused to accept the exhortation to accept the Christian faith made by Fray Vicente de Valverde, according to a Quechua account:

> Fray Vicente entered . . . carrying a cross in his right hand and a breviary in the left. And he said to the Inka Atahualpa that he (Vicente) also is an ambassador and messenger from another lord, very great indeed, and a friend of God, and he [Atahualpa] should become his [God's] friend and adore the cross and believe the gospel of God and that everything else was not worthy of adoration, that it was false.
>
> The Inka Atahualpa responded that he did not have to adore anyone except the sun, which never dies . . . and gods who also have their law: those he obeyed. . . . Fray Vicente called out and said: Here, gentlemen, these gentile Indians are against our faith! And Don Francisco Pizarro and Don Diego de Almagro, on their part, raised their voices and said: Go forth, warriors, against those infidels who oppose our Christian faith! (in Léon Portilla 1987, 144)

The Spanish chronicler of the conquest of Peru and personal secretary of Pizarro, Francisco de Jerez (1947, 332–33), relates this scene with different details. He admits, however, that the order to attack Atahualpa and his warriors was given after Valverde informed Pizarro that the Inka chief "had thrown the sacred scriptures to the ground." Following the messianic cry of "Santiago" [Saint James], the Castilian artillery and cavalry attacked by surprise, causing the Inka warriors to flee, and allowing for the imprisonment of the Inka monarch. Pizarro then explains the providential and religious cause of his victory:

> We came to conquer this land so that all may come to know God and His holy Catholic faith . . . and so that you will understand and abandon the diabolical and beastly life you lead. . . . And if you have been taken prisoner and your people scattered and killed, it is because . . . you threw on the ground the book where God's words are, therefore Our Lord allowed your pride to be wounded and did not permit an Indian to hurt any Christian.[10]

He who carried the cross becomes the legitimizing agent of the one who uses the sword; the requirement of conversion becomes the death sentence.

Symptomatic of the close link between religious and military power in the conquest of the Americas is the description given by Robert Ricard (1986, 265–66) of the convents and monasteries that the friars built in Nueva España during the first years of evangelization:

The convent of the sixteenth century, besides its primary aim, had two purposes: to serve as a fortress if needed and as a refuge for Spaniards in the not remote case of an Indian uprising. In that way the two conquests were mutually allied and strengthened: the spiritual and the military. And this explains, also, the military value of many convents . . . true fortified castles.

Therefore, when Doctor Luis de Anguis, professor of the Decretal Chair of the University of Mexico, protested in a letter to Felipe II (February 20, 1561) because of what was in his opinion the excessive size of the monasteries and convents, he received a reply that was more military than religious: "They answered that they built them that way so that when necessary they could serve Y. M. as a fortress" (in Cuevas [1941] 1975, 262).

Alonso de Ercilla relates in his epic *La Araucana* (1569–1589) (1984 [1945], 34:582–83 [302–03]) the conversion and final torment of Caupolicán, the last of the great Araucan chiefs who rebelled against Spain. His sudden acceptance of the Christian faith, after his defeat and arrest, caused great joy among the Spaniards, who after instructing him in his new religion, baptizing him, and celebrating his conversion, proceeded nevertheless to execute him in a horrendous way: by impalement and transfixment with arrows.

> Yet, God changed him in a moment,
> Working with His Hand Almighty.
> Bright with faith and understanding,
> He desired a Christian's christening.
> Piteous joy did he elicit
> From surrounding folk Castilian,
> Causing all admiring wonder,
> Awing red barbarians present.
> On that mournful day, yet happy,
> Solemnly they then baptized him,
> And whilst scanty time permitted,
> In the true faith gave instructions.
> Dense platoons of armored gentry
> Hemmed him in and soon escorted
> Him out to suffer death accepted
> In the hope of God's hereafter.

In other respects, the battle between the cross (friars and ecclesiastics as defenders of the Indians) and the sword (conquerors and colonists) is one of the most interesting chapters in the long and labyrinthian relationship between Church and state, between spiritual and worldly powers. Occasionally the envangelizers tried to redeem the soul of the American native without chaining the body, but this was not the general practice. The most famous example of peaceful evangelization was the religious activity of Las Casas in Vera Paz, Guatemala.

With a decree in 1526 the Spanish Crown tried to control and moderate the violence of the sword by requiring the inclusion of religious men or clerics in every expedition. Thus, the armed actions against the natives required the previous authorization of the religious "signed with their names" (in Konetzke 1953, 1:92, 94). Demetrio Ramos (Ramos et al. 1984, 716) has assessed the outcome in the following way: "The system of 1526 failed. . . . The moral power of the two 'religious men or clerics' on which rested the responsibility of conscience, had no efficacy at all."

The theological-juridical idea of the *just war*, promoted by Saint Augustine, had the double and difficult task of moderating the cruelty of war and at the same time admitting that on some occasions a nation could, and even should, use arms in response to a grave injury (see Russell 1975). Spanish theologians and jurists tried to demonstrate that the armed conflict against the indigenous peoples fulfilled the criteria for a just war. Sepúlveda was an extreme case, but Vitoria did the same, while defining and restricting the reasons and causes. In general, Spanish scholars made the just war concept the conceptual fundamental axis for their analysis of the double confrontation for Catholic armies at that time: against Turks and Muslims, on the one hand, and against the indigenous peoples, on the other. From Vitoria to Spanish Jesuit theologian Francisco Suárez, the problem of the legitimacy of the war against the "infidels" was central to Castilian academic circles.

Although for those thinkers, the main criterion for determining the legality of a military conflict derived from the injury received and not vindicated (Vitoria: "La única y sola causa justa de hacer la guerra es la injuria recibida" [The one and only just cause to make war is the injury received] [in Urdanoz 1960, 825]), it was easy to devalue infidels and gentiles based on the religious motives of virulent holy wars. In that case, the Spanish theologians sometimes approved of extremes of horrendous cruelty. The Jesuit Luis de Molina in *De iustitia et iure* (2.122, n. 4, in Höffner 1957, 455) recommends the killing of infidel enemies,

> if from it [the killing] there is some usefulness for the church, and even for the guilty ones. For example, when dealing with gentiles, those who can hardly be expected to convert or abandon their sinful life. In that case, it would be without doubt holy and legitimate to kill them all or, at least, as many as would be considered necessary to achieve that aim. On the one hand, such an execution would be just in itself, and, on the other, a manifestation, also, of love of God and neighbor. It would serve the good of the church and of the executors of the order and even of the executed ones themselves, for death would impede them from continuing to accumulate sin on top of sin. They would suffer less punishment in the eternal flames than if they had continued to live in this world.

This reference shows the subtle line separating the just war from the holy war, and the ferocity and violence that always accompanies the holy war.

Las Casas adopted the opposite position: the wars the Indians wage against the Spaniards are just. Two indispensable factors are missing from the Spanish wars to rate them as legitimate: a just cause ("No war is just if there is no cause for declaring war. . . . But the infidel people [the Indians] . . . have not done any damage to the Christian people for which they deserve to be attacked by war" [Las Casas 1942, 515]) and true authority (the attacks by the conquerors, according to Las Casas, have been carried out without true royal consent).

For Las Casas the Indian wars on the Spanish, on the contrary, fulfill the formal criterion that grants them legitimacy: they are declared by the true authority of the territories in question, are for defense, and respond to incalculable damages that have not been vindicated. The Spaniards are blind and cannot see that:

> [The wars] were, are, and always will be unjust, evil, tyrannical, and detestable wherever for such a cause and under that title [i.e., refusal to accept the *Requerimiento*], they are or will be waged against the inhabitants and dwellers of the Indies; they are condemned by all natural, human, and divine law; therefore, wars of these infidels against every Spaniard and against every Christian who starts such a war are very just. (Las Casas 1986, 3.3.58:30)
>
> They have the very highest cause of all, and many other causes in all justice which they, the Indians, have by natural, divine, and human law, and that is to quarter them if they have the strength and arms needed, and to throw them out of their lands, because of their very unjust behavior, filled with every iniquity, and condemned by all the laws that are in force among them . . . reason, therefore to make war against them (the Spaniards). (Las Casas 1989, 101)

The wars of the Spaniards violate all the natural rights of the indigenous nations and constitute, also, a repugnant procedure contrary to the one that ought to be followed in the conversion of the natives. This, according to Las Casas, should be characterized by persuasion of their understanding and attraction of their will, both absent from armed conflicts. Faced with the opinion of those who alleged that war would achieve more positive results, such as the eradication of cannibalism and idolatrous human sacrifice, he replied that generally there are more victims as a result of armed conflict than those who could be saved from cannibalism or ritual sacrifices, and that the desire to impose the faith by force was more in keeping with the followers of Mohammed than with the Christians.

It is an error, however, to label the posture of Las Casas as "extreme pacifism," as Urdanoz has done (see 1960, 629, n. 269). Although he considers armed conflict "the worst evil" and "a plague of the body and the soul" (Las Casas 1974, 298, 360), it is a distortion of his position to classify it as pacifism, if that term is understood as the unconditional rejection of any military action. Two observations need to be made here.

First, Las Casas distinguishes between the use of arms for defending the state and the nation from external aggressors, which he considers valid, and armed action for the spread of the Gospel, which is illegal.

> But do not think that as a result armed conflicts are forbidden to Christian princes when needed for the defense of their republics. For it is one thing to speak about the way the law of Jesus Christ should be preached, and therefore of assembling, propagating, and preserving Christianity where it reigns spiritually, and it is something else to speak of ways of preserving a human republic in accordance with right reason, which tells us that sometimes it is necessary to undertake war to defend it and free it from tyranny. (Las Casas 1942, 491)

Secondly, Las Casas holds that there are times when a prince may defend or preach the Christian faith by means of war. Three traditional examples that he supports are: (a) the recovery of the Holy Land—reason for the Crusades; (b) the reconquest of the Iberian peninsula from the Moors; and (c) in general, the battle against the Muslims, "enemies of the faith, usurpers of Christian kingdoms" (Las Casas 1965, 1037).[11] Those are, in his opinion, defensive actions against the offenses committed by Muslims against Christianity. Even at times when there can be a truce, for example, against the Ottoman Turks, that does not alter the fact that "we have a just war against them, not only when they are actually waging it against us but even when they stop, because we have a very long experience of their intention to harm us; so our war against them cannot be called war but legitimate defense" (Las Casas 1986, 1.1.25:134).

Las Casas is willing to go further and justify armed action to defend the preaching of the Gospel and the missionaries from the aggressive actions of hostile infidels: "Our war would be just against them if they maliciously pursue or disturb or impede our faith and Christian religion, or without legitimate cause kill its priests and preachers" (ibid.). But it has to be proven that there is no genuine "legitimate cause" for the violent action of the infidels and the resistance to preaching is done "maliciously" and not in response to injustice previously committed by Spanish Christians (1974, ch. 25, 168–75).

In his extensive apologia against Sepúlveda, Las Casas accepts in principle the tenet of Vitoria on the legality of utilizing arms to defend the innocent victims who are sacrificed by infidels on the altars of their gods and those executed for cannibalistic purposes. However, in his opinion, reality contradicts the appropriateness of such armed intervention since it would be accompanied by greater damage to more innocent people than the few instances, according to his unique accounting system, of those who are sacrificed or eaten by the peoples of the Americas (ibid., 185–94).[12] Faithful to his usual style, he gathers extensive quotes from theological and juridical authorities to demonstrate the injustice of such military ventures.

He is also ready to validate wars aginst the heretics (such as the famous wars against the Albigensians and Hussites). "The Apostolic See may grant and cede the kingdoms of heretics to the Catholic Monarchs . . . and give them [Catholics] orders to war against them and eradicate them." Of course, this is granted on one condition: "that it can be accomplished without great loss, killings, and damages," which is in keeping with the war criterion of proportionality (Las Casas 1965, 1037).[13]

Las Casas establishes a distinction in the treatment of the heretics and the infidel natives. The first can be compelled by ecclesiastical and state force as a result of disobeying their baptismal vow, not the second. Thus, he tries to evade the relevance of the quotes that Sepúlveda uses from the epistles of Saint Augustine in which he defends the state repression of heretics.

> It is of little use for the doctor [Sepúlveda] to use against the Indians what Saint Augustine said of the heretics, since the heretics can be subjected by force to the faith which they promised by baptism, for they are already subjects of the church. This is not true of the Indians because they are not subjects as they have not received baptism. (Las Casas 1965, 381)

In respect to the basis of this key distinction between "infidel" and "heretic," it is my opinion that we need to modify John Phelan's (1974, 298) judgment that Las Casas tried to "replace an Augustinian idea with a Thomistic one" by insisting that being an orthodox Christian is not a prerequisite for the validity of one's political and personal rights, "an idea for a long time identified with Saint Augustine." More precisely, what Las Casas is proposing is that the Augustinian thesis is valid with respect to the heretics, but not to the infidels whose separation from the Christian faith comes from "invincible ignorance."

Las Casas is walking on very orthodox paths. Aquinas expounded the distinction between heretic and infidel. Cardinal Cayetano (Tomás de Vio Caietano) made a further distinction: namely, the category of infidel with invincible (i.e., inculpable) ignorance, and therefore guiltless for being pagan. The distinctions of the latter became the restraining wall against the universalist theocratic concepts that advocated the holy war against infidelity, for infidelity was an alleged intolerable offense against God.[14] In a key passage, Cayetano distinguished between the infidels who by law and by fact (*de iure et de facto*) are under the jurisdiction of Christianity, those who by law but not by fact are, and those who neither by law nor fact are legitimate subjects. The natives of the New World belonged to the third category:

> The owners of these lands, although infidels [those who have not committed any injury against Christianity], are their legitimate owners . . . [and] their infidelity does not deprive them of their dominion, for dominion ensues from natural law and infidelity from divine law, which

does not destroy natural law. . . . No king nor emperor, not even the Roman church itself, can wage war against them to occupy their lands and dominate them in temporal matters, for there is no cause for a just war. . . . Whereas we would seriously sin if we wished to spread the faith in Jesus Christ in this manner, and would not obtain legitimate jurisdiction, but rather would be committing grave robbery and would be obliged to make restitution for these unjust opponents and owners. To those infidels there should be sent good men who by their preaching and example would convert them to God and not such as those who oppress them, despoil them, scandalize and subject them, and make them twice the children of Hell, in the style of the Pharisees.[15]

At the same time, however, the cruel persecution of the heretics is justified. Aquinas (*Summa* 2-2.10.8), after insisting that the infidels should not be obliged to convert "because the act of faith belongs to the will" (*quia credere voluntatis est*), says of the heretics and apostates that they "should be subjected even to bodily compulsion so that they may fulfill what they have promised and profess what they at one time received."

Las Casas does not separate himself from that intolerance of theological heterodoxy. After repeating the dogmatic motto *extra ecclesiam nulla salus* (outside the church there is no salvation), he warns that, unlike the American natives, "the heretics should be expelled from the church by means of spiritual punishment, excommunication. If they stubbornly persist in their error, they should be consumed by the flames," since there "cannot be salvation in the absence of the holy Catholic faith" (Las Casas 1967, 1.3.45:238; 1974, 163–64, 304–12).[16] That was the common doctrine of the theologians of the Roman Church in general. Domingo de Soto, critic of the attempts to enforce the conversion of the natives by war, also established the distinction between the infidels who never had the Christian faith preached to them and the heretics. Against the latter, punishment is legitimate—even capital punishment: "Certainly it is licit to compel the second ones [the heretics] with threats and terrors; and even to inflict capital punishment. . . . But not so against the first [the infidels]."[17]

However, the wars against the natives do not fall within any of the categories outlined above. The American natives "are not Turks nor Moors who pester and maltreat us" (Las Casas 1986, 3.3.120:241). They are not heretics either. The norms of the just war do not apply against the infidels who do no harm to Christianity. After a long time of confrontations between Christian Europe and the Islamic "infidels," many have made the mistake of identifying infidelity as a legitimate cause for war.

It is from there the confusion comes that we now have. Some advocate the extension of what the doctors [scholars] affirm of the Moors and Turks, persecutors of the Christian name and violent occupiers of the kingdoms of Christianity, to the infidels who never knew nor were obliged to know that there were Christian people in the world, and therefore had never offended them. (Las Casas 1965, 1039)

Juan de Zumárraga, bishop of Mexico, also expressed his criticism of armed invasions against the Indian nations, insisting in a letter of April 4, 1537, after hearing the account of the situation in Peru from one of the friars, "that the conquest be taken away . . . ; they are an opprobrious injury to Christianity and our Catholic faith. In all this land what has happened has been only butchery" (in Cuevas 1975, 83; also cited by Isacio Pérez Fernández in Ramos et al. 1984, 132–33).

A Franciscan follower of Las Casas, Fray Gaspar de Recarte, in a brief of September 24, 1584, stressed the injustice of the Castilian wars of conquest, and, in contrast, the justice of the wars of resistance and defense on the part of the natives:

> Because the infidel natives, by natural law and the law of nations, are legitimate and true lords of these lands and kingdoms, they can justly *manu armata* [by armed force] impede entry into their lands to all and every [person] who wishes to come into them against the expressed or implied will of those Indians, and proceed against them as enemies and violators of the natural law and law of nations, even to the point of killing them if necessary. . . . And the Spaniards cannot resist them *manu armata*, even under the title of defense. (in Gómez Canedo 1977, 282)

This, however, was a minority view. Another Spanish bishop, Vasco de Quiroga, expressed the predominant opinion on the favorable interrelation between the sword and the cross to constitute an *imperium fidei* [the rule of the Christian faith] in the "testimonial of erection of the Cathedral of Michoacán," his diocese:

> It pleased the Divine Will to place at the head of the kingdoms of Spain such famous heroes, who did not only defeat the swords and war machinery of the barbarians, but who, generous with their lives and their patrimony, penetrated . . . unknown and very remote regions and having defeated the monster of idolatry, they planted everywhere, amid the clapping and happy anticipation of the Christian religion, the gospel of life, for the universal triumph of the banner of the cross. (in Zavala 1971, 263–64, 448)[18]

It is the sword of the conquerors that allows the "universal triumph of the banner of the cross" that is carried by the religious. The *imperium fidei* is extended through force and the violence of war. Pope Clement VIII, on the first centenary of the first Columbian journey, in the bull *Excelsia divinae potentiae*, celebrates

> the conversion of such an extraordinary number of New World countries . . . Nueva España, America, Brasil, Peru, and all the vast adjacent lands.
> Let us bless God for all this, then, for in His great mercy He has willed, in new ways, to call men also during this time to cease being children of wrath so that they can be led to living hope and to the knowledge of His Son Jesus Christ, Our Lord.

The unity of the faith and the nation could not be absent. The pope, on March 21, 1592, exhorts the inhabitants of the conquered lands to be fully loyal to the Spanish Crown:

> In conclusion, we warmly commend you in the Lord to show fidelity and obedience to our very dear son in Christ, Felipe the Catholic King of Spain and the Indies, your prince, to whom the Apostolic See granted power and the mission to procure the salvation of those nations. (in Terradas Soler 1962, 118–20)

Notes

1. Although Sepúlveda blamed Las Casas, above all, for the ban against his *Demócrates segundo*, the host of opponents was wider. Cano, theologian at Salamanca, wrote in 1548, "Your doctrine cannot be admitted with such certainty as not to be able to judge it as all just and very reasonable. This criterion is followed by the schools of Salamanca and Alcalá, which unanimously have refused to grant license for the publication of your book" (in Höffner 1957, 323).

2. This lack of critical judgment is seen in the attempts to highlight the historical importance of Vitoria. It taints the otherwise very fertile analysis by Fernando de los Ríos (1957). Something similar could be said of Scott's (1934) work.

3. See Lockhart 1972 (36–37) for a critique of the attempts to describe the social reality of Spanish colonization through the false shortcut of reading contemporary legal codes.

4. The thesis regarding the "most complete success" explains Manzano's opposition to the publication of the *Tratados* of Las Casas ("Brevísima relación" "Octavo remedio," etc.) in 1552. In his opinion, this was unnecessary since the Dominicans were winning the fight against the *encomenderos* and colonists; it was imprudent since "the consequences would be fatal to the national cause," for they gave rise to the "black anti-Hispanic legend . . . the most horrendous deceit registered by the annals of humanity." The only thing it accomplished was to "strike a mortal blow at the good name of the Spanish nation as soon as they fell into the hands of foreigners, especially heretics" (ibid., 229, 233, 250). It seems a tactful criticism, but soon Manzano reveals the deeper reason for his repudiation of *Tratados* by labeling them works "plagued by the most dangerous and grave errors" (ibid., 248). In reality, in spite of his frequent praise for Las Casas, he disagrees deeply with the vision the bishop of Chiapas had about the relationship between Spaniards and the natives. In Manzano's opinion that relationship was fundamentally beneficial, in spite of some considerable abuses. That was not the perspective of Las Casas. Manzano's critique is not original. It had already been expressed in 1555, with no less animosity, by Motolinía, who thought that the Dominican friar "dishonored . . . the Spaniards with his writings" (Benavente 1984, "Carta a Carlos V," 211). It was repeated in Peru by *"Anónimo de Yucay"* (439–43), for whom the books of Las Casas "defamed the Christian nation, and among Christians, the Spaniards," thus helping "the English and French heretical Lutherans . . . who say that the Spanish King is a tyrant, . . . that we are thieves in the Indies." The heretics, who are themselves led in reality by "greed for gold and silver," then proceed in armed confrontation against the Castilian overseas empire. The idea that the "black legend" would not have existed had Las Casas

not written his *Tratados* is arguable. Friederici ([1925] 1986, 1:393) states that "his pages do not contain, in substance or nature, anything that we cannot read in other works." Those who affirm that Las Casas, especially in his *Brevísima relación*, is the principal culprit of the "black legend," are also mistaken. There were other factors that provoked anti-Spanish stereotypes in England and the Low Countries. Religious antagonism prevailed, as did the threat that the Dutch Calvinists and English Protestants felt in the face of the fierce Catholic fervor of Felipe II in assuming his role as the scourge of "heresies." More influential among the European Protestant audience than the *Brevísima relación* were the many accounts that painted a gloomy picture of the Spanish Inquisition. See Maltby 1982.

5. See Pérez de Tudela 1958 for a keen criticism of the common affirmation that the New Laws represented a total victory for Las Casas.

6. Salas (1986, 59), in his essay on Anglería, sees in these words of the Italian humanist "all the drama of a wise and Christian legislation [that] fails because of distance and human ambition and greed that flow unrestrained in the newfound lands. . . . rudely creating a way of life . . . a reality that in many respects had nothing to do with the *Leyes de Indias*."

7. Much has been said about the breakdown in morality in the passage from Europe to América at the beginning of the conquest and colonization, even causing the coinage of the pregnant concept of "tropicalization of the white man." Although Bataillon (1976, 364) prefers "criollización," to indicate that we are dealing more with a social process than a climatological one, the first phrase seems to me appropriate. It points to the dissolution of ethical inhibitions, which are always fragile and precarious in the presence of the seductive influence of the vegetation and flora of the American jungle, as is so often dealt with in Latin American literature.

8. I consider Hanke's (1967, 28–32) panegyric to the "freedom of speech in [sixteenth-century] Spain" to be hyperbole. It is no accident that many works written during the second half of that century were unpublished for several centuries.

9. Spanish chroniclers and theologians debated with their customary intensity the justice and legitimacy of Atahualpa's execution. Acosta (1952, 2.18:211) censures it, not out of legal concerns but because of missionary convenience. It would have been preferable, he suggested, to have his collaboration so as to evangelize the natives. "Our people gravely erred in the death of Atabalipa [sic], Inka prince, . . . and if the good will of the prince had been gained, the entire Inka empire would have soon received the faith easily."

10. Oviedo (1851, 4.3.48.6:373) recounts that Vicente de Valverde was killed by the natives of the islands of Puná. The tone of divine revenge in the narrative is interesting: "God allowed time and Indians to avenge the imprisonment and death of prince Atabalipa [sic], in which affair the religious superior Fray Vicente had been the intercessor so-called." Valverde was named bishop of Cuzco in 1536 by Carlos V, who gave Valverde the title of "protector e defensor de los yndios de la provincia [del Peru]" (in Armas Medina 1953, 122, n. 51).

11. In later reflections about African slavery he arrived at the important conclusion that not all Muslims are necessarily "enemies of the faith, usurpers of Christian kingdoms."

12. Contrary to his exaggerated arithmetic of Spanish cruelty, Las Casas understands that the aborigines did not sacrifice more than "thirty, a hundred, or a thousand" persons in a year, and not all of them necessarily "innocent" (ibid., 205). Note that Motolinía (1984, 3.11:167), not at all sympathetic toward Las Casas, recognizes that "the avarice of our Spaniards was more to blame for the

destruction and depopulation of this land than all the [human] sacrifices, wars, and homicides that took place there during its time of infidelity."

13. On another occasion he mentions the possible legitimacy of the war against infidel princes who are tyrants and cruel. In that case, the Supreme Pontiff can admonish them to change their despotic ways. If his request is not heeded, "the Supreme Vicar of Christ can order those tyrants who do not make amends or who resist to be compelled by war." This is reminiscent of one of Vitoria's reasons for legitimizing the Spaniards' wars against the natives: defense of the innocent. This perspective would bring him close to the Spanish scholastic Dominicans of the sixteenth century—to Christian humanitarian imperialism—but he never develops it fully (Las Casas 1965, 1009).

14. See his key work: *Secunda secundae partis summae totius theologiae d. Thomae Aquinatis, Thomae a Vio Cajetani commentariis illustrata.* Printed in 1517 for the first time, it was widely read due to the many manuscripts in circulation and the many references made to it. The distinction between infidels is in the commentary to part 2-2.66.8.

15. Ibid. It is included in Leturia 1959 (1:164) and in Silvio Zavala's introduction to the treatise by López de Palacios Rubios and Paz (1954, lxxxv–lxxxvi). Las Casas cites it in Latin in his "Tratado de las doce dudas" (1965, 490) and in *Los tesoros del Perú* ([1563] 1958, 260). Although in this passage Cayetano does not make explicit mention to the controversies over the Indies, Las Casas (1986, 2.3.38:563) alleges that he wrote it after being informed by the Dominican friar Hierónimo de Peñafiel about the abuses committed against the natives of the Americas. This text was very influential with many Dominican theologians, among them Vitoria, who developed the same idea in *De indis* (1538) in a section dedicated to a discussion of illegitimate Spanish domination over "the barbarians of the New World"; Bartolomé Carranza, in his lecture *An infideles possint habere dominium super fideles* (1539); Melchor Cano, in his treatise *De dominio indiorum* (1546) (the last two are in Pereña 1956, 38–57, 90–147, respectively); and Fray Miguel de Benavides, in his statement, "Ynstrucción para el govierno de las Filipinas," in Hanke and Millares 1977 (241). On Cayetano, see Carro 1944 (1:397–408).

16. In his *Apologia* against Sepúlveda, Las Casas indicates that in the lost first book of his work *Del único modo de atraer a todos los pueblos a la verdadera religión* he delved in detail into the distinction between heretics, who can be compelled to fulfill their baptismal vows, and infidels, who do not know Christianity and cannot be forced to obey ecclesiastical precepts (Las Casas 1974, 312).

17. "Et quídem illos secundos non solum minis et terroribus cogere licet, verum . . . capitis suplicio plectere. Priores autem non item" (And indeed it is licit to compel the latter by threats and terror, even . . . inflict capital punishment on them. This may not be done with the former). *In quartum sententiarum commentari*, Salmanticae, 1570 (1:271). Cited in Latin in Castañeda Delgado (1974, 137). Höffner (1957, 114–18) shows there was unanimity among the great scholastic Spanish theologians of the Golden Age (Vitoria, Soto, Bañz, Suárez) in favor of persecution and execution of heretics.

18. Vasco de Quiroga seems to have been a bishop dedicated to the well-being of the natives. Fray Juan de Zumárraga, bishop of Mexico, wrote about him to the Council of the Indies on February 8, 1537: "The deep love that this good man shows them, which he proves with the works and benefits he continually performs on their behalf with great spirit and perseverance . . ." (in Cuevas 1975, 76).

Resources

Acosta, José de, S.J. 1952. *De procuranda indorum salute (Predicación del evangelio en las Indias, 1588)*, "Proemio." Ed. Francisco Mateo, S.J. Madrid: Colección España Misionera.

Anglería, Pedro Mártir de. 1964–65. *De orbe novo*. Latin edition, 1530. *Décadas del nuevo mundo*. 2 vols. Translated by Agustín Millares Carlo and Foreword by Edmundo O'Gorman. México, D.F.: Porrúa. References are for volume, decade, book, and page. [*The Decades of the New World or West India*, by Pietro Martire d'Anghiera. Translation from G. F. de Ovieda y Valdés (1478–1557), R. J. Eden (1480/1491-c. 1534), and Antonio Pigafetta (1480/1491-c. 1534). Ann Arbor, Mich.: University Microfilms, 1966.]

Armas Medina, Fernando de. 1953. *Cristianización del Perú (1532–1600)*. Sevilla: Escuela de Estudios Hispano-Americanos de la Universidad de Sevilla.

Bataillon, Marcel. 1976. *Estudios sobre Bartolomé del las Casas*. Barcelona: Península.

Benavente, Toribio de. Known as Motolinía. 1984. *Historia de los indios de la Nueva España: Relación de los ritos antiguos, idolatría y sacrificios de los indios de la Nueva España, y de la maravillosa conversión que Dios en ella ha obrado*. Ed. Edmundo O'Gorman. México, D.F.: Porrúa. "Carta a Carlos V" found here, 203–21.

Carro, Venancio D., O.P. 1944. *La teología y los teólogos juristas españoles ante la conquista de América*. 2 vols. Madrid: Escuela de Estudios Hispano-Americanos de la Universidad de Sevilla.

Castañeda Delgado, Paulino. 1974. "Los métodos misionales en América. ¿Evangelización pura coacción?" In *Estudios sobre Fray Bartolomé de Las Casas*, André Saint-Lu et al. Sevilla: Universidad de Sevilla.

Cuevas, Mariano. 1975. *Documentos inéditos del siglo XVI para la historia de México* [1914]. México, D.F.: Editorial Porrúa (Biblioteca Porrúa, 62).

Ercilla, Alonso de. 1984. *La Araucana*. La Habana: Editorial Arte y Literatura. [English lines are from: *The Araucaniad*, trans. Charles Maxwell Lancaster and Paul Thomas Manchester. Nashville: Vanderbilt University Press, 1945. Numbers in brackets in citations correspond to English ed. page numbers.]

Fabié, Antonio M. 1879. *Vida y escritos de don Fray Bartolomé de Las Casas, Obispo de Chiapa*. 2 vols. Madrid: Imprenta de Miguel Ginesta. [Reprinted in the *Colección de documentos inéditos para la historia de España*. Vols. 70–71. Vaduz: Kraus Reprint, 1966.]

Friede, Juan. 1976. *Bartolomé de las Casas: Precursor del anticolonialismo*. México, D.F.: Siglo XXI.

Friederici, George. 1986. *El carácter del descubrimiento y de la conquista de América: Introducción a la historia de la colonización de América por los pueblos del Viejo Mundo*. México, D.F.: Fondo de Cultura Económica. [Der Charakter der Entdeckung und Eroberung Amerikas durch die Europäer. Stuttgart-Gotha: Verlag Andres Perthes, A.G., 1925–1936.]

Ginés de Sepúlveda, Juan. 1951. *Demócrates segundo o de las justas causas de la guerra contra los indios*. Bilingual ed. Introduction, editing, notes, and Spanish translation by Angel Losada. Madrid: Consejo Superior de Investigaciones Científicas.

Gómez Canedo, Lino. 1977. *Evangelización y conquista: Experiencia franciscana en Hispanoamérica*. Contains "Carta a Carlos V," by Franciscan friar Francisco Vitoria, 223–25. México, D.F.: Porrúa.

González Rodríguez, Jaime. 1984."La Junta de Valladolid convocada por el Emperador." In Demetrio Ramos et al., 199–227.

Hanke, Lewis U. 1967. *La lucha española por la justicia en la conquista de América*. Madrid: Aguilar. [*The Spanish Struggle for Justice in the Conquest of America*. Philadelphia: University of Pennsylvania Press, 1949.]

Hanke, Lewis U., and Agustín Millares Carlo, eds. 1977. *Cuerpo de documentos del siglo XVI sobre los derechos de España en las Indias y las Filipinas*. México, D.F.: Fondo de Cultura Económica.

Höffner, Joseph. 1957. *La ética colonial española del siglo de oro: Cristianismo y dignidad humana*. Madrid: Ediciones Cultura Hispánica.

Jerez, Francisco de. 1947. *Verdadera relación de la conquista del Perú y provincia del Cuzco, llamada la Nueva Castilla, conquistada por Francisco Pizarro, capitán de la sacra católica real majestad del Emperador nuestro señor (1534)*. Vol. 26, Ediciones Atlas. Madrid: Biblioteca de Autores Españoles.

Konetzke, Richard. 1953. *Colección de documentos para la historia de la formación social de Hispanoamérica, 1493–1810*. 3 vols. Madrid: Consejo Superior de Investigaciones Científicas.

Las Casas, Bartolomé de. O.P. 1942. *Del único modo de atraer a todos los pueblos a la verdadera religión*. México, D.F.: Fondo de Cultura Económica.

———. 1958. *Los tesoros del Perú*. Ed. Angel Losada. [First edition: *De Thesauris in Peru*, 1563.] Includes amendment to "Tratado comprobatorio" found in his *Tratados*, 85–349. Madrid: Consejo Superior de Investigaciones Científicas.

———. 1962. *Tratado de Indias y el doctor Sepúlveda*. Caracas: Biblioteca Nacional de la Historia.

———. 1965. Prologue to *Tratados*, by Lewis Hanke and Manuel Giménez Fernández. Transcription by Juan Pérez de Tudela and translations by Agustín Millares Carlo and Rafael Moreno. 2 vols. México, D.F.: Fondo de Cultura Económica. These documents are found here: *"Aqui se contiene una disputa o controversia,"* 1:217–459; *"Octavo remedio,"* 2:643–849; *"Tratado comprobatorio del imperio soberano y principado universal que los reyes de Castilla y León tienen sobre las Indias,"* 2:914–1233; *"Treinta proposiciones muy jurídicas,"* 1:460–499.

———. 1967. *Apologética historia sumaria*. 2 vols. Ed. Edmundo O'Gorman. México, D.F.: Universidad Nacional Autónoma.

————. 1974. *In Defense of the Indians. The Defense of the Most Reverend Lord, Don Fray Bartolomé de las Casas, of the Order of Preachers, Late Bishop of Chiapa, Against the Persecutors and Slanderers of the Peoples of the New World Discovered Across the Seas.* Trans. and ed. Stafford Poole, C.M. De Kalb: Northern Illinois University Press.

————. 1986. Introduction and editing of *Historia de las Indias*, by Lewis Hanke. México, D.F.: Fondo de Cultura Económica. [*History of the Indies: Selections.* New York: Harper & Row, 1971.]

————. 1989. Introduction and notes to *Brevísima relación de la destrucción de Africa: Preludio de la destrucción de Indias. Primera defensa de los guanches y negros contra su esclavización*, by Isacio Pérez Fernández, O.P. Salamanca-Lima, Editorial San Esteban-Instituto Bartolomé de las Casas.

León Portilla, Miguel. 1987. *El reverso de la conquista: Relaciones aztecas, mayas e incas.* 16th ed. México, D.F.: Editorial Joaquín Moritz.

Leturia, Pedro de, S.J. 1959. *Época del real patronato, 1493–1800.* Vol. 1 of *Relaciones entre la Santa Sede e Hispanoamérica, 1493–1835.* Caracas: Sociedad Bolivariana de Venezuela; Rome: Universidad Gregoriana.

Lockhart, James. 1972. "The Social History of Colonial Spanish America: Evolution and Potential." *Latin-American Research Review* 7, no. 1 (Spring): 6–45.

López de Palacios Rubios, Juan, and Matías de Paz. 1954. *De las islas del mar océano* (1–209); *Del dominio de los reyes de España sobre los indios.* Published in one volume with an introduction by Silvio A. Zavala and trans. Agustín Millares Carlo. Buenos Aires-México, D.F.: Fondo de Cultura Económica.

Maltby, William S. 1982. *La leyenda negra en Inglaterra: Desarrollo del sentimiento antihispánico, 1558–1660.* México, D.F.: Fondo de Cultura Económica.

Manzano Manzano, Juan. 1948. *La incorporación de las Indias a la corona de Castilla.* Madrid: Ediciones Cultura Hispánica.

Mendieta, Gerónimo de. 1980. *Historia eclesiástica indiana* [1596]. 3rd facsimile ed. México, D.F.: Editorial Porrúa.

Milhou, Alain. 1975–76. "Las Casas frente a las reivindicaciones de los colonos de la isla Española." *Historiografia y bibliografia americanistas.* 19–20:11–67.

Motolinía. *See* Benavente, Toribio de.

Ots Capdequí, José María. 1986. *El estado español en las Indias.* 7th reprint. México, D.F.: Fondo de Cultura Económica.

Oviedo y Valdés, Gonzalo F. de. 1851. *Historia general y natural de las Indias, islas y tierra firme del mar Océano.* Madrid: Real Academia de Historia. References are to volume, part, book, chapter, and page.

Pacheco, Joaquín F., Francisco de Cárdenas, and Luis Torres de Mendoza, eds. 1864–1884. *Colección de documentos inéditos relativos al descubrimiento, conquista y organización de las antiguas posesiones españolas de América y Oceanía, sacados de los Archivos del Reino y muy espe-*

cialmente del de Indias. Vols. 1–31. Madrid: Real Academia de la Historia.

Pereña Vicente, Luciano. 1956. *Misión de España en América (1540–1560).* Includes *De iustitia belli adversus indos* (1548), by Diego de Covarrubias, and Bartolomé de Carranza's 1540 lecture in Valladolid. Madrid: Consejo Superior de Investigaciones Científicas.

Pérez de Tudela, Juan. 1958. "La gran reforma carolina de las Indias en 1542." *Revista de Indias* (Madrid) 18: 73–74; 463–509.

Phelan, John Leddy. 1974. "El imperio cristiano de Las Casas, el imperio español de Sepúlveda y el imperio milenario de Mendieta." *Revista de Occidente* 141 (diciembre): 292–310.

Ramos, Demetrio. 1984. "El hecho de la conquista de América." In *La ética. See* Ramos et al., 1984.

Ramos, Demetrio, et al. 1984. *La ética en la conquista de América.* Vol. 25, *Corpus Hispanorum de Pace.* Madrid: Consejo Superior de Investigaciones Científicas.

Ricard, Robert. 1986. *La conquista espiritual de México. Ensayo sobre el apostolado y los métodos misioneros de las ordenes mendicantes en la Nueva España de 1523–24 a 1572.* México, D.F.: Fondo de Cultura Económica.

Ríos, Fernando de los. 1957. *Religión y estado en la España del siglo XVI.* México, D.F.: Fondo de Cultura Económica.

Russell, Frederick H. 1975. *The Just War in the Middle Ages.* Cambridge: Cambridge University Press.

Salas, Alberto Mario. 1986. *Tres cronistas de Indias: Pedro Mártir de Anglería, Gonzalo Fernández de Oviedo, Fray Bartolomé de las Casas.* 2nd ed. corrected and enlarged. México, D.F.: Fondo de Cultura Económica.

Sauer, Carl Ortwin, 1984. *Descubrimiento y dominación española del Caribe.* México, D.F.: Fondo de Cultura Económica.

Scott, James Brown. 1934. *The Spanish Origin of International Law. Francisco de Vitoria and His Law of Nations.* London: Oxford University Press.

Sepúlveda. *See* Ginés de Sepúlveda.

Soto, Domingo de. 1967. *De la justicia y del derecho* (1556). 4 vols. Introduction by Venancio Diego Carro. Trans. Marcelino González Ordoñez. Madrid: Instituto de Estudios Políticos. Refrences are given by volume, book, question, article, and page.

Terradas Soler, Juan. 1962. *Una epopeya misionera: La conquista y colonización de América vistas desde Roma.* Madrid: Ediciones y Publicaciones Españolas.

Urdanoz, Teófilo, O.P., ed. 1960. *Obras de Francisco Vitoria: Relaciones teológicas. Edición crítica del texto latino, versión española, introducción general e introducciones con el estudio de su doctrina teológico-jurídica.* Madrid: Biblioteca de Autores Cristianos.

Vitoria, Francisco de. 1967. *Relectio de indis o libertad de los indios.* Edited by Luciano Pereña Vicente and J. M. Peres Prendes. "Carta de

Francisco de Vitoria al P. Arcos," Appendix I, 137–39. Vol. 10, *Corpus Hispanorum de Pace*. Madrid: Consejo Superior de Investigaciones Científicas.

————. 1967. Introduction to *Relecciones. Del estado, De los indios y Del derecho de la guerra*, by Antonio Gómez Robledo, ix–xc. México, D.F.: Editorial Porrúa.

Ybot León, Antonio. 1948. "Juntas de teólogos asesoras del estado para Indias 1512–1550," *Anuario de estudios americanos* 5:397–438.

Zavala, Silvio. 1971. *Las instituciones jurídicas en la conquista de América*. 2nd ed. revised and enlarged. México, D.F.: Porrúa.

————. 1984. *La filosofía política en la conquista de América*, 3rd ed. revised and enlarged. México, D.F.: Fondo de Cultura Económica.

2

The Ordenanza del Patronazgo of 1574: An Interpretative Essay

Robert C. Padden

By midsixteenth century the Spanish Crown had issued scores, if not hundreds, of decrees concerning the regulation of the Catholic Church. Under the concept of the Patronato Real, the Crown claimed temporal control over the Church, including the king's right to appoint bishops, archbishops, and parish priests as well as the right to collect the ecclesiastical tax, or tithe. Robert Padden looks into the political aspects of the debate over the royal patronage and the behind-the-scenes maneuvering at its implementation.

The promulgation of the Ordenanza del Patronazgo was not an isolated event but rather part of a larger Crown program that sought to codify royal law dealing with the New World. This effort at codification was initiated by Juan de Ovando, president of the Council of the Indies and an important adviser to King Philip II. Other sets of ordinances also emerged from this effort, although the universal code of law that Ovando sought would not come into being for a century. The other major set to appear in the 1570s was the Ordinances for Population and Settlement.

The Ordenanza del Patronazgo was an attempt on the part of the Crown to interpose itself between the papacy and the Church in the Americas. It also sought to control the power of the regular clergy, both by restricting direct access to the papacy and by moving the regulars from the rural parishes back into urban monasteries.

Robert Padden is emeritus professor of history at Brown University. Among his publications is the popular Hummingbird and the Hawk, *an account of the conquest of Mexico. He also has written several important essays on the history of early colonial Mexico and its role in Spanish imperial designs.*

At the accession of Isabella in 1474 the Church in Castile lay prostrate for the most part before the will of the papacy. Greater and lesser

From *The Americas* 12 (1956): 333–54. Reprinted by permission of the Academy of American Franciscan History.

benefices were controlled from Rome, foreigners were commonly appointed to the highest dignities, and tribunals of justice were rendered impotent by interminable appeals to Rome. No less were the Castilian nobles accustomed to usurping royal authority in the civil and political branches of government. Castile was a patchwork of private jurisdictions and privileges of which Isabella was no more than a titular sovereign.

As private rights of patronage and justice formed the basis of medieval politics, so did they provide a foundation for development of a national state. Immediately following the successful conclusion of the war which was caused by her succession, Isabella moved against the nobles, replacing their seignorial tribunals with her own. It was a victory of public justice, in the name of the queen, over justice privately wielded. This was the beginning of modern Spain and the absolute monarchy.

By 1482, Isabella was prepared to challenge the papacy. In that year Pope Sixtus IV conferred the bishopric of Cuenca on his nephew. The queen refused to accede, and, taking advantage of Roman corruption, suggested the convention of a general reform council to investigate the condition of the Church. Unwilling or unable to bear examination, Sixtus IV adopted a conciliatory attitude which ultimately led him to confer on Isabella all rights of presentation to higher ecclesiastical dignities in Castile. The following year she gained the right to reform and control the Spanish Inquisition.[1] The arsenal of absolutism was now complete. Progressively, Isabella suppressed private justice and old feudal privileges, replacing them with royal administrative laws. Through her powers of ecclesiastical presentation, the Church acquired the identity of a vast and loyal bureaucracy. As Ferdinand and Isabella consolidated their kingdoms and pressed to the south, Catholicism became synonymous with the new nationalism, and Mohammedanism and Judaism were crushed beneath its weight. In this unity of national and religious sentiment it was inevitable that the Church and the Holy Office should become quasi-political agencies of the Crown, and so it came to pass that secular churchmen became recognized as civil servants.

By the time of their deaths, Ferdinand and Isabella had formulated a basic attitude towards both Church and State which endured for over two hundred years. Increasing centralization of royal ecclesiastical authority and diminishment of papal influence in temporal affairs were firmly established as constants of Spanish monarchical policy. This continuity is fundamental to the understanding of the Church that was founded in the Spanish Indies.

With the discovery of the New World, the Catholic kings accepted a perpetual obligation of evangelization.[2] Although both Crown and papacy were ignorant of the geographical extent of the newly discovered lands, it was evident that distance alone would make the cost of evangelization great. The Crown, in asssuming financial responsibility, was given control of the tithe which might be levied in the New World.[3] A more precise knowledge of the Caribbean was afforded after Española was permanently settled, and it soon became apparent that formal ecclesiastical organization was necessary for evangelization of the natives and the spiritual welfare of the Spanish colonists. This need was satisfied by the bull *Universalis Ecclesiae*, which gave the Crown the privileges of founding churches and presenting all persons for ecclesiastical appointment.[4]

By virtue of these concessions the Crown achieved a tight managerial control over the Church in the Indies. Technically, the colonial Church was founded on the spiritual authority of the papacy under the political aegis of the Spanish Crown. This implied a partnership of responsibility, but the Crown's attitude towards such an entente was apparent from the beginning. In 1493 the pope sought to establish his authority in the New World by sending a nuncio to Española. Ferdinand and Isabella sternly warned him not to send a representative without their express permission.[5] Such vigilance was constant. In 1528 the nuncio in Madrid secretly sent a collector of *espolios* to Española. The king found it out and ordered the audiencia to restrain him, seize his papers, and forward them to the Council of the Indies.[6] This policy of isolation was extended to include papal decrees. From the late fourteenth century, Spanish monarchs had enjoyed the right to inspect and approve papal decrees before permitting publication in their realms. In 1538, Charles V applied this power of exequatur to his possessions in the Indies, making it illegal to publish or make use of a papal pronouncement without first submitting it to the Council of the Indies for approval.[7] In a sense the Council of the Indies became a curia to the Crown, while the Roman curia was barred from direct participation in the religious affairs of the Indies.

We may think it strange that the papacy, so great a temporal and spiritual power, would divest itself of its share of authority in the temporal management of the colonial Church. Certainly the Crown used a great deal of influence and persuasion in obtaining fiscal control and exclusive rights of patronage. But these privileges, however significant they later became, were relatively insignificant at the time of concession. The whole of the Caribbean, in an ecclesiastical sense, was of less import than the meanest bishopric in Spain. Subsequent exploration of Tierra Firme gave evidence of wealth and vast Indian populations; this caused the "Indies" to be multiplied both in size and significance. On the basis of his yet imperfect knowledge, Ferdinand ordered his ambassador in Rome to request erection of a bishopric in the vicinity of Darién. Anticipating subsequent erections and the need of a central ecclesiastical authority answering to himself, he further ordered the ambassador to seek concession of a patriarchal office, appointive by the Crown, and resident on the mainland.[8] The pope complied with his first request, but refused to grant the patriarchate with authority of ecclesiastical office. The papacy, like the Crown, was becoming aware of the magnitude of the Indies, and this refusal signified the conclusion of papal concessions which could bolster the Crown's independence in administration of the colonial Church.

It was the conquest and transitory wealth of Mexico, rather than Tierra Firme, which ultimately revolutionized the European conception of the Indies. With the spoils of Peru closely following those of Mexico, Spain's fortune in the Indies was made, and the material significance of the New World for the Old was manifest. But political dominion and economic exploitation, so much the talk and envy of the European powers, comprised only one side of the golden medallion. The Spanish Crown was also confronted by the greatest evangelical challenge in modern history.

The Valley of Mexico, first conquered in point of time and yielding a vast indigenous population, became a proving-ground for evangelical method and ecclesiastical organization in the ever-widening sphere of Spanish domination. This preeminence survived further conquest and Mexico remained as the ecclesiastical focal point of the overseas empire through the sixteenth century. In discharge of his obligation of evangelization, Charles V relied almost exclusively on friars of the Mendicant Orders. Members of the Franciscan Order were sent out in 1524; Dominican friars arrived in 1526, and Augustinians in 1533. Episcopal organization followed swiftly. In 1528 a bishopric of Mexico was created; in 1545, after the erection of three additional dioceses, Oaxaca, Michoacán, and Chiapas, the bishopric of Mexico was elevated to archiepiscopal rank. During this period of proliferous growth, episcopal office was usually occupied by friars. Secular clergymen were nearly always present, but their numbers were limited and their evangelical skills were generally inferior to those of the Mendicants. When passing mention is made of the Church in Mexico prior to 1550, it must of necessity refer to Mendicant organization, rather than to what is commonly thought of as a well-developed secular clergy.

By 1550, however, the secular clergy had grown in numbers and had adjusted itself to the conditions of colonial life. As they gained strength, the seculars sought to curtail the ecclesiastical privileges and immunities by means of which the friars had undertaken the evangelization of Mexico and currently ministered to both Indians and Spaniards. The friars, on the other hand, were not of a mind to relinquish any of their privileges at the demand of secular bishops. The friars were proud of their accomplishments and considered assimilation of their position by a small and frequently inferior clergy to be nothing short of ridiculous. On this basis there was a gradual development of conflict between secular bishops and their clergy and the Mendicant Orders.

Conflict over Jurisdiction

An omnipresent cause of conflict in Mexico was argument over episcopal jurisdiction. As missionaries in a heathen land, the Mendicants wielded extraordinary ecclesiastical authority. They could freely grant absolution, officiate at marriages, administer all sacraments, and practice the care of souls. If there was no bishop, or if they found themselves beyond two days' journey of a bishop's residence, they could perform many acts which normally required the office of a bishop. In effect, every friar was virtually a bishop in his own right. These privileges were set forth and guaranteed in the bull *Omnimoda*, which served as a charter of Mendicant rights.[9]

The coming of bishops did not give occasion for immediate questioning of these privileges. Most of the early bishops were themselves Mendicants, and they commonly subordinated episcopal office to their prime objective of evangelization. Friars continued to exercise their privileges as though there were no bishops, and the technical limitation of two days' journey went largely unobserved. With development of a secular clergy and hierarchy, this practice was brought to question and challenged. By 1551 the bishoprics of Guatemala, Michoacán, Oaxaca, and Nueva Galicia were administered by secular prelates,[10] and exercise of Mendicant privileges under their very noses was decried as usurpation of episcopal office. The bishops sought to reduce the friars' privileges well beyond their immediate vicinities, and the friars, with equal vigor, defied the bishops on their own doorsteps.

Conflict over the Tithe

Another perennial issue was the tithe. The bishops sought to include the Indians in the general tithe that was levied on the Spanish population. Such an increase of income, they argued, was needed in order to support a properly organized Church and to provide for enlargement of the secular clergy. They were strenuously opposed by the friars, who favored neither growth of the secular clergy nor increase of the financial burden already borne by the Indians.[11] This was a fundamental argument. The bishops realized that their own authority was measured by the strength of the secular Church. Consequently, they were determined to develop its strength in spite of all opposition. The Mendicants received most of their material support from the Indians. Alms and contributions of labor and produce sustained the evangelical system. If the Indians were to be subjected to the general tithe, in addition to the tribute which they already paid, the secular Church would of necessity divert a large proportion of the Mendicants' sustenance to its own use. Fearful of losing their independent income, hence their ecclesiastical independence, the friars resisted the bishops by every means at hand. This was not merely an economic consideration. The friars sincerely believed that the independence of their organizations was the keystone of the Indians' conversion and salvation. This conviction, in view of the fate of the Caribbean Indians, was based upon historical reality.

The friars, having been the first to enter the field in numbers, occupied vast mission districts which they closed to the entry of both seculars and friars of a different Order. When the bishops attempted to extend their authority into these areas and to place their priests in rural *doctrinas*, sharp and often violent conflict ensued. Documentary fragments of the period seem to indicate a rampant spirit of vindictiveness. Robert Ricard tells of two Franciscan friars who raised an army of 1,600 Indians, arming them with bows, arrows, and shields. In the middle of the night they attacked a secular church, razing the structure and burning its remains. It was reported that one Indian was killed in the action. In 1550, during a dispute between the bishops of Michoacán and Nueva Galicia over diocesan limits, a band of seculars from Michoacán invaded Nueva Galicia territory, sacked and pillaged a church, and put the friars to flight. In 1559 a group of vandals, allegedly seculars, made a night attack on a Dominican convent in Puebla during which they manhandled the friars, knocked the prior's teeth out, and escaped with whatever they could lay their hands on.[12] Episcopal determination and Mendicant intransigence made discord all-pervasive. By 1555 dissension was epidemic in the Mexican Church.[13]

Some Reasons behind the Mendicants' Attitude

One cannot read through correspondence of the period without being struck by the singular contempt in which Mendicants held the secular clergy.[14] Although conflict was extremely bitter on a personal basis, I believe this feeling of disdain was owing more to ideological discord than to disputes over purely temporal and material issues. The Franciscans, who led the evangelization of Mexico, maintained a theory of ecclesiastical primacy. They believed themselves and the other Mendicants to be the only genuine apostles in New Spain. Before the formal arrival of the Franciscans in 1524, evangelization was conducted by both seculars and religious. Clérigo Juan Díaz, Mercedarian Fray Bartolomé de Olmedo, and Fleming Franciscans Juan de Tecto, Juan de Aora, and Pedro de Gante conducted services in Mexico City and were noted for their charitable ministrations to the Indians.[15] The later Franciscans acknowledged the good work done by their predecessors in Mexico and in the Caribbean, but denied them apostolic status. The differentiation which made the year 1524 a baseline of apostolic demarcation arose from a distinction of ecclesiastical authorities.

Only the Franciscans of 1524 and the Mendicants who followed them were in possession of papal authority. Those who had preceded them and the seculars who followed were merely possessed of royal license; hence, they were not apostles.[16] The manner in which this authority, embodied in the *Omnimoda*, was ushered into the New World is indicative of the reverence owed it. The Franciscan apostles of 1524 were limited to twelve in number, with one prelate, because that was the number with which Christ had undertaken the conversion of all mankind. Saint Francis, too, had led twelve apostles. Having reached the shores of New Spain, the apostles walked barefooted to Mexico City where Hernán Cortés humbled himself before them. To the friars this was not so much the spirit of imitation as it was that of participation in the continuum of Christian tradition. They were symbolically uniting themselves with historical experience. This was the very soul of their enterprise.

In Mendicant practice, the seculars were always excluded from apostleship, and their attempts at evangelization were generally derided or viewed as a nuisance.[17] Occasionally a worthy secular was lauded in the pages of Mendicant chronicles, but this was a great exception to a general rule. The Mendicants felt that seculars, lacking in tradition and training and too closely associated with the laity, were unfit for evangelization. The seculars quite naturally did not agree.

Papal Concessions to Mendicants

The *Omnimoda* was supranational. It was, if you please, a very piece of the rock of Saint Peter. In unbroken descent it passed from Rome to the General of the Franciscan Order, thence to members of the Order and to other Mendicants.[18] The seculars possessed nothing comparable to it. Their sole authority was the king's will. Coming from a thoroughly nationalized Church, of which the king was ruler in all but faith and morals, they did not bear an apostolic tradition. Royal patronage, as exercised through the ecclesiastical bureaucracy, was both the beginning and end of professional service. Everyone, and this included the friars, had to have royal permission in order to go to the Indies. After their arrival, seculars remained under the royal thumb as it was manipulated by the episcopal hierarchy. The friars, on the other hand, joined their own organizations and the immunities and privileges which the Middle Ages had bestowed upon them. And they had their *Omnimoda*.

Disparagement of royal license as an ecclesiastical authority was symptomatic of the Mendicants' attitude towards the Crown. They willingly recognized its political authority but hedged from its ecclesiastical pretensions. Especially did they consider their internal organizations exempt from royal interference. Theirs was not a position easily maintained. Viceregal office threatened them on one side, the secular Church on the other. Between these two arms of the state, the Mendicants strove to preserve their ecclesiastical independence. Never did the friars entertain the idea of compromise. As apostolic delegates of the pope and ultimately the servants of God, they could not and would not come to terms with royal mercenaries.[19]

Tentative Settlement

Both regulars and seculars constantly sought a definitive settlement of the struggle in which they were engaged. In 1555, Archbishop Alonso de Montúfar convened the first Provincial Council and attempted to subordinate the Orders to his control. No clergyman, regular or secular, was henceforth to practice the care of souls, or hear confessions, without previous examination by the episcopacy to ascertain fitness for such duties. No monastery was to be built without a bishop's license, nor was any friar to celebrate Mass in a monastery which had been built without such license. Henceforth, all residents, including the Indians, were to pay the general tithe; anyone opposing its levy was to be excommunicated.[20] Thunderous Mendicant protest caused the Crown to disallow the Council's measures.[21] The Archbishop was determined, and in 1559 the Crown issued *cédulas* which gave him the right to inspect the records and properties of the parish churches under Mendicant jurisdiction.[22]

In 1565, Montúfar convened a second Provincial Council in order to implement the reforms of Trent. Happily for him, the Tridentine reforms of monastic organizations placed all persons charged with the care of souls under his jurisdiction.[23] The Orders refused to acquiesce and the Crown, in order to avert ecclesiastical disaster, was forced to obtain from the pope a suspension of Tridentine reforms for the viceroyalty of New Spain.[24]

In their appeals to the Crown for a satisfactory settlement of outstanding questions, the friars invariably cited their ancient monastic immunities and the *Omnimoda*. At the same time, the seculars had recourse to canon law and customary usage of the Spanish Church. Both appealed with reference to a definite and, to them, inviolate framework of ecclesiastical rights. To Philip II, in whose reign this whole question was to be definitively answered, ecclesiastical right was little more than what the Crown desired it to be. As Philip labored to maintain a tight control over the Spanish Church, he was frequently opposed by its bishops, who enjoyed certain traditional rights and exemptions from royal authority. The bishops were by no means independent, but they preserved a sufficient measure of customary practice, made legal by the passing of time, with which to obstruct an arbitrary royal will. This was not the case in the Indies. The colonial Church was new, without age and accumulation of customary privilege. It was simply a feudatory of the Crown, without the protection of a contract.

When Philip interceded for the benefit of one party or the other, it was a moderative gesture rather than a settlement. The *cédulas* which reaffirmed the right of Mendicants to exercise the privileges stated in the *Omnimoda* merely gave the Crown's permission for that exercise, but did not recognize an inherent autonomous right. In the same manner, episcopal authority might be employed only with the Crown's permission. This was a temporizing policy, designed to protect the Crown's ecclesiastical prerogatives. By withholding recognition of regular and secular claims of inherent authority, neither faction could acquire the basis necessary to development of customary privilege with ultimate legal foundation.

After 1565 it became apparent that a temporizing policy could no longer serve. In spite of suspension of Tridentine reforms, the conflict became more intense. The bishops increased their attack on Mendicant privileges and the friars retaliated. The king's failure to substantiate the claims of either side caused both to seek their own kind of victory. Something else which caused Philip to ponder the whole Mexican situation was a renewal of papal interest in the evangelization of the Indies. The Council of Trent had absorbed papal interest and energy. When it closed in 1563, the popes were relieved of onerous responsibilities for it and could pay greater attention to the problems of evangelization. Philip feared, and rightly so, that his heretofore silent partner in the overseas Church would speak aloud.

Difficulties of Settlement of Conflict

A resolution of the ecclesiastical problem in Mexico involved much more than either regulars or seculars seemed to realize. The services of both were indispensable to the Crown. Simple suppression of one or the other would not provide a solution, nor could immediate suppression be accomplished in any case. Any adjustment of privileges or episcopal reorganization would of necessity require papal sanction, and this fact brought the Mexican question into relationship with the host of religious and political complexities in which Philip II and the Roman curia were deeply involved. The Mexican conflict, although far removed, was problematically related to the diplomacy of empire.

Philip's consideration of this problem was of a political nature. As such, that part of it which involved the secular Church was indeed slight. The seculars, by law and habit subordinated to the Patronato, could be elevated or reduced according to his desire, so long as he did not attempt to alter the papal decretals upon which the secular Church had been founded. But Mendicant organization was quite a different matter. The *Omnimoda* provided the friars with a legal claim of exemption from the Crown's ecclesiastical arm, the secular Church, and their ancient exemptions freed them from laical supervision. Technically, the Mendicants served in the Indies at the pleasure of the Crown. Their passports could be revoked at any time. But what did the friars care for these political controls? From the very beginning they paid more heed to their own provincial limits than they did to diocesan limits; they supported themselves in large measure through the direct offerings of the Indians; in election of superiors and placement of friars in *doctrinas*, they acted under their own authority, rather than through the channels of the Patronato. In practice the prerogatives of the Crown were considered to be theory rather than fact.

There was but one direct course of action that Philip could take in this situation. He could forbid exercise of the *Omnimoda*'s privileges. In effect, this had been the action of Mexico's Provincial Councils, and with disastrous results. If pushed too far, the regulars in Mexico could withdraw, and neither the Crown nor the secular Church could prevent it. The problem, then, was to find a course of indirect action which would change the conditions under which the Mendicants served rather than to remove the basis of their service.[25]

In formulating a solution to this problem of conflict within the Mexican Church and the question of ecclesiastical supremacy which it suggested, Philip relied almost exclusively on the juridical genius of Juan de Ovando. A dedicated regalist, Ovando served for many years in the bureaucracy of the Inquisition. In 1567, Philip appointed him investigator of the Council of the Indies. He was nominated to the presidency of the Council in 1571, at which time he emerged as the dominating figure in formulation of all policies of colonial government.[26] He held this position until his death in 1575.

Ovando's interest in ecclesiastical problems appears to have antedated his investigation of the Council of the Indies. While conducting the probe, he also worked on the first volume of his ordinances, *De la gobernación espiritual*, completing it early in 1569.[27] The work contained twenty-two titles, embracing almost every aspect of divine worship and ecclesiastical government. The titles concerning erections and tithes are of paramount interest, since they state part of a plan for the resolution of regular-secular conflict in the Indies.

Ovando's Plan

Ovando postulated a radical division of the Church. According to his plan, the erection of metropolitan cathedrals in the Indies would continue according to traditional form, that is, with full cabildo, benefices, and episcopal organization. Secular prelates would continue to have a hand in collection and distribution of the tithe. In areas where Spaniards were sparsely settled, or where a majority of parishioners were Indians, both churches and bishoprics were to be constituted and governed according to the rule of one of the three Mendicant Orders. The governing rule was to be that of the dominant Order in the area, and the friars were to be allowed to exchange monasteries and properties between themselves so that homogeneous bishoprics could be created. All secular churches which might not be self-supporting were also to be put under the jurisdiction of the friars. In all subsequent erections only one Order would be permitted to enter a bishopric. The friars were to hold their appointments to parish and *doctrina* at the pleasure of the king, and were to be removable by the prelates and bishops. In order to free all religious from the trouble of collecting the tithe and first fruits, thereby, in Ovando's view, affording them more time for spiritual endeavor, the Crown's fiscal agents would levy and collect the tithe without the aid or intervention of the friars. Income would be doled out from a central treasury and administered by royal officials. The Crown would further reserve the right to distribute the tithe as it pleased.[28]

This was an ideal solution from the Crown's point of view. The abilities of the Mendicants could be exploited in the fullest measure and the seculars, groping for strength of stature, could be maintained at a manageable size. Conflict between the Orders over mission districts would likewise be eliminated. The cost of the colonial Church would also be reduced, since many of the secular benefices would be extinguished. Although they would win control of the largest portion of the Church, this plan did not point to a Mendicant victory. Inherent in the plan was a subtle weakening of the friars' missionary status. They would tend to be transformed from papal-sponsored missionaries into civil servants of the Crown. The administrative laws of the State would largely replace papal grants of privilege.

Ovando prepared two texts of his *Gobernación espiritual*. While the original text contained his plan for the division of the Church, the second merely repeated the traditional formula for erections of churches and bishoprics and administration of the tithe.[29] Although he was in a position to dictate the terms of ecclesiastical policy to the Council, Ovando appears to have desired secrecy. In order to maintain secrecy and, at the same time, to gain the cooperation of the Council in administering the vast Indian empire, he offered the Council the second copy for its emendation and approval.[30] He also gave the Council the first section of his second volume of ordinances which concerned the organization and operation of the Council. By August, 1571, both works had been approved, and were submitted to the Crown for signature. At the time of submission, Ovando appended his *consulta*, or final report on his investigation of the Council and a summary of observations concerning policies. Since the *consulta* was privy between himself and the king, he inserted materials of which the Council had no knowledge. In addition to laws for operation of the Council, he proposed controls and restraints over its members which he knew the Council would have contested.[31] He avoided the scrutiny of the Council in the same manner by submitting under separate cover a copy of his plan to reorganize the overseas Church.[32] Philip received the *consulta* and the projected legislation. He quickly signed the ordinances for government of the Council, but the second text of *Gobernación espiritual*, apparently provided for the sole benefit of the Council, was summarily rejected.[33]

This plan of reorganization, if it was to subordinate the Orders to the Crown's ecclesiastical authority, was in need of a condition to its implementation. While willing to accept any sort of hegemony, the friars would be quick to recognize the subtle implications of the reorganization, and would move to resist the coils of the Patronato. With papal support their resistance could be effective. I have no doubt that Ovando saw this quite clearly, realizing that the historic relationship between the friars and the papacy stood between Philip II and absolute domination of the colonial Church.

Patriarchate of the Indies

In Ovando's diplomatic strategy, restoration of the Patriarchate of the Indies became the *sine qua non* of the whole plan of reorganization. Since first developed by Ferdinand in 1513, this idea had not left the minds of Spanish kings. In 1560, Philip, disturbed by reports of ecclesiastical conflict, tried to obtain the appointment of two Patriarchs, one each for Mexico and Peru.[34] In this attempt Philip was no more successful than Ferdinand had been. As the proposals for a Patriarchate were revived by Ovando, the office acquired greater significance. Aside from faith and morals, it was to be the supreme ecclesiastical authority of the Spanish Indies; its See was to be located in the royal court at Madrid. It was, of course, to be appointive by the Crown.[35] This was the wedge that Ovando intended to drive between the Mendicants and the papacy. If Rome, in the interest of faith, desired the proposed expansion of Mendicant organization in the overseas Church, concession of the Patriarchate was to be the price it must pay.

To gain such a concession required two things: the right pope and the right moment, neither of which was offered during the pontificate of Pope Pius V.[36] Shrewd, dedicated, an ascetic of renown, Pope Pius lived by a single maxim: Catholics had fallen into Protestantism because they had scorned the authority and jurisdictional prerogative of the Church. Strengthening of papal authority, in his estimation, was the foundation of the Counter Reformation.[37] With this attitude he was an inflexible foe of lay power in ecclesiastical affairs, and nowhere was this power in greater evidence than in the Spanish states of Naples and Sicily. Philip was dedicated to the preservation of his most powerful weapons, the right of exequatur, *recurzo de fuerza*, by means of which any subject under sentence of an ecclesiastical court could appeal to royal justice, and the *Monarquía sícula*, a traditional right of the King of Sicily to administer the Church through a lay tribunal.[38] In resistance to royal ecclesiastical authority, Pope Pius made full use of the bull *In Coena Domini*. This bull was published annually, assessing heavy penalties against those who transgressed the jurisdictional rights of the Church and certain clerical prerogatives of the Roman curia. Each year the penalties were made more painful until Philip, in 1568, refused to allow the bull to enter Naples and Sicily.[39] Bitter jurisdictional conflict between Pope Pius and Philip was a normal state of affairs.

At the same time that Pius opposed Philip in Italy he sought to strengthen his influence in the Indies. He looked with extreme interest on the complaints and reports which were being received from New Spain. In April, 1568, he instructed his nuncio in Madrid to call on the king and sound him out on the idea of establishing nunciatures in the Indies. Philip's response to the nuncio's queries was firmly negative.[40] Nunciatures, indeed! The king was at the zenith of political power and was determined to push through Ovando's plan for reorganization of the Church. In October of 1568, just as Philip and Ovando were readying their arguments for concession of the Patriarchate, Pius suddenly took a new tack in his proposals to the Crown. Through his nuncio he assured the king that he would attempt nothing in the Indies without the knowledge of the Crown.[41] This was a stunning feint, apparently calculated to put Philip in a defensive position. If the pope was not to tamper with the overseas establishment, neither was the Crown. The precise timing of this maneuver and its effect would strongly suggest that information leaked from the inner sanctum of the Spanish court had reached the ears of the pope.

Because of this sudden turn of events, Philip gave up any illusions he might have had of gaining the desired concession from Pius V. In his instructions to Francisco de Toledo, in December of 1568, he stressed the desirability of establishing the Patriarchate, but because of the difficulties involved in obtaining it, or even suggesting it, he felt that the matter would better be postponed until a more auspicious occasion and a better state of affairs might be afforded it.[42]

The Patriarchate: New Attempts

Pope Pius V died early in May, 1572. Hugo Buoncompagni was elected Pope Gregory XIII shortly thereafter. Pope Gregory was an entirely different personality; quiet, almost diffident, he appeared to have none of the characteristics of his predecessor. Don Juan de Zúñiga, Philip's ambassador, an almost infallible judge of character and situation, described him as wishing to live quietly, willing to let the world go as it might.[43] In

September, 1572, Philip ordered Zúñiga to proceed with the request for the Patriarchate.

Philip's letter of instruction to the ambassador indicated the line of argument he was to follow. Concession of the Patriarchate was proposed as a first principle in maintaining the faith in the Indies. Without this concession, Philip expressed serious doubts concerning the adequate provision of spiritual guidance. The slowness of communications made government of the overseas Church difficult. If the Patriarchs at court were free to provide immediate solutions to problems, argued the king, they could be sent out with the first returning fleet. Referral to Rome for solutions made prompt attention impossible, with the result that solutions had to be formulated by the Council of the Indies or civil officialdom in the Indies. This, according to Philip's argument, was the greatest reason for concession: ". . . we hold it to be highly unbefitting," he said, "that lay tribunals should interfere in ecclesiastical affairs."[44]

Partial disestablishment of the secular Church and the creation of Mendicant churches and bishoprics were requested on the argument that the seculars had failed miserably in their duty to the faith. These measures were proposed as the *only* way in which the Church could be founded in the Indies on a permanent basis. The seculars, the king charged, failed to establish the Church through their selfish greed and insatiable thirst for riches.[45]

The pope was to be further asked to issue a bull which would prohibit the Orders from holding property or wealth in any form except that which might be allowed to the monastery; other holdings were to be confiscated, and the friars were to be prohibited from asking or receiving anything from the Indians, even though it were willingly offered. The Crown, recently having obtained from the General of the Franciscan Order the privilege of appointing a commissioner to reside at court and aid in the administration of the Order in the Indies, further requested confirmation of that privilege and its extension to the other Orders.

These were the essential points in the proposed reorganization, all of which were to be sought in the name of the faith. All these things and many more could be easily arranged, said Philip, *if* the pope would concede the Patriarchate; thus it was upon that point that his ambassador was most urgently to insist.[46]

By December, Zúñiga was able to send a comprehensive report to the Crown. He reported the pope to be ill pleased over jurisdictional conflict in Italy. His Holiness, he said, was very resentful because the king, through holding him in slight esteem, had undertaken things that he had not dared in the time of Pius V. As for the Patriarchate, continued Zúñiga, it was extremely doubtful that the pope would concede it with the requested faculties because he feared that the Spanish Crown would be converted into another *Monarquía sícula*. He advised Philip to content himself with the powers he already had, rather than to seek enlargement of them from Gregory XIII.[47]

By the tone of this report it becomes evident that Zúñiga, in his first reports, had failed to perceive the true character of Pope Gregory. Nor had Philip guessed what lay behind his mask of serenity. In assuming an aggressive initiative the Crown had erred egregiously. An example of Philip's highhanded attitude is found in his dealings with Cristóbal Capitefontium, General of the Franciscan Order. Shortly before the death of Pius V, Philip had sent a personal emissary to negotiate with the General for the privilege of appointing a commissioner to reside at court and aid in administration of the Order in the Indies.[48] Under circumstances which are not clear, the General agreed, whereupon Philip made an appointment.[49] When Gregory became pope he was presented with a *fait accompli* rather than a request for the privilege. The pope's reaction was reflected by General Capitefontium who quite suddenly, and without regard to agreement, transferred the jurisdiction of the Franciscans in the Indies from the hands of Philip's appointee to those of the Commissary General of Spain.[50]

In the course of the following months Zúñiga maintained pressure on the pope in the hope of gaining the Patriarchate. Gregory finally relieved the pressure by moving to turn the whole question over to a congregation of cardinals for discussion and suggestion. This, of course, was the very thing that Philip wanted least; the curia would in effect be legislating for the Church in the Indies. On June 11, 1573, Philip instructed Zúñiga to avoid the transfer which was threatened.[51] Ovando's carefully contrived plan for reorganization of the colonial Church had failed.

Discord in the Mexican Church grew apace while the Crown formulated its plans and negotiated for an organic settlement of the problem. Philip's temporizing policy was successful in gaining time for diplomacy, but it also served to prolong and intensify the struggle. Ovando's plan posed the most expeditious solution to the problem because it took advantage of the preponderance of Mendicant organization and authority in the Church, merely changing the nature and basis of this authority. The seculars in Mexico and, for that matter, throughout the Indies, could easily have been manipulated to conform to the new order of things if the plan had succeeded. The failure of Ovando's plan, however, made necessary a sharp reappraisal of Mendicant authority and the balance of power in the Mexican Church.

The Ordenanza of 1574

In his arguments for the Patriarchate, Philip had posed the Mendicants as the only instruments that could preserve the faith and found the Church, and he had deplored the interference of laymen in ecclesiastical affairs, but the essence of the patriarchal idea, as it was correctly perceived by Pope Gregory, was laid bare by diplomatic defeat. Within the year Ovando drafted a declaration of patronage that was to serve as a charter for the gradual but inexorable secularization of the Mendicants. On June 1, 1574, the Crown promulgated its Ordenanza del Patronazgo: this date may be taken as both the apogee of Mendicant authority and influence in the Church of the Indies and the beginning of its end.

The Ordenanza, composed of twenty-three chapters, was a frontal attack on Mendicant privilege.[52] Both regulars and seculars were to be subordinated in every respect to the ecclesiastical authority of the Crown and its viceroys. While the seculars found little that was novel in this pronouncement, the regulars recognized a potential destruction of their position. The mission fields which they monopolized were to be opened to both secular clergymen and lay persons as *doctrineros*; all such positions were to be filled through *oposición*, with presentation by the viceroy and canonical installation by the archbishop. Prelates of the Orders were to keep perpetual lists of all monasteries and areas of occupation, including a census of inhabitants and a muster of employed friars, giving names, qualifications, and duties. Copies of the lists were to be given to the Crown, viceroy, and episcopacy so that friars could be reduced in number or added, depending on the needs. Before removing a friar from his position, or placing him in one, the provincials were to clear the matter with the secular prelate and governor. All regular prelates were to show their patents to the viceroy before assuming either office or jurisdiction.

The friars received the Ordenanza with disbelief, then sought to resist it with an obstinacy that was born of both defiance and dismay. In a statement to the viceroy the Franciscans offered to continue their ministrations to the Indians under the conditions to which they had been accustomed, but, they warned, if they were either to submit to the new laws or forfeit their bulls of privilege, they would choose the latter course and withdraw from the work of evangelization.[53] In essence their objections were based upon a fear of episcopal and lay authority and its effect upon mendicity. The intromission of a foreign authority between friar and Mendicant prelate, it was feared, would destroy the fundamental Mendicant vow of obedience. It would be better, they said, to flee to the mountains than to surrender the administration of their Order to secular and civil hands.[54]

In spite of Mendicant protest and evasion the Crown's ecclesiastical policy remained unchanged after 1574. The gradual suppression of their privileges was never sharp enough to cause the friars to withdraw; neither did it allow them to construct an adequate defense. The Council of the Indies maintained a steady flow of legislation which amplified the Ordenanza and placed further restrictions on the independence of the friars. The secular Church, basking in the sun of royal favor, grew enormously. Although the friars retained a measure of autonomy on the borders of empire, their independent authority within the Church was steadily diminished until, by 1600, the secular Church was master in New Spain. The Jesuits, through their function of training secular priests, were an important factor in the rapid growth of the secular clergy. Not long after entering Mexico they acquired the status of a third force in the ecclesiastical balance of power. Their work on behalf of the secular clergy and their evangelical rivalry with the other Mendicants made them a useful interim support for the secular Church. It may well be that such a potentiality was considered by the Crown when it sent them to Mexico in 1572.[55] At any rate, the influence of the Jesuits in Mexico was increasing while the older friars were experiencing a forced emulation of the fates of Columbus and Cortés in the service of the Spanish Crown—one of conquest, achievement, and rejection at the hand and pleasure of the agency which they had served. There is more than a little irony in realization that the Jesuits, as useful instruments of royal supremacy, would suffer the fate of the earlier Mendicants in due course of time.

Notes

1. Vicente de la Fuente, *Historia eclesiástica de España* (6 vols.; Madrid, 1873–74), V, 69–72, passim; William H. Prescott, *History of the Reign of Ferdinand and Isabella the Catholic* (revised ed.; 3 vols.; Philadelphia, 1881), I, 314–18, 350.
2. See the bull *Inter Caetera* in Roberto Levillier, *Organización de la iglesia y ordenes religiosos en el virreinato del Perú en el siglo XVI* (2 vols.; Madrid, 1919), II, 7–8.
3. *Eximiae devotionis*, Nov. 16, 1501, Levillier, II, 35.
4. Dated June 28, 1508, ibid., pp. 38–40. Following this concession, three bishoprics were erected on Española. In 1511 they were abolished in favor of two new erections on Española and one on Puerto Rico. All were suffragan to the Archiepiscopal See of Seville. The decretals of erection may be seen in Francisco Javier Hernáez, *Colección de bulas, breves, y otros documentos relativos a la iglesia de América y Filipinas* (2 vols.; Brussels, 1879), I, 24–26. Because of the distances involved and the need for ready replacements in vacant benefices, an adjustment to the means of appointment was made between the Crown and the prelates of the Antilles in 1512. In accordance with this agreement, known as the Concordat of Burgos, the bishops were allowed to make inferior appointments without the interference of civil officials. The appointee was merely obliged to present the Crown's approbation of his appointment to the viceroy or governor within a year and a half. This came to be a custom whereby prelates made canonical institution in the name of the king without his knowledge and approval. Ibid., pp. 21–24.
5. *Boletín de la Real Academia de la Historia*, XIX (July, 1891), 183.
6. Juan de Solórzano y Pereira, *Política indiana* (Madrid, 1647), *lib.* iv, *cap.* xi.
7. *Recopilación de leyes de los reynos de las Indias* (4 vols.; Madrid, 1791), *lib.* I, *tít.* 9, *ley* 2.

8. King to Mossén Gerónimo de Vich, July 26, 1513, Lesmes Frías "El Patriarcado de las Indias occidentales," *Estudios Eclesiásticos*, II, No. 5 (1922), 25–26.

9. Issued by Pope Adrian VI, May 10, 1522. This wide jurisdiction was given in order to facilitate evangelization. The *dieta*, or one day's journey by land, was set at seven leagues by Roman law. Spanish usage set the distance at ten leagues, or about thirty miles. Hernáez, I, 379, 387.

10. Ernesto Schäfer, *El consejo real y supremo de las Indias* (2 vols.; Seville, 1935–1947), II, 203–4.

11. The following missives are illustrative of opposing viewpoints: Archbishop Alonso de Montúfar to the Council of the Indies, May 15, 1556, *Epistolario de Nueva España, 1505–1818* (16 vols.; Mexico, 1939–1942), VIII, 72–78 (hereafter cited as *Epistolario*); "Respuesta que los religiosos de las tres Ordenes de la Nueva España dieron en el año de 1557," Joaquín García Icazbalceta, *Nueva colección de documentos para la historia de México* (5 vols.; Mexico, 1886–1892), IV, 1–18; also see Robert Ricard, *La conquista espiritual de México*, trans. Angel María Garibay (Mexico, 1947), pp. 442–44. The question of whether or not the Indians should be included in the general tithe was of wide interest. Laymen frequently became embroiled in the argument, adding their opinions to those of the seculars and religious. In 1562 the cabildo of Mexico City besought the Crown for a final ruling which would end the interminable conflict and confusion. *Actas de cabildo del ayuntamiento de México* (77 vols.; Mexico, 1884–1905), 1562, p. 11.

12. Ricard, pp. 440–41. A temperate analysis of the evils afflicting the Church is found in the report of Dr. Luís de Anguís, *provisor* of the archdiocese of Mexico. Mariano Cuevas, *Documentos inéditos del siglo XVI para la historia de México* (Mexico, 1914), pp. 250–76. For partisan attitudes see the following: Archbishop of Mexico and Bishops of Michoacán and Oaxaca to the King, April 30, 1562, *Epistolario*, IX, 171; Gerónimo de Mendieta to the King, Oct. 8, 1565, Icazbalceta, *Nueva colección*, I, 38–40.

13. There was much crossing of factional lines. The infinite number of shifting animosities, splits among and between the Orders, differences among seculars, and hundreds of differing opinions make generalizations imperative if the story is to be told. *Regulars and seculars* are used generically for purposes of discussion, and are not intended to convey the impression of homogeneous action or opinion. The conflict, in an abstract sense, was inexorable and absolute. In a concrete sense it was modified by circumstance.

14. Example is provided in the correspondence of Gerónimo de Mendieta, Icazbalceta, *Nueva colección*, I, 38–40, 1–34, 108–12, *passim*. Also see Provincials of the Three Orders of the King, Feb. 25, 1561, *Cartas de Indias* (4 vols.; Madrid, 1877), I, 147–50, and Fray Juan de San Román to Juan de Ovando, Mar. 16, 1571, Icazbalceta, *Nueva colección*, I, 97–98. The friars habitually charged the seculars with incompetence, ignorance of native languages, and ecclesiastical immorality. The venerable Mendieta, in a moment of hyperbole, ventured the opinion that the Indians would be extirpated before they could become Christians if the regulars should withdraw from Mexico (Mendieta to Juan de Ovando, 1571, Icazbalceta, *Nueva colección*, I, 108–13). Contrary to these charges and assertions, by 1565 there were vast numbers of secular clergymen engaged in effective rural evangelization. They used all the native dialects and appear to have been satisfied with small remuneration for their services. See Luís García Pimentel, *Descripción del arzobispado de México hecha en 1570 y otros documentos* (Mexico, 1879) and *Relación de los obispados de Tlascala,*

Michoacán, Oaxaca, y otros lugares en el siglo XVI (Mexico, 1904), also "Relación del distrito y pueblos del obispado de Tlaxcala," *Epistolario*, XIV, 70–101. It must of course be remembered that interested parties to the conflict usually wrote polemically; consequently the truth does not always appear at the surface.

15. Luís Alfaro y Peña, *Relación de las iglesias y conventos de México* (Mexico, 1863), p. 47; Juan de Torquemada, *Monarquía indiana* (3 vols.; Mexico, 1945), III, 424–25, 35–39.

16. Torquemada, III, 4–5.

17. This paragraph represents impressions founded on the reading of countless letters and chronicles. Individual citations in addition to those already given would, I think, serve only the cause of pedantry.

18. Pope Leo X issued a bull in 1519 which established a principle of communication of privileges between Mendicants. Hernáez, I, 375–76.

19. This fundamental distinction between mercenaries and apostles was made before the Franciscans formally set foot on Mexican soil. Torquemada, III, 14. Although with distaste, the seculars admitted their mercenary status. Archbishop Alonso de Montúfar to the Council of the Indies, May 15, 1556, *Epistolario*, VIII, 77.

20. Francisco Antonio Lorenzana, *Concilios provinciales* (Mexico, 1769), *caps.* 8, 9, 35, 90.

21. Torquemada, III, 264–266; Vasco de Puga, *Cedulario* (2 vols.; Mexico, 1878), II, 294–96.

22. *Recopilación, lib.* 1, *tít.* 15, *ley* 29; *lib.* 1, *tít.* 2, *ley* 20.

23. *El sacrosanto y ecuménico Concilio de Trento*, Ignacio López de Ayala, trans. (Paris, 1857), pp. 367–70, 378–79.

24. Lucas Ayarragaray, *La iglesia en América y la dominación española* (Buenos Aires, 1935), pp. 54–55; Hernáez, I, 399; *Recopilación, lib.* 1, *tít.* 14, *leyes* 47, 67. Fernando de Armas Medina, *Christianización del Perú (1532–1600)* (Seville, 1953), p. 493, believes that this suspension was also enacted in Peru. He is contradicted by Solórzano (*lib.* iv., *cap.* xvi) who emphatically stated the opposite. In my opinion it is extremely doubtful that conditions existed in Peru which necessitated such a measure. Although Mendicants antedated seculars in Peru, they never succeeded in massing the organizational strength that they did in Mexico. Conflict between Mendicants and episcopal forces was universal in the Indies, but only in Mexico did it acquire so exaggerated a spirit of anarchy. By 1565 the secular Church in Peru was at least as powerful as either the civil administration or the combined Orders. Indeed, one of Viceroy Francisco de Toledo's most imperative tasks was to effect reduction of the overweening authority of the secular Church.

25. Since there are no known sources which in themselves explain Philip's motives in formulating ecclesiastical policies for the colonial Church, it is necessary to infer them from the evidence which is at hand. In relating what is often disparate evidence, I offer what is in essence a hypothetical explanation, both of Philip's policies and their consequences. The tentative nature of such an explanation is apparent. If it will serve to stimulate differing opinion and further research the object of its inception will have been fulfilled.

26. Very little is known about the personal life of Ovando and his relationship with the Crown. Even after he assumed direction of the Council, documentary evidence remains rare, so that in his official capacity he is often shrouded in mystery. For authoritative information concerning Ovando see José de la Peña Cámara, "Nuevos datos sobre la visita del licenciado Juan de Ovando al Consejo de Indias, 1567–68," *Anuario de Historia del Derecho Español*, XII (1935), 425–

38; "La copulata de leyes de Indias y las ordenanzas ovandinas," *Revista de Indias*, II, No. 6 (1941), 121–46; "Las redacciones del libro de la gobernación espiritual," ibid., II, No. 5 (1941), 93–15.

27. "Relación del estado en que tiene el licenciado Ovando la visita del Consejo de Indias," *Antecedentes de la recopilación de Indias: Documentos sobre la visita del Consejo de Indias por el licenciado Juan de Ovando*, ed. Victor Manuel Maurtúa (Madrid, 1906), p. 4 (hereafter cited as "Relación").

28. These titles are reproduced in Peña's "Las redacciones del libro de la gobernación espiritual," pp. 111–15.

29. The second text is found in Maurtúa's work, *Antecedentes de la recopilación de Indias*. Unfortunately, the author reproduced it without criticism or annotation. Since I have been unable to compare the texts myself, I am dependent upon the judgment of Mr. Peña as to the primacy of the first text and the authorship of Ovando, neither of which seems to be open to doubt. Because Mr. Peña views the two texts in a context different from mine, we disagree in assigning significance to the differences between them.

30. Ovando, "Relación," p. 4

31. "La consulta de le visita del Consejo de Indias con su Magestad," Maurtúa, pp. 9–11.

32. Ibid., p. 17.

33. Peña, "Las redacciones del libro de la gobernación espiritual," p. 93. The Council's copy was simply a restatement of the laws under which conflict in Mexico was taking place. Since the Crown hoped to provide an organic solution to its problems, perpetuance of the old laws at this time would have been inconsistent with its aims.

34. Lesmes Frías, "El Patriarcado de las Indias occidentales," p. 33.

35. Philip II to Don Juan de Zúñiga, Sept. 9, 1572, Ayarragaray, p. 105. Restoration of the Patriarchate was also discussed by a special junta convened in 1568 by Philip to discuss the ecclesiastical problems of Peru and to draw up instructions for the new viceroy-elect, Francisco de Toledo. The *actas* of this junta have never been found, hence, it is difficult to say with certainty what relationship, if any, existed between the junta and Ovando's formulation of policies. Although Ovando does not appear to have been a member of the junta, he was undoubtedly aware of its deliberations. It is my guess that he utilized ideas from many sources in formulating royal policy, the ultimate nature of which was dictated by the Crown.

36. 1566–1572.

37. Luciano Serrano, *Correspondencia diplomática entre España y la Santa Sede* (4 vols.; Madrid, 1914), III, xliv.

38. Ibid., pp. xli–xlv.

39. Rafael Altamira, *Historia de España* (4 vols.; Barcelona, 1906), III, 406; Serrano, III, xlviii–lv.

40. Serrano, II, 390; also see Pedro de Leturia, "Felipe II y el pontificado en un momento culminante de la historia hispanoamericana," *Estudios Eclesiásticos*, VIII, No. 7 (1928), 61–63.

41. Serrano, II, 472, n. 1.

42. King to Francisco de Toledo, Dec., 1568, Frías, "El Patriarcado de las Indias occidentales," p. 36.

43. Quoted in Leturia, "Felipe II y el pontificado," p. 66.

44. Philip II to Don Juan de Zúñiga, Sept. 9, 1572, Ayarragaray, pp. 108–9.

45. Ibid., pp. 112–13.

46. Ibid.; see pp. 104–13 for details of these and lesser proposals.

47. Quoted in Leturia, "Felipe II y el pontificado," p. 67.

48. Philip II to Capitefontium, Feb. 19, 1572, Levillier, I, 74–75.

49. Philip II to Capitefontium, June 11, 1572, ibid., p. 76. Perhaps by coincidence, a pay warrant was ordered by the king for 300 ducats in favor of Capitefontium for "cosas de nuestro servicio y bien." At the date of issue, Sept. 3, 1572, the General appears to have been in France (ibid., p. 77).

50. See Philip's complaint in Ayarragaray, pp. 67–68.

51. King to Zúñiga, Frías, "El Patriarcado y las Indias occidentales," pp. 39–40.

52. *Ordenanza del Patronazgo*, Diego de Encinas, *Cedulario indiano* (4 vols.; Madrid, 1945–1946), I, 83–86.

53. "Respuesta que los padres . . . de la Provincia del Santo Evangelio dieron al señor visorrey Don Martín Enríquez sobre los artículos enviados del Consejo de España en que pretendían obligar los religiosos a ser curas," Dec. 12, 1574, Icazbalceta, *Nueva colección*, IV, 198–202.

54. "Memorial de inconvenientes," 1574, ibid., pp. 205–12.

55. Archbishop Pedro Moya de Contreras, writing to Ovando in 1574, fervently praised the work of the Jesuits, describing them as the chief means whereby the secular Church would gain hegemony over the Mendicants (*Epistolario*, XI, 207–8). Also see Schäfer, *El consejo real y supremo de las Indias*, II, 242. The Jesuits served a similar function in Peru, although under different circumstances (Armas Medina, *Christianización del Perú*, pp. 43–46).

3

The Ordenanza del Patronazgo in New Spain, 1574–1600

John F. Schwaller

While Robert Padden sought to place the Ordenanza del Patronazgo in the larger political context of imperial Spain, John Schwaller looks at the local ramifications of its implementation. This article, in comparison with Padden's, demonstrates the changing interest and focus of historians. In the 1950s and 1960s, scholars commonly had recourse to royal decrees and official correspondence and chose to look at issues of policy on an imperial level. Many of the primary sources were published and thus relatively easily available. By the 1970s scholars began to rely more heavily on archival materials, and their interest shifted from imperial policy to the tension between this policy and local concerns.

Schwaller outlines the particulars of the Ordenanza del Patronazgo and how ecclesiastical and royal officials in Mexico sought to implement it. What is clear is that the policy had different implications for different participants. The archbishop sought to improve the quality of the parish clergy through the system of competitive exams called for in the decree, while the viceroy used the policy as a means to draw the Church more firmly under the direct supervision of the state. Individual clerics interpreted it as granting them what constituted lifetime parochial appointments.

John Schwaller has written extensively on the history of the Catholic Church in sixteenth-century Mexico, including two books: The Origins of Church Wealth in Mexico *and* The Church and Clergy in Sixteenth-Century Mexico. *He is currently associate provost and vice president for academic affairs and professor of history at the University of Montana.*

The history of the Church in Mexico has seen an ongoing confrontation between the secular and the regular clergy. During various periods one or the other side would achieve ascendancy, only to decline at a

From *The Americas* 42, no. 3 (January 1986): 253–74. Reprinted by permission of the Academy of American Franciscan History.

later date. The religious orders have chronicled the exploits of their brothers and friars, yet to this day the activities of the secular clergy have remained largely unknown. One critical period in the development and expansion of the secular clergy occurred between the promulgation of the Ordenanza del Patronazgo in 1574 and the end of the sixteenth century. In this quarter century many of the basic institutions of the diocesan establishment came into being, and in general the whole ecclesiastical hierarchy felt the changes. This essay specifically will focus on the implementation of the Ordenanza del Patronazgo and its effect on the secular clergy.

In 1571 the Jesuits arrived and began their ministry. At about the same time, the Holy Office of the Inquisition was founded in Mexico, which likewise had repercussions among the clergy. The consecration of a new archbishop, Moya de Contreras, a little later, continued the pattern of change and reform. But perhaps the most striking event of the period was the promulgation on June 1, 1574, of the Ordenanza del Patronazgo. Only the canons and decrees of the Third Provincial Council, in 1585, would have a greater impact on the clergy.

The arrival of Moya de Contreras to serve first as Inquisitor, and later as archbishop, and the promulgation of the Ordenanza del Patronazgo are two events which are intimately linked in the history of the Church and of the Spanish administration of the Indies. Don Juan de Ovando, Moya de Contreras's former mentor and patron, oversaw the creation of the Ordenanza. Ovando, Moya, and others formed part of a coterie active in the court of Philip II. The writing of the famous *Recopilación de las Leyes de Indias* dates from the efforts of Ovando.[1] While the initial effort to codify legislation pertaining to the New World failed, several major codes did result for this attempt. Included among these were the Ordenanza del Patronazgo and the laws of exploration and discovery.

The politics and policies behind the promulgation of the Ordenanza have been fully explored by Robert C. Padden in his interpretative essay.[2] The thrust of the laws clearly demonstrated the Spanish monarch's intention to limit the parochial duties of the regular clergy and to support the seculars while increasing his own absolute control over the entire ecclesiastical system. The king claimed control only over the diocesan hierarchy of the Church, and not over the mendicant orders. By enforcing certain decrees of the Council of Trent which mandated that the regular orders recognize the local jurisdiction of the bishop and become subject to his authority, the monarch would come indirectly to regulate the mendicants. In the New World the bishops received their appointments from the monarch; and thus through the bishops, the king had a method of controlling the regular clergy.

The Ordenanza del Patronazgo consisted of twenty-three articles. Many of these had been issued singly and in groups before 1574. While setting out on a reorganization and internal reform of the Church, the laws also sought to return the mendicants to the monasteries and strip them of their parochial authority. While the Ordenanza did, in fact, call for the secularization of the rural parishes, this had to wait two centuries before fulfillment. Beyond this, the laws placed all ecclesiastical matters more closely under the oversight of the monarch as patron. The viceroy served as vice patron in taking charge of administrative matters under royal purview while the audiencia continued to serve in a supervisory judicial function, interpreting the bull of erection and assuring that the ecclesiastical courts followed due process. The laws also mandated the initiation of competitive exams, *oposiciones*, to fill the newly created rural benefices, *beneficios*. The benefices differed from the earlier simple curacies in that they carried with them a guaranteed salary and that the cleric could hold the post for life without fear of being hastily removed by a new bishop. The *oposición* and benefices were the most commonly suggested remedies for what critics saw as a lax, ill-prepared, and venal diocesan clergy.

Archbishop Moya de Contreras, upon receiving the laws, put himself fully behind the *oposición* system by vacating parishes and convoking competitions. Other bishops, while ostensibly supporting the new system, had serious reservations. Because the documentation for Mexico is more complete, this essay will first take a detailed look at the process of the implementation of the Ordenanza del Patronazgo there, and then of the suffragan dioceses.

The institution of the benefice dates from Roman times. As it relates to the Church, the institution took on its structure between the fifth and seventh centuries. By the sixteenth century, canon law had long recognized the importance of the benefice and a whole corpus of regulations had grown to govern it. Basically the benefice consisted of three things: 1) the obligation to discharge an ecclesiastical office (the spirituality), 2) the right to enjoy the fruits attached to the office (the benefice), 3) and the fruits themselves (the temporalities). Under canon law, the patron of the benefice had the right to appoint, nominate, or present the cleric who would enjoy the benefice. The local bishop, under whose jurisdiction the benefice existed, then judged the sufficiency of the candidate to serve the benefice. Once evaluated and found fitting, the bishop confirmed the cleric in the benefice, the act of collation. Then, through canonical installation, the bishop committed the cleric to the cure of souls attached to the office, the spirituality. After receiving the collation and canonical installation, the beneficiary had to take physical possession of his benefice. After that, the beneficiary could serve and enjoy the benefice in perpetuity.[3]

Moya de Contreras supported the new system mandated in the Ordenanza on two grounds.[4] By guaranteeing them a good wage and a permanent position, bright young men might more readily enter the clergy than pursue other careers. Likewise, the system of competitive exams ensured that the most qualified priest received the benefice. Filled with enthusiasm, Archbishop Moya de Contreras convoked the first *oposición* on January 24, 1575.[5] Moya took advantage of this new system also to implement some of the reform legislation of Trent. To oversee the *oposiciones*, he appointed a tribunal of leading clerics. In addition to its duty in selecting parish priests, the tribunal also examined candidates for holy orders and ecclesiastical notaries. The tribunal consisted of Dr. Esteban del Portillo, canon of the Mexican cathedral, and provisor-vicar general of the archdiocese, Dr. D. Juan de Zurnero, archdeacon of the cathedral, Dr. Francisco Cervantes de Salazar, canon of the cathedral and professor of Rhetoric at the university, and Canon Alvaro de Vega of the Puebla cathedral but who also served as Visitor General of the archdiocese.

According to the regulations set by the archbishop, the tribunal met three days a week in the archiepiscopal residence to conduct its business. It kept a record book of the meetings containing the edicts of parochial vacancy and registries of candidates for orders, candidates for the benefices, and Church notaries. With each of these entries, the secretary of the tribunal would write the date and a full explanation for any action taken in each and every instance. Moya ordered that no one could participate in the competition without having first filed a statement of *limpieza de sangre* and a *relación de parte y de oficio*: "información de *moribus et vita.*" Part of the royal legislation pertaining to parish clergy had always encouraged the appointment of the descendants of the conquerors and others with experience in the New World. The Ordenanza also mandated this.

In keeping with these precedents, Moya charged the tribunal with investigating the particular merits of each competitor, if he were a descendent of a conqueror, and how long he had served in Indian parishes, both within and outside of the archdiocese of Mexico. Since the ability to speak an Indian language was of primary importance in selecting rural parish priests, the tribunal had to ascertain the ability of all candidates in Nahuatl and Otomí, the two most prevalent native languages in the archdiocese. As well, they tested each cleric in the administration of the sacraments, moral theology (cases of conscience, *casos de conciencia*), and in plain chant. Since the Council of Trent and other ecclesiastical bodies established a university education as a goal for all priests, the tribunal had to examine the candidate in whatever discipline he declared competency, giving him twenty-four hours for preparation, stipulating beforehand the point for examination. Lastly, the tribunal had to find out if the competitor owned a new breviary and could officiate using the new missal of Pius V. Moya then went on to outline the specific details to be required of candidates for holy orders and ecclesiastical notaries.

On the same day, January 24, 1575, Archbishop Moya de Contreras also promulgated the edicts of *oposición*.[6] Moya had vacated the various parishes affected by this action on January 15, and within four days candidates had appeared for the competition, although, as one can see, the mechanism to deal with it was not in place until five more days had passed. At that point, priests had until March 8 to apply for participation. Rather than confront the chaos inherent in vacating and filling all parishes at the same time, Moya spread the exercise across almost three years. The first parishes affected included Zumpango de la Laguna, Huipuztla, Tepequaquilco, and the Mexico City parish of Santa Veracruz. The position of sacristan for Santa Veracruz was also included in the competition, the only time a sacristy would be presented.

By February 28, all candidates had come forward. In his letter to the Crown, to be more fully explained later, Moya expressed his deep distress at the turnout. He had good reasons for disappointment. The Mexico City parish of Santa Veracruz in fact had two benefices open, and only two candidates appeared. The tribunal found neither of them suitable. In the case of Zumpango, four competitors came forward; again the examiners accepted none. In the face of such a failure, Moya and the tribunal decided to make temporary appointments until more qualified priests came forward. Thus on March 8, 1575, Carlos de Herrera was declared beneficiary of Zumpango and Bach. Juan de Arrieta was appointed to Santa Veracruz. In the case of Herrera, the tribunal recommended a temporary appointment until either someone more capable appeared or until Herrera himself improved.[7] As it turned out, Herrera improved, the tribunal found him competent, and on December 22, 1575, he received his canonical institution to the benefice.[8]

In short order, the tribunal decided on the parish of Huipuztla on March 12, 1575. Three priests had presented themselves for this position, including two who had also applied for Santa Veracruz and Zumpango. The board of examiners now found an applicant who fulfilled its expectations, and certified Mateo López Vendaval as sufficient to receive presentation and collation.[9] On March 26, the tribunal decided to review the qualifications of all the priests who had applied, evaluate all of the posts, and come to some firm decisions. This attempt did not change their earlier opinions of the candidates, and again only López Vendaval received unanimous approval. With this, the tribunal formally submitted his name to Archbishop Moya de Contreras.[10] At this point a whole new machinery went into action.

According to the Ordenanza del Patronazgo, only the king had the right to fill ecclesiastical benefices. These included the dignities of archbishop and bishop, members of the cathedral chapters, down to the lowliest parish priest. The Ordenanza did not just mandate the competition but also required all beneficiaries to receive royal approval. Clearly neither the king nor the Council of the Indies had the means to evaluate the thousands of parish priests in the New World, and so they delegated this power to the viceroy, as vice-patron. The system of competitive exams served to help the vice-patron select the candidate whom he would, in turn, present to the bishop. Thus, the archbishop forwarded López Vendaval's name to the viceroy for official confirmation. In later competitions, when both the number and quality of the candidates had improved, to maintain the fiction that the king actually did the choosing, the archbishop would present two names to the viceroy. Nevertheless, the viceroy nearly always chose the proper candidate.[11]

Upon certification by the viceroy, the beneficiary returned to the archbishop, once again, carrying a royal provision. The prelate, in this case Archbishop Moya de Contreras, then prepared the ecclesiastical documents to endow López Vendaval with the benefice: the collation (*colación*) and the canonical institution. The former gave the beneficiary the right to collect the revenues of the benefice, while the latter canonically endowed him with the right to exercise the office. Following this, the priest had to physically take possession of the parish. This ritual included the public proclamation of all the previous documents (royal provision, collation, and canonical institution) in the main village of the parish. The beneficiary then had to physically open the doors of the church, ascend to the altar, and perform some act, such as preaching or praying, to demonstrate that he had actually taken possession.

After the somewhat shaky start endured by Moya de Contreras and his examination tribunal, the *oposición* system of competitions mandated in the Ordenanza continued to serve the archdiocese relatively well. The next round of competitions sought to select beneficiaries for the parishes of Tepotzotlan, Jiquipilco, and Huitzquiluca. Although only four candidates stepped forward for the offices, at least three suitable ones emerged from the exam. Following that, competitions continued on a regular basis for the rest of the colonial period. The number and quality of candidates improved with time. For instance, in the case of Iguala, in the archbishopric, in both 1581 and 1585, eleven men presented themselves as candidates.[12]

On March 30, 1575, Archbishop Moya de Contreras sent in a description of the first *oposiciones* and a letter to the president of the Council of the Indies explaining the outcome.[13] This letter clearly demonstrated Moya's desires on the question and his explanation for the rather disheartening results. He placed most of the blame at his predecessors' feet, although his colleagues, the other bishops, also received some criticism. Moya complained that had he been in charge earlier, he would not have ordained many of the current deacons and subdeacons because of their unsuitability. Likewise, unsuitable priests when stripped of their posts in the archdiocese merely went to the neighboring dioceses and found employment. He further charged that the suffragan bishops ordained too many unsuitable individuals without credible *congruas*.[14] To put things in their proper perspective, and to have a chance to undermine the mendicants, Moya also complained that if one examined the orders closely, especially the Franciscans, one would find as much ignorance and human frailty as among the seculars.

Beyond these rather bleak sentiments, Moya held out several rays of hope. They can be summarized in education and better work incentives. Moya noted that even without benefices he had, in general, appointed more and better qualified priests than his predecessors, especially either Archbishop Montúfar or the *sede vacante*. But his great hope lay in the educational facilities of the capital. He pointed out the two Jesuit colleges and the Colegio de Omnium Sanctorum (Todos Santos) as prime examples of the improved educational opportunities available. Another large component of the growing system of higher education was the University of Mexico, which had opened some twenty years earlier.

For Moya, the preparation of clerics only addressed one side of the question. Beyond that, he hoped to provide the priests with a living wage and job security, and for Moya this meant further benefices. In the letter of March 30, 1575, however, he lamented that while the salaries paid to the rural curates were already quite low, on average 150 *pesos de oro de minas*, the priests also had to rely on the Indians for food. Nevertheless, he pointed out that at least seventy priests already lived in rural areas of the archdiocese, but even with the promise of benefices, they did not apply as candidates for the competitive exams, even given a generous forty-day filing period. Lastly, he expressed the hope that in the future there would be qualified personnel for the benefices available and hoped that even better opportunities might be offered to young priests.

The reaction to the Ordenanza del Patronazgo varied from diocese to diocese and official to official. Needless to say, the regular clergy expressed total opposition to the order. Moya mentioned the beginning of this hostility in an early letter to the president of the Council of the Indies.[15] In this letter, Moya indicated that Viceroy Martin Enríquez might accede to the pressure placed on him by the regulars. In fact, Enríquez did come out against the Ordenanza and in favor of the regulars. This is all the more poignant because Moya and Enríquez had both served as protégés of the head of the Council of the Indies, Juan de Ovando.

Writing to Ovando, on 14 March 1575, the Bishop of Puebla-Tlaxcala, Don Diego de Romano, indicated that Moya and Enríquez had entered into open hostilities toward one another. Romano suggested that both would probably send along their own versions of the confrontation. Romano suggested that Ovando intervene, make peace between them, and make them stop acting like schoolgirls.[16] Bishop Romano, although seeming to be a paragon of calm in a world of upheaval, in actual fact had serious misgivings himself about the Ordenanza.

In this letter, he practiced the technique of *reductio ad absurdum* in arguing against certain features of the Ordenanza. As noted in the study of the first competitions in Mexico, the Ordenanza implied that sacristans would be subjected to the same process as curates. In his argument, Romano stated that using this logic, then every ecclesiastical post which fell under the Royal Patronage would have to be filled through competitive exams and receive the approval of the viceroy. That would mean a never-ending process of presentations and selection. In a somewhat humorous observation, Romano reflected that since Viceroy Enríquez was fond of detail, this process would surely please him: "como es tan amigo de menudencias no hay quitalle desta."[17] Following this line of reason, then, every choirboy would have to compete for his office and face approval by the viceroy. On a more serious note, Romano proposed that only the curacies fall under the jurisdiction of the Ordenanza. Basically, he suggested that the viceroy take charge of endowing the cleric with the benefice, and allow the ecclesiastical officials to continue to control the canonical obligations. In fact, this was the division of authority which ensued.

Bishop Romano wrote several letters to the King, the Council of the Indies, and Ovando over the next few years detailing the implementation of the Ordenanza in Puebla-Tlaxcala. The earliest mention of topics covered by the Ordenanza came in October, 1574. In that letter, Romano discussed the problems which he had had with the regular orders. Beyond that, he called for stability in the appointment of beneficiaries and in the control of the regulars in the parishes. He anticipated traveling to Mexico City in November to attend the consecration of Moya de Contreras as archbishop. At that point the assembled bishops could discuss the problems, and probably evaluate the impact and implementation of the Ordenanza.[18]

The next letters from the Bishop of Puebla-Tlaxcala date from December, 1574. The first, dated December 10, specifically dealt with the Ordenanza; the second, of December 11, covered relations with the regulars.[19] Commenting on the ordinances, Romano expressed his reservations about giving so much control over local clerics to the viceroy. He suggested that this power, if subject to the whims of advisers and retainers within the viceregal household, could seriously undermine the overall quality of the parish clergy. Secondly, the granting of benefices allowed a far greater degree of permanence than curates had previously enjoyed. By granting this lifetime appointment, the bishops would lose much of their control over the curates, by being unable to remove them. Concerning other topics in the Ordenanza, Romano complained that needing to secure viceregal permission before building chapels, churches, and other ecclesiastical structures posed real inconveniences, due to the distance between most cathedrals and the capital.

The first indication of the battle between Enríquez and Moya appeared in the December 10 letter when Romano complained that the hostilities had now spread to the other bishops, and that Enríquez shunned them, too. This corroborates other information which suggested that Enríquez grew to favor the regular clergy at this time. Part of this letter and all of the December 11 one complained about the regulars. Central to Romano's argument was the notion that the regulars should give up those parishes which they could not administer. He suggested that one friar could serve one thousand Indians in those areas where too few friars lived and worked; seculars should go to serve the rest of the population. In the second letter, he repeated his fear that Enríquez had buckled under to the demands of the regulars.

Bishop Romano wrote two letters while engaged in actively filling the newly created benefices. The first of these, March 14, 1575, has already been discussed. The second, March 20, 1575, was directed to the king and Council of the Indies.[20] In this more public letter, he proudly announced that he had implemented the Ordenanza. Beneficiaries served the majority of the *partidos.* Yet the main problem with the implementation lay in the opposition of the regulars to the entire notion embodied in the ordinances. Romano complained that Enríquez had delayed the enforcement of the law at every turn. He repeated his challenge that the regulars should give up those parishes which they could not adequately serve.

The implementation of the Ordenanza in Puebla-Tlaxcala reappeared in the correspondence of the bishop in 1579, 1581, and then again in 1582–83. The letter of 1579 complained about the permanence enjoyed by the beneficiaries, especially those carrying appointments directly from Spain, a point to be discussed later.[21] In 1581, Bishop Romano addressed a particular problem. The grain-producing region surrounding Tepeaca had recently become so popular that Spaniards had begun to settle it in large numbers. These Spaniards requested that the bishop supply them with a curate. They expressed their willingness to build a church and to pay a reasonable salary. In keeping with the dictates of the Ordenanza, the bishop requested approval from the viceroy, who denied the request on the grounds that Tepeaca fell under the jurisdiction of the Franciscans, and to create a secular parish there would break the principle of no religious group interfering in the territory of another. The bishop argued that he had no desire to remove anyone, but merely add priests as the need arose.[22]

The religious establishment had reached a solution to a similar problem in Atlixco and Huexotzingo where the bishop added secular curates to minister to the Spanish population, while the Franciscans continued to serve the Indians. In both of these cases the initial appointment of the secular cleric had occurred in about 1568, long before the Ordenanza. Nevertheless, with the creation of the benefices, both of these Partidos received beneficiaries.[23] The marginal notations to the 1581 letter indicate that the Council of the Indies was busy formulating legislation to follow up on the Ordenanza.

The letters of 1582–83 responded to several royal communications. The king had requested specific information about the various parishes, hospitals, offices in the cathedral, and a host of other details related to the ecclesiastical estate, as well as questions about the implementation of the patronage. Bishop Romano's replies to these orders repeated much of what he had written in earlier letters. Although Romano had some reservations about the overall impact of the law, he did go forward in implementing it.

In the winter of 1583, the king sent individual decrees clarifying some aspects of the Ordenanza to each of the bishops of New Spain. The order to Puebla-Tlaxcala was dated January 29, while the one to Mexico carried the date of March 31.[24] The *cédula* came as a direct result of Bishop Romano's 1581 letter about the Franciscans in Tepeaca. The monarch detailed the good work done by the regular orders in their early apostolic missionary activity. He warmly praised their accomplishments at Christianizing the Indians and establishing Spanish society in the colony. Then, noting this job well done, he observed that with the decline in Indian numbers caused by recent pestilence, and other factors, the regulars were no longer needed to help in the parochial administration of the colony. Thus in the future, where possible, the bishops would see that the regulars returned to their monasteries, and that secular priests took their place in the parishes as qualified secular priests came available. The decree was a wonderfully worded statement telling the regulars that their very success had eliminated the need for their efforts. The decree clearly indicated to all the bishops that the king had every intention of following through with his program of secularization. The implementation of the system of benefices neared completion after the receipt of this order.

The other bishops of New Spain seemingly found little to write about with reference to the Ordenanza. The Bishop of Oaxaca, Don Fr. Bernardino de Albuquerque, protested loudly, both over the loss of power to his office and, to a lesser degree, the loss of power to the religious orders. Mostly he felt that the king had crippled the power of the bishops by requiring them to seek viceregal approval in their parochial appointments. He further expressed his fear that the Church would become weakened and impoverished, leaving the curates unqualified and probably ineffectual.[25]

The Bishop of Michoacan, Don Fr. Juan de Medina Rincón, wrote his letter on March 20, 1576. Like the others he feared losing power to the viceroy; he clearly felt that the Ordenanza violated the traditional clerical immunity from supervision by secular authorities. The bishop suggested that if the Church needed reform, the monarch should send a special investigator or secure a papal nuncio.[26] By 1582, Medina Rincón had not changed his opinion of the whole system. He rather begrudgingly implemented the system of benefices, but only in those parishes under the royal Crown. In Spanish communities and in Indian villages under encomenderos, he refused to place beneficiaries, preferring to continue to appoint curates to serve at his pleasure. He characterized the beneficiaries as an embarrassment and most inconvenient. So far, neither Enríquez nor his successor, the Conde de Villamanrique, required him to place only beneficiaries, and he felt that was best.[27]

Lastly, the Bishop of New Galicia, Lic. Don Francisco Gómez de Mendiola, after a career as a royal justice, seemed to lack the same indignation over what his episcopal colleagues saw as royal usurpation of their authority. The one letter which deals with the Ordenanza dates from 1584.[28] In it Mendiola mostly complained about the regulars, and the problems in finding well-qualified secular priests.

The position of Viceroy Enríquez seemed to vacillate on the question of the Ordenanza. In the five years between the receipt of the ordinances and the time he left the post of viceroy, Enríquez failed to clarify his stand. The correspondence of the period, especially that of Archbishop Moya de Contreras and Bishop Romano, indicates that Enríquez sought to postpone enforcement of some aspects of the Ordenanza until the religious orders could mount an effective counterattack.[29] The brunt of his opposition, then, seems not to have centered on the question of royal patronage so much as over the issue of the secularization of the parishes.

Dissension broke out between the archbishop and viceroy during the implementation period. Writing in April, 1575, Moya described a bitter confrontation with the viceroy. According to the archbishop, Enríquez called in the provisor and accused the ecclesiastical authorities, namely, Moya, of violating the royal will by refusing to vacate and fill all the benefices at once, even though the archbishop reported that all had agreed to a slower process. The viceroy took the offensive and threatened to remove all of the seculars and replace them with regulars.[30]

In extracts from a letter from the viceroy to the Crown, written in March, 1575, Enríquez indicated that he tentatively favored the *oposición* system. He felt that although the system suffered from tremendous problems, only time would resolve them. He wrote further that reform could not occur until the system began operation.[31] A year later, Enríquez clarified his position in a letter to the king in March, 1576. By this time the viceroy embraced the idea that the Ordenanza could not be implemented in one dramatic sweep. The core of his opposition remained his support of the regulars. While the tone of the letter indicated that he generally agreed with the Ordenanza in theory, he did not fail to point out the countless small problems.[32]

Four years later, in his formal advice to his successor, Enríquez continued to manifest reservations about secularizing the parishes. He emphasized that things in Mexico differed greatly from Spain. With specific reference to the secular clergy, he reiterated his opinion that it would be a long time before the regulars left the parishes, and that until that time the viceroy should take great care in selecting competent religious to serve curacies.[33] Nevertheless, his advice suggests a degree of control over the religious orders which few viceroys commanded. While the viceroy opposed many aspects of the Ordenanza, he did not block the implementation of the *oposición* system, nor the creation of benefices. He acted in accordance with the law by providing royal provisions to those curates selected through the process, and otherwise saw to the orderly transition. He did accomplish the suppression of the secularization program, thereby guaranteeing the religious orders a place in the parishes for centuries to come.

The strongest supporter of the system was Archbishop Moya de Contreras. As he came to take on more and more power, in the political and ecclesiastical realm, he could better supervise the implementation of the system by the suffragan bishops. In the period from 1575 to 1579, Moya filled benefices in 54 parishes. This affected 68 priests, since ten parishes supported multiple curacies, and some curacies were filled twice. While the register book which Moya ordered kept for the archdiocese of Mexico contains the appointments to parishes up until the middle of 1582, after that only the examination records continue. Using this as a basis for analysis, some limited observations can be made about the early system of filling benefices through competitions.[34]

While one of the goals of the system was to create a modicum of stability in the appointment system, considerable movement from parish to parish occurred in the early years. After their initial hesitance, the priests became enthusiastic about the system, applying for new benefices as soon as they came open. In twenty-three of the parishes, the initial beneficiary left before 1582. This tended to appear more in towns under encomenderos than in parishes under the royal Crown. Twenty-two parishes fell completely under encomenderos, the royal Crown and encomenderos shared nine, while the remainder (twenty-three) fell under the Crown or were Spanish communities. Of the purely encomienda villages, half saw two or more beneficiaries between 1575 and 1582. Only eleven of the thirty-two mixed parishes had more than one curate in the period. The reason for this continued mobility related to priests' desires to acquire the best post. Priests seem to have had less enthusiasm about serving an encomienda town, as a result of the difficulty with which the priest could collect his pay. The encomenderos paid the priest directly. Recourse against the encomenderos required a civil suit involving time and expense. Thus, if the encomenderos were unwilling to pay the curate, the priest faced a very difficult situation. A quick perusal of the archival documents turns up a number of viceregal and audiencia orders to encomenderos to pay the parish priest back wages.[35] In the last instance, often the authorities allowed the priest to collect his pay directly from the Indians, out of the tribute destined to the encomendero. Priests in Crown villages had less trouble. Either they or their agent had to appear at the royal treasury in Mexico City no more often than three times a year to collect the salary.

Observations on improvements in the quality of priests serving the rural parishes seem to bear out Moya's optimism. According to reports sent to the king as part of the visitation of Juan de Ovando (1569–1571), of the 95 priests listed for the archdiocese, 22 had university degrees, the vast majority of them simple baccalaureates.[36] Six years later, during Moya de Contreras's incumbency as archbishop, another listing of 155 priests included 45 who held university degrees.[37] This means that during this time the percentage of reported clerics having university degrees rose from 23 percent in 1569 to 29 percent in 1575.

A similar trend can be seen in the neighboring diocese of Puebla-Tlaxcala following the implementation of the Ordenanza. In 1571, again with information from the Ovando reports, only 7 percent of the 42 priests listed had finished a university degree.[38] This can be compared to a report filed in 1582 for the diocese of Puebla-Tlaxcala.[39] Of the 118 priests, 24 (or 20 percent) had university degrees, a significant rise in the overall quality of the clergy included in the reports.

This specific rise in university training repeated itself throughout New Spain. In 1598, according to the pay records for the parish priests in villages under the royal Crown, 37 percent of the curates held university degrees. This is well demonstrated by the competition held in 1596 for the parish of Chiapa de Mota; all four of the competitors held university degrees, and two of them held dual baccalaureates.[40] In fact, one veteran priest, who had twenty years' parochial service to his credit, withdrew from the competition because he feared his lack of university training would be held against him.

Another area where measurement is possible is knowledge of an Indian language. Since this required subjective reporting by someone, comparisons are exceedingly difficult. By taking this into consideration, however, a trend emerged. In the case of the two reports from the archbishopric of Mexico in 1569 and 1575, more clerics were described as knowing at least one Indian language in the latter year, 54 percent compared to 65 percent. The data for Puebla do not really provide a useful comparison, but at least 65 percent of the priests described in the 1582 report commanded at least one Indian language. In the case of parish priests in villages under the Crown across the whole *gobierno* the problem is more complex since pay records do not indicate language ability. Nevertheless, by identifying priests with available biographies, 75 percent of those so isolated did speak at least one Indian language. Again, using the 1596 *oposición* in Chiapa de Mota as an example, the ecclesiastical judges based their decision on the fact that the chosen priest spoke both Nahuatl and Otomí, while the runner-up spoke only Nahuatl. The parish was a bilingual one. Thus, in this aspect as well, the Ordenanza and the more stringent policies of the king and prelates alike seem to have had their effect.

The members of the secular clergy expressed great enthusiasm in supporting the program. While the number of *opositores* remained relatively small in the first few years of implementation, by the 1580s each new competition drew larger numbers of applicants. In 1583, the Congregación de San Pedro, a religious sodality of secular priests, drew up testimony in favor of the full implementation of the Ordenanza, the full secularization of all parishes, including those held by the regulars. The questionnaire for the testimony posits that the territory had a large pool of well-qualified and -trained priests eager to take over parochial duties. The priests further described the *oposiciones* as attracting many candidates, thus guaranteeing the quality of the ultimate winner. The testimony then proceeded to complain of the religious orders' excesses. The complaints included charges of vanity, brutality, ignorance, and pride. In many ways the arguments made by these secular priests were exactly the same as those traditionally made by the regulars. Over ninety secular priests, and a few lay persons, signed the petition.[41]

A look at the careers of some priests demonstrates the change which the Ordenanza del Patronazgo made in their lives. The career of Cristobal Gil spans the two periods. Gil was a native son of Oaxaca, born in 1539. His father, Martín Gil, a conqueror, and mother, Isabel de Añoz, originally came from Antequera in Spain. From the time he entered the priesthood in 1565, until 1581, he served a variety of different parishes, including Talistaca, Mitla, Pochutla, and Amoltepec. The king appointed him as a canon of the cathedral chapter of Oaxaca, but low revenues prevented him from earning a living there. The exact thread of his career between 1581 and 1589 is missing. In the latter year he won the benefice of Tetiquipa, and served it for the rest of the century and, one imagines, the rest of his life. Thus the difference between the two periods implied a good degree of stability for Gil.[42]

Often beneficiaries spent their entire career in one parish. Luis Hidalgo de Montemayor, born in Puebla to the early settlers Gonzalo Hidalgo de Montemayor and Juana de Caceres, entered the priesthood about 1568. He served two parishes, at least, before the implementation of the Ordenanza. In 1576, he entered the competition for Xalacingo, and won. He continued to serve the parish well into the seventeenth century.[43] Likewise, Diego Onez de Santa Cruz, another native son of Puebla, entered the priesthood about 1573. He won the benefice of Tetela in Puebla-Tlaxcala in 1576, taking possession in September of that year. He served it for the rest of the century. In 1586, he competed for the benefice of Miztepec. In that competition he was found to know Nahuatl, and only a little Mixteca, the language of the parish. The winner of the competition was a Portuguese, Francisco Home, from Oporto, who had several advantages over Onez de Santa Cruz. Home had received his baccalaureate, knew Latin, Mixteca, and a little Nahuatl.[44] Thus in the specific areas of need for the parish of Mixtepec, Home was more qualified, and won the spot.

Following 1575, most beneficiaries received their posts from the viceroy through the system of competitive exams. Nevertheless, the king, as patron, reserved the right to appoint whomever he pleased to any benefice. Some benefices ultimately came to fall totally under the direct appointive power of the monarch, as vested in the Council of the Indies. Specifically, by the end of the sixteenth century the curacies of the cathedrals were regularly filled by appointees with royal provisions, rather than through the competitive exam system. In other instances whenever a royal appointee arrived, usually the beneficiary selected locally had to make way, since the royal decree took precedence over an order of the viceroy.

Such an incident occurred in 1581 when three priests arrived from Spain carrying royal provisions to the benefices of Acapulco, Temazcaltepec, and the parish of Santa Catalina in Mexico City. When the three clerics displayed their appointments to the viceroy, he forwarded them on to the archbishop. The viceroy had neither the power nor the interest to intervene in the issue. This placed the resolution of the situation squarely in the lap of Archbishop Moya de Contreras.[45] The archbishop likewise had to obey the royal order. All he could do was remove the beneficiaries who already served the parishes and then grant the posts to the newcomers.

In the process Moya followed the regulations outlined in the Ordenanza del Patronazgo as carefully as he could. He proceeded to test the three priests, newly arrived from Spain. The results of their examinations before the tribunal of experts hardly pleased the three hopefuls. Andrés Pérez de Ayala, presented to the Acapulco benefice, failed the exam, although Moya suggested that with some study he could pass it later. Unless the cleric passed the exam, the archbishop could not canonically grant him the authority to administer the parish. The royal provision gave him the right to the fruits of the benefice but no canonical power to administer it. Juan Montaño, appointed to the benefice of the Temazcaltepec mines, decided not to take the exam right away, preferring to study beforehand. He made a wise choice, since the previous time he had taken the exam, in 1576, he had failed. Montaño eventually passed the test. Pérez de Ayala succeeded on the second time he took it. The last of the three, Hernando Yáñez, had no difficulty with the exam, and received appointment to the parish of Santa Catalina. Although not of the highest quality, all three of the appointees finally proved their ability, received the canonical documents, and took possession of their benefices.

Although in many ways lucky to have the jobs at all, the three priests then initiated legal proceedings to have all the other beneficiaries in their parishes dismissed. It so happened that all three *partidos* needed several curates because of their size. Acapulco had three, plus a chaplain for the fort; Temazcaltepec and Santa Catalina had two. In each instance one beneficiary had already lost his post to make room for these royal appointees. Not satisfied, Pérez de Ayala, Yáñez, and Montaño then declared that their provisions gave them the exclusive and absolute right to the whole parish. While Yáñez and Pérez de Ayala demanded that the other priests leave the parish, Montaño merely declared his right to all the revenues without demanding the removal of the other beneficiary. He later recanted, and joined the other two in their position. Neither the viceroy nor the archbishop accepted the arguments which the three put forward, and all parties initiated a letter campaign to the king and Council of the Indies.

Moya de Contreras, writing to the king, expressed his amazement that three such unqualified priests could have received presentations to such important parishes. In strong language for the period, Moya urged the king to examine appointees in Spain before issuing provisions and not place the burden on officials in the New World. He further remarked that it bothered him to have to remove beneficiaries placed by competitive exams, and that replacing them with less-qualified personnel weighed heavily on his conscience. The entire system had been created to help improve the quality of the local clerics, forcing them to compete in open examinations. The viceroy, unusually agreeable to his often adversary, in his letter to the monarch expressed the same concerns, especially emphasizing that good priests selected through competitions had lost their jobs in making room for these unqualified appointees. Viceroy Enríquez continued that the incident had sent shock waves throughout the clerical establishment. While initially the beneficiaries had felt their jobs to be at last secure, they now realized that through a whim, faulty bookkeeping, or pure oversight, the monarch could replace them. Enríquez ended his letter by urging the king to use the system of competitive exams to fill the posts locally. While he did have reservations about the Ordenanza as a whole, he recognized that the exam system did ensure that the best qualified and worthy persons received the appointments, thus fulfilling the monarch's moral obligation.

The viceroy and the archbishop absolutely refused to allow the royal appointees to take over the entire parish, as they had demanded. The king upheld that position. In a reply to Moya de Contreras's letter, the king ordered the archbishop to examine all candidates who arrived with royal provisions. He noted that while in some cases a locally appointed beneficiary might need to be removed to make way for the royal appointee, it did not give the royal appointee the right to the whole parish, in the case of multiple benefices. The monarch made it perfectly clear that he had no desire to remove qualified priests from where they were needed.[46] The incident had one other effect: it set off a rash of petitions to the king and Council of the Indies from the beneficiaries. The only assurance that a beneficiary could have that he would not be replaced was to secure a royal confirmation of his post.

Increasingly after 1550, and certainly by 1575, some benefices fell exclusively to the Crown in Spain. The first of these tended to be the curacies in the cathedral of Mexico. By the end of the century, usually at least one, if not two, of the cathedral curates had appointments from the king. The cathedral of Puebla received a few direct royal appointments to its curacies, but not to the degree of Mexico. The other posts which regularly saw direct royal appointments were the chaplaincies attached to the garrisons at San Juan Ulua, in the port of Veracruz, and at Acapulco.

Some beneficiaries selected locally succeeded in acquiring royal confirmation of their appointment. One of these was Juan de Molina Valderrama. Molina Valderrama served the parish of Orizaba. The town was important because of the large complex of sugar haciendas developed there, and the large sugar mill owned by Don Rodrigo de Vivero, whose descendants would become the Counts of the Orizaba Valley. A cousin of Viceroy Don Luis de Velasco, the younger, Molina Valderrama was born in Osuna in Andalucía. He came out to the New World, and was ordained in Puebla in 1577. One of his first appointments was as vicar of Cuzcatlan. By 1581, the bishop made him vicar of Orizaba. Undoubtedly he began to petition the Crown for royal confirmation, which was forthcoming in 1586.[47] In a letter to the king, the Bishop of Puebla protested the action claiming that Orizaba had never been constituted as a benefice, and that his initial appointment of Molina Valderrama merely responded to a temporary need.

The actions of Molina Valderrama demonstrate the successful subterfuge of the established hierarchy. The case of Juan González de Urbina reflects a more standard proceeding. González was born in Mexico in about 1545. His father, Andrés González, and maternal grandfather, Pedro Vázquez de Toledo, were both conquerors. González first served as one of the choir chaplains in the cathedral of Mexico after his ordination in 1574. The next year he became vicar of Atitalaquia, until a beneficiary could be selected. In that round of competitions, he won the benefice of Chiapa de Mota, which he served for three years, until what he considered a superior post became available. In the competition, González emerged successful, winning the benefice of Atlacomulco in 1579. After working in that benefice for several years, he petitioned the Crown for confirmation of the appointment, garnering it in 1590. Royal treasury records indicate that the parish escheated to the Crown on October 25, 1595, upon the death of the encomendero.[48]

While stability tended to rule after the implementation of the Ordenanza, some priests still had to serve at the pleasure of the bishop. Only a very few benefices would become vacant each year. Thus, some well-qualified priests had to bide their time until they could secure a parish. Juan Bautista Belliza had just this difficulty. Belliza was a native son of Mexico, born in about 1560 to Alonso de Belliza and Doña Isabel de Prado. His paternal grandparents had both entered religious orders in their old age. His grandfather, García de Belliza, a conqueror of New Galicia, became a Franciscan, while his grandmother, Beatriz Enríquez, entered a convent. Juan Bautista studied as a youth with the Jesuits, with various scholars in Mexico, and served for nine years in the household of Bishop Mendiola of New Galicia. Belliza entered the priesthood in 1584, and immediately began to serve curacies. For the next eleven years, he moved from pillar to post as a *cura vicario* of Tlatlauquitepec, Mixtepec, Chocana, Ayutla, Pochotitlan, and possibly others. Finally, in 1596, he won the benefice of Guatusco, and took possession of it on March 12. He qualified for the office, having learned Nahuatl as a child, studied other disciplines for many years, and was a descendent of a conqueror.[49]

The reaction of the encomenderos to the administrative changes does not appear in the available documents. For them, the changes brought about by the Ordenanza dealt with matters beyond their control anyhow. Under the older system, the bishop had appointed the local curate; the encomendero merely paid the salary of whomever it might be. Usually because of declining revenues from the encomienda, the encomendero would attempt to moderate the amount he had to pay and delay the payment as much as possible. The king reflected this same attitude when, after the epidemic of 1576, he requested royal officials to investigate the possibility of decreasing the number of curates, since the number of Indians had declined.

One curious exception to this trend appeared in 1595 when the encomendero, Pedro Múñoz de Chaves, of the village of Jiquipilco, northwest of Mexico City, suggested that an additional benefice be created. In his petition to the provisor, Múñoz noted that the parish had over twelve miles between villages and that he was willing to pay the extra beneficiary. This proposal came in the wake of the death of the longtime curate, Francisco de Aguilar. Clearly, Múñoz felt that the ecclesiastical authorities could just as easily hold a competition for two benefices as for one. Ultimately, Múñoz did not produce the specific information needed by the provisor, and the whole question went into abeyance. Múñoz did demonstrate his sincerity when he drew up a formal obligation to pay the additional beneficiary from the tributes of the village, should one be appointed.[50]

The changes brought about by the implementation of the Ordenanza del Patronazgo restructured the career patterns of the secular clerics. These changes had a further effect in reordering the hierarchy within the ranks of the clergy. The *beneficiado* became an important figure within the whole structure of the Church. Before the Ordenanza, the secular clergy consisted of the upper clergy, including the cathedral chapter and the episcopal staff, and the lower clergy, the local curates. After the implementation, the lower clergy had three sections. The highest of these contained the beneficiaries. After them came the simple curates, who tended to be trained and qualified priests who had been unable to win a competition. The bishops used these men to serve as interim curates. In fact, in the period after 1575, the term *cura vicario* signified a temporarily assigned priest, serving at the pleasure of the bishop. The third group within the lower clergy, then, included those individuals who, for one reason or another, could not receive even a temporary assignment. Some priests chose not to serve rural parishes, preferring to seek their fortune in the cities. Others so lacked in training or integrity that a bishop would not appoint them even for brief periods. As more men entered the priesthood in the late sixteenth century, the bishops could afford to be more selective in all of their appointments since the system of competitive exams tended to guarantee that only the qualified would receive benefices.

While the major goal of the Ordenanza del Patronazgo—the secularization of the rural parishes and the bringing of the regular clergy under the control of the monarch—did not succeed, the secondary aims did. Within ten years after the promulgation, nearly every parish had become a benefice in every diocese of the *gobierno* of Mexico and competitive exams had been convened to select curates. The impact of this legislation on the secular clergy was great. In the development of the Church in Mexico, the seculars began to gain the ascendancy in the 1570s, due in no small part to the Ordenanza. The guarantees of job security and salary inherent in the benefices encouraged more youths to enter the clergy. The overall quality improved, as more young men, born and raised in New Spain, entered the clergy. These native sons brought with them the ability to speak an Indian language. Furthermore, the University of Mexico, since its beginning in 1553, produced many able priests. The educational facilities of the colony increased greatly after 1571 with the establishment of the Society of Jesus. The introduction of this new religious order merely signaled the first moments of yet a new confrontation between seculars and regulars, the peak of which would come in the mid-seventeenth century. Thus the promulgation of the Ordenanza, and the establishment of the Jesuits and the Holy Office, marked the end of one era and the beginning of another.

Notes

1. Clarence Haring, *The Spanish Empire in America* (New York, 1947), pp. 103–105.
2. See Chapter 2 in this volume.
3. *Catholic Encyclopedia*, 16 vols. (New York, 1907), vol. 2, "Benefice," p. 473.
4. The papers dealing with the first *oposiciones* can be found in three places. The registry book and *oposición* records are in the Archivo Arzobispal de Mexico (AAM), Ordenes Sacros, I. Moya's letters and reports to Spain are in Archivo General de Indias, Seville (AGI), Mexico, 336-A, doc. 117. Several of these have been published in Francisco del Paso y Troncoso, *Epistolario de la Nueva España*, 16 vols. (Mexico, 1939–42), vol. 11, pp. 237–260.
5. AGI, Mexico 336-A, doc. 117 a & b, 24 Jan. 1575, "Nombramiento & Instrucción"; Paso y Troncoso, *Epistolario*, 11, pp. 237–239.
6. This chronology is based on the letter of Moya to Ovando, AGI, Mexico, 336-a, doc. 117, 30 Mar. 1575; Paso y Troncoso, *Epistolario*, 11, pp. 244–249. The daily record is in AAM, Ordenes Sacros, I.
7. AGI, Mexico, 336-A, doc. 117 d, "Oposición de Zumpango y Huipuztla," 8 Mar. 1575; Paso y Troncoso, *Epistolario*, 11, p. 243.
8. John F. Schwaller, *Partidos y Párrocos bajo la Real Corona en la Nueva España, Siglo XVI* (Mexico, 1981), p. 508.
9. AGI, Mexico, 336-A, doc. 117 d; Paso y Troncoso, *Epistolario*, 11. p. 243.
10. AGI, Mexico, 336-A, doc. 117 e, "Presentación," 26 Mar. 1575; Paso y Troncoso, *Epistolario*, 11, pp. 241–242.
11. Records of the early presentation can be found in AAM, Ordenes Sacros, I.
12. Ibid.
13. AGI, Mexico, 336-A, doc. 117, Moya to Ovando, 30 Mar. 1575; Paso y Troncoso, *Epistolario*, 11, pp. 244–248.
14. Ibid., "a titulo de unos beneficios mentales y imaginados o de unos patrimonios fingidos."
15. AGI, Mexico, 336-A, doc. 109, Moya to Ovando, 20 Dec. 1574; Paso y Troncoso, *Epistolario*, 11, pp. 204–210.
16. AGI, Mexico, 343, Romano to Ovando, 14 Mar. 1575 "cada uno escrivira a V Sa; facil cosa sera entrando la autoridad de V Sa por medio q. tengan paz, quitados puntos y niñerias."
17. Ibid.
18. AGI, Mexico, 343, Romano to Ovando, 25 Oct. 1574.
19. AGI, Mexico, 343, Romano to Ovando, 10–11 Dec. 1574.
20. AGI, Mexico, 343, Romano to King in Council of the Indies, 20 Mar. 1575.
21. AGI, Mexico, 343, Romano to King in Council of the Indies, 1 Nov. 1579.
22. AGI, Mexico, 343, Romano to King in Council of the Indies, 23 July 1581 and 24 Dec. 1581.
23. Peter Gerhard, *A Guide to the Historical Geography of New Spain* (Cambridge, 1973), pp. 57 and 142; Paso y Troncoso, *Epistolario*, 14, 92; Francisco del Paso y Troncoso, *Papeles de la Nueva España*, 7 vols. (Madrid, 1907), vol. 5, p. 262; AGI, Mexico, 284, Juan Vizcaino.
24. AGI, Mexico, 1064, Libro 2 (F-2), ff. 91v-92, 100v-101

25. AGI, Mexico, 357, Albuquerque to King in Council of the Indies, 12 Mar. 1577.

26. AGI, Mexico, 374, Medina Rincón to King, 20 Mar. 1576.

27. AGI, Mexico, 374, Medina Rincón to King, 4 Mar. 1582 and 3 Nov. 1582.

28. AGI, Guadalajara, 55, Mendiola to King, 3 Ap. 1584.

29. AGI, Mexico, 336-A, doc. 109, Moya to Ovando, 20 Oct. 1574; Paso y Troncoso, *Epistolario*, 11, pp. 204–210.

30. AGI, Mexico, 336-A, doc. 118, Moya to Ovando, 22 Ap. 1574; Paso y Troncoso, *Epistolario*, 11, pp. 256–261.

31. AGI, Mexico, 19, doc. 151, Enríquez to King, 8 Mar. 1575.

32. *Cartas de Indias* (Madrid, 1877), pp. 315–322.

33. Lewis Hanke, ed., *Los virreyes* (Madrid, 1977), I, pp. 205–206.

34. The subsequent discussion of the impact of the Ordenanza is based on data found in AAM, Ordenes Sacros, I. This is corroborated, where possible, by data from the Royal Treasury accounts published in Schwaller, *Partidos*.

35. AGN, General de Parte, 2, f. 167, exp. 717; f. 176, exp. 751; f. 183, exp. 779.

36. Luis García Pimentel, *Descripción del arzobispado de México hecha en 1570* (Mexico, 1897), pp. 317–399.

37. *Cartas de Indias*, pp. 196–218.

38. Paso y Troncoso, *Epistolario*, 14, pp. 72–101.

39. AGI, Patronato, 183, Num. 1, Ramo 3, "Relacion de los clerigos."

40. AGN, Bienes Nacionales, 992, exp 2, "Oposición de Chiapa."

41. AGI, Mexico, 217, doc. 34, 17 Ap. 1583.

42. AGI, Mexico, 210, doc. 27; AGI, Mexico, 282, Cristóbal Gil.

43. AGI, Patronato, 183, Num. 1, Ramo. 3.

44. Ibid., AGI, Mexico, 343, Romano to Villamanrique, 8 May 1586.

45. The papers dealing with these appointments and the ensuing controversy come from: AGI, Mexico, 20, doc. 81; AGI, Mexico, Ramo 2, 26 Oct. 1581; AGI, Mexico, 336-A, doc. 156.

46. AGI, Mexico, 1064, Libro 2 (F-2), f. 107v, 29 Ap. 1583.

47. AGI, Mexico, 286, Molina Valderrama; AGI, Patronato, 183, Num. 1, Ramo 3.

48. AGI, Mexico, 214, doc. 12; AGI, Mexico, 215, doc. 14; AGI, Mexico, 284; AGI, Mexico, 287; AGI, Mexico, 289; AGI, Mexico, 293, all Juan González de Urbina; *Cartas de Indias*, 220; AAM, Ordenes Sacros, I.

49. AGI, Mexico, 221, doc. 3: AGI, Mexico, 290; AGI, Mexico, 293; AGI, Patronato, 183, Num. 1, Ramo 3, all Juan Bautista Belliza.

50. AGN, Bienes Nacionales, 1044, exp. 13.

II

Parochial Issues

4

The Spiritual Conquest Reexamined: Baptism and Christian Marriage in Early Sixteenth-Century Mexico

Sarah Cline

The extent of the evangelization of the natives of the New World has been an issue for recent scholars. If the natives were as thoroughly converted to Christianity as the early religious chronicles implied, why does there seem to be such a presence of native practices in Latin American Christianity? Sarah Cline analyzes a series of censuses that were drawn up in the 1540s in central Mexico. These censuses are of tremendous importance for several reasons. First, and most critical, they were written in Nahuatl, the native language of the Aztecs. Second, they come from an area close to some of the major efforts at evangelization. The Franciscans working in the Cuernavaca Valley were assumed to have been as thorough as any other order at implanting Christianity among the natives. And third, the censuses date from a period that is some fifteen years removed from the Conquest. On the one hand, fifteen years is less than a generation, so the older members of the society had been born prior to the arrival of the Spaniards. On the other hand, fifteen years would seem to be a long time in terms of conversion to Christianity.

Cline's conclusions demonstrate that the evangelization was not as thorough as the friars might lead us to believe. Nevertheless, there were strong indications that Christianization had begun to take hold in a dominant and definitive manner. Cline's study marks a shift in interest of scholars from documentation provided by the Spaniards, to that more closely related to the native perspective. Earlier researchers were content to rely totally on documentation written in Spanish. By the mid-1970s, however, scholars began to explore the wealth of documentation found in native

From *Hispanic American Historical Review* 73, no. 3 (August 1993): 453–80. © 1993 by Duke University Press. Reprinted by permission of Duke University Press.

languages, especially Nahuatl. While the author of the censuses used by Cline is unknown, the fact that it was written in Nahuatl indicates that natives played an active role.

Sarah Cline has studied the impact of evangelization on the natives of the Cuernavaca Valley in The Book of Tributes. *She is also known for her important study of the history of early colonial Mexico,* Colonial Culhuacan, 1580–1600. *She is professor of history at the University of California, Santa Barbara.*

S ome interesting historical research has been conducted on late colonial Nahua views of conversion based on information in local-level
Nahuatl documents; but a similar study of the early colonial era has not
been attempted previously.[1] Like so much information from the conquest
period, descriptions of the initial evangelization, even from the Spanish
point of view, are sketchy. Other than reports from early missionaries—
such as Fray Toribio de Benavente Motolinia, who described the
Franciscans' mass baptism of natives—little is known about the pace of
conversion and the social contours of the baptized population.[2]

A corpus of six Nahuatl-language household censuses from the
Morelos region, ca. 1535–40, collectively titled the Libro de Tributos,
gives unique insight into aspects of conversion, particularly baptism and
Christian marriage, from an indigenous point of view.[3] This body of documents, closely examined, can help construct a fuller picture of the conversion process than that presented in Robert Ricard's classic study, *The
Spiritual Conquest of Mexico*, which is based on Spanish sources.[4] Ricard
did not consider the effectiveness of early conversion and baptism to be a
central issue in the course of evangelization; but his dismissal of the question should not end the examination of this moment in colonial history.[5]

The Morelos censuses, moreover, are the earliest and perhaps the only
Nahuatl source for such information.[6] Until this study, no empirical analysis of Christian evangelization has been based on local-level, native-
language documentation. This type of source has allowed scholars to advance their understanding of Indian culture from the inside. Indians, or at
least a select group of Indian males, were taught to write the Nahuatl
language in Latin letters as part of colonial policy. Consequently, Indians
generated many records in Nahuatl for the colonial administration,
but also created many for their own use. These include indigenous histories and other formal texts; but most useful for historians have been the
community-centered texts, such as indigenous town council records, wills
and testaments, bills of sale, and other mundane documents, such as these
censuses.[7]

The process of conversion, or "spiritual conquest," has been studied
primarily from the point of view of the Spanish religious. The methods

and techniques of the first generation of Franciscans, Dominicans, and Augustinians in Mexico were examined by Robert Ricard in the early part of this century.[8] In many ways, Ricard's picture resembles what the religious orders themselves painted. *The Spiritual Conquest* includes a chapter titled "The Virtues of the Founders." Yet Ricard's work is significant for delineating the problems facing the regular clergy in New Spain, as well as their usually practical solutions.

More recently, some scholars have challenged the Ricardian view as incomplete, and have begun exploring indigenous viewpoints using selected texts produced by the friars. A theoretical framework for Indian responses to Christianity has been outlined by J. Jorge Klor de Alva, and the degree to which indigenous thought and beliefs shaped Indians' acceptance and understanding of Christianity has received sophisticated analysis from Louise Burkhart.[9] Burkhart has gone farther than any other scholar in showing how indigenous beliefs shaped the form and content of the Christian message, not just in its reception by the Nahuas but in its original framing by the Spanish religious.

Background of the Spiritual Conquest

The "spiritual conquest," the attempt by the Spanish clergy to convert the indigenous peoples of the New World to Christianity, was seen as a necessary companion to the military conquest. For Spaniards of the late fifteenth and early sixteenth centuries, militant Christianity was an integral part of the world view, stemming from their successful struggle to reconquer Spain. It turned their overseas expeditions into missions of discovery, conquest, settlement, and conversion. Conversion was politically important, for it was the legal basis for the Spanish crown's overseas empire.[10] The first phase of religious efforts, in the Caribbean (1492–1519), was not conspicuously successful, since the indigenous population was on the road to extinction. Systematic proselytizing began in Mexico with the mendicant orders—Franciscans, Dominicans, and Augustinians—shortly after the fall of Tenochtitlan.[11]

The Spaniards' experiences attempting to convert Jews and Muslims on the Iberian peninsula set the precedents for strategies utilized in the New World.[12] On the other hand, the New World populations differed from the Jews and Muslims, who had had contact with Christianity and rejected it. The Indians were to be won to Christianity by preaching and example, not coercion. Moreover, expulsion of those who refused baptism was not an option, as it had been in Iberia. The complex civilization of the Nahuas of Central Mexico put missionary efforts to the test, but dense populations were rapidly converted to the rudiments of Christian belief and practice.

In central Mexico the Spanish administrative structures, both civil and ecclesiastical, were based on the organization of native political structures, particularly the *altepetl*, or province-sized city-state.[13] In the civil sphere, the largest altepetl became the basis for the colonial structure of *cabeceras*, or head towns, with outlying settlements as *sujetos*, or subject communities. In the conquest period, the labor of these native communities was awarded to Spaniards in encomiendas. As for the church, sometime in the early sixteenth century it organized *doctrinas*, with resident clergy in the main settlements, and outlying population clusters designated *visitas*. The visitas were an integral part of the ecclesiastical structure, but their residents saw the clergy only at intervals.[14]

Precisely when these colonial structures were formally established is unclear. The territory was divided among the three main mendicant orders, which assumed the major responsibility for evangelizing the Indians. Because the Franciscans arrived first in 1524, they had first choice; but the Dominicans quickly asserted themselves after their arrival in 1526. The Augustinians, arriving last in 1533, often staked out territories unclaimed by the other two orders.[15]

The Morelos Censuses

The set of early sixteenth-century Nahuatl censuses covers six Morelos communities: Huitzillan, Quauhchichinollan, Tepoztlan, Molotlan, Tepetenchic, and Panchimalco. The three volumes of census material are well known to specialists, and portions of them have been published.[16] Although they have been examined carefully for information on social and economic structure, their record of baptisms and Christian marriages has been largely overlooked. Pedro Carrasco points to the large number of unbaptized persons as evidence for the early dating of the censuses, but does not pursue the matter further.[17] The data on individuals' baptismal status and, to a lesser extent, the number of couples joined in Christian marriage, can be analyzed to trace the contours of the spiritual conquest in a central Mexican region aproximately 20 years after the fall of Tenochtitlan.

Just as the Ricardian view has its limitations, the Morelos censuses present an incomplete picture, both from the indigenous side and for the entire central Nahua region. To begin with, except for Tepoztlan, the exact location of these towns cannot be pinpointed, although Carrasco has suggested the others may have been near Yautepec.[18] The scholarly literature generally agrees in placing all of these towns in the domain awarded to the conqueror Hernando Cortés, the Marquesado del Valle de Oaxaca. Because it was part of the Marquesado, Morelos had fewer Spaniards, and in some ways the area was relatively isolated from Central Mexico. The censuses are not dated, but all appear to have been composed at the same time, probably sometime between 1535 and 1540, to resolve a dispute between Cortés and the crown.[19]

Not knowing the precise location of five of the six towns also raises the question of which religious order evangelized them. All three mendicant orders operated in Cortés's Morelos domain. The Franciscans established themselves in Cuernavaca in 1525, the Dominicans soon after in Oaxtepec (1528), and the Augustinians in Yecapixtla (1535). The Dominicans are known to have established monasteries in Tepoztlan (ca. 1556) and Yautepec (ca. 1550); they were doubtless operating there before the church buildings were constructed.[20] If Carrasco's supposition is correct, it is likely that the Dominicans were responsible for evangelization in all the census towns. The matter is relevant because the Franciscans and the Dominicans had different philosophies of evangelization. The Dominicans emphasized more instruction before baptism than the Franciscans did.[21] The order in charge in a given place could therefore affect the baptismal rates. Despite this and other difficulties in using the censuses, however, these records are extremely valuable for their abundant information on the Nahuas' acceptance of some Christian forms.

The census data were undoubtedly collected for tribute purposes, and they are presented in two forms: house-to-house enumerations and final summaries of specific categories of information. With some variations, the enumerations list the head of household (usually a senior male) and all his dependents, along with their relationship to him. The age of each unmarried child is generally given. A person's baptismal status is noted, and in some cases couples sacramentally married are indicated as such. In the Tepoztlan census (volume 550), the listings for children are not as complete, giving information only on the oldest unmarried child. Married children are listed with their spouses; unmarried younger children have no enumeration for gender, age, or baptismal status. All the censuses specify the size of the household's fields and the amount and periodicity of tribute deliveries.

Although information on baptism (and sometimes Christian marriage) is given in the individual household listings, it is not found in the final summaries, apparently because it has no economic significance. The summaries indicate only the numbers of people in different civil categories: married couples, with no distinction between Christian marriages and other unions; widows; single persons; and minor children, as well as total tribute goods delivered.[22]

One set of questions for analyzing the census data focuses on the dynamics of baptism: who was baptized first and why; whether baptism affected household structure and economic arrangements; how baptism affected married couples; whether baptismal rates differed between males and females, adults and minors; how Christian names and naming patterns evolved; and how the baptized indigenous perceived the unbaptized.

Other questions involve Christian marriage: how extensive it was at this period, who entered such unions, and what were the Indians' attitudes toward and expectations of this institution. The patterns that emerge yield a picture of baptism and marriage in the indigenous context to determine how it affected individual lives, the larger social and economic structure, and the pace of the spiritual conquest.

The censuses reveal significant variations not only in the total number baptized in different places, but also the age and gender of those baptized. In addition, patterns of Christian marriage seem to vary from one community to another. From these data, researchers can speculate about the presence and effectiveness of clergy in the region.

Baptismal Patterns

Comparing the tribute levies of households that included baptized persons and those that did not indicates that baptism caused no obvious economic impact, good or bad. Both the baptized and the unbaptized had similar-sized fields and tribute requirements. Since the censuses were apparently compiled for economic reasons, the fact that information on baptism and Christian marriage was collected even in the individual household listings is notable. Such information must have had social significance that warranted recording it, yet apparently it had no economic ramifications.

Spanish sources provide some idea of whom the friars first sought to baptize. Just as the Spaniards used the standard technique of capturing the cacique to hasten military conquest, the friars meant to facilitate large-scale religious conversion by targeting indigenous rulers for baptism. This followed the European practice of converting the monarch so that his subjects would follow suit.[23] Colonial Mexican texts by Nahuas prominately record the conversion of rulers. Even if the purported early baptism of the Indian lords of Tlaxcala is not historically accurate, it is a celebrated episode in that polity's history. In Texcoco, its ruler, Ixtlilxochitl, and some others were said to have been baptized by Fray Martín de Valencia in 1524, perhaps after instruction by Fray Pedro de Gante. Children were also targeted for baptism, particularly rulers' sons.[24]

The Morelos censuses contain evidence that native elites were targeted for baptism, presumably so as to exert pressure on their subjects to convert also. The dynastic rulers (*tlatoque*; singular *tlatoani*) of Huitzillan, Quauhchichinollan, and Tepoztlan, as well as the rulers of Molotlan, Tepetenchic, and Panchimalco were baptized. What is more interesting in these rulers' households, however, is that in a number of cases not all members were baptized. The Huitzillan *tlatoani*'s household comprised 20 people, 11 of whom were baptized. Six of his 8 children were baptized, only the youngest 2 were not. The *tlatoani* had 6 concubines, just 3 of whom were baptized. There were also various unbaptized dependents.[25] The ruler of Quauhchichinollan was baptized, but in his household of 17 only 3 others were, including a concubine, a brother, and a dependent's child.[26] In Tepoztlan, however, the ruler's household of 10 had just one unbaptized person, a slave.[27] Molotlan's ruler's household had 15 people, only 2 of whom were not baptized.[28] Of all the rulers' households, only in those of Tepetenchic and Panchimalco was everyone baptized.[29] Although these are high rates of baptism, unbaptized adults were present even in these elite residences. Therefore the decision to be baptized could have remained an individual one for adults.

The rulers' households in turn are an index to baptismal patterns in the larger communities (see Table 1). Quauhchichinollan, followed by Huitzillan, had the fewest baptisms overall, while Molotlan, Tepetenchic, and Panchimalco all had high percentages. Tepoztlan's data are problematic because the information on children is more limited, but the rate of adult baptism is high.

Table 1: Numbers of Nahua Baptized

	Male	*Female*	*Total Baptized*	*Total in Census*	*Percentage*
Huitzillan	77	50	127	1,464	9
Quauhchichinollan	34	5	39	971	4
Tepoztlan*	870	828	1,698	3,123	—
Molotlan	382	425	807	1,057	76
Tepetenchic	337	342	679	813	84
Panchimalco	447	488	935	1,191	79

*Incomplete data. Gender and baptismal status unknown for 521 children.

The distribution of the baptized varied from one community to another (Table 2). Tepetenchic had the highest percentage of households with everyone baptized—more than half; Panchimalco and Molotlan also had significant numbers in that category, as did Tepoztlan, from available data. Quauhchichinollan had no household at all with everyone baptized, and the two cases in Huitzillan were highly unusual two-person households—baptized couples with no dependents.[30] Households comprising a mixture of baptized and unbaptized were close to half in Tepoztlan, Molotlan, Tepetenchic, and Panchimalco, with Huitzillan and Quauhchichinollan again lagging. The unbaptized constituted the majority in Quauhchichinollan, with more than three-quarters of the households showing no one baptized, closely followed by Huitzillan. The number of unbaptized households in Molotlan, Tepoztlan, Panchimalco, and Tepetenchic was negligible, especially Tepetenchic, with just 3 cases out of 116.

Table 2: Baptismal Status by Household

| | Baptized[a] | | | | | | Unknown[b] | | Total House- holds |
| | All | | Some | | None | | | | |
	No.	%	No.	%	No.	%	No.	%	
Huitzillan	2	1	54	30	114	63	10	6	180
Quauhchichinollan	0	0	25	19	104	77	6	4	135
Tepoztlan[c]	218	39	298	54	36	7	0	0	552
Molotlan	48	38	65	50	15	12	0	0	128
Tepetenchic	61	53	52	45	3	2	0	0	116
Panchimalco	69	41	87	51	13	8	0	0	169

[a]These are broad groupings. The category "some baptized" ranges from households with only one baptized to those with only one unbaptized.
[b]Household enumerations are only fragments, due to manuscript damage.
[c]Data incomplete for children. Data in the "all" and "some" categories should be taken as provisional, based on available information.

In the households with a mixture of baptized and unbaptized, the analysis of who was unbaptized gives further insight into the dynamics of conversion. Table 3 compares the numbers of unbaptized in mixed households, showing that generally in Tepetenchic, Molotlan, Panchimalco, and to the extent known, Tepoztlan, only one or two people were unbaptized in a given household, whereas in Huitzillan and Quauhchichinollan the unbaptized generally constituted the majority of household members. The latter two communities show no clustering of baptized members in a few households, and the other four show no clustering of unbaptized. In Huitzillan and Quauhchichinollan some of the mixed households could be quite large, with as many as 14 unbaptized members. How isolated the one or two baptized felt in this situation is not known.

In the four communities with high percentages of baptized, the unbaptized in mixed households provide a means to understand conversion at an advanced but still incomplete stage. Table 4 indicates that in those communities the mixed households included more unbaptized adults than children. Children are lumped into a single category, since gender cannot always be determined by the Nahuatl given name. Children in these four communities accounted for less than a quarter of the unbaptized, and a great number of these were newborns.

A much larger number of household heads were unbaptized. Panchimalco had 49, one a woman (29 percent); Molotlan 28 (22 percent); Tepetenchic 22 (19 percent); and Tepoztlan 158 (29 percent). Clearly, heads of households were not dictating the baptismal status of household members, but it is even more interesting that frequently the head was the only one not baptized. Given that the majority of the population in these four communities was baptized, the continuing non-Christian status of household heads in the community at large may indicate either that they were not targeted for baptism or, if they were, they resisted it.

Table 3: Numbers of Unbaptized in Mixed Households

Number unbaptized per household	Households					
	H	Q	Tepoz	M	Tepe	P
1	1	0	120	25	20	38
2	4	0	97	21	16	27
3	4	1	34	10	6	10
4	6	1	30	4	3	5
5	5	5	8	1	4	3
6	3	1	4	1	2	2
7	5	2	2	2	1	1
8	2	2	2	0	0	0
9	10	5	0	1	0	1
10	5	3	1	0	0	0
11	1	3	0	0	0	0
12	3	1	0	0	0	0
13	1	1	0	0	0	0
14	4	0	0	0	0	0
Total mixed households	54	25	298	65	52	87

H = Huitzillan, Q = Quauhchichinollan, Tepoz = Tepoztlan, M = Molotlan, Tepe = Tepetenchic, P = Panchimalco

Table 4: Gender and Age of Unbaptized in Mixed Households

	Tepoztlan[a]	Tepetenchic		Molotlan		Panchimalco	
	No.	No.	%	No.	%	No.	%
Men	257	42	37	54	36	91	49
Women	304	47	41	71	47	42	34
Children	65[b]	25	22	26	17	32	17
Total	626	114	100	151	100	185	100

[a]Household enumerations include data for first child only.
[b]Baptismal status of 521 children unknown.

A small but noteworthy group of the unbaptized were slaves. Only a few slaves resided in Tepoztlan, Huitzillan, and Tepetenchic, and many of them were unbaptized. The entire Huitzillan census lists just 1 slave, in the *tlatoani*'s household, where the slave was one of 9 unbaptized residents.[31] The Tepoztlan *tlatoani*'s household, however, contained 6 slaves, just 1 of whom was unbaptized. The community as a whole included 17 unbaptized slaves and 13 baptized; of the baptized, all but one were women. The baptized were concentrated in five households and the unbaptized in 9 households.[32] Tepetenchic had 6 slaves: 3 baptized, 3 unbaptized.[33]

Slaves in early colonial central Mexico generally had held that status since the pre-Hispanic era. Slavery came to an end fairly early in the central region, though it continued in frontier areas, especially targeting natives who fiercely resisted pacification.[34] Slaves in pre-Hispanic society could marry and hold property on their own, but how much their subordinate status changed in the colonial period is unclear. Why many of the slaves in the Morelos censuses are unbaptized is not known. Did the clergy put less effort into converting them? As the foregoing examples have shown, rulers and household heads apparently did not coerce adults in their units to convert; the evidence that unbaptized slaves shared households with baptized residents may enhance the perception that adult baptism was an individual choice. Perhaps continued non-Christian status for these native slaves was a form of resistance. On the other hand, slave owners might have kept their slaves away from the clergy, controlling the slaves in a manner not possible with kin or other dependents. Or perhaps slave status brought with it some form of ostracism similar to the treatment of outside groups in Nahua communities. Here that treatment might have been applied to exclude slaves from the higher status of the baptized.

Huitzillan and Quauhchichinollan

The two communities where fewer people were baptized present sharply different patterns from the other four. The contrast suggests that the conversion process was captured at two different points: the initial contact by the religious in Quauhchichinollan and Huitzillan, and the more advanced stage in the other four communities. The critical factor is the frequency of contact with the Spanish religious. This cannot be proven definitively, since the censuses contain neither explicit testimony of contact with the religious nor specific evidence for these communities from the religious themselves. In general, however, in the early sixteenth century, the Nahua population was dense (although reduced by epidemics) and the number of Spanish religious was small. These conditions had changed by the end of the century, with a smaller indigenous population and sufficient clergy to minister to them.[35]

It is generally accepted that by this later time, everyone in the area close to Mexico City was baptized or passing as such. The *Códice franciscano* reports that the friars dealt with the delicate matter of Indians passing themselves off as baptized. When the friars became aware of the situation, they would secretly baptize those Indians.[36] In the latter sixteenth century, the usual practice was for all central Mexican Indians to be baptized, and its lack was hidden and cause for further subterfuge.

In the earlier period, however, the data are relatively reliable, and those for Quauhchichinollan and Huitzillan can be comparatively analyzed. The Huitzillan census is divided into two distinct sections.[37] The first part consists of 41 households closest in the listings to the *tlatoani*'s household. The second part consists of 139 households. The distinction between the first and second sections is quite useful. In both communities, the baptized are a small percentage of the total population (see Table 1). Quauhchichinollan had a population of 971, of which only 39, or about 4 percent, were baptized. The total population of Huitzillan was 1,464, with 274 in the first section and 1,190 in the second. The baptized were 20 percent of the population in the first section and just 6 percent of the second section (Table 5). The Quauhchichinollan census and the second section of the Huitzillan census are thus roughly comparable.

Table 5: Gender and Age of Baptized

| | Huitzillan | | | | Quauhchichinollan | |
| | Section 1 | | Section 2 | | | |
	No.	%	No.	%	No.	%
Men	8	14	13	18	6	15
Women	12	22	13	18	3	8
Total adults	20	36	26	36	9	23
Boys	26	47	30	42	28	72
Girls	8	15	16	22	2	5
Total children	34	62	46	64	30	77
Total males	34	62	43	60	34	87
Total females	21*	38	29	40	5	13
Total baptized	55	100	72	100	39	100

*One female could not be identified as adult or child. She is included only in the total of females.

In neither Quauhchichinollan nor Huitzillan were adults the majority of the baptized population. Quauhchichinollan and the second section of Huitzillan reported relatively few adult women baptized. The first section of Huitzillan, with its higher percentage of baptized, shows more baptized women than men. Children were the majority of the baptized, and overwhelmingly they were boys. This confirms Motolinia's reports about the targeting of children.[38] Quauhchichinollan shows a great imbalance between baptized males and females. Huitzillan's data show more males than females being baptized, but the percentage difference is not as glaring. In sum, in these two communities, the typical baptized person was a boy.

The age breakdown of the baptized minors also deserves attention. In Huitzillan and Quauhchichinollan, for both boys and girls, the largest number of baptized were between 6 and 10 years old—a very impressionable age. If the Huitzillan and Quauhchichinollan censuses are taken as models of how baptism was introduced, they indicate that infant baptism was not the norm initially. In only one case in either of these censuses is a child baptized at less than a year old: one Tomás was born "half a year ago" (*ya tlacoxivitl. yn tlacat*).[39]

Judging from the relatively few unbaptized children in the other communities, infant baptism probably became standard as contact with clergy increased. In Panchimalco, for example, census entries indicate a baptized child was "born last year" (*ya monamicti yn tlacat*). Even more common was the dating of a baptized child's birth to a certain number of days (usually in multiples of 20).[40] According to the *Códice franciscano*, in the second half of the sixteenth century parents would bring children to be baptized on Sundays at Mass and Thursdays at Vespers, but when this custom was established is unclear.[41]

The baptism patterns for households differed slightly between Quauhchichinollan and Huitzillan (Table 6). In Quauhchichinollan the most common household situation was that just one person was baptized. This was not the case in Huitzillan, where often several members of a household were baptized. In Quauhchichinollan, 74 percent of the households with baptized had just one baptized person, and it was rarely the household head. In the first section of the Huitzillan census (the one with the closer connection to the *tlatoani*), only 26 percent of the households with baptized had just one baptized member, while in the second section 47 percent fell into that category. The higher number of Huitzillan baptized in the *tlatoani*'s household (11) and the larger number of households with multiple baptized residents in section one suggest that the *tlatoani*'s baptism did indeed have an influence on his subjects, although it was not decisive. A possible conclusion is that the religious targeted the *tlatoani*'s district first for evangelization.

Table 6: Number of Baptized per Household

Number baptized per household	Huitzillan		Quauhchichinollan
	Section 1	Section 2	
1	6	15	16
2	6	12	6
3	3	4	1
4	3	4	2[b]
5	1	1	0
11	1[a]	0	0
Total households with baptized	20	36	25
Total households in census	41	139	135

[a] *Tlatoani*'s household
[b] One is *tlatoani*'s household

As to who was baptized in Quauhchichinollan and Huitzillan, it was, as noted earlier, fewer adults than children; but who they were is worth examining. In the first section of Huitzillan it was common—though not the rule—for the householder himself to be baptized. In Quauhchichinol-lan, however, just six men were baptized at all, and of these only two were household heads. The category "other" in Table 7 includes a variety of kin, encompassing many complex household situations that are reflected in the size of this category.[42]

Table 7: Baptized Person's Relationship to Household Head

	Huitzillan		Quauhchichinollan
	Section 1	Section 2	
Self	7	6	2
Wife	7	3	0
Concubine	3	0	1
Son	12	18	13
Daughter	6	10	1
Brother	4	3	10
Sister	0	0	0
Nephew	3	3	3
Niece	0	5	1
Brother-in-law	3	5	0
Sister-in-law	1	6	1
Other	9	13	7
Total baptized	55	72	39

For the adults in the community, the baptism of children may not have been initially significant. The baptism of the male household head was clearly important, as seen in collective designations of baptismal status; but whether these notations were judgments by the census taker or by the household member or members giving the information is unclear. In the Quauhchichinollan census, which has the largest percentage of un-baptized people, scribes wrote the phrase "None of the residents here is baptized" (*y nica chaneque ayac mocuatequia*) as the opening formula for the household.[43] Frequently this blanket statement was incorrect; the households did have baptized members. Examination of the households indicates that in none of the cases of incorrect identification was the house-hold head the baptized person. With the exception of two instances, none of the unacknowledged baptized was an adult.[44] A very interesting case is a household where five members were baptized, including the only couple in the whole census to be married sacramentally, but the enumeration be-gins, "no one is baptized here."[45] The importance of the baptismal status of the head of household (almost always an adult male) thus emerges; children and non-household heads counted for less.

The overall baptismal patterns for couples indicate that most part-ners had the same status (Table 8). In Molotlan, Tepetenchic, Panchimalco, and Tepoztlan, most people were baptized; and this trend also appears in couples' baptismal patterns (and since the Tepoztlan data are complete for adults, the information on partners' status is comparable to the other censuses). Both partners baptized constituted the clear majority in Tepoztlan, Molotlan, Tepetenchic, and Panchimalco. Unbaptized couples were the majority in Huitzillan and Quauhchichinollan, where virtually no one was baptized. For the four communities that were more mixed, unbaptized couples still constituted a significant minority (see percentages in Table 8). Mixed couples were a minority overall in these four communities. In Panchimalco the wife baptized and the husband not was more usual (19 percent) than vice versa (4 percent). There is one example of a Panchimalco household with three couples in which the wives are baptized but the husbands are not.[46] Overall, the differences in the other communities are not as lopsided as in Panchimalco.

In Huitzillan and Quauhchichinollan the baptismal status of parents and minor children often differed. Households included unbaptized parents and baptized children, frequently when there was just one child.[47] A number of unbaptized parents had all their children baptized.[48] More frequently, though, only some minor children were baptized.

Where some children were baptized and others not, no clear pattern emerges. Sometimes the only one baptized was the oldest, but in other cases, the only minor child not baptized was the oldest.[49] The unbaptized oldest child often appeared where the parents were unbaptized. In one family with five children, the only one not baptized was a 15-year-old son.[50] It might be speculated that it was his own decision not to be baptized. Another unusual situation is a family with three children. The two minors, aged 6 and 3, were baptized, but the married eldest daughter, Teyacapan, was unbaptized and married to a baptized man. Since Teyacapan was surrounded by her baptized husband and siblings, her unbaptized status is noteworthy.[51] If familial pressure was exerted for her to be baptized, she seems to have resisted it.

When only the youngest child was not baptized, perhaps lack of opportunity rather than lack of desire was at work. This was doubtless the case in Molotlan, Tepetenchic, and Panchimalco, with their high baptism rates. Even in Huitzillan, with its lower overall rate, there seems to be some evidence of this. The *tlatoani* and his wife had six of their seven children baptized; only the youngest was not.[52] In Huitzillan and Quauhchichinollan, however, the baptism of the youngest or younger two, but not the oldest, was not unusual.[53] Perhaps the older the child, the more personal the choice.

Christian Names and Naming Patterns

Upon baptism a person took or was given a Christian saint's name. Where the census listing does not explicitly say a person is baptized, the listing

Table 8: Couples' Baptismal Patterns

	Huitzillan	Quauhchichinollan	Tepoztlan	Molotlan	Tepetenchic	Panchimalco
Husband + /Wife +	7	1	517 (61%)	170 (66%)	137 (78%)	185 (67%)
Husband + /Wife −	9	2	72	14	4	11
Husband − /Wife +	7	0	62 (16%)*	22 (14%)*	12 (9%)*	55 (23%)*
Husband − /Wife −	273 (92%)	276 (99%)	198 (23%)	50 (20%)	22 (13%)	46 (15%)
Total	296	279	849	256	175	297

+ Baptized, − Unbaptized
*Combined percentage +/− and −/+

of a Christian name is a sure indicator of baptism. In some cases siblings within the same family had the same saint's name, which might suggest that the Christian name was not what the person was usually called. It might also imply that the cleric did not know his parishioners well, for he might have hesitated to baptize siblings with the same name. Individuals clearly knew their Spanish baptismal names, however, because the census reproduces them.

While it was unusual for siblings to bear the same baptismal name, it was common for mothers and fathers to have the same baptismal name as their same-gender children. For men, this was a change from pre-Hispanic practice, for it was rare for men to have the same Nahuatl name as their sons. Women's Nahuatl names, however, were quite stereotypical, birth-order names (Tiacapan, "oldest"; Tlaco, "middle child"; and Xoco, "youngest"). Duplication of women's Nahuatl and Christian names was frequent within the same nuclear and certainly the same extended family.

Certain phrasing in the censuses may suggest that the Nahuatl name was used as a term of address. One notation says, "She has a child, baptized, named Perico; his local name is Qualchamitl."[54] In the Molotlan census the Nahuatl name is referred to as the *macehualtoca* or "commoner name."[55] There is clearly a perceived difference between the Nahuatl name and the Christian. It is unclear whether one or the other was used by preference, but the distinction was drawn. Another entry reads, "Mexicatl's second younger sibling is named Nicolás; his old-style name is Teuctlamacazqui."[56] Nicolás was a resident of Quauhchichinollan, where few people were baptized, so he may have made a special point of his two names. His Christian commitment was quite strong, for the previous year he had married sacramentally (*teoyotica omonamicti*), the only such union recorded in Quauhchichinollan. By the end of the sixteenth century, the use of Christian given names without Nahuatl ones was quite common. Some Nahuas even took standard Spanish surnames as well.[57]

During the late sixteenth century in the Nahua community of Culhuacan, men's baptismal names showed greater variety than women's; but in nearby Coyoacan, this apparently was not the case.[58] In the Morelos censuses the pattern resembles the one found later in Culhuacan. A closer look at the male baptismal names in the Morelos censuses reveals that they are quite stereotypical. The inventory of all baptismal names comes to a total of 42 men's names and just 20 women's names, but no single community used every name.[59] The dubbing of some Indians with more unusual baptismal names, such as Damián, Calisto, and Ambrosio, may mean that the cleric had special favorites or that Indians were given saint's names corresponding to the saint's day on which they were born or baptized.[60]

Looking at the data on Christian names for men, it is not surprising that Huitzillan and Quauhchichinollan, with their very small baptized populations, had a very narrow repertoire (Huitzillan, 13; Quauhchichinol-lan, 8). The other communities, Tepoztlan, Molotlan, Tepetenchic, and Panchimalco, list between 25 and 31 names. Even so, a few men's names were popular and accounted for the majority. The name Domingo led in all communities, with the all-time high in Quauhchichinollan, where 12 (35 percent) of the 34 baptized males had that name. The Yautepec region was a Dominican stronghold, which may account for the high proportion of Domingos and may lend weight to the supposition that the communities of unknown location were in the Yautepec area. The names Juan, Francisco, and Martín were also popular in all communities. One consideration obviously of no influence in the choice of a baptismal name was the current political ruler of Spain: no one was called Carlos.[61]

Female baptismal names showed little variety; Magdalena was the most popular. In Huitzillan 30 (63 percent) of the 48 baptized females bore that name, while in other communities it represented between 30 and 36 percent of females. It is interesting that the name was not especially common among Spanish women at this time. María was the second most popular name overall, and in Tepoztlan it just beat Magdalena. Ana and Juana were the other two names commonly given. In other parts of central Mexico, María, Magdalena, Ana, and Juana were still popular at the end of the sixteenth century.[62]

Christian Marriage

If data on baptism are copious in the Morelos censuses, evidence of Christian marriage is much less so. Permanent conjugal unions were a standard part of the pre-Hispanic social fabric, but these unions differed from Christian marriage in some important ways. Divorce was permissible, and so was marriage to more than one wife simultaneously. What's more, concubines had a recognized status. Christian marriage was a lifelong, indissoluble union to one spouse, though remarriage after being widowed was permissible. In practice, concubinage existed in European Christian society, but it was not morally permissible.

The mendicants tried to institute the Christian sacrament of marriage, but they were far less successful, even superficially, than they apparently were with baptism.[63] Fray Alonso de Molina's *confesionario* of 1569 goes into considerable detail about preparing the couple for the sacrament of marriage and about the relationships that prohibited marriage.[64] Molina drew up his confessional manual after the Council of Trent (1545–63), which codified various aspects of Catholic marriage practices, to counter Protestant views of marriage and divorce.[65] Molina's manual makes it explicit that both prospective partners had to be baptized. The Morelos censuses, however, deal with pre-Trent practices, so the parameters of nuptial practice are not clear. Certainly with the few people baptized in

Huitzillan and Quauhchichinollan, a minimum requirement for Christian marriage was generally not fulfilled.

Language may be an indicator of shifts in native perceptions of what constituted marriage. The phrase for Christian marriage in early sixteenth-century Nahuatl is *teoyotica omonamicti*, which can be rendered as "took a match through divinity or sacrament." By the later sixteenth century, the modifier *teoyotica*, "through divinity or sacrament," was usually omitted, so the early form found in the Morelos censuses is notable. More commonly, these early censuses refer to marriage with the term *cihuatia*, "acquire a woman"; *oquichtia*, "acquire a man"; or the plural reflexive *ana*, "to take" (for example, *manque*, "they took each other"). Usually the last phrase was followed by a specification of how long a couple without children had been married. A man's wife was called *icihuauh*, "his woman," and a woman's husband *ioquich*, "her man," a variation of the more standard form *ioquichhui*. These usages seem to have been applied to men and women with recognized Christian marriages.

A Nahuatl term for spouse, *-namic*, often found in late sixteenth-century documents, does not appear in this form in any of the Morelos censuses; it may have developed later, when Christian marriage was more firmly established. It is standard by the 1580s, when people would call their partner *nonamic*, "my spouse," and sometimes, with greater effect, *nonamictzin*, "my honorable spouse."[66] In the Morelos censuses the verbal form of *-namic*, *namictia*, was coming into use with the phrase *teoyotica omonamicti*, "married through divinity or sacrament," meaning Christian marriage; and the negative, *amo monamicti*, "not married." The *tlatoani* of Quauhchichinollan is described as not being married (*amo monamictia*) but having three concubines.[67] In Huitzillan the phrase *ayamo namiqueque*, "they do not yet have spouses," also appears.[68] It may well be that this terminology for marriage is a postconquest development and specifically linked to the Christian concept of sacramental marriage.

Overall, the number of couples whose marriages are explicitly said to be Christian is small. No one at all in Huitzillan apparently had a Christian marriage, and in Quauhchichinollan just one couple did; surprisingly, not the *tlatoani*.[69] For Huitzillan and Quauhchichinollan, the absence of the notation about couples with recognized Christian unions is consistent with the baptismal data. But both Panchimalco and Tepoztlan, which had high rates of baptism, list only two couples whose unions are explicitly noted as sacramental.[70] Tepetenchic had just four such couples.[71] In all these cases, the census taker went out of his way to indicate the difference between Christian marriages and others, but the comparison is not necessarily straightforward.

Only in the Molotlan census do phrases appear suggesting that Christian marriage was the norm. Census entries in other locations might imply that Christian marriage was not standard. Dynastic rulers in Panchimalco, Tepoztlan, and Tepetenchic are among the very few identified as having been married sacramentally.[72] And as noted earlier, the *tlatoani* of Quauhchichinollan is described specifically as not being married, though he has three concubines. Despite its census pattern, however, Molotlan's ruler is not explicity identified as having a union sanctified by the church.[73] Even more interesting is that five households had varying numbers of couples described as "not married through divinity" (*ha[m]o teoyotica monamictia*).[74] Only five couples are positively described as married sacramentally.[75] For all other Molotlan couples, nothing is said one way or the other about the nature of their marital bonds; but it is quite possible that Christian marriage actually was standard here and that only its lack was noteworthy.

The importance of the husband in the Indians' view of marriage (perhaps the male Indians' view) is suggested by the phrasing in a Tepetenchic household enumeration. One Francisco was married to a woman named Juana, and the passage ends, "Francisco was married through divinity" (*deoyotica omonamicti y frcv*).[76] This focus on the husband is consistent with the censuses' use of the male head of household as the point of reference for enumerations.

One highly unusual notation about a Molotlan marriage is in Nahuatlized Spanish. In translation the entry reads: "Domingo Pantli and his wife named Marta Teyacapan do not yet have children; he has been married two years" (*domingo pa[n]tli yn izivauh ytoca maltha teyacapan a[m]o pilhuaque tus anos casato*).[77] The phrase specifying the number of years married, *tus anos casato*, is an entirely standard way for a Nahuatl speaker to render the Spanish phrase *dos años casado*.[78] In these very early Nahuatl texts, which contain virtually no Spanish loanwords, this Spanish phrase indicates a certain level of contact between the Indian scribe and the Spaniards—enough for the Spanish word for "married" (*casado*) to make its way into the scribe's active vocabulary. Because language is embedded in culture, this Nahuatl-speaker's use of a Spanish phrase to indicate married status is especially noteworthy.[79] It is interesting that the couple in question is not specified as being married sacramentally. As explained earlier, in Molotlan the implication of such an omission may be that it was a Christian marriage rather than not. In this case, the Spanish phrasing implies Christian marriage, which was the Spanish norm.

The native practice of having more than one wife or a wife and concubines was something the mendicants had a good deal of difficulty stamping out—and it still has an underground existence today in some parts of central Mexico.[80] Having several wives was an index of status for men and was still standard in some communities in the early postconquest period. In Huitzillan, even though the *tlatoani*, don Tomás, had a wife (*içivahu*), he also had six concubines (*imecava*), three of whom were baptized.[81] In Quauhchichinollan the ruler, don Martín, was said to be not married (*amo monamictia*) but had three concubines (*yeyti imecava*), one of whom was baptized.[82] In Molotlan the ruler had five wives, four of whom were baptized (*yziguagua macuiltin navinti omocuatequia*).[83] The norms of Christian marriage were indeed met by some rulers, for the rulers of Tepoztlan, Tepetenchic, and Panchimalco were married sacramentally, had only one wife, and had no other partners, such as concubines.[84] In those three communities, moreover, the rate of baptism was high.

Baptism did not deter couples from living in polygynous unions. Several census listings show baptized men having two wives, both of whom were also baptized.[85] None of these unions was said to be a Christian marriage, which was expected to be a lifelong union with one partner or, at least, one partner at a time. It might be asked when baptism took place for people in polygynous relationships. Was it before or after the unions were established?

In 1530, the crown attempted to regulate converted Indians' marriage patterns by legislation, setting punishments for a man taking a second wife while the first still lived. Clearly, in the Morelos region between about 1535 and 1540, this decree seems not to have affected practice. Indians were forthcoming in stating their true situations. It is noteworthy that the 1530 royal decree allowed unbaptized Indians to follow their traditional patterns, but by 1551 the rule applied to all Indians regardless of baptismal status.[86] The clergy's concern with stamping out the practice of polygyny reportedly often resulted in the practice of men sacramentally marrying their first or favorite wife.[87]

As for Indian views of Christianity, the question of belief cannot be probed deeply, for the texts generally do not provide the means to do so. There is only a hint about one baptized Indian's attitude toward the unbaptized. A scribe for the Panchimalco census noted that "no one is baptized, they do not know Our Lord God" (*ayac[mocuat]equia amo quiximaty y totecuio y dios*).[88] The phrasing is entirely standard, and this is the earliest known example of it in local-level texts. In the censuses the more usual entry simply indicates that someone is not baptized (*amo mocuatequia*). It is also interesting that the scribe uses the Spanish loanword *dios* for God—indicating again the impact of Spanish Christian ideas and vocabulary. It has been said that the friars used Spanish loanwords in Nahuatl discourse to make the distinction between Christian and indigenous non-Christian concepts; but what actually occurred on either side of the cultural exchange is unclear.[89] As noted previously, the very fact that the censuses record the baptismal status of individuals, and to a lesser degree the number of Christian marriages, indicates that for the census takers as well as the natives who were enumerated, individuals' Christian status counted for something.

Conclusions

In light of the notion that Nahuas flocked to Christianity in the aftermath
of conquest for a variety of political, religious, and psychological reasons, how can the Morelos census material be interpreted? It is likely that
the Indians were predisposed to convert, because the pattern in pre-
Hispanic central Mexico was that conquered populations took on the gods
of the conquering power. James Lockhart has viewed colonial-era Nahuas
as needing less to be persuaded than instructed.[90] In the Morelos censuses
the baptismal patterns vary, and perhaps the sacramental marriage patterns as well. This leads to the conclusion that the communities stood at
two different stages of the conversion process; Quauhchichinollan and
Huitzillan essentially at the beginning and Molotlan, Tepetenchic,
Panchimalco, and Tepoztlan at a later but not final stage. Although neither Spanish nor Nahua records can confirm the assumption, the variations in patterns seem to be tied directly to differences in the frequency
and level of contact with the clergy. This in turn suggests that low rates of
baptism and sacramental marriage in some communities can be explained
as a function of clerical contact rather than indifference or resistance.
Thus the notion of Nahuas readily accepting Christianity is generally supported by the data if communities had increased contact with the religious. Resident or frequently visiting clergy could baptize and catechize
the Indians, perform the sacraments, and reinforce the notion of Christian
marriage to one wife.

If Quauhchichinollan and Huitzillan are taken as models of communities in the early stages of evangelization, then the Indians cannot be
said to have embraced Christianity en masse. In households, baptism was
by ones and twos, and in the community at large it was scattered, although
concentrated somewhat in the *tlatoani*'s district in Huitzillan. The other
four communities, Molotlan, Tepetenchic, Panchimalco, and Tepoztlan,
show high rates of baptism, with the very old and the very young well
represented in the unbaptized population. These communities had a few
pockets of unbaptized households, but generally the unbaptized appeared
by ones and twos in individual households. Baptism was standard practice, but the pace and the means by which this standard was achieved are
not made explicit. The friars themselves noted variation in rates of baptism, with what we might now call quantum leaps in numbers of Christians; the period 1532–1536 was particularly important in central Mexico.[91]

The ideal of Christian conversion was that baptism should be a voluntary decision by each person regardless of class or gender. In Europe,
where Christianity was tied to secular politics, conversion of the ruler
meant that his subjects became Christians as well; but that European pattern was not replicated in Mexico. This is perhaps the most important

conclusion from this study of Morelos baptism patterns. The mendicant orders, particularly the Franciscans and Dominicans, who had already been involved in missionary efforts in Iberia, seem to have returned to the ideals of the early church, stressing personal religious commitment. Admittedly, in early colonial Mexico some native rulers were targeted for baptism nevertheless, and so particularly were their sons, who in the early period were seen as potential candidates for the Christian priesthood.[92]

The variation in baptismal status even in the highest-ranking Morelos households suggests that the ideal of conversion as an individual decision may have been attained to a considerable extent. The hope of the religious orders was to baptize as many as possible as soon as possible, especially because the demographic disaster was under way in Mexico as it had been in the Caribbean. But in central Mexico, apparently, the mendicants were not converting by coercion. Judging from the Morelos censuses, high-ranking converts and households were not coercing their subjects or dependents. Nor were they obstructing conversion, except possibly among their slaves. Higher rates of baptism for the *tlatoani*'s people in Huitzillan suggest that even if the *tlatoani* did not directly coerce baptism, his own baptism did influence others, if for no other reason than that the friars likely were concentrating on him and his district first.

The higher initial rate of baptism for males, like the targeting of rulers, may have brought social pressure to bear on Morelos families; but evidence may show that household heads resisted baptism later, in the more advanced stage of the spiritual conquest. The higher rate for minors, particularly boys, in the communities least touched by Christianity indicates the long-term interests of the clergy. These census data confirm reports by the friars themselves.

The baptismal patterns of both adults and children give insight into the dynamics of conversion. The like-baptismal status of couples suggests that the marital bond was strong and that it influenced the decision whether or not to be baptized. With parents and children, the difference in baptismal status can be variously interpreted. It may have been parents' positive response to the opportunity to have their children baptized; their neutrality toward the friars' efforts to baptize the young; or their inability to prevent them. Given all the other indicators, the last possibility seems unlikely. For adults, baptism of children simply may not have seemed particularly important initially, as indicated by the cases in which households were misidentified as containing no baptized members. Actually, the misidentified households generally did not contain baptized adults.

While the decision to be baptized was probably the individual's, particularly for adults, it is unclear how much the baptismal name was an individual choice and whether it was important. It is notable that these names were either freely volunteered by household members or elicited by the census takers. Clearly, as a marker of baptized status, the baptis-

mal name was a more specific way to distinguish one person from another. In Morelos, there was greater choice of male names than female,
echoing pre-Hispanic practice; but beyond that, further insight cannot be
gained. The endless numbers of Domingos, Franciscos, and Juans;
Magdalenas, Marías, and Juanas may have been simply the fashion of the
day. The occasional pocket of non-stereotypical names may well indicate
a friar with a favorite saint at work, naming his parishioners, showing
the effect of individual priests in native communities. But the choice of
name may not have mattered much in any case. Certainly in the early
sixteenth century, siblings bearing the same Christian name and the wider
persistence of Nahuatl names could indicate that Christian names were
unimportant.

The paucity of positively identified Christian marriages in the Morelos
censuses is difficult to interpret. However, the evidence of multiple wives
and concubines even among the baptized indicates the difficulty in changing patterns of a fundamental social institution. The friars themselves reported the difficulty, for they met considerable resistance on this matter.
Pre-Hispanic patterns such as polygyny and concubinage were at odds
with Christian ideals of marriage. The cases of polygynous unions where
all partners were baptized suggest that Christian practice had penetrated
only so far, and Spanish legal restrictions hardly at all. On the other hand,
a new Nahuatl terminology for marriage seems to have been emerging.
Explicit Christian marriage was worthy of mention in some of the censuses, while its lack was noteworthy in others. This is possible evidence
that Christian marriage was becoming the norm in some places, while in
others it may have been unusual.

Perhaps in those places where Christian marriage is explicitly noted,
the friars were preoccupied with the Indians' conversion to Christianity
at the most fundamental level; that is, baptism. It may be that they saw
continued instruction in the catechism after baptism as the most practical
next step, and fulfillment of Christian expectations concerning marriage
as something that could wait for a further stage of consolidation.

The outward signs of Christian practice, measured by baptism and
Christian marriage, thus show great variation from place to place within
a given region a generation after the military conquest of Mexico in 1521.
The information on baptism and Christian marriage comes to us as a by-
product of more secular concerns—to count the native population and to
assess tribute. But the impact of efforts to convert the Nahuas is seen in
the very inclusion of that information in a secular census. Baptismal status and sometimes Christian marriage became identifying markers for
natives.

Even though historians must generally engage this information on
religious commitment in the aggregate rather than on the individual level,
it represents, nevertheless, thousands of individual decisions reached

through largely unknown means. It can be posited that where the religious had greater contact with the populace, the rate of conversion was higher. But why some people were baptized in places where there was no sustained contact with the friars or any economic or social pressure is unclear. While the task of changing even the outward signs of religious affiliation was a major one, the long-term enterprise of reinforcing and ensuring the Indians' orthodox belief was much more daunting.[93]

Notes

1. Stephanie Wood, "The Cosmic Conquest: Late Colonial Views of the Sword and the Cross in Central Mexican Títulos," *Ethnohistory* 38:2 (1991), 176–95; James Lockhart, *The Nahuas After the Conquest: A Social and Cultural History of the Indians of Central Mexico, Sixteenth Through Eighteenth Centuries* (Stanford: Stanford Univ. Press, 1992), 203–60.

2. Fray Toribio de Benavente Motolinia, *Memoriales o libro de cosas de la Nueva España y los naturales de ella* (Mexico City: Universidad Nacional Autónoma de México, 1971), 116–28, 150, 188. My thanks to Monica Orozco for the page references.

3. Libro de Tributos, Museo Nacional de Antropología e Historia, Archivo Histórico, Mexico City (hereafter abbreviated as MNAH-AH), Colección Antigua, vols. 549–51. Volume 549, Huitzillan and Quauhchichinollan, 63 folios; volume 550, Tepoztlan, 97 folios; volume 551, Molotlan, Tepetenchic, and Panchimalco, 122 folios. This article cites archival material that has been published by household number, and still-unpublished material by volume and folio number (see note 16). My thanks to James Lockhart for bringing these censuses to my attention in 1975, and for help in resolving problems of translation.

4. Robert Ricard, *The Spiritual Conquest of Mexico: An Essay on the Apostolate and the Evangelizing Methods of the Mendicant Orders in New Spain, 1523–1572*, trans. Lesley Byrd Simpson (Berkeley: Univ. of California Press, 1966).

5. Ibid., 94.

6. I am unaware of any other existing source with similar information. Newly discovered Nahuatl documentation does come to light from time to time; for example, the Culhuacan wills in Nahuatl resided in a private collection and remained generally unknown to the scholarly community until their publication. They were published as *The Testaments of Culhuacan*, ed. S. L. Cline and Miguel León-Portilla (Los Angeles: UCLA Latin American Center Publications, 1984).

7. The importance of local-level, native-language documentation has been established in recent years. See Frances Karttunen, "Nahua Literacy," in *The Inca and Aztec States, 1400–1800: Anthropology and History*, ed. George A. Collier, Renato I. Rosaldo, and John D. Wirth (New York: Academic Press, 1982), 395–417. On the many types of extant documentation, see James Lockhart, Arthur J. O. Anderson, and Frances Berdan, *The Tlaxcalan Actas: A Compendium of the Records of the Cabildo Tlaxcala, 1545–1627* (Salt Lake City: Univ. of Utah Press, 1986). Full-length studies based on Nahuatl documentation include S. L. Cline, *Colonial Culhuacan, 1580–1600: A Social History of an Aztec Town* (Albuquerque: Univ. of New Mexico Press, 1986); Robert Haskett, *Indigenous Rulers: An Ethnohistory of Town Government in Colonial Cuernavaca* (Albuquerque: Univ. of New Mexico Press, 1991); and Lockhart, *Nahuas After the Conquest*.

8. Ricard, *Spiritual Conquest*. This work was begun in 1922; it was first published in 1933 in French. See the translator's preface, vii.

9. J. Jorge Klor de Alva, "Spiritual Conflict and Accommodation in New Spain: Toward a Typology of Aztec Responses to Christianity," in Collier et al., *Inca and Aztec States*, 345–66; Louise M. Burkhart, *The Slippery Earth: Nahua-Christian Moral Dialogue in Sixteenth-Century Mexico* (Tucson: Univ. of Arizona Press, 1989).

10. For the political implications of conversion, see Charles Gibson, *Spain in America* (New York: Harper and Row, 1966), 15–19.

11. Cortés requested that Franciscans and Dominicans be sent to New Spain rather than the secular clergy, partly because the regulars were better educated, had experience with evangelization, and were perceived as having higher moral standards. Since administration of the sacraments usually came under the secular clergy's jurisdiction, papal approval of the special arrangement had to be obtained. Hernán Cortés, *Letters from Mexico*, trans. Anthony R. Pagden (New York: Grossman Publishers, 1971), 332–34; Ricard, *Spiritual Conquest*, 20–21.

12. E. Randolph Daniel, *The Franciscan Concept of Mission in the High Middle Ages* (Lexington: Univ. Press of Kentucky, 1975); R. W. Southern, *Western Views of Islam in the Middle Ages* (Cambridge: Harvard Univ. Press, 1962); R. I. Burns, "Christian-Islamic Confrontation of the West: The Thirteenth-Century Dream of Conversion," *American Historical Review* 76 (1971), 1386–1434; Norman Daniel, *Islam and the West: The Making of an Image* (Edinburgh: Edinburgh Univ. Press, 1962); Joseph F. O'Callaghan, *A History of Medieval Spain* (Ithaca: Cornell Univ. Press, 1975).

13. See Charles Gibson, *The Aztecs Under Spanish Rule* (Stanford: Stanford Univ. Press, 1964); and Lockhart, *Nahuas After the Conquest*.

14. This study uses the term *clergy* to denote all religious personnel involved in the evangelization, though it focuses on the regular clergy. On the visitas, see James Lockhart and Stuart Schwartz, *Early Latin America: A History of Colonial Spanish America and Brazil* (Cambridge: Cambridge Univ. Press, 1983); Ricard, *Spiritual Conquest*; and Gibson, *Aztecs Under Spanish Rule*.

15. Ricard, *Spiritual Conquest*, 20–23, 61–82.

16. The censuses for Molotlan and Tepetenchic, both in MNAH-AH, vol. 551, have been published in full by Eike Hinz and his colleagues Claudine Hartau and Marie-Luise Heimann-Koenen, eds., *Aztekischer Zensus. Zur indianischen Wirtschaft und Gesellschaft im Marquesado um 1540: Aus dem "Libro de Tributos" (Col. Ant. Ms. 551) im Archivo Histórico, México*, 2 vols. (Hanover: Verlag für Ethnologie, 1983). The Huitzillan and Quauhchichinollan censuses (MNAH-AH, vol. 549) will appear in S. L. Cline, *The Book of Tributes: Early Sixteenth-Century Nahuatl Censuses from Morelos* (Los Angeles: UCLA Latin American Center Publications, forthcoming). The Tepoztlan (MNAH-AH, vol. 550; Bibliothèque Nationale, Paris, Manuscrit Mexicain 393) and Panchimalco (MNAH-AH, vol. 551) censuses remain unpublished. Pedro Carrasco has published an excerpt of the Molotlan census, "La casa y la hacienda de un señor tlalhuica," *Estudios de Cultura Náhuatl* 10 (1972), 22–54, as well as a series of descriptions and analyses of the material: "Tres libros de tributos del Museo Nacional de México y su importancia para los estudios demográficos," in *XXXV Congreso Internacional de Americanistas, México 1962, Actas y Memorias, 1964*, 3:373–78; "Family Structure of Sixteenth-Century Tepoztlan," in *Process and Pattern in Culture: Essays in Honor of Julian H. Steward*, ed. Robert A. Manners (Chicago: Aldine, 1964), 185–210; "Estratificación social indígena en Morelos durante el siglo XVI," in *Estratificación social en la Mesoamérica prehispánica*,

ed. Pedro Carrasco and Johanna Broda (Mexico City: Centro de Investigaciones Superiores, Instituto Nacional de Antropología e Historia, 1976), 102–17; "The Joint Family in Ancient Mexico: The Case of Molotla," in *Essays on Mexican Kinship*, ed. Hugo Nutini et al. (Pittsburgh: Univ. of Pittsburgh Press, 1976), 45–64.

17. Carrasco, "Family Structure," 186.

18. Carrasco, "Estratificación social," 102–3.

19. The analysis of the census data here assumes the dating is contemporaneous. Carrasco, "Estratificación social"; Hinz et al., *Aztekischer Zensus*; and Cline, *Book of Tributes*, all believe that the censuses were completed ca. 1535–1540. See also Cline's detailed discussion of the dating.

Cortés had been awarded in encomienda 23,000 tributaries in 22 named towns. The dispute concerned what constituted the tributary unit. The crown, attempting to curb Cortés's power, wanted a small unit, such as the nuclear family; Cortés sought as large a unit as possible, such as the household, which could be complex. A commission of six was constituted to resolve the dispute, and the census of Cortés's domain was undertaken. Scholars consider the Morelos censuses to be a direct result of this dispute. G. Micheal Riley discusses the dispute in *Fernando Cortés and the Marquesado in Morelos, 1522–1547: A Case Study in the Socioeconomic Development of Sixteenth-Century Mexico* (Albuquerque: Univ. of New Mexico Press, 1973), 28–34.

20. Peter Gerhard, *A Guide to the Historical Geography of New Spain* (Cambridge: Cambridge Univ. Press, 1972), 96; Ricard, *Spiritual Conquest*, chap. 3.

21. Ricard, *Spiritual Conquest*, chap. 4.

22. The final summaries are found, respectively, in MNAH-AH 549, fol. 36r, v, fol. 63v; MNAH-AH 550, fol. 1r, v; Hinz et al., *Aztekischer Zensus* 1:139–40 (fol. 44r), 2:117 (fol. 79v); MNAH-AH 551, fol. 113v.

23. J. N. Hillgarth, *The Conversion of Western Europe, 350–750* (Englewood Cliffs: Prentice-Hall, 1969).

24. On Tlaxcala, see Diego Muñoz Camargo, *Historia de Tlaxcala* (Mexico City: Editorial Innovación, 1978). On Texcoco, see Fernando Alva Ixtlilxochitl, *Obras históricas*, Mexico (1891–92), 1:399, cited in Ricard, *Spiritual Conquest*, 84. Motolinia also notes the importance of children for indoctrination and the targeting of elites' sons for education. *Memoriales*, 38, 439, 444.

25. Cline, *Book of Tributes*, Huitzillan (H) 1.

26. Ibid., Quauhchichinollan (Q) 1.

27. MNAH-AH 550, fol. 5v.

28. Hinz et al., *Aztekischer Zensus* 1:Hh1.

29. Ibid., 2:Hh1.

30. Highly complex households are the norm in most of the Morelos censuses; couples residing alone are very rare.

31. Cline, *Book of Tributes*, H1.

32. MNAH-AH 550, fols. 5r, 6r, 33v, 34v, 37v, 44v, 47v, 48v, 55r.

33. Hinz et al., *Aztekischer Zensus* 2:Hh2, Hh47, Hh48.

34. Gibson, *Aztecs Under Spanish Rule*, 154.

35. The sufficient number of secular religious personnel was an argument the secular clergy used to wrest control of parishes from the mendicant orders.

36. *Códice franciscano, siglo XVI. Nueva colección de documentos para la historia de México* (Mexico City: Editorial Salvador Chávez Hayho, 1941), 81.

37. The Quauhchichinollan census is bound between the two sections of the Huitzillan census. At what point the volumes were put together and why an error occurred in the foliation is unclear. The first 41 households in Huitzillan were

probably geographically closer to the *tlatoani*'s, but the text provides no confirmation of this.

38. Motolinia estimates that the Franciscans had baptized "more than one hundred thousand persons, most of them children" *(Mis compañeros tienen hasta hoy bautizados más de cada cien mil personas, los más de ellos niños)*. Since he uses *niños*, it is unclear whether he means children or just boys. *Memoriales*, 444.

39. Cline, *Book of Tributes*, H#15. (# indicates the second section of Huitzillan.)

40. MNAH-AH 551, fol. 81r.

41. *Códice franciscano*, 82.

42. The complexities of household structure and kinship are the main topics of analysis in the published literature.

43. Cline, *Book of Tributes*, Q48.

44. Ibid., Q13, Q14, Q17, Q38, Q43, Q47, Q58, Q62, Q65, Q66, Q109.

45. Ibid., Q17.

46. MNAH-AH 551, fol. 108v.

47. Cline, *Book of Tributes*, H2, H20, H22, H39, H#11, H#15, H#22, H#43, H#45, H#59.

48. Ibid., H3, H33, H#10, H#52.

49. Ibid., H4, H24, H32, H#5, H#10, H#54, H#55, H#61, H#133, Q17, Q31, Q45: and H#61, H#113.

50. Ibid., H#61.

51. Ibid., H#113.

52. Ibid., H1. The *tlatoani* also had another unbaptized child, two years old, probably by another woman.

53. Ibid., H#22, H#36, H#42, H#57, Q14, Q35, Q109.

54. *"hoca / ypilci / vmoquatequi ytoca pelicco y nican itoca qualchalmitl,"* Ibid., H17. The phrase *nican itoca*, translated in this study as "local name," more literally means "here name."

55. Hinz et al., *Aztekischer Zensus* 2:Hh35, Hh50, Hh51, Hh53, Hh57, Hh113.

56. *"ynic umeti ycava / mexicatl - ytoca / niculas yvevetoca / tecuitlamacazqui,"* Cline, *Book of Tributes*, Q17.

57. Cline, *Colonial Culhuacan*, 117; Rebecca Horn, "Indian Women in Mexican Parish Archives: Naming Patterns in Seventeenth-Century Coyoacan" (Paper presented at the Pacific Coast Branch of the American Historical Association, Portland, Ore., 1989).

58. Cline, *Colonial Culhuacan*, 117; Horn, "Indian Women."

59. Men's names are Agustín, Alonso, Ambrosio, Andrés, Antón, Baltasar, Bartolomé, Bernardino, Blas, Calisto, Clemente, Cristóbal, Damián, Diego, Domingo, Esteban, Felipe, Francisco, Gabriel, Gerónimo, Gonzalo, Hernando, José, Juan, Julio, Lucas, Luis, Marcos, Martín, Mateo, Miguel, Nicolás, Oreden, Pablo, Pedro, Perico, Sebastián, Tomás, Toribio, Vicente. Women's names are Agustina, Ana, Ana María, Angelina, Anica, Catalina, Francisca, Juana, Juliana, Inés, Isabel, Lucía, Luisa, Magdalena, María, Marta, Mencia, Mónica, Rocín, Verónica.

60. William B. Taylor has found such a pattern for eighteenth- and early nineteenth-century Mexico. See "The Virgin of Guadalupe in New Spain: An Inquiry into the Social History of Marian Devotion," *American Ethnologist* 14:1 (Feb. 1987), 9–23.

61. Carlos was not a common name at the beginning of the sixteenth century in Spain, and when it came into use in the second half of that century it was used among people of high rank. A notable indigenous example in New Spain was don

Carlos Ometochtzin, a Texcocan noble, who was tried for apostasy in 1534 by the episcopal inquisition of Fray Juan de Zumárraga and then executed. In general, the Spanish monarch's name was not a usual choice for an Indian's baptismal name, but a number of Indian nobles did take elite Spanish surnames after 1550.

62. Cline, *Colonial Culhuacan*, 117. Magdalena seems not to have been a popular name in late sixteenth-century Culhuacan, however.

63. Ricard, *Spiritual Conquest*, 110–16.

64. Alonso de Molina, *Confesionario mayor en la lengua mexicana y castellana* (1569: reprint, Mexico City: Universidad Nacional Autónoma de México, 1984), fols. 45r–58r.

65. James A. Brundage, *Law, Sex, and Society in Medieval Europe* (Chicago: Univ. of Chicago Press, 1987), 494–503; W. Van Ommerer, "Tametsi," *New Catholic Encyclopedia*, 18 vols. (New York: McGraw-Hill, 1967–89), 13:929.

66. Cline, *Colonial Culhuacan*, 60.

67. Cline, *Book of Tributes*, Q1.

68. This is a rare and combined form of *-namic*. Ibid., H#129.

69. Ibid., Q17.

70. MNAH-AH 551, fol. 77v; 550, fols. 5r, 33v.

71. Hinz et al., *Aztekischer Zensus* 2:Hh1, Hh47, Hh114.

72. MNAH-AH 551, fol. 77v, 550, fol. 5r, Hinz et al., *Aztekischer Zensus* 2:Hh1.

73. Hinz et al., *Aztekischer Zensus* 1:Hh1.

74. Ibid., Hh8, Hh11, Hh13, Hh15, Hh28.

75. Ibid., Hh20, Hh33, Hh37, Hh71, Hh73.

76. Ibid., Hh114.

77. Ibid., Hh19.

78. The *t* for *d* substitutions are standard. Nahuatl has no distinction between voiced and voiceless consonants, so substitutions of *b* for *p*, *d* for *t*, and *g* for *k* are typical. For an extended discussion of linguistic questions, see Frances Karttunen and James Lockhart, *Nahuatl in the Middle Years: Language Contact Phenomena in Texts of the Colonial Period* (Berkeley: Univ. of California Press, 1976).

79. For sopisticated analysis of culture change as measured by language, see Lockhart, *Nahuas After the Conquest*.

80. Ricard, *Spiritual Conquest*, 110–16; Hugo Nutini, "Polygyny in a Tlaxcalan Community," *Ethnology* 4 (1965), 123–47.

81. Cline, *Book of Tributes*, H1.

82. Ibid., Q1.

83. Hinz et al., *Aztekischer Zensus* 1:Hh1.

84. MNAH-AH 550, fol. 5r; Hinz et al., *Aztekischer Zensus* 2:Hh1; MNAH-AH 551, fol. 77v.

85. MNAH-AH 551, fols. 80v, 97v, 98r.

86. Woodrow Borah and Sherburne Cook, "Marriage and Legitimacy in Mexican Culture," *California Law Review* 54:2 (1966), 955.

87. Ricard, *Spiritual Conquest*, 113–15.

88. MNAH-AH 551, vol. 112v.

89. Certainly Molina's *confesionario*, as well as the works of Sahagún and others, have the highest proportion of Spanish loanwords in the Nahuatl for Christian concepts or practices. For an extended discussion of the problems in translating Christian religious concepts into Nahuatl, see Burkhart, *Slippery Earth*.

90. Lockhart, *Nahuas After the Conquest*, 203–4.

91. According to Ricard, around 1529 "evangelization made an immense jump, and it is certain the average number of baptisms was much greater between 1532 and 1536 than between 1524 and 1532." Ricard, *Spiritual Conquest*, 91.

92. The failure of the Colegio de Santa Cruz Tlatelolco (founded 1536) was a bitter disappointment to the Franciscans, who had hoped to train caciques' sons for the priesthood. The training of the young men there did produce a core of educated Indians literate in Nahuatl, Spanish, and Latin.

93. The reinforcement of Christian belief has been the subject of considerable interest. Some scholars of native culture have pinpointed the confessional as a key mechanism for changing native beliefs and actions. Confessional manuals in Spanish and Nahuatl provide insight as to how this might have operated. See J. Jorge Klor de Alva, "Colonizing Souls: The Failure of the Indian Inquisition and the Rise of Penitential Discipline," in *Cultural Encounters: The Impact of the Inquisition in Spain and the New World*, ed. Mary Elizabeth Perry and Anne J. Cruz (Berkeley: Univ. of California Press, 1991), 3–22. The "primitive" Inquisition and the later exclusion of the Indians from the jurisdiction of the Holy Office (established in 1571) are examined by Richard Greenleaf in two works: "The Inquisition and the Indians of New Spain: A Study in Jurisdictional Confusion," *The Americas* 22 (Oct. 1965), 138–66; and *The Mexican Inquisition of the Sixteenth Century* (Albuquerque: Univ. of New Mexico Press, 1969). The role of the Office of the Protectorate, to which baptized Indians were subject, as a reinforcer of Christian practice has been examined by Roberto Moreno de los Arcos, "New Spain's Inquisition for Indians from the Sixteenth to the Nineteenth Century," in Perry and Cruz, *Cultural Encounters*, 23–36.

5

Individualization and Acculturation: Confession among the Nahuas of Mexico from the Sixteenth to the Eighteenth Century

Serge Gruzinski

Of the Catholic sacraments, Penance provided the missionaries with an opportunity to come to a deeper understanding of their native parishioners. Nevertheless, as Serge Gruzinski points out, the act of confession, which initiates Penance, was poorly understood by the natives. For Christians, the moral and ethical implications of religion are not always evident, but for the natives of the New World, they were often incomprehensible. Yet most native groups had a strong moral tradition, with severe penalties for violations of standards. The Nahua, for instance, held out the option of punishing drunkenness with death. To them, moreover, the Christian notion of sins of intent was completely foreign.

For Gruzinski, the act of confession also strengthened the colonizers' hold over the colonized. The Spanish imperial state, utilizing the Church as an agent, sought not only to control the physical reality of the natives but their moral and ethical world as well. Gruzinski also demonstrates a new methodological orientation in the study of the Church in colonial Latin America. His work can be seen as one of the first of the school of "subaltern" studies wherein scholars focus their attention not only on the impact of the colonial experience on the native people but also on how the state manipulated and reconceptualized them. He looks into the many means whereby the imperial state was able to manifest its hegemony in the everyday lives of its colonial subjects.

Serge Gruzinski is one of the most important scholars working in the early colonial period. His The Conquest of Mexico: The Incorporation of

From Asunción Lavrin, ed., *Sexuality and Marriage in Colonial Latin America* (Lincoln: University of Nebraska Press, 1989), 96–115. © 1989 by the University of Nebraska Press. Reprinted by permission of the University of Nebraska Press.

Indian Societies into the Western World *has become a standard for scholars looking at cultural change in the wake of the Conquest.*

Beginning with the concept of confession within the Roman Catholic Church, the focus of my analysis will follow that of Michel Foucault in his *History of Sexuality*, in which he discusses the scope and the Western heritage of the sacrament of penitence. Foucault convincingly demonstrates that, beginning with the sixteenth century and the Counter-Reformation, confession became a more pressing and invasive practice, an anchor of power in which "forms of subjection and schemes of knowledge develop in constant fluctuation." An example of the new strategy is that established by the church in New Spain within the framework of colonial domination. As a result, we have the development of a discourse centered on sex and the flesh; upon it revolved both power and knowledge.[1]

Confession can go beyond the church's spiritual goals, its objectives of dominion, and its systems of categories and interventions that would lead to the notion of "sexuality." Confession can also become an instrument for expressing church-approved forms of individualization and guilt, eroding the traditional ties and interpersonal relations of colonized societies. This has already been suggested by ethnographers studying the changes of confession in western Africa and inquiring into the dissolving and contradictory effects of certain forms of confession among ethnic groups in the process of acculturation.[2]

In the light of these different but complementary studies, the reading of manuals written to facilitate the confession of the Indians in New Spain, especially the Nahuas (or Aztecs), reveals facts that might have otherwise been inadvertently overlooked or regarded as obvious and trivial. Thus, for example, confession imposes on the indigenous penitent a series of fixed categories to evaluate his own acts and thoughts. These categories form a system of values that claims to be universal and leaves no margin for the most minimal improvisation, since they are supported by written texts and thus protected from the hazards of oral transmission.

Confessors impose upon the indigenous penitent an order of enunciation: "Put your sins in order," "Tell your sins in order."[3] This indisputable order, a "natural" one for the Catholic priests, leads to hierarchical series: the Ten Commandments, the five commandments of the church, the seven capital sins, the five senses, etc. These series are partially balanced by a dualistic principle that counterposes the seven virtues to the seven sins; in turn, it subdivides the sin category into mortal and venial sins and aligns the three potencies of the soul against its three enemies. In other words, the Indians were forced to pass from systems of multiple references, varying according to their ethnic group, location, social group, and ritual context, to a single conceptual framework, lacking geographical roots and incapable of apprehending "the other" in his cultural and intellectual specificity.

As an example, let us examine the concept of the soul. The Indians saw their own pre-Hispanic concept of three vital entities, whose harmonious interrelation determined the physical, mental, and moral equilibrium of the person, replaced by the Christian notion of the soul.[4] This transposition presented untold difficulties, not only because of the inextricable character of the concepts and the systems supporting them, but also because of the radically different manner of apprehending them. On the one hand, we have a uniform system (the Christian) with a strictly defined content that demands the unqualified adhesion to faith. On the other hand, we have among the indigenous societies a network of notions expressing themselves in their rites and influencing their behavior, but without being the object of systematic elaborations such as those achieved by the Western researcher.[5] Furthermore, Christianity is inseparable from writing, which permits it to assign a definite place to all beings and things. The midsixteenth-century "equivalences and oppositions of propositions" of Alonso de la Vera Cruz illustrate the systematic character that writing confers upon Western thought.[6] The indigenous cultures seem to handle a more flexible and mobile form of thought, open to alternative solutions and constructed upon a broad range of oppositions, distinctions, and parallelisms.

We assume that a concept such as free will must have perplexed the Indians as much as that of the soul. Confessionals are particularly insistent on this point. "You will not say that the devil forced or provoked you to sin; neither will you say that my friend or my relative made me sin. Inasmuch as I did what he ordered me, I am guilty for what I did and for my own folly."[7] Such are the words of Fr. Alonso de Molina in 1565; ten years later the Augustinian Juan de la Anunciación put the following words on the lips of his penitent: "I deprived myself of my Father God on my own will."[8] These are formal texts based on a fundamental assumption of sixteenth-century Catholicism: the Indian should act on his own will, and thus he is responsible for his own behavior. He has to put aside his surroundings, his social group, the weight of his tradition, and the external forces that used to influence his behavior, such as the power of a god's ire, the incantations of a witch, the envy of a neighbor or a relative, the ill-omened emanations of a sexual deviant or a transgressor of prohibitions. In other words, by centering on the "subject"—in the Western meaning of the word—the interrogation of the confession breaks down the ancient solidarity and social networks, as well as the physical and supernatural tics. Thus, the belief in a family force, related to the *tonalli* (fate) and vital to the cohesion of the group and the well-being of the family components, all but disappears.[9] It is obvious that this interruption (discontinuity or suspension) of the past, the customs, and the environment is related to the appearance of the omniscient and all-powerful figure of the Catholic priest.

This process of "desterritorialization," or brusque break with the traditional context, was supported by a system of psychological mechanisms designed to explore the penitent's conscience. The first one was introspection. "It is very necessary first to learn what is inside your soul, which is not what it seems outwardly; know thyself . . . the right knowledge is the knowledge of yourself."[10] The ancient Greek dictum was thus transferred to the newly converted Nahuas through the pen of Alonso de Molina. The process began with a questioning of the self that led the penitent of Juan de la Anunciación to state, "I am not the one I used to be."[11] This questioning, perhaps banal to us, establishes the relationship of the subject to himself within the Western humanist perspective and even Erasmian thought. As we know, Bishop Juan de Zumárraga, and Molina in his translations, were both inspired by the writings of Erasmus of Rotterdam.[12] There could be no wider gap between the autochthonous, largely peasant cultures and the discourse of the confessor.

Introspection cannot take place without previous memorization. Thus, it is indispensable to "know and remember all the sins," "bring into memory all the sins."[13] This memorization does not suffer mere approximation; it has to be exact, exhaustive, copied from an arithmetic model, "as a lord taking account from his mayordomo." This exercise comprehends the entire course of life, concerning itself with actions as well as "thoughts, desires, intentions." It is an attempt to master the new categories, to read into the past actions through the individualistic filter of the Christian ethic—that is to say, to organize such material according to a concept of "Western" time, perceived as a concatenation of causes and personalized consequences that shape the singular and irreducible trajectory of the biographical self.[14]

This reading and deciphering lead to the selection of the appropriate formulation of the sins, the manner "in which you will tell them."[15] Certain limits must be respected, however: "you will think about them fast, and survey them briefly." Under no circumstances should this dangerous mental gymnastics give way to pleasant but perverse deviations to avoid exerting the required self-censorship. These mental operations had to give the subject a feeling of guilt, a profound internalization of that feeling. "It is very necessary to know thyself as a sinner, to cry for your sins." "Tell your sins with feelings and crying; declare them with an abundance of tears and deep sighs." The penitent takes charge of the drama of guilt, not only by assimilating the concept of evil (sin) but also by modifying his own consciousness of evil and misfortune. This process is not specific to New Spain in the sixteenth century. It takes place, in one way or other, in the acculturation and transitional processes of traditional cultures facing modern Western cultures.

As a final step in the process of accepting guilt the Indian is invited to disclose his transgressions: "I wish to cast out all my sins before the priest." This disclosure precedes the eventual resolution of the anguish created by the "guilty" conscience and exacerbated by the questioning during confession. Two rites, absolution and penitence, allow the penitent to reach his "medicine" and his "consolation."[16] Such is the intellectual and psychic base upon which rests the practice of Catholic confession. It requires two fundamental prerequisites: the assimilation of an exotic conceptual apparatus, and the acceptance by the Indians of their position as Western *subjects* in a double sense: as vectors of an embryonic individualism and as ideologically and psychologically dominated subjects of the Catholic confessor.

Thus conceived, the device for domination has several fields of application: the body, sex, the world of dreams, personal fantasies, and even work. Let us begin with the body or, rather, the new image of the body introduced by the confessor. Affected by broadly negative connotations, the body is a form of anti-soul. "The third enemy of the soul is our body; the soul seeks its heavenly salvation, and the body, earth and mire, is always wishing for dirty carnal things."[17] This concept is placed within a binary frame that assigns the dyad "soul-heaven" an antithetic place to that of "body-hell." The intellect—or reason—is the exact counterpoise of the body.[18] It is obvious that Christianity imposed a narrow game of synthetic categories and an abstract dichotomy, whereas the Nahuas conceived a series of multiple components that broke down at the time of death to lead to different destinations (mansions).[19] Nevertheless, both cultures agreed on the need to impose the concept of mastery over the body to reinforce, among other goals, their control over society. Whether the weakness of the bureaucratic and political controls—in the pre-Hispanic world—or the cultural distance—in the case of the church—encouraged the choice of the body in preference to other objectives will remain an unanswered question. It is significant, however, that slightly over fifteen percent of Molina's *Confesionaro mayor* is devoted to the body and sexuality, while only one percent deals with the more urgent and threatening subject of idolatry.[20] To remedy the "lewdness" of the flesh, the church imposed the sacrament of Christian marriage, which represents a uniform institutional tie, both personal and public. Its celebration altered a traditional allocation of roles by implicating only the church and the engaged couples. The church reserved for itself the definition of the forbidden degrees of relatedness (*parentesco*), and the impediments or negative elements of the ceremony, while the contracting parties enjoyed complete freedom in the election of their partners. Thus, the concept of the marital union as part of a cosmic vision dominated by the play of fate (*tonalli*) disappeared.[21] The intervention of the authorities of the community was forbidden; the relatives, the lineage, and the matchmakers lost the essential role that Nahua tradition had assigned them. Similarly, the consorts were all by themselves within the conceptual space of indissoluble monogamy. "We advise fathers and mothers that once they have married their children, not to be concerned with them and therefore stop meddling with them or talking to them about each other, because they may break the marriage with hatred and ill-will."[22] Christianity promoted conjugal intimacy, intensified spiritual and affective communication among the spouses, established a complete parity and reciprocity on the subject of sexual relations within marriage, and assigned the confessor the task of watching over the functioning of the conjugal pair.

The confessor's inquiry also delineated the narrow space of the nuclear family: the duties of the parents towards their offspring and the obligations of the children towards their parents. The family circle, thus restricted, substituted for polygamy and lineages and transformed the nature of the relationships, which ceased being interchangeable. The affinal relations were better defined, although excluded from any possible sexual or matrimonial relationship, while the ties between father, mother, and child were more firmly fixed. Confessionals consider only the "modern" family model in which the classic oedipal triangle may develop.

It would be a mistake to reduce confession to a critical examination of the subject's behavior. Its intention is to penetrate into thoughts and into the most intimate and subjective experiences, with special predilection for sexual fantasies. Let's listen to Molina: "How many times do you think dirty lustful thoughts? Do you try to forget and discard them? Do you return quickly to yourself or do you wish to carry them out?" In other words, the penitents, men or women, were entreated to express the particulars of their fantasies, their attempts to repress them, or their fickleness in trying to carry them out. Thus the explicit apology of self-repression: "It is an abominable sin that you committed . . . because you did not wish to restrain yourself or return to yourself when your vicious flesh coveted without shame the filthy pleasure."[23] Mental pleasure, "the filthy pleasure inside your heart," is also reviled.[24]

Even more subtly, the inquiry attempted to induce the penitents to establish correspondences among desires, thoughts, illicit relationships, condemned forms of seeking sexual pleasure (whether or not the relationship was licit or not), pleasurable dreams, and the mental images of couples in their legitimate union.[25] Undoubtedly the confessors in New Spain attempted to subject their penitents to a veritable "technology of the flesh" and pleasure. It is also true that this "sexuality device"—to use Foucault's term—combines the imperatives of salvation with an unlimited will to maintain vigilance over the individual.[26] I wish to focus here on the process of individualization and will use the case of masturbation to illustrate it.

The first sources tell little about the "solitary pleasure," which seems to escape the systematic and violent repressions applied to sexual deviations and perversions. It makes a timid appearance in Molina's *Confesionario mayor* (1569) as an insignificant two percent of the text devoted to the Sixth Commandment. In 1575, Juan de la Anunciación devoted five percent of the questions on this commandment to masturbation, alluding to rather than describing it. Almost a quarter of century later, in 1599, the Franciscan Juan Baptista uses a tenth of that same part of the confessional's questionnaire to deal with the topic, addressing both men and women. Finally, in 1611, one-fourth of the questions of the Dominican Martín de León are concerned with masturbation, carefully avoiding a separation of the act from the thought accompanying it: "When you did that, did you have as an object of thought a married, a single, or a virgin woman?"[27] Later in the seventeenth century (1673) the Franciscan Agustín de Vetancurt was similarly preoccupied with the subject, devoting twenty-seven percent of his questions on the Sixth Commandment to the subject of autoerotism.[28]

It may be argued that these percentages are either the result of prurient arithmetic or the reflection of the obsessions of the confessionals' authors. Nevertheless, we must not forget that in western Europe late marriage and an increasing repression of illicit heterosexual relations seem to have heightened the practice of the solitary pleasure among the youth of the period under review.[29] Nine years after the publication of Vetancurt's work, in 1682, a French manual did not hesitate in placing this "deviation" among the most frequent capital sins.[30] The intensification and internalization of desire and guilt in onanism propitiated an exacerbation of the individual sensitivity and encouraged psychological withdrawal and further individualization. Paradoxically, in his efforts to uproot that "vice," the Mexican confessor continued to impose a conception of the self deeply Western and individualistic.

For the confessor, fantasy and dream were very close. As an involuntary activity, dreams escaped the sphere of sins, as long as the Indian denied any meaning to them and did not use them to foster erotic fantasies. It sufficed that he stopped believing in dreams. Diego Durán, however, was more demanding: "It is necessary that in dealing with dreams, they be examined on what it was that they dreamed . . . and thus, it is necessary that on this subject we ask: What did you dream?"[31] In the same vein, the doors to the consumption of pulque or hallucinogens such as mushrooms, *ololiuhqui*, and *peyotl* were tightly shut. What were before sources of revelations, of knowledge, of communication with the gods are rejected as folly or madness, confining the individual to the narrow circle of Western reality and its boundaries, which may be trespassed only exceptionally.

We should not assume that the model imposed by the church in sixteenth-century New Spain limited itself to familial, sexual, or mental patterns. We should not forget the interest shown in regulating economic activities through numerous advisory remarks delineating, in individual-istic terms defined by the medieval church, the relation of the indigenous to property, wealth, and temporal goods.

The penitential discourse developed through time, evolving toward more diversified and sophisticated definitions, as if trying to enmesh the penitent in the increasingly tighter nets of confession. Thus, for example, in the eighteenth-century confessional of Gerónimo Thomás de Aquino Cortés y Zedeño, there is a pronounced intensification of guilt about the sexual act. The questionnaire adds, and describes in detail, new zones of pleasure and perversions such as exhibitionism, voyeurism, sadism, and fetishism.[32] New objects took an unusual profile, such as male virginity, child sexuality, other conflicts within the family circle, and the incestu-ous desire for the mother, which is openly quoted in the confessional of Carlos Celedonio Velázquez de Cárdenas.[33] In successive and continued steps, confessionals brought together more intimately family and sexual-ity in a century in which, according to Foucault, the family became "the obligated center of affection, sentiments, and love" and "the most active focus of sexuality."[34]

Altogether, the rite of confession went beyond the spiritual sphere to become a complex enterprise of dominion and control over bodies and minds, an enterprise of "desterritorialization" that alienated the individual from his culture and his environment and imposed upon him an expla-nation of sorrow and sin expressed in a single form of speech with uni-versalist pretensions. It is obvious that the diffusion of confession was contemporary to the fall of the Indian societies and the installation of the colonial order. It would be difficult to deny that confession contributed in an indirectly and intellectual manner to the erosion of mental, social, and familial structures and to the crumbling of ancestral codes and an-cient forms of solidarity that regulated the functioning of pre-Hispanic societies.[35]

Indian Reaction

Given the constrictions of space, I will stress only some of the responses to the exigencies of confession, without aspiring to draw a total picture. After a bright beginning—according to the Franciscan chroniclers—the number of confessants in the second half of the sixteenth century offered an unflattering picture. Towards 1566, over eighty percent of the adult population died without confession in the Archbishopric of Mexico. In Tlaxcala, only twenty percent of the faithful confessed annually. In other parishes the frequency of the sacrament varied between six and forty percent of the Indian population. In the city of Mexico, the number was less than ten percent in 1556.[36]

The attitudes of the minority who practiced confession allow us to assess the mental and conceptual obstacles faced by the penitents. According to the works of the Franciscan Juan Baptista and the Dominican Martín de León, published in 1600 and 1611 respectively, the concepts of classification and categorization of sins were badly assimilated. The Indians failed to distinguish between venial and mortal sin; they even failed to recognize the difference between a meritorious creed and guilt.[37] They used to answer in an "incoherent" fashion to the confessors. For example, they "easily say something now and something else later in the confession; an Ave María within another."[38] They could not provide an accurate assessment of the number of their transgressions: "Sometimes they say they have sinned twice, and they add everything else in the confession."[39]

Without the comprehension and assimilation of the conceptual frame of Christianity, any attempt to keep account of the number of sins became foolish and senseless. The Indians stuck to numbers arbitrarily chosen. The effort made to fulfill the rite and please the confessor seems to alter completely the content of the answers; it was almost impossible to them "to order their remembrances in succession." Faced with this report we should not discard the possibility that such behavior was part of a deliberate attitude. Under a superficial conformity lie alienation and indifference, similar perhaps to those described by Richard Hoggart in contemporary popular situations.[40]

In fact, the vicissitudes of acculturation determined the capacity for assimilation and produced the most bizarre reactions. Some Indians ignored the rules of confession. Others, in an excess of scruples, lost themselves in irrelevant details.[41] Yet others never succeeded in overcoming the psychologically anguishing conditioning required for confession. Mentioning the "confusion" of the penitent, Martín de León comments: "He goes to confession so confused that he does not know what he says."[42] Thus, "a thousand absurdities," contradictions, and misunderstandings were added to the mental confusion of the subject. Incapable of attributing their failures to the cultural distance between themselves and the Indians, confessors conceived the difference as inferiority, lamenting the small capacity, the dullness and rusticity, and the ignorance and lack of understanding of the indigenous penitents. Nonetheless, at least in the work of Juan Baptista, an underlying optimism softens the contempt of the colonial discourse: "Their dullness is not natural, but due to lack of instruction by able and discreet persons."[43] Martín de León, more disillusioned, proposed to limit the exigencies of confession: "It is necessary that we adjust ourselves, more in this matter than in others, to their lowly and narrow understanding."[44]

It would be a mistake to confine the dialogue created by the confession to the alternatives of domination or incomprehension, making the Indian penitents mere passive, confused, and ignorant receptors. By the end of the sixteenth century we find knowledgeable Indians—possibly principals—"well versed and Hispanized," in the words of Juan Baptista.[45] They succeeded in deflecting, and even distorting, the discourse of the confessor, facing him with astute answers. "They tell stories. To confess a sin they first give a thousand excuses to lessen and mask it to make it look less bad, and for that purpose they use fastidious words so as not to be understood."[46] Although the tactics used varied, all gave evidence of the Indians understanding and their assimilation of the Christian categories. They were also a form of sabotage of the dominant discourse, drowning it "in a multitude of words and unnecessary stories."[47] They manipulated the rules of confession, toying with the attenuating circumstances of sin. Their astuteness takes surprising forms. When facing confessors insisting on formulating their questions in an intelligible and accessible manner, the penitents use a language of their own, wilfully unusual and disconcerting.[48] The verbal exuberance, the making up of guilt, the terminological hermetism, or the plain lie intended to confuse the priests in the very same field they chose and imposed: the religious discourse.[49]

At the beginning of the eighteenth century the situation had changed very little. The author of *El farol indiano*—published in 1713—echoed the complaints of Juan Baptista and Martín de León: "the majority of them ignore the manner of a good confession."[50] Fifty years later, another confessor wondered, "with the exception of a few, all Indians confess themselves badly."[51]

Although these critiques denounced not the limited practice of the rite but its deficient quality, for part of the population the Christian set of values continued as confused as it was at the end of the sixteenth century. "They take what is bad for good, and vice versa," stated Manuel Pérez. "For confession, the Indians examine their conscience very superficially or not at all." He cited obstacles similar to those cited in the sixteenth century by others: the difficulty in remembering their actions and thoughts, of offering an account of their transgressions, or of distinguishing between venial and mortal sin.[52] There is also a repetition of the adjectives used by the confessors: pejorative, not to say racist, expressions, not tempered by the hope of any betterment. "The Indian at the knee of the confessor is quite unfit."[53] Even more severe is the author of *Ayudante de cura*, who in 1766 does not spare a single disparaging adjective, citing their ignorance, dullness, lack of capacity, fickleness, and great infidelity.[54] Elsewhere he states: "We cannot give them understanding." It is inconceivable and, worse, hazardous, to attempt reasoning with them, since "to attempt showing them their inconsistencies . . . is to confuse them."[55] This amounted to arguing that the Indian penitents had remained impervious to Western logic as it is developed in the confessional interrogatory.

Along with these judgments, however, we find other different and even contradictory observations. At the beginning of his *Farol indiano*, Manuel Pérez expresses his own perplexity: "These are rustic but otherwise able people." He does not know whether to lament "the inconveniences of their rusticity or their ability."[56] Both Manuel Pérez and Andrés Pérez de Velasco agree in differentiating two kinds of Indians, following a city/countryside dichotomy instead of the social classification adopted by Juan Baptista. Urban Indians (Mexico City, Puebla, and their vicinities) were more able than those "who should be held as purely Indian on account of their rusticity and ignorance." The former, more *ladino*, seemed to be more familiarized with the sacrament of confession. "They have discretion enough to examine their own conscience, to explain their guilt, to assume its gravity . . . they know well what sin is."[57] The responses of the Indians were, nevertheless, varied. Some handled the notion of sin according to a logic of their own that differed sensibly from the criteria of the Church. This corroborates the indigenous assimilation of the process of conscience examination. These people seem to have elaborated a specific casuistry of their own by combining the Catholic rituals, such as the obligation to fast on Saturdays, to attend mass, and to abstain from eating meat while sick, with prohibitions against drinking pulque, lying with their wives during Holy Week, or spitting after taking communion, etc.[58] While the Church explained these practices as the mistakes of "erring minds," we may ask whether they were not the efforts of the Indian penitents to interpret and assimilate the dogma, since they are important and "ordinary" enough to take fifteen titles and over twenty pages of *Farol indiano*.

Paradoxically, far from softening or depleting the meaning of the ecclesiastical prescriptions, the practices that the Indians accused themselves of neglecting extended those obligations and strengthened the prohibitions of Roman Catholicism. Thus, from the sin of believing in dreams, one passed to the sin of dreaming; from the sin of drunkenness, to that of drinking pulque. They erroneously chastised themselves for eating eggs and drinking milk before paying for the Bull of *Santa Cruzada*; they assumed as sin eating meat on Wednesday, "while carrying the scapulary of the Virgin," excessively valorizing the cult of Mary. They also denounced nonexistent incests committed by presumed affinal relatives (*compadres*) who were not related, since "they call all relatives *compadres* and *comadres*."[59] The inflation of the spiritual affinal relations and the exaggeration of the ritual prescriptions—whether they were respected or not—distorted the logic of Catholicism. Such practices reflect a rigorous perception of ecclesiastical law, which could mean both the need for stricter rituals or the obsessive fear of not complying with them. In some instances, however, the motivation raises some doubts. The Indians aspired to copy the religious usages of the Spaniards and the *gente de razón* in general, in an obvious attempt at cultural identification and social promotion. Thus, they assumed that not attending mass on Saturdays, or eating beef during Lent, was a form of evil requiring penitence. In other instances, the Indian interpretation of the Christian norms may have led to new forms of sin hierarchization, such as when they assumed witchcraft to be a mortal sin.[60]

They could also find new forms of expressing transgressions. To emphasize the gravity of drunkenness, the penitent confessed: "I committed the seven mortal sins."[61] Their interpretation of sin might also guide them to more misleading assumptions. According to Pérez de Velasco, "it seems that most Indians assume that sins are only those committed during Lent . . . such as eating meat, becoming drunk, skipping mass, or incurring sensuality, which are among them the most common faults."[62] Using the transgressions defined by the church and the Christian periodization, the penitents constructed a code that favored the observance of liturgical time, rather than addressing the act itself. This resulted in a displacement of prohibitions—such as those related to fasting and mass—and a complete misunderstanding of the sexual and alcoholic transgressions. Their reasoning was the effort of attempting to put some order and logic in the maze of ecclesiastical rules that, although based on a universal concept of sin, showed some notable variations according to the ethnic origin of the penitent.

The manipulation of the Christian norms produced subtle and Machiavellian arguments that would prove the knowledge and assimilation of the exigencies of the Catholic ethics and confession. For example, when the male Indian pretended to gain a woman's favor, "he tells her—and the woman believes it—that it is a greater sin not to give in to him, because such behavior raises his desire and makes him sin; should the woman give in, he would commit only one sin."[63] By using such apt casuistic augmentations, the Indians appropriated the Christian logic of guilt, twisting it for the satisfaction of personal ends and showing an astuteness comparable to that used by priests (*solicitantes*) urging the favors of their defenseless female penitents.[64] Using Foucault's reasoning, we could point to the use of the same discourse—that of confession—to fulfill opposite strategies, encouraging criminal behavior and escaping completely from the grip of the institution originating it.[65]

The free election of a marital partner was an important factor in the process of individualization, and on this point the treatises of the eighteenth century suggest the presence of an evolution. They remind applicants of "the freedom demanded by this sacrament" and expose cases of

Indian women who married without or against their parents' will, or who obtained the dissolution of betrothal (*esponsales*). They point to the conflictive situations created between parents and children-in-law, suggesting that couples acquired a significant degree of autonomy after marriage. They probe into conjugal intimacy, pointing to women who gingerly denied sexual relations to their husbands.[66] However, we are far from being able to state that the family (the parents of the engaged couple) lost the role it had enjoyed in pre-Hispanic times. It was not uncommon for parents to oppose the union: "fathers and mothers are continuously putting obstacles to their children's marriages."[67] It was just as common for the family of the bride to arrange her marriage, fixing the conditions to their own benefit. Sometimes the future son-in-law had to agree to reside in the home or in the neighborhood of his fiancée—a form of uxorlocality— and sometimes he was obliged to serve "for a fixed period of time" in the house of his in-laws. This was a common practice in the rural areas.[68]

On the other hand, both in the rural and the urban areas, the practice of resorting to matchmakers, who had a very important role in pre-Hispanic societies, was still in use.[69] Their presence at this late period confirms the weight retained by the relatives in concerting a marital alliance. We have some indications of problems in the understanding of the Christian norms, however. One of them is the early age of the couple: "as soon as they are ten or eleven years old they think of nothing but marriage."[70] In remote areas such as the southern coast of Guerrero, the parents represented the groom.[71] Indians misunderstood the nuptial rites, assuming that "marriage was not the expression of consent and giving hands, but the reception of nuptial blessings."[72] In general, the key moment of marriage for the Indians was not the religious ceremony, but the betrothal. As soon as the matchmakers had performed their tasks, the groom began not only to serve in the bride's home but also to carry out sexual relations with her, a practice attributed to their promiscuity as much as to their desire to verify the bride's virginity. "They have in great dishonor to marry a woman who is not a virgin (*doncella*) . . . and this is why they communicate [carnally] with them before marriage, and if they find the woman nonvirginal (*corrupta*) it is difficult to proceed with the marriage."[73] These premarital relations were allowed by the parents, much to the scandal of the helpless confessors. Under these circumstances, only the groom enjoyed personal autonomy and power in the decision to marry, while women remained confined to an obscure and silent role. These observations should be broadened by taking into consideration Indians' "procedures of escaping" the strictures of ecclesiastical marriage, including bribing false witnesses, pretending to be married without the benefit of the ceremony, or using to their advantage the corruption of local officials (*alguaciles*) to continue to live in concubinage.[74] Such practices, introduced in the urban zones and among the more mobile indigenous sectors, undermined the sacrament of marriage and became modes of adaptation that suggest—as in the case of confession—the understanding of the Christian model.

It is riskier, if not impossible, to assess the impact of confession on the subconsciousness of the indigenous penitents. The insistent attempt to eradicate the belief in dreams—denounced in all confessionals throughout the colonial period—seems to have yielded some fruit, although not the expected one. It succeeded in lending a guilty character to most oneiric activities. As we have seen, the Indians confessed their dreams as if they had committed a grave sin. Pérez de Velasco, author of *Ayudante de cura*, gives us a significant piece of information: "To confess their lewd dreams they say that the dream deceived them."[75] The wording used by the Indians suggests that they knew the difference between a "lewd" dream and other dreams, but the preoccupation for the meaning—or false meaning— continued to dominate the indigenous mind, against the will of the confessors, who rejected what they judged irrelevant petty oneiric images.

In the same text, Pérez de Velasco points to the ambiguity of the Nahuatl word *elehuia*, used by the penitents. It could express, at the same time, the heterosexual impulse, the thought, and the act.[76] Curiously, we do not find the same continuity in the practice of masturbation. While the Indians entertained sexual fantasies, they did not satisfy them by masturbating. At least, this is what both Pérez and Pérez de Velasco inform us, attributing the absence of masturbation among Indians "to the great easiness with which they can obtain women."[77] Masturbation is thus almost the only sin from which Indians escaped, despite all the bad traits they were accused of. Why, then, the increasing interest of confessionals, from Molina's to Vetancurt's, in solitary pleasure? If we consider the curiosity of the confessors on this subject as a mere projection of European anxieties, and the above-mentioned observations of two confessors as a reflection of an indigenous reality, then we could interpret the infrequency of onanism as a symptom of the failure of the individualization process, or as the absence of the privatization of pleasure due to the persistence of collective behavioral patterns.[78]

Doubtless, the practice of confession became a refined tool of ideological subjection and of dominion over the individual, although its scope remains to be more fully investigated. Confession may be regarded as a device to bring the Indian faithful within the boundaries of a process that remained spiritual in its goals. Without denying this dimension, I must underline the complementary purposes of confession as "consolation and medicine," as explained by Alonso de Molina. In this perspective, the rite of penitence appears more as a side effect of colonial domination than as one of its generating forces. Confession offered a structure of support and comfort amidst the disturbances of deculturation. In other words, confession became a defensive and therapeutic mechanism, capable of appeasing not only the anguish raised by its own practice but also the traumas generated by colonial rule. Furthermore, by conferring a meaning to the new order, to the new misfortunes, and to the multiplicity of new cultural references overtaking the indigenous reality, confession helped create a buffer between the traditional cultures and the naked violence of colonial exploitation. If we fail to take into account the ambiguity of this Catholic rite, we run the risk of remaining ignorant about the adaptive strategies conceived by certain sectors of the indigenous population, and of overlooking attitudes and activities that reflect the capacity of reception, assimilation, and recreation on the part of the indigenous cultures in colonial society.

Notes

1. Michel Foucault, *Historia de la sexualidad*, vol. 1: *La voluntad de saber* (Mexico City: Siglo XXI, 1977) (French edition, Paris: Gallimard, 1976). See, especially, pp. 54 ff.
2. See, for example, Marc Augé et al., *Prophétisme et thérapeutique: Albert Atcho et la communauté de Bregho* (Paris: Hermann, 1975).
3. Fr. Juan de la Anunciación, *Doctrina cristiana muy cumplida donde se contiene la exposición de todo lo necesario para doctrinar a los indios . . .* (Mexico City: Pedro Balli, 1575), p. 142; Martín de León, *Camino al cielo en lengua mexicana . . .* (Mexico City: Diego López Dávalos, 1611), p. 109. The first volume of a project collecting all colonial catechisms for the instruction of the Indians is now available. See Juan Guillermo Durán, ed., *Monumenta catechetica hispanoamericana* (siglos XVI–XVIII) (Buenos Aires: Publicaciones de la Facultad de Teología de la Universidad Católica Argentina, 1984). On the general process of Westernization, acculturation, and evangelization, see Serge Gruzinski, *La colonisation de L'Imaginaire: Sociétés indigènes et occidentalisation dans le Mexique espagnol, xvie–xviiie siècle* (Paris: Editions Gallimard, 1988); Serge Gruzinski, "Confesión, alianza y sexualidad entre los indios de Nueva España," in *El placer de pecar y el afán de normar*, by Seminario de Historia de las Mentalidades (Mexico City: Joaquín Mortiz, 1988), pp. 169–215.
4. Alfredo López Austin, *Cuerpo humano e ideologia: Las concepciones de los antiguos nahuas*, 2 vols. (Mexico City: Universidad Nacional Autónoma de México, 1980), 1:285–318, and passim.
5. I have in mind the works of Alfredo López Austin, such as that cited in the preceding note, or that of Christian Duverger, *L'esprit du jeu chez les Aztèques* (Paris: Mouton, 1978).
6. See, for example, *Recognitio summularum* (Mexico City: Juan Pablos, 1554). See also Ernest J. Burrus, "Alonso de la Vera Cruz: Pioneer Defender of the American Indians," *Catholic Historical Review* 70, no. 4 (October 1984): 531–46. This work provides a short biographical survey and analysis of the main writings of this sixteenth-century Augustinian theologian.
7. Alonso de Molina, *Confesionario mayor en lengua mexicana y castellana* (Mexico City: Antonio de Espinosa, 1569), pp. 12–13.
8. Juan de la Anunciación, *Doctrina*, p. 141; Martín de León, *Camino*, p. 113.
9. López Austin, *Cuerpo humano*, 1:281–961.
10. Molina, *Confesionario*, pp. 5, 6.
11. Juan de la Anunciación, *Doctrina*, p. 141.

12. Antonio Rubial García, "Evangelismo y evangelización: Los primitivos franciscanos en la Nueva España y el ideal del cristianismo primitivo," *Anuario de Historia* 10 (1978–79): 95–124. See also, Juan de Zumárraga, *Regla cristiana breve* (Mexico City: Editorial Jus, 1951), and his *Doctrina cristiana: Suma de lo qu e más conviene predicar y dar a entender a los indios* (Mexico City: Impressa por mandado del Ro. Señor Don Fray Juan Zumárraga, 1545–46). Molina translated this work into Nahuatl.

13. Molina, *Confesionario*, pp. 6v, 8v, 9.

14. I am using here the concepts developed by Marie-Cécile and Edmond Ortiguez in *Oedipe africain* (Paris: Plon, 1966).

15. See Molina, *Confesionario*, pp. 7, 11, 8v, 15, respectively, for these citations.

16. Ibid., pp. 14, 17.

17. Juan de la Anunciación, *Doctrina*, p. 215; Molina, *Confesionario*, p. 23.

18. Juan de la Anunciación, *Doctrina*, pp. 217–18. See also in Molina, *Confesionario*, p. 115, the opposition of the concepts of the weakness of the flesh and the fervent desires of the soul. Martín de León, in his *Camino del cielo*, mentions the sickness of the body deriving from the sickness of the soul (1:362).

19. López Austin, *Cuerpo humano* 1:362

20. Molina, *Confesionario*, p. 20.

21. López Austin, *Cuerpo humano*, 1:342

22. Juan de la Anunciación, *Doctrina*, p. 67.

23. Molina, *Confesionario*, pp. 33v, 80v.

24. Juan de la Anunciación, *Doctrina*, p. 87.

25. Ibid., p. 88.

26. Foucault, *La voluntad de saber*, p. 153.

27. Martín de León, *Camino*, p. 115v.

28. Fray Agustín de Vetancurt, *Arte de la lengua mexicana* (Mexico City: Francisco Rodríguez Lupercio, 1673).

29. Jean-Louis Flandrin, *Le sexe et l'Occident: Evolution des attitudes et des comportments* (Paris: Seuil, 1981), pp. 297ff.

30. *Instructions pour les confesseurs du diocèse de Chalon-sur-Saône* (1682), Cited in Flandrin, *Le sexe et l'Occident,* p. 297.

31. Diego Durán, *Historia de las Indias de Nueva España e Islas de la Tierra Firme*, 2 vols. (Mexico City: Editorial Porrúa, 1967), 1:132; Juan de la Anunciación, *Doctrina*, p. 114.

32. Gerónimo Thomás de Aquino Cortés y Zedeño, *Arte, vocabulario y confesionario en el idioma mexicano como se usa en el obispado de Guadalajara* (Puebla: Colegio Real de San Ignacio, 1765).

33. Carlos Celedonio Velásquez de Cárdenas y León, *Breve práctica y régimen del confesionario de indios . .* (Mexico City: Bibliotheca Mexicana, 1761).

34. Foucault, *La voluntad de saber*, p. 143.

35. We could ask to what extent the immigrant (*naboría*) Indian, disjoined from his community and offering his labor in the mining communities, the homes, and the haciendas of the Spaniards, resembles the imaginary interlocutor of the confessionals for Indians. The mobility and autarchy of the former is close to the autonomy demanded from the latter. See, for example, *Provinces of Early Mexico*, ed. Ida Altman and James Lockhart (Los Angeles: University of California Press, 1976), pp. 18–19.

36. Francisco del Paso y Troncoso, *Epistolario de Nueva España*, 16 vols. (Mexico City: Editorial José Porrúa e Hijos, 1940), 10:132; 8:74.

37. Juan Baptista, *Advertencias para los confesores de los naturales* (Mexico City: M. Ocharte, 1600), pp. 3–3v.

38. Martín de León, *Camino*, p. 101.
39. Baptista, *Advertencias*, p. 2v.
40. Richard Hoggart, *The Uses of Literacy* (London: Chatto and Windus, 1957).
41. Martín de León, *Camino*, p. 110.
42. Ibid., p. 102.
43. Baptista, *Advertencias*, pp. 4v, 5, 6, 59.
44. Martín de León, *Camino*, p. 104.
45. Baptista, *Advertencias*, p. 13v.
46. Martín de León, *Camino*, p. 110 v.
47. Ibid.
48. Or more simply, they lie. See Agustín de Vetancurt, *Teatro americano* (Mexico City: Maria de Benavides, 1698), p. 91. It is also worthwhile to mention dilatory tactics consisting of blaming third persons: "They spend a lot of time without confessing a personal sin but, instead, talking about those of their husbands, neighbors." (Manuel Pérez, *Farol indiano y guia de curas de indios . . .* [Mexico City: Francisco de Rivera Calderón, 1713], p. 76.)
49. Anthropologist Jack Goody has raised an important question about the impact of the written discourse on oral cultures; this remains to be answered in the Nahua case. See Jack Goody, *The Domestication of the Savage Mind* (Cambridge: Cambridge University Press, 1977), p. 153. We are thinking of the confessionals that, according to Fr. Diego Valdés, some Indians read and also of the learning techniques developed by the Indians, using paintings and stones. See Esteban J. Palomera, *Fr. Diego Valadés, OFM: Su obra* (Mexico City: Editorial Jus, 1962), pp. 256, 308.
50. Manuel Pérez, *Farol indiano*, p. 16.
51. Andrés Pérez de Velasco, *El ayudante de cura . . .* (Puebla: Colegio Real de San Ignacio, 1766), p. 45.
52. Manuel Pérez, *Farol indiano*, pp. 16, 27.
53. Ibid., p. 19.
54. Pérez de Velasco, *El ayudante*, p. 66.
55. Ibid., pp. 63, 67.
56. Pérez, *Farol indiano*, p. 1.
57. Pérez de Velasco, *El ayudante*, p. 67.
58. Ibid., pp. 26ff.
59. Ibid., p. 77.
60. Ibid., p. 61.
61. Ibid., p. 50.
62. Ibid., p. 75.
63. Ibid., p. 44.
64. See Jorge René González Marmolejo, "Clérigos solicitantes, perversos de la confesión," in *De la santidad a la perversión*, ed. Sergio Ortega (Mexico City: Editorial Grijalbo, 1986), pp. 239–52.
65. Foucault, *La voluntad de saber*, p. 133. See also Pierre Bourdie, *Sens pratique* (Paris: Editions de Minuit, 1980), for the concept of "the logic of practice."
66. Manuel Pérez, *Farol indiano*, p. 186.
67. Ibid., p. 168.
68. Ibid., p. 158; Pérez de Velasco, *El ayudante*, p. 87.
69. Serge Gruzinski, "Matrimonio y sexualidad en México y Texcoco en los albores de la conquista," in *Seis ensayos sobre el discurso colonial relativo a la comunidad doméstica* (Mexico City: Instituto Nacional de Antropología e Historia, 1980), pp. 17–59.
70. Manuel Pérez, *Farol indiano*, p. 129.
71. Ibid., 149.

72. Pérez de Velasco, *El ayudante*, p. 89.
73. Manuel Pérez, *Farol indiano*, p. 160.
74. Ibid., pp. 134, 154.
75. Pérez de Velasco, *Ayudante*, p. 53.
76. Ibid, p.51.
77. Manuel Pérez, *Farol indiano*, p. 85; Pérez de Velasco, *Ayudante*, p. 51.
78. On the importance of the role of the community among the Indians, see William B. Taylor, *Drinking, Homicide and Rebellion in Colonial Mexican Villages* (Stanford: Stanford University Press, 1979), pp. 154, passim: "the Indian concept of the individual . . . in contrast to Hispanic concepts, stressed the responsibility to the community over self-realization." See also Margarita Loera, *Calimaya y Tepemaxalco: Tenencia y transmisión hereditaria de la tierra en dos comunidades indigenas en la época colonial* (Mexico City: Instituto Nacional de Antropología e Historia, 1977). This work underlines the persistence of the communitarian concept of territorial property.

6

The Battle for Bodies and Souls in the Colonial North Andes: Intraecclesiastical Struggles and the Politics of Migration

Karen Vieira Powers

Important distinctions accompanied racial designations. Likewise, the clergy were divided into two general categories, the seculars and the regulars. Karen Powers analyzes racial designations, especially between Indians and mestizos, as well as conflict among the religious orders and the secular clergy in the context of the region of modern-day Ecuador.

In the populations studied by Powers there were two "anomalous" groups—that is, populations that did not fit easily into categorization by the Spaniards. These included forasteros, *Indians who had migrated out of their traditional homes into other areas; and* castas, *also known as mestizos, persons of mixed Spanish-Indian ancestry who could not be classified strictly as either native or Spaniard. Powers looks at the two groups and the conflict between the regular clergy (in this case, the Franciscans) and the secular clergy over which would minister to and, in many ways, dominate them.*

Powers sees the forasteros *and* castas *as threats to Spanish spatial and racial notions of colonial rule. At the same time, the secular clergy were able to use this intrusive social group as a means to gain leverage over the better organized and historically better established regular clergy. This study offers important insight into the multiple levels upon which we can evaluate the tensions within the Church and society in colonial Latin America.*

Karen Powers is professor of history at Northern Arizona University. She has studied the process of Spanish settlement and acculturation in

From *Hispanic American Historical Review* 75, no. 1 (February 1995): 31–56. © 1995 by Duke University Press. Reprinted by permission of Duke University Press.

colonial Ecuador in Andean Journeys: Migration, Ethnogenesis, and the State in Colonial Quito.

This study uses intraecclesiastical conflict in the Audiencia of Quito as a vehicle for exploring the relationship between migration and political change from approximately 1534 to 1700. First, it analyzes how lower caste agency, in the form of Indian population movements and resultant mestizaje, subverted the race-based political order of the colony. Second, it examines how the products of migration, *forasteros* and *castas*, helped shape the colony's local political universe and then were themselves conscripted into elite conflicts (in this case with regard to the church).[1]

The essay aims to achieve these objectives in two ways. First, it closely examines the lived experiences and ideological discourse of the lower clergy regarding the systemic "problems" arising from Indian migration and mestizaje in the province of Latacunga, in the Audiencia of Quito. Second, it delineates the role of that province's *forasteros* and *castas* in the classic power struggle between the regular and secular clergy. Embedded in this analysis is an assessment of the relative importance of politicoeconomic and ideological motivations for the conflict.

According to the existing literature, the regular-secular controversy in Spanish America originated in papal decrees that entrusted the conversion of New World peoples to the regular clergy and inverted the traditional balance of power between ecclesiastical branches.[2] The religious orders, formerly relegated to simple preaching, were granted special dispensation to administer the sacraments in the Americas and to perform duties normally reserved for secular priests and even bishops.[3]

Toward the beginning of the seventeenth century, a declining Indian population and a growing secular clergy combined to create a relative shortage of benefices. These demographic and economic conditions exacerbated existing politico-ideological sentiments, leading the seculars to covet the Indian charges of the relgous orders and to devise strategies to "take back power"; that is, to return the hierarchy to its "proper" order. Similarly, the regulars formulated counterstrategies to maintain the status quo. Although the crown theoretically supported episcopal authority and the preeminence of the secular clergy from the Ordenanza del Patronazgo (1574) on, patrimonial politics dictated vacillating royal policies that kept the ecclesiastics in a state of turmoil for two centuries.[4]

In the province of Latacunga, this conflict was waged as a protracted dispute between the Franciscans and the secular priests about which branch had jurisdiction over the region's growing *forastero* and *casta* population.[5] The archival data related to this dispute permit us to follow the conflict from the mid-sixteenth century, when the newly empowered

Franciscans first established their *doctrinas*, to the turn of the eighteenth century, when the shift to secular preeminence was secured. More important, the Latacungan dispute provides an empirical window through which to see how both the desegregation of the colonial order and the historic regular-secular controversy were played out "on the ground."

Lower Caste Agency and the Breakdown of the Segregated Colonial Order

The catalytic nature of migration is illuminated if it is examined in the theoretical context of Spanish imperial organization in America. In the North Andes, as in all areas of the New World, the colonizers reconstructed an accentuated version of the corporate society of their homeland and superimposed it on a multiracial colonial situation. Spaniards, Indians, Africans, and their myriad interracial progeny were incorporated into a race-based social hierarchy—a legal caste system conceived in Iberian organicism, informed by its intersection with preexisting, indigenous sociopolitical organization, and exacerbated by the relations of European colonialism.[6] The conquest of one race by another placed the conquerors' race on top and that of the conquered on the bottom, giving the former the "natural" right to collect tribute and labor services from the latter.

This division was further manifested by the spatial segregation of the two groups, in agreement with the political organization of the colony, into two separate republics based on race: the republic of the Indians and the republic of the Spaniards. Within this construct, Spaniards were required by legislation to live in Spanish-style cities in polity with other Spaniards; Indians were to remain in Indian towns in the countryside, where they would constitute an easily accessible labor pool and where tribute collection and Christian indoctrination could be carried out more efficiently. It was a construct intended to facilitate colonial exploitation and to preserve cultural and racial "purity." Its smooth functioning, however, depended on a stationary Indian population and the physical integrity of the Indian towns. Migrations, especially those during the seventeenth century, caused this construct to break down, converting an Indian survival strategy into an important force in the evolution of a more fluid colonial society.

Lower caste agency, in the form of migration, became a determining factor in shaping the racial, cultural, and politicoeconomic texture of the colonial world. It subverted the segregated political order of the colony not only by creating large groups of Indians who lived out of polity (*forasteros*), but by accelerating the processes of race mixture and transculturation, thereby increasing the numbers of *castas*. While the *forasteros* moved spatially, eventually turning the dual republic concept on its head, the *castas* migrated within the racial hierarchy, throwing the original caste system into disarray. These spatial and socioracial migrants represented a shared challenge to the colonial order that was not lost on Spanish officials, who often referred to them, both disparagingly and worriedly, as *la gente suelta*.

The rapid growth of these "deviant" groups during the sixteenth and seventeenth centuries posed a threat to elite hegemony—the *forasteros* by undermining the forced labor system and the *castas* by pressuring the elite monopoly on economic resources and social privileges.[7] More pointedly, contemporary observers even alluded to the dark potential of *la gente suelta* to bring down the empire through intercaste alliances.[8] Though official phobia was, for the most part, unfounded, it nevertheless demonstrates the impact that lower caste agency and the resulting aberrations of space and race had on the colonizers. The case of Latacunga provides an opportunity to see in detail the turmoil that migration and its products, the *forasteros* and *castas*, caused for one set of colonial actors, the clergy of the Audiencia of Quito.

The Clerical Struggle in Latacunga

In sixteenth-century Latacunga, as elsewhere in Spanish America, the division of parishes was racially specific. The religious orders ministered to the overwhelming majority of indigenous peoples, while the secular clergy were assigned to the Spanish colonists.[9] At first, this division was a near-perfect reflection of the colony's formal separation into parallel Spanish and Indian states. As Indian migration and race mixture proceeded unabated in the sixteenth and seventeenth centuries, however, the synchrony of race and space was obfuscated. A growing number of people, for reasons of either residence or mixed racial origin, no longer fit into the original construct of separate Indian and Spanish states or the ecclesiastical organization that mirrored it. This led to a clerical struggle over the demarcation of parish lines.

The clergy's attempts to grapple with the breach between theory and practice were embodied in the dispute over ecclesiastical jurisdiction. Their scramble for parishioners in the new demographic context generated numerous and varied arguments that reflected both the economic and ideological evolution of a dynamic colonial politics. At first, the clergy attempted to insert old corporate precepts into new spatial arrangements by pressing for a division of parishes based on previous concepts of space, on racial types, or on levels of acculturation to either Spanish or Indian norms. Later, they forsook the corporate criteria in favor of more pragmatic organizational rules based on residence and even on the will of the parishioners—thereby acknowledging the agency of the colonized peoples, in this case the *forasteros* and *castas*, as a contending political force.

The Beginnings of Discord, 1550–1630

The Franciscans and Augustinians entered the corregimiento of Latacunga shortly after the conquest, with papal license for their orders to set up Indian *doctrinas* in the region. They operated with complete autonomy for at least two decades, because the Bishopric of Quito was not established until 1545 and its officials were prevented from exercising real authority until the close of Peru's civil wars. In 1550, Bishop Garci Diez Arias arrived to take up his duties and began to appoint seculars to some Indian *doctrinas*, including one in the province of Latacunga, the town of Angamarca.[10] With the inception of episcopal authority and these secular appointments came the first seeds of ecclesiastical discord.

The period from the 1560s to the 1580s was one of steady growth for the Indian *doctrinas*, as both locally inspired *reducciones* and those ordered by Toledo were carried out with at least some degree of success. Although some Indian migration occurred, these years were characterized largely by the spatial integrity of the *doctrinas*; that is, the clergy instructed the indigenous peoples in the Christian faith and administered the sacraments to them in specific physical spaces into which they had been aggregated—Indian towns.

As in other parts of Spanish America during these years, a tacit alliance continued (despite the Ordenanza del Patronazgo) between the royal bureaucracy and the religious orders, a political configuration that was to change considerably in the seventeenth century. This alliance was reinforced by frequent reports of irresponsible and abusive behavior on the part of the secular priests, leading to a general consensus in the Audiencia of Quito that Indian *doctrinas* were best entrusted to the regular clergy.[11] It was also a time when dense indigenous populations and a severe shortage of religious personnel still plagued many regions—a dilemma that prompted Bishop Fray Pedro de la Peña, a Dominican, to establish a seminary for creoles in Quito in order to increase the number of secular priests.[12] In short, these various circumstances served to maintain the status quo.

By the 1580s, this brief nucleation and segregation was being displaced by a number of structural changes that led to ecclesiastical strife. The epidemics of 1585–91 caused severe Indian depopulation in the Audiencia of Quito; at the same time, the number of secular priests graduating from Quito's seminary increased from 75 in 1576 to 300 in 1588.[13] The resulting imbalance led the secular clergy to turn its attention to the Indian *doctrinas* and to devise strategies for making inroads into the domain of the religious orders. Some of these strategies derived from increased migration rates between the Spanish and Indian republics. The drop in native population and the concurrent growth of the Spanish population had stimulated land and labor conflicts that in turn accelerated intersphere migration.

In Latacunga, as well as other areas in the Viceroyalty of Peru, migration also brought Spaniards into Indian towns, and thereby provided the secular clergy with an opening for its expansionist schemes. As the division between the Spanish and Indian republics began to break down, bishops and prelates throughout the viceroyalty assigned secular clergy to Indian parishes to minister to the new Spanish population. Presumably, these appointments were made to ensure secular control at least over the Spaniards. But the strategy often resulted in two clergymen from different ecclesiastical branches being placed in a single parish, and that created bitter conficts.[14] As the years went by, the secular priests attempted to expand their power base in the Indian towns by extending their jurisdiction to include everyone living "out of context"—mestizos, mulattos, blacks, and Indian *forasteros*—in other words, *la gente suelta*.[15]

The decade of the 1580s, then, saw the initial stages of a protracted feud. In 1583, the crown issued an imperial decree that favored the position of the secular priests; after strong resistance on the part of the religious orders, however, it reversed the decree in 1585. In the Audiencia of Quito, however, continued secular usurpation of regular *doctrinas* prompted a delegation of Franciscans to travel to Spain in 1586 to protest their case directly before the king. The crown ordered the secular clergy to leave the Indian towns in the hands of the religious orders and confine its ecclesiastical activities to the Spanish *asiento* of Latacunga.[16] The Franciscans were ordered to request authorization from the secular clergy to minister to the Spaniards residing in their jurisdictions.[17]

Arguments based on both New World and Old World ideologies were very much in evidence in the discourse surrounding this episode in Latacunga. In the 1590s, the church of San Vicente was constructed and the secular benefice established in the Spanish *asiento*. Both events took place under protest from the Franciscans, who claimed that the order had administered Latacunga since the time of the conquest and that the secular clergy had no right to be there in the first place.[18] The order offered the usual claims of "conqueror" status and "seniority in the Indies" as strong indicators of its legitimacy.[19] The seculars responded with familiar rhetoric, calling the regulars imposters.[20] In response to charges that they were encroaching on the friars' jurisdiction over the *forastero* and *casta* populations, the seculars conceded that the Franciscans should be permitted to continue ministering to the *originarios* (Indians who remained in their communities of origin) of the Indian towns, but jurisdiction over the rest of the population should now pass to the "real" priests.[21]

At the same time, the arguments of both ecclesiastical branches were informed by principles of Iberian corporatism and Spanish American segregationism. At first, this meant a pure and simple issue of physical space. Essentially, any (literal) body living in Spanish space should belong to the priests of the Spaniards, and anybody living in Indian space should belong to the priests of the Indians. Thus in 1602 the Franciscans tried to prove that the Spanish *asiento* of Latacunga was originally an Indian town, thereby laying claim to its growing number of *forasteros* and *castas* without radically changing the rules of ecclesiastical organization.

The assertion that Latacunga was originally a native village was taken quite seriously, as demonstrated by the careful investigation by the *visitador* of the bishopric. The *visitador* arrived with instructions to demolish the *asiento* if it was found to be an Indian town, and to relocate the Spaniards to the Valley of Cunchibamba. He summoned all the Spanish *vecinos* and old Indian caciques of the area and prompted them to testify about the status of the *asiento* of Latacunga as far back as the time of the Inca. The *visitador*'s eventual decision—that Latacunga had never been an Indian town—legitimated Spanish occupation and saved the *asiento* from demolition.[22] Subsequently, the Franciscans turned to race-based arguments, holding that all Indians, whether residing in Spanish or Indian space, belonged to them.

The seculars, however, were equally determined to gain ground, especially after the royal decree of 1586. For example, although his assignment of 1619 limited his ministry to the *forasteros* residing in the Spanish *asiento*, the secular priest Antonio Basante del Río tried to extend his jurisdiction to include all *forasteros* within a two-league radius of the *asiento*. In 1626, the bishop of Quito ordered Basante to desist under threat of excommunication and a fine of one hundred pesos, but in 1629, he was cited again as overstepping his bounds in relation to the *forasteros*.[23]

In 1632, the Franciscans reverted to the position based on space, informing the king that in spite of various royal decrees confirming their right to administer the sacraments to both Indians and Spaniards, the bishops and prelates continued to place secular clergy in charge of ministering to the Spaniards who resided in their towns. The Franciscans presented as a precedent the 1623 royal decision in favor of the Franciscans of Cajamarca, which stated that the order had been in "possession" of the region for 80 years and that the secular clergy should therefore be removed. In response, the crown reiterated the measures outlined in its resolution of 1586: the secular clergy should withdraw to the Spanish *asiento*, and the Franciscans should request their permission to serve the Spaniards of their *doctrinas* on a case-by-case basis.[24]

To the arguments based on space and race the secular clergy added another that focused on culture. It posited that persons who dressed like Spaniards should belong to the secular clergy, and those who dressed like Indians to the religious orders. While this argument was based not on biological race but on the degree to which interstitial groups had acculturated to either Spanish or Indian norms, it still attempted to maintain some semblance of the segregated corporate structure. At the same time, however, it contained an implicit recognition of the extent to which this construct had broken down. Not only had migration and race mixture given rise to new spatial arrangements and new racial groups, but they had caused a desynchronization of race and culture. Furthermore, parish lines based on levels of acculturation represented a liberalization of the colonial order. A division of jurisdiction based on how people dressed was a division based on self-definition. People would no longer be categorized solely according to race or space, but rather according to their cultural perceptions of themselves, further complicating the original struggle with alternate criteria for determining social identity. Clearly, the migrants and race mixers had unknowingly challenged the corporate order and had emerged victorious.[25]

It might seem that such an ingenious solution would settle matters once and for all; but the controversy continued to rage, now over the specifications of Spanish and Indian garb. More to the point, a debate ensued over just how acculturated to Spanish norms an Indian or *casta* needed to be to belong to a Spanish parish, and how acculturated to Indian norms to belong to an Indian parish.

In 1632, for example, when an episcopal order put all mestizos, men and women, who wore Indian garb under the Franciscans' jurisdiction, the secular clergy objected on the grounds of degree of acculturation. The priest of the Spanish *asiento* stipulated that this order should include only mestizas who wore an *anaco* and not those who wore a *faldellín*.[26] The *anaco* was a long, wraparound skirt of Indian origin while the *faldellín* was a hybrid fashion worn by Indians and mestizas that more closely approximated the European-style skirt. Unfortunately for the secular clergy, however, the *visitador* chose another article of clothing as pivotal. He declared that all mestizas who wore a *lliclla* (shawl) were under the jurisdiction of the Indian *doctrineros*.[27] Since the shawl was worn by almost all Indians and mestizas, the seculars came away with very little reward for their trouble.

The Simmering Controversy, 1640–1660

As the seventeenth century wore on and structural tensions became more acute, Latacunga's intraecclesiastical conflict escalated, and its protagonists' arguments became more transparent. At the heart of this intensification was the proliferation of *forasteros* and *castas*. In many parts of the Audiencia of Quito, accelerated migration resulted in an Indian population that was 50 percent *forastero* by the mid-seventeenth century.[28] Because demographic movement was increasingly oriented toward the Spanish republic, it produced a corresponding rise in the incidence of mestizaje.[29] In addition, migration to Spanish *obrajes* (textile workshops), haciendas, and urban centers meant that Indians were moving away from the domain of the religious orders and toward that of the secular priests.

This particular migration flow threatened the position of the regulars more than at any other time, and facilitated the encroachment of an ever-growing secular clergy.[30]

From the 1640s on, secular attempts to usurp the regulars' Indian power base (and secondarily their *casta* parishioners) became more brazen, as did Franciscan reactions. In 1641, the order petitioned the audiencia to protest the actions of the secular priest of Latacunga, don Fernando Ruiz Adame, who they asserted was intruding on their jurisdiction over the *forasteros*. Adame had apparently extended the boundaries of his parish to include not only his predecessor's claim to the *asiento* and two leagues around but also the Franciscan towns of San Felipe and San Sebastián, where he administered the sacraments to the *forasteros* and collected fees from them.[31] Finally, in 1645, his successor, Antonio de Plasencia, pushed the secular claim to the limit when he insisted that he should have the right to minister to all the *forasteros* of the whole corregimiento of Latacunga.[32]

Plasencia resorted to the argument based on physical space to support the contention that all people living in the *asiento* of Latacunga, regardless of racial type, should be under his jurisdiction. He reiterated that Latacunga had been Spanish since its founding and that the Franciscans had no right to administer the sacraments there, not even to the Indian *forasteros*.[33] Plasencia attempted to use the old rules, based on a settlement pattern that no longer pertained, to turn the tide in his favor.

The Franciscans continued to play two cards simultaneously. They claimed that by virtue of several royal decrees, they had jurisdiction over everyone living within the borders of their Indian parishes, whether Indian, Spaniard, mestizo, mulatto, black, or *zambo*, using the same argument as did Plasencia: they were in charge of a physical space called an Indian town, and any "body" in it was theirs.[34] But when it came to the *forasteros* residing in the Spanish *asiento* of Latacunga, the friars insisted that they should have jurisdiction over these migrants because they were Indians. They deployed the old racial argument as well as the spatial one.

That parishes should still be divided along racial lines in spite of the spatial disintegration of the Indian *doctrinas* became a central argument in Franciscan efforts to harness the *forastero* poplation to their jurisdiction. In the early 1640s, Fray Juan Bohórquez, a Franciscan *doctrinero* from the Indian town of Puxillí, added substance to this claim by traveling to the *asiento* of Latacunga to take a census of the Indians living on Spanish haciendas and in Spanish households. He then claimed that they were *forasteros* from his *doctrina* and were therefore under his jurisdiction.[35] Bohórquez was followed by many other Franciscan *doctrineros* from the Indian towns of the corregimiento, all with the same project. Their efforts were paralleled by an attempt by the head of the Franciscan monastery in Latacunga to aggregate Indian and mestizo *forasteros* into a centralized *doctrina* in the Spanish *asiento*. If the *forasteros* and *castas* would not return to Indian space, the Franciscans would come to them.

As the battle proceeded, it assumed increasingly violent characteristics. Witnesses for both sides testified about ugly scenes in which one ecclesiastical branch of the *asiento* mounted raids on the *doctrinas* of the other. The Franciscans, for example, sent their Indian officials to the *doctrina* of the secular clergy to remove the *forasteros* by force in the midst of religious services. Catechumens were dragged away by their hair or persuaded to leave with punches to the face and threats of eternal damnation.[36]

Besides creating rival *doctrinas* in the Spanish *asiento*, the mendicants resorted to ministering systematically to the Spaniards who resided in the Indian towns without bothering to request permission from the secular clergy. They also extended their jurisdiction to include the Spanish haciendas in their vicinities and pressured the owners to pay fees whether the friars provided services or not.[37]

In the 1650s, the secular clergy revived the argument based on levels of acculturation. Although the edict of 1632 had awarded possession of the "mestizos in Indian garb" to the religious orders, the seculars continued to intrude on the Franciscans' jurisdiction over this population and attempted to justify their usurpation with old arguments based on race. They insisted that since the good of a mixture always drowns out the bad, the mestizos' Spanish blood predominated over their Indian blood, and it was for this reason that the mestizos were not incorporated into Indian censuses or made to pay tribute. This led the seculars to assert that any person whose name did not appear on an Indian census should be considered a Spaniard regardless of acculturation level, and should therefore be classified under the seculars' jurisdiction.[38]

In 1658 the Franciscans responded, once again with the spatial argument. This time it focused only on mixed-blood women. The mestizas, the order contended, did not change their place of residence simply because they were mestizas; they rarely left the side of their Indian mothers. Therefore, by virtue of domicile, they should remain members of the Indian *doctrinas*. The Indian censuses listed the mothers of these mixed-blood women; therefore the mestizas should be considered accessories of their mothers and subject to the regular clergy.

The Franciscans then extended this argument to the *forasteros*. Any *forastero* whose mother or father was listed on the census of a Franciscan town should come under the jurisdiction of the Franciscans, no matter where that person was living.[39] This argument incorporated both the racial and spatial precepts of colonial corporatism and reflected the ecclesiastics' constant attempts to reconstruct the old order in new racial, spatial, and cultural parameters.

Although the ultimate goal of these arguments was the aggrandize-ment of one ecclesiastical branch or the other, the arguments also express the lower clergy's ideological struggle to understand and deal with the breakdown of a societal order based on segregated Spanish and Indian states. We see them in this dispute, especially its sixteenth-century phase, asking all the difficult questions of the period: Where do the *forasteros* and *castas* fit into the corporate structure? Now that these people have broken out of the categories into which the Spanish regime placed them, how should they be recategorized—according to space, race, or degree of acculturation?

Finally in 1658, the bishop, don Alonso de la Peña y Montenegro, and the audiencia attempted to settle the issue, taking into account the new spatial and racial realities. The jurisdiction of each ecclesiastical branch was minutely outlined as follows:

1. The secular clergy of the Spanish *asiento* of Latacunga had juris-diction over all Spaniards, blacks, mulattos, *zambahigos, tente en el aires, saltatrases,* and mestizos who dressed in Spanish garb. Spanish garb was to consist of *capa* (cloak), *calzón* (breeches), and *ropilla* (doublet) for men; and *saya* (European skirt), *bluzón* (blouse), and *manta* or *mantilla* (head covering) for women. The seculars also had jurisdiction over all Indian *forasteros* and mestizos who dressed in Indian garb; this consisted of the *manta* (men's shawl) for men and the *lliclla* and *faldellín* for women. The jurisdiction of the secular clergy covered the whole *asiento* and one league around it.

2. The head of the Franciscan monastery in the Spanish *asiento* of Latacunga was to have jurisdiction over all native Indians of the *asiento,* all Indians in the *asiento* who came from the Franciscan towns of the corregimiento, and all mestizos, men and women, who were from the Franciscan towns and wore Indian garb. (These last two groups were not to be considered *forasteros* because they were in Latacunga only for rea-sons of temporary employment.)

3. The Franciscan *doctrineros* in the Indian towns of the corregimiento of Latacunga had jurisdiction over all Indians, whether natives or *forasteros*; all Spaniards; and any other category of person (probably all the racial types referred to above) who lived in or had their homes inside the borders of the Indian towns.[40]

The tedious detail of the bishop's decree is emblematic of both the complexity and the simplicity of the new colonial order. In the mind of a Spanish bureaucrat like de la Peña, Latacunga's spatial and racial terrain could be portrayed only in terms of its deviation from an imperial system based on dual republics and a race-based hierarchy. Underneath his pre-cise and intricate description, however, the new bishop really was dictat-ing that all people, regardless of race or cultural affiliation, who had taken up permanent residence in the Spanish *asiento* of Latacunga were to be considered under the jurisdiction of the secular clergy; and all people who had taken up permanent residence in the Indian towns of the corregimiento were to be under the jurisdiction of the Franciscans. Put simply, jurisdiction would no longer be defined by Indian or Spanish space or by race or culture, but by territorial residence.[41] Though written in the language of the original corporate system, the bishop's decree embodied an official recognition and acceptance of the spatial organization, racial composition, and cultural variations of a new colonial order—an order that had arisen in part from the agency of the ruled. In short, the historical actions of *forasteros* and *castas* had redesigned the stage of imperial organization and, as will be shown, had dictated new roles and behaviors for its actors.

Elite Manipulation of Lower Caste Agency

Lower caste agency, in the form of spatial and socioracial migration, eventually produced politicoeconomic conditions at the local level that some colonial sectors manipulated to acquire, maintain, or enhance power, or even to challenge the position of traditional elites.[42] The rest of this article will focus on how *la gente suelta* contributed to the changing configurations of colonial politics and then were themselves utilized as political pawns in one elite conflict—the conflict between the regular and secular clergy.

The Battle for Bodies and Souls, 1660–1680

During this period, a marked shift occurred in the Latacungan struggle that placed the *forasteros* at its center and the *castas* on its margins. This shift may have resulted from the *forasteros'* numerical superiority over the *castas* by this time, but a more documentable factor is their improved economic status. In 1614, the *forasteros* of the Spanish *asiento* of Latacunga were described as a poor, transient population that could not be depended on to sustain a *doctrina*.[43] Their depiction as a marginal group of undesirables, however, contrasts sharply to the central position they held in the ecclesiastical dispute of the 1660s and 1670s. What happened in the interim to cause such a reversal?

   Because of Spanish land divestment and excessive labor exactions, migration had continued unabated throughout the corregimiento, giving way to vast absenteeism in the Indian towns. As a consequence, the viability of the mita broke down, and increasing numbers of enterprises had to depend on individual contract labor. Not only did new enterprises arise, based on *forastero* labor, but many establishments that had formerly operated with *mitayos* were now worked increasingly with free-wage labor.

The large private *obrajes* of don Alonso Melgarejo and don Diego Ruiz de Rojas, the community *obraje*, the royal gunpowder factory, and numerous small *obrajuelos* were among the enterprises in the *asiento* that attracted and maintained large migrant work forces.[44]

All these employment opportunities for migrants, and the higher wages they received as an enticement, evidently created conditions for stabler *forastero* communities—communities of people capable of paying tribute and ecclesiastical fees and, because of improved living standards, no longer prone to move on when pressed for those exactions. Indeed, the crown *forasteros* (those who had been aggregated into crown *parcialidades*), though they composed only 4.2 percent of the corregimiento's population in the 1670s, paid 30 percent of the district's total tributes.[45] In addition, numerous *forasteros* who lived in the *asiento* of Latacunga either were not yet attached to the crown or were listed as absent on the rolls of other districts.[46] This meant that they were free of all formal obligations and therefore likely prey for the clergy and other local interest groups.

Both the regular and the secular clergy responded to these changing structural conditions not only by attempting to adapt the spatial conception of the *doctrina* to new demographic imperatives, but also by formulating strategies to minimize the financial hazards of less integrated parishes. The following case study is revealing.

Changes in ecclesiastical income and working conditions can be measured in part by comparing the financial records of five Franciscan *doctrinas*—Mulaholó, Saquisillí, San Sebastián, Alaques, and San Miguel—for the years 1598 and 1672.[47] What is immediately apparent from such a comparison is that, at least on paper, the lower clergy was receiving significantly less remuneration for ministering to many more Indians.[48] In addition, considering that Latacunga's rate of tribute payment for the 1670s was a mere 39 percent, it is doubtful that the *doctrineros* received even the compensation listed in fiscal records.[49] Indeed, lawsuits abounded in which *doctrineros* and their superiors complained about nonpayment of stipends during this period of demographic bedlam, financial crisis, and increasing corruption. The lower clergy, however, formulated a survival strategy by harnessing the *forastero* population to its parishes and siphoning off some of the *forasteros*' goods and services. The mechanisms that accomplished this require some detailed examination.

Ecclesiastical remuneration in the corregimiento of Latacunga fell into three distinct categories. Encomienda Indians paid an annual salary that was subtracted from their tributes; crown *forasteros* paid a flat annual fee of one peso; and unattached *forasteros* paid the clergy separate fees for each individual service or transaction, a system called *a obenciones*.

The first category had, by the mid-seventeenth century, become a totally unsatisfactory method of remuneration because of the escalating tribute arrears of encomienda Indians and the corruption of public officials.

In addition, as tribute records of 1672 demonstrate, payment under this system amounted to only two-fifths of a peso annually for each tributary Indian and included all ecclesiastical services, not only for the individual but also for every family member and all other tribute-exempt members of the community.[50]

The second category, that of the crown *forasteros*, represents a vast improvement over the first. Each tributary Indian paid one peso annually—an amount that did not depend on the rate of tribute payment because it was collected separately. Extrapolating from the 1672 statistics, ecclesiastical remuneration for the 539 crown *forasteros* in the corregimiento of Latacunga would have been 539 pesos a year.[51] The same number of encomienda Indians would have produced only 216 pesos, making the payment rate of the crown *forasteros* 2 1/2 times greater.

The third category, however, was clearly the most lucrative. The unattached *forasteros* represented an independent operation for the ecclesiastics. The latter did not have to wait until appointed times of the year for remuneration from these Indians, but could replenish their coffers at regular intervals, rendering services throughout the year and collecting fees on an ad hoc basis.[52] Since the fees were not adequately monitored, clergy could also change them arbitrarily and charge whatever the traffic would bear. Furthermore, fees were collected from each *forastero* for each service and not just from the head of the family, as they were in the other two categories. If crown *forasteros* paid 2 1/2 times more than encomienda Indians, a payment rate three to four times greater for unattached *forasteros* would not be outside the realm of possibility.

In addition to the direct monetary gains that could be exacted from *forasteros*, the latter's labor was also of more than passing interest to the clergy. In flagrant violation of ordinances prohibiting them from engaging in entrepreneurial activities, priests operated all manner of businesses, often with the unpaid labor of their parishioners. Although all Indians were subject to these illicit labor demands, the *forasteros* constituted an especially desirable workforce because they were exempt from the mita, in need of subsistence, and often officially "invisible."[53] Indeed, the Franciscans of the five towns examined for this study operated lucrative illegal *obrajes*, allegedly with unpaid labor, which provoked lay charges of unfair competition in the textile market.[54] The battle for the bodies and souls of Latacunga's *forasteros*, then, was a battle for the economic viability of the clergy.[55]

In 1661, the regular-secular controversy reached fever pitch in a vicious struggle over burial fees.[56] The secular priest of the Spanish *asiento* of Latacunga charged that the Franciscan *doctrinero* of the Indian town of San Felipe had dispossessed him of the dead body of one of his *forastero* parishioners and then had buried it and collected the fee. He demanded that the body be disinterred so that he could rebury it in his parish and collect his rightful remuneration.[57]

After that episode, Indian spies were employed to report on the health of *forastero* parishioners; when one died, the clergy and their Indian accomplices rushed to the home, confiscated the body, and buried it before their ecclesiastical opponents had a chance to respond. Body snatching became the subject of numerous complaints by both secular and regular clergy throughout the 1660s.[58] The conflict over the *forasteros* of Latacunga had sunk to new depths; the clergy now fought over the right to fleece the relatives of the dead.

Ecclesiastics from both branches also attempted rhetorically to manipulate the definition of *forastero*.[59] In spite of official decrees delineating *forastero* status, the contenders stretched the definition in order to expand their jurisdiction, or narrowed it to limit their losses. Depending on the circumstances, *forasteros* could include not only Indians from the towns of the same corregimiento but even *mitayos* who happened to be working temporarily outside their communities of origin. The intent was not just to augment the size of parishes but to designate larger numbers of Indians as *forasteros* so as to collect higher fees.[60]

A third mechanism that enriched the coffers of the church was the double collection. Since *forasteros* were generally listed on the censuses of their original towns as absent Indians and usually included in the town's doctrinal stipend, the collection of high ecclesiastical fees in their places of residence meant that the church was at times remunerated twice for migrant Indians. Judging from the number of official pronouncements against double collection, it appears to have been a general practice by the mid-seventeenth century.

In Latacunga, the secular clergy accused the Franciscans of devising a deliberate strategy to collect double fees. They alleged that the abbot of the Franciscan monastery in the Spanish *asiento* had established a *doctrina* for *forasteros* who worked in the *obrajes* and on nearby haciendas and was collecting fees from them. Reportedly, these Indians came from the Franciscan towns—some were even *mitayos*—and the *doctrineros* in those towns were also paid a stipend for the same Indians.[61]

Clearly, migration, though initially an Indian survival strategy, came to mean not only survival but profit for the ecclesiastics. The *forasteros*, however, became not only a target of extortion but an axis on which the machinations of sectoral politics revolved.

The Politics of Indian Migration

Although agency as a historical concept is ordinarily applied to the underdogs of a society, in seventeenth-century Spanish America, lower caste agency was paralleled by a form of elite agency; namely, creole empowerment. Originally ranked beneath peninsular Spaniards in the colonial hierarchy, by the second half of the century creoles were moving toward hegemony in government, the economy, and the church. Through population growth, a rising awareness of their differences from Iberians, and structural conditions increasingly advantageous to their local autonomy, creoles upset the delicate balance of an imperial legal system predicated on containing them. In short, the creoles, too, were migrants of a sort.

Throughout the Viceroyalty of Peru, this was a time when the colonial state passed from royal control into the hands of creole elites. The seventeenth-century crisis of the Spanish crown led to, among other corruptions, the sale of public offices and the regularization of ill-gotten lands through *composición*. This in turn resulted in a general weakening of royal authority and a "creolized" state that operated for the politico-economic benefit of local interest groups.[62] In the church, this new colonial politics was played out in the regular-secular controversy.

The Audiencia of Quito was no exception to these trends. By the end of the sixteenth century, a creole identity had already emerged there, playing a significant role in the alcabala riots of 1592–93. During that rebellion, Quito's population was clearly divided on the basis of geographic origins: peninsular Spaniards tended to support the tax, while American-born Spaniards opposed it.[63] The mostly creole secular clergy participated heavily in the uprising, preaching insurrection from its pulpits and inciting parishioners to defend the *patria*.[64] The mixed creole and European population of the religious orders, however, was divided in its sentiments and tempered in its actions by the loyalist bent of its superiors, most of whom were still peninsular Spaniards in those years.[65]

Throughout the seventeenth century, the uncertain political position of the regular clergy was demonstrated by the endless turmoil inside and between the orders over creole-peninsular supremacy. As in many parts of Spanish America, the divisive practice of the *alternativa* provoked one conflict after another, not only pitting Spaniards against creoles inside the monasteries but spilling over into the lay sectors, most of whose sentiments rested with regular creole factions.[66] In addition, the predominantly pro-creole orders (the Dominicans and Augustinians) allied with one another against the royal bureaucracy, which was often supported by the Spanish-dominated orders (the Franciscans and Mercedarians).[67] In short, as society moved toward the creolization of church and state, the religious orders remained divided, ambilvalent, and at times reactionary. The more homogeneous secular clergy, however, was squarely allied with elite creole causes.[68]

A related project that eventually operated in tandem with that of the creoles was the consolidation of episcopal authority in Quito. The Patronato Real and the Omnimoda severely circumscribed the power of early Spanish American bishops in relation to both the royal bureaucracy and the religious orders. Federico González Suárez reports that episcopal authority in Quito was flouted in the extreme by both audiencia officials and the regular clergy. Perhaps the bishops' unenviable position is best illustrated by the words of Bishop Fray Pedro de Oviedo (who served from 1629 to 1646), who often stated, "There are two bishops in Quito: the provincial of the Franciscan order and I."[69]

Aside from political jurisdiction, the bishops worried about the debased financial position of the secular church, a problem intimately related to the religious orders' monopolization of resources. The regular clergy (especially the Franciscans) not only controlled the largest and richest *doctrinas* in the audiencia, gaining privileged access to liquid capital and labor, but also amassed large tracts of land and other properties, all of which were exempt from the *diezmo*.[70] As the assets of the religious orders expanded the revenues of the royal treasury, the ecclesiastical cabildo shrank, along with the resource base available to the total creole population, both lay and clerical. Over the course of the seventeenth century these trends reached a critical juncture, causing a confluence of episcopal, creole, and royal interests. The religious orders were powerless to confront this new political configuration; their preeminence depended on former crown strategies to obstruct creole hegemony through vacillating policies that no longer obtained.

By the 1660s, the seculars were numerically equal to the mendicants, and still coveted the latter's Indian charges.[71] Undoubtedly, Quito's newly creolized state made common cause with episcopal authorities to manipulate the controversy in favor of the secular clergy, the overwhelming majority of whom were creoles attached to powerful families. Bishop de la Peña's administration had made extraordinary efforts to energize the secular seminary, thereby enhancing episcopal authority. Nevertheless, five hundred of the audiencia's seven hundred secular priests went without benefices, and the situation placed extreme pressure on the bishop to remedy the "unequal" distribution of *doctrinas*.[72]

The quest for both creole hegemony and secular preeminence in Quito was facilitated by Indian migration to secular space and by episcopal decisions favoring secular jurisdiction over the growing *forastero* and *casta* population. An examination of the ecclesiastical decrees and related discourse is instructive. Bishop de la Peña's 1658 decree dividing jurisdiction over the *forasteros* and *castas* by residence might seem equitable, but when examined in light of the extensive Indian migration to the Spanish republic (secular space), it clearly assigned many more parishioners to the secular clergy than ever before. In 1669, the bishop went a step further and decreed that any Indian who migrated to the Spanish sphere to perform contract labor would come under the jurisdiction of the secular clergy, even if originally from a Franciscan town, while *mitayos* residing in the Spanish sphere would continue to belong to the Franciscans.[73] De la Peña's rationale was that the *mitayo* had been forced to leave the Indian sphere and intended to return when the work was done, while the contract laborer had made a voluntary decision to detach himself from his community, which was his natural right as a free individual.[74]

That parish lines should be drawn according to the Indians' free will and freedom of movement represented a complete about-face on the part of the church hierarchy, which until this point had consistently recommended the forced repatriation of *forasteros*.[75] In addition, because ecclesiastical organization was but a microcosm of the larger colony, it can be said that this policy shift reflects a considerable weakening, by 1669, of the segregated corporate structure and its replacement with a more fluid colonial order.

What the decree also reflected, however, was the progression of creole and episcopal hegemony in the Audiencia of Quito. By 1669, Indian migration and *forasterismo* had reached massive proportions in Latacunga, undermining the mita and making contract labor the predominant work form.[76] Thus, to declare all "voluntary contract laborers" who had migrated to the Spanish sphere (in other words, *forasteros*) to be under the jurisdiction of the seculars was to swell the seculars' ecclesiastical domain. This in turn further advanced the cause of creole hegemony, not only by shifting ecclesiastical fees to the secular church but also by channeling labor toward non-regular enterprises. In short, this pronouncement signaled the demise of the regulars' preeminence in the Audiencia of Quito.

The reform of the regular *doctrinas* had been an episcopal preoccupation for more than 60 years (1606–1669). Bishops Rivera, Santillán, Sotomayor, Oviedo and Ugarte had all worked arduously—although with differing styles—to curb regular clergy privileges and consolidate episcopal authority.[77] Not until de la Peña's administration, however, were significant inroads made, and these only by going "through the back door." Episcopal decisions that awarded the demographic and financial benefits of the *forasteros* and *castas* to the secular clergy were a way of achieving secular control (that is, creole control) over a substantial part of the lower caste population without having to make a frontal assault on the domain of the religious orders. The church hierarchy did not need to engage in the formal expropriation of regular *doctrinas* and reassignment of them to secular priests, as it did in other areas of Spanish America.[78] In the Audiencia of Quito, and specifically in the province of Latacunga, the bishop could simply manipulate ecclesiastical jurisdictions by taking advantage of migration to the Spanish sphere and accelerated mestizaje, then legitimate that manipulation with liberal rhetoric derived from the sixteenth-century School of Salamanca.[79] The substance of this ideological discourse, however, is questionable. Both civil and bureaucratic portrayals of the secular clergy as a bunch of criminals in ecclesiastical garb multiplied after their "coup" of 1669. Pedro Jiménez de Vélez, a secular priest himself, wrote to the Council of the Indies in 1681 that even bigamists, bastards, and adulterers were being ordained in the bishopric of Quito.[80] This is in keeping with the creoles' growing domination of bureaucratic positions and their subsequent treatment of government as "booty," so prevalent in documentation of official fraud in late seventeenth-century Quito and elsewhere.[81]

Although the secular priests made enormous gains with the edict of 1669, control over *forasteros* living in the Spanish sphere was not enough. Later that year, a secular priest of the Spanish *asiento* of Latacunga would press for additional jurisdiction over the *forasteros* residing in the Indian towns. Don Pedro Flores de Hinojosa attempted to legitimate his claim by reviving old charges that the Franciscans had only temporary rights to the administration of souls. Their privileges in America should be limited to the Indians whose names appeared on the census rolls; the *forasteros* should belong to the ecclesiastical patrimony of the Holy See, and therefore to the seculars.[82]

Flores's case is an illustration of the emptiness of late seventeenth-century ideological justifications for what were primarily politicoeconomic motives. By 1669, these secular priests of the Audiencia of Quito were overwhelmingly creole, and formed part of a political process aimed at wresting de facto control of the colony away from the crown so that creoles could rule in their own interests. Yet Flores saw fit to hark back to Old World ideas about privilege; that is, the preeminence of the secular clergy based on the patrimony of Saint Peter. Perhaps this discourse derived from genuine passions in the sixteenth century; but when inserted into the politicoeconomic context of the late seventeenth century, it rings hollow. Indeed, it seems more likely that men of the cloth used such rhetoric to cover material aspirations and self-interest in a cloak of ecclesiastical dignity.

What was in store for members of the lower clergy like Flores, however, was not what they expected. In the late seventeenth century, the colonial church and state, not dominated by creole elites, attempted to regularize ecclesiastical remuneration by establishing a uniform stipend for *forasteros* and devising complicated rules intended to assess more accurately the clergy's income.[83] These measures were not necessarily intended to protect the Indians' financial assets, but rather to ensure that those assets filtered up to the hierarchy.[84] In 1669, Bishop de la Peña ordered that all *forasteros* of the Audiencia of Quito pay an annual stipend of one peso.[85] In 1684, the viceroy, the Duke de la Palata, echoed this order and also stipulated that the payment be collected by the corregidor and discounted from the priests' salaries. This measure was intended to impose an intermediary between the *doctrineros* and the *forasteros*, thereby preventing ecclesiastical gorging and private collections.[86] The church hierarchy and the state had apparently caught on to the new economic mechanisms of the lower clergy, and attempted to redirect toward themselves some of the proceeds of the *forastero* population.

Conclusions

The mass migrations that took place in the Andes as a response to the Spanish regime exemplify the most rudimentary form of human resistance, physical movement. These movements, among other forms of lower caste agency, ensured that colonization would be not a static imposition but a dialogical process. Not only did migration blur the spatial division between the Spanish and Indian republics, but it also fostered the racial diversification of the original three-tier caste system. By challenging imposed categories of space, race, and culture, *forasteros* and *castas* subverted the segregated imperial order and contributed to the formation of a more fluid colonial society.

In addition, lower order agency, in the form of Indian migration and mestizaje, played a determining role in the colony's shifting political fortunes. The ascendency of one sector over another often depended on each group's ability to harness the resources of *la gente suelta* to its own project. This political trend was evident in Latacunga, where the weaker ecclesiastical branch, the secular clergy, was able to use the spatial and socioracial migrants as a vehicle for intruding on the prerogatives of the more established power holders, the religious orders. Clearly, the *forasteros* and *castas* had become the unknowing conscripts in an intraecclesiastical war in which the New World supremacy of one branch over the other hung in the balance. Furthermore, because the regular-secular conflict was intimately connected to creole empowerment, the manipulation of *la gente suelta* had import beyond the ecclesiastical domain.

The seventeenth-century expansion of the *forasteros* and *castas* led to systemic contradictions that reached critical proportions in the eighteenth century. Growing elite phobia resulted in more restrictive legislation intended to put *la gente suelta* back in their "proper" places. In 1720, Indian status was redefined according to territorial affiliation instead of ethnic origins in an attempt to harness the *forasteros* more tightly to the extractive system. The *castas'* empowerment was curtailed by measures such as restricted admission to universities and craft guilds, as well as the marriage law of 1776. Nevertheless, the breach between ascriptive categories and actual behaviors is nowhere more evident than in the so-called repressive environment of the eighteenth century. The *casta* and *forastero* populations not only continued to grow but also continued to find ways to subvert the system. Migration and mestizaje had accumulated 2 1/2 centuries of momentum. The challenge of *la gente suelta* to the colonial order was irreversible.

Notes

1. *Forasteros* were Indians who migrated away from their communities of origin to escape tribute and forced labor. Their descendants were also called *forasteros*. Here, *casta* is used to describe all people of mixed race; that is, any person who was neither a Spaniard nor an Indian.

2. The literature on the dilemmas arising from this inversion is vast. See esp. Victoria Hennessey Cummins, "Imperial Policy and Church Income: The Sixteenth-Century Mexican Church," *The Americas* 43 (July 1986), 87–103; Robert Charles Padden, "The Ordenanza del Patronato, 1574: An Interpretative Essay," *The Americas* 12 (Apr. 1956), 336–54; Stafford Poole, "The Third Mexican Provincial Council of 1585 and the Reform of the Diocesan Clergy," in *The Church and Society in Latin America*, ed. Jeffrey Cole (New Orleans: Center for Latin American Studies, Tulane Univ., 1984), 21–23; John Frederick Schwaller, "Implementation of the Ordenanza del Patronazgo in New Spain," in ibid., 39–50; Robert Ricard, *The Spiritual Conquest of Mexico, 1523–1572* (Berkeley: Univ. of California Press, 1966); Antonine Tibesar, *Franciscan Beginnings in Colonial Peru* (Washington, D.C.: Academy of American Franciscan History, 1953).

3. Although, according to David A. Brading, the religious orders often enjoyed more prestige in sixteenth-century Europe than did the secular clergy, their functions were limited. According to Antonine Tibesar, the mendicant orders went from being restricted to preaching on street corners in Europe to declaring themselves inquisitors in the Americas. Brading, *The First America: The Spanish Monarchy, Creole Patriots, and the Liberal State, 1492–1867* (Cambridge: Cambridge Univ. Press, 1991), 235; Tibesar, "The Early Peruvian Missionary Effort," in *The Roman Catholic Church in Colonial Latin America*, ed. Richard Greenleaf (New York: Alfred A. Knopf, 1971), 55.

4. The Ordenanza del Patronazgo called for the gradual secularization of the mendicants' *doctrinas*. Nevertheless, the religious orders' strong resistance and their de facto power obstructed its enforcement, in some places for as long as two centuries.

5. Pleito del licenciado Antonio de Plasencia, cura beneficiado del asiento de Latacunga, 1645, Archivo Nacional, Quito (hereafter cited as ANQ), Presidencia de Quito, fols. 8–153; Tierras de Latacunga, 1627–1799, Archivo Municipal de Quito (hereafter AMQ), fols. 4–36.

6. At this time, Iberian society itself assumed castelike features as the racist doctrine of *limpieza de sangre* became a criterion for social advancement. Angus MacKay, *Spain in the Middle Ages: From Frontier to Empire, 1000–1500* (New York: St. Martin's Press, 1977), 186–87; Henry Kamen, *Spain, 1469–1714: A Society of Conflict* (London: Longmans, 1991), 106.

7. Because labor quotas were levied on Indians only in their communities of origin, the *forasteros* became exempt from the mita (forced labor system) by moving away.

8. In 1585, the Jesuit Acosta, alarmed by the proliferation of the *casta* population, warned of a possible mestizo-Indian alliance that could bring down the Spanish cities of the Indies one by one. In 1660, the Audiencia of Charcas cautioned that Upper Peru, from Cuzco to Potosí, was at great risk because of the proliferation of mestizos and *forasteros* who might ally with one another to foment an insurrection. Thierry Saignes and Thérèse Bouysse-Cassagne, "Dos confundidas identidades: mestizos y criollos del siglo XVII," in *Quinientos años de mestizaje en los Andes*, ed. Hiroyasu Tomoeda and Luis Millones (Osaka: Museo Etnológico Nacional del Japón, 1992), 29–30, 38.

9. Los curatos y doctrinas de la Audiencia de Quito. 1598, Archivo General de Indias, Seville (hereafter AGI), Quito, leg. 76. Only one Indian *doctrina* in the Corregimiento of Latacunga belonged to a secular clergyman, that of Angamarca.

10. José María Vargas, *Historia de la iglesia en el Ecuador durante el patronato español* (Quito: Editorial Santo Domingo, 1962), 34–35.

11. In 1565, President Hernando de Santillán credited whatever Christianization had taken place in Quito to the religious orders, adding that the seculars assumed *doctrinas* and then did not fulfill their obligations. Vargas, *Historia de la iglesia*, 55.

12. The seminary was established in 1566 and had ordained 75 secular priests by 1576. Vargas, *Historia de la iglesia*, 99. With no solid support from the crown and highly circumscribed authority over the religious orders, most bishops, whether secular or regular themselves, supported the growth of the secular clergy as their only chance of enhancing episcopal power.

13. This growth resulted largely from the efforts of Pedro de la Peña's successor, Bishop Fray Luis López de Solís, who energized the seminary. Vargas, *Historia de la iglesia*, 124.

14. Pleito de Antonio de Plasencia, fols. 27–30.

15. This appears to have been a widespread phenomenon, because between 1585 and 1586, the Franciscans of Latacunga, Cajamarca, and Jauja all presented identical petitions of complaint that the secular clergy had usurped their rights to the Spaniards, mestizos, mulattos, and *forasteros* residing in their *doctrinas*. Ibid.

16. Both the province and the Spanish seat (*asiento*) of the province were called Latacunga. To avoid confusion, the Spanish seat will be referred to as the *asiento* of Latacunga.

17. Pleito de Antonio de Plasencia, fols. 23v–26v.

18. Ibid., fols. 21–22, 43.

19. The regular clergy's claims to ecclesiastical primacy were often based on what James Lockhart describes as the highest value of New World ideology: seniority in the Indies. A clear example of this is the case of the Franciscans of Cajamarca, who, in their petition of 1623, represented themselves as the "conquistadores" of the *doctrinas* and pointed out that they had "conquered" the *doctrinas* at the high cost of their health, blood, and lives, and without the help of a single secular clergyman. James Lockhart, *The Men of Cajamarca: A Social and Biographical Study of the First Conquerors of Peru* (Austin: Univ. of Texas Press, 1972); Pleito de Antonio de Plasencia, fols. 27–30.

20. Throughout Spanish America, the crux of the seculars' argument was that the regular clergy had no right to the patrimony of Saint Peter; they were not authorized to administer the sacraments. They had received this right in America, through a special bull granted by Pope Adrian VI, only because of extenuating circumstances—a scarcity of priests and hordes of "infidels" in need of conversion.

21. Pleito de Antonio de Plasencia, fol. 107v.

22. Ibid., fols. 61, 87.

23. Ibid., fol. 33.

24. Ibid., fols. 23v–26v.

25. One might argue that the word *victorious* is a bit strong, considering that the eighteenth century would witness elite attempts to put these groups "back in their place." Nevertheless, since most restrictive legislation was ineffective in containing the growth of the *forastero* and *casta* populations, it can be said that their challenge to the colonial order went uninterrupted until independence.

26. Pleito de Antonio de Plasencia, fol. 40.

27. Ibid.

28. See Karen Vieira Powers, *Andean Journeys: Migration, Ethnogenesis, and the State in Colonial Quito* (Albuquerque: Univ. of New Mexico Press, 1995), chap. 2.

29. Statistics on the numbers of *castas* in the seventeenth-century Viceroyalty of Peru are hard to come by, but qualitative data suggest a very high rate of growth: Saignes and Bouysse-Cassagne, 40.

30. Under Bishop Alonso de la Peña y Montenegro (1653–1687), the criteria for ordination were loosened, freeing Quito's seminary to ordain hundreds more secular priests. Vargas, *Historia de la iglesia*, 287.

31. Pleito de Antonio de Plasencia, fol. 34.

32. Ibid., fol. 17.

33. Ibid., fol. 61.

34. Ibid., fols. 21–22.

35. Ibid., fol 66.

36. The most vivid accounts of violence were those reported in 1645 and 1658. Ibid., fols. 84, 120–21.

37. Ibid., fols. 59–87.

38. Ibid., fol. 107.

39. Ibid., fols. 120–21.

40. Tierras de Latacunga, 1627–1799, fols. 4v–7v; Pleito de Antonio de Plasencia, fol. 130.

41. This decree was not unlike the viceregal decree of 1720 redefining the legal status of Indians, including *forasteros*, according to territorial affiliation instead of ethnic origins. Ann M. Wightman, *Indigenous Migration and Social Change: The Forasteros of Cuzco, 1570–1720* (Durham: Duke Univ. Press, 1990), 43–44. It should be recognized, however, that these redefinitions were often conveniences of the Spanish regime and may have had little to do with how indigenous peoples and *castas* defined themselves.

42. For details on this last phenomenon, see Karen Powers, "Resilient Lords and Indian Vagabonds: Wealth, Migration, and the Reproductive Transformation of Quito's Chiefdoms, 1500–1700," *Ethnohistory* 38 (Summer 1991), 226–49; and idem, "Indian Migration in the Audiencia of Quito: Crown Manipulation and Local Co-optation," in *Migration in Colonial Spanish America*, ed. David Robinson (Cambridge: Cambridge Univ. Press, 1990), 313–23.

43. Tierras de Latacunga, 1627–1799, fols. 20–28.

44. For details on structural changes in the seventeenth-century Audiencia of Quito, see Karen Powers, "Indian Migration and Sociopolitical Change in the Audiencia of Quito" (Ph.D. diss., New York Univ., 1990), chap. 2

45. Powers, *Andean Journeys*, chap. 3.

46. Statistics on the total number of *forasteros* in Latacunga are unavailable. From abundant documentation in the ANQ, however, it is clear that the province was a target for in-migration during this period, and sheltered a large *forastero* population. See Powers, "Resilient Lords."

47. In 1598, their combined tributary population was 2,500 Indians, and they yielded 1,550 pesos in stipends plus 4 1/2 *camaricos* (provisions) annually. The value of a *camarico* varied from place to place. In his study of the Audiencia of Guatemala, Adriann Van Oss calculated that *camaricos* (called *raciones* in Guatemala) were often equal to the Indians' tribute obligations to the crown, and afforded friars a very comfortable life. In 1672, the same *doctrinas* had 4,317 tributary Indians and provided 1,768 pesos a year, which comprised both the stipends and the *camaricos*, now *camaricos de plata* (cash substitute). Curatos y doctrinas de la Audiencia de Quito, 1598; Adriann C.Van Oss, *Catholic*

Colonialism: A Parish History of Guatemala, 1524–1821 (Cambridge: Cambridge Univ. Press, 1986), 27, 86; Cartas cuentas de Latacunga, 1672, ANQ, Indígenas, caja 11.

48. "On paper" because seventeenth-century tributary figures in the Audiencia of Quito were highly inflated, due to unorthodox census-taking procedures, migration, absenteeism, and the regime's failure to subtract deceased and absent Indians from the tribute rolls. See Powers, *Andean Journeys*, chap. 3.

49. Rate cited in Robson Brines Tyrer, *Historia demográfica y económica de la Audiencia de Quito: población indígena e industria textil, 1600-1800* (Quito: Banco Central del Ecuador, 1988), 290.

50. John L. Phelan claims that *doctrineros* received four hundred pesos a year for every four hundred tributaries, but he uses more general data to support his argument. When the treasury records for specified locales are examined, the amount totals two-fifths of a peso per tributary. Phelan, *The Kingdom of Quito in the Seventeenth Century: Bureaucratic Politics in the Spanish Empire* (Madison: Univ. of Wisconsin Press, 1967), 172; Cartas cuentas de Latacunga, 1672.

51. Cartas cuentas de Latacunga, 1672. These records do not list the doctrinal stipend for the crown *forasteros*, but starting in the 1620s with the *visita* of Matías de Peralta, they were assessed a doctrinal stipend of one peso annually.

52. Pleito de Antonio de Plasencia, fols. 19 and 23; Tierras de Latacunga, 1627–1799, fols. 20–28. Fees were officially fixed, but more often than not they depended on the discretion of the priest. In addition, some clergy charged the customary annual stipend of one peso for routine services plus fees for baptisms, marriages, and burials.

53. On the use of *forasteros* as invisible workers, see Powers, "Resilient Lords."

54. Phelan, *Kingdom of Quito*, 75.

55. Antonio Acosta calculates for Peru that a seventeenth-century *doctrina* with an *obraje* could yield between 7,348 and 11,048 pesos annually from all forms of appropriation—or up to nine times the value of the Indians' royal tributes. Considering the comparative analysis of fees as discussed here and the labor potential of *forastero* parishioners, the latter would most likely have yielded even more than their *originario* counterparts (the official members of the *doctrina*). Acosta, "Religiosos, doctrinas, y excedente económico indígena en el Perú a comienzos del siglo XVII," *Histórica* 6 (July 1982), 28.

56. Excessive burial fees were one of the most often cited ecclesiastical abuses of the colonial period, and commonly absorbed all of the deceased's possessions, leaving the survivors disinherited. During the sixteenth century, the prime targets for this type of exploitation were described as wealthy Indians. By the mid-seventeenth century, however, the victims were described more often than not as *forasteros*, implying that the latter were perhaps better able to pay these excesses than their *originario* counterparts. Cédula del 3 de septiembre de 1586, and Cédula del 6 de abril de 1588, AMQ, Colección de cédulas reales dirigidas a la Audiencia de Quito, fols. 318 and 435; Cabildo del 30 de diciembre de 1588, AMQ, Colección de documentos sobre el obispado de Quito, 1583–1594, fol. 389.

57. Pleito de Antonio de Plasencia, fols. 145–53v.

58. Ibid.; Tierras de Latacunga, 1627–1799, fols. 29–32.

59. In the 1620s the audiencia issued a decree that only Indians who resided outside their original corregimientos should be considered *forasteros*; in 1695 this was changed to all Indians who lived outside their towns of origin.

60. Pleito de Antonio de Plasencia, fols. 8–153.

61. Ibid., fols. 46–46v, 107; Tierras de Latacunga, 1627–1799, fols. 33–36.

62. On creole empowerment in the Viceroyalty of Peru, see Kenneth Andrien, *Crisis and Decline: The Viceroyalty of Peru in the Seventeenth Century* (Albu-

querque: Univ. of New Mexico Press, 1985). On Quito, see Powers, *Andean Journeys*, chap. 3.

63. Federico González Suárez, *Historia general de la república del Ecuador* (Quito: Imprenta del Clero, 1892), 3:231.

64. Ibid., 3:304–5.

65. Perhaps this ambiguity is best illustrated by the contradictory behavior of the Franciscans. Some creole friars were actually involved in gunpowder production, while their superiors colluded with the royal administration to put down the rebellion and provided a safe refuge for the president and oidores of the audiencia. Ibid., 3:222, 232.

66. The alternativa was a system the crown imposed on the religious orders whereby creoles and peninsulars took turns being elected to high offices. It ensured that, even though the creoles predominated, the peninsulars would wield power disproportionate to their numbers. In Quito, the Dominicans had the alternativa by 1617. The Franciscan order apparently did not have it until the 1680s, even though creole Franciscans outnumbered peninsulars by the mid-seventeenth century. Antonine Tibesar, "The Alternativa: A Study in Spanish-Creole Relations in Seventeenth-Century Peru," *The Americas* 11 (Jan. 1955), 220–81.

67. The Franciscans were especially cooperative with the royal administration during these episodes. In the Dominican conflict over the alternativa in 1627, for example, the audiencia imprisoned the creole Dominican and Augustinian rebels in the Franciscan monasteries of the city. Phelan, *Kingdom of Quito*, 181; González Suárez, *Historia general*, 3:335.

68. This polarization may also have been informed by vague distinctions of social rank that favored the secular clergy. Vargas, *Historia de la iglesia*, 172–73; González Suárez, *Historia general*, 3:335.

69. González Suárez, *Historia general*, 3:407, 4:200.

70. By the mid-seventeenth century, the religious orders owned more than half the cultivable surface of the audiencia. Vargas, *Historia de la iglesia*, 136.

71. González Suárez reports almost one thousand friars in the audiencia by the late seventeenth century. Vargas reports about seven hundred secular clergy by the 1660s and eight hundred by 1681, so their numbers must have begun to approximate each other by the second half of the seventeenth century. González Suárez, *Historia general*, 4:443; Vargas, *Historia de la iglesia*, 287.

72. Vargas, *Historia de la iglesia*, 288.

73. Tierras de Latacunga, 1627–1799, fol. 19.

74. This emphasis on individual free will and natural law is reminiscent of the Salamancan philosophy so prevalent in the bishop's guide for parish priests and *doctrineros*. Alonso de la Peña Montenegro, *Itinerario para párrocos de indios* ([Madrid, 1663] Quito: Corporación de Estudios y Publicaciones, 1985).

75. The reversal may have resulted from the creolization of the secular clergy. Most seventeenth-century bishops supported creole causes, since the majority of seculars under them were creoles. J. I. Israel, *Race, Class, and Politics in Colonial Mexico, 1610–1670* (London: Oxford Univ. Press, 1975), 86.

76. Absentee rates in the Indian towns of Latacunga had reached between 50 and 85 percent by the 1670s. Powers, *Andean Journeys*, chap. 2.

77. González Suárez, *Historia general*, 4:201.

78. In the 1640s, for example, Bishop Palafox of Puebla, Mexico, resolved this dilemma by depriving the mendicants of 37 *doctrinas* and replacing them with 150 seculars. Brading, *First America*, 235.

79. On Salamancan ideas about labor and free will, see Nicolás Sanchez-Albornoz, "El trabajo indígena en los Andes," *Revista de Historia Económia*

Ecuatoriana 2 (Dec. 1987), 153–81; Marjorie Grice-Hutchinson, *Early Economic Thought in Spain, 1177–1740* (London: G. Allen and Unwin, 1978).

80. Vargas, *Historia de la iglesia*, 287. Although Jiménez de Vélez' statement may contain some hyperbole, he nevertheless makes a point.

81. Powers, *Andean Journeys*, chap. 3. Especially widespread was the manipulation of census and tribute statistics by creole officials for purposes of government extortion.

82. Pleito de Antonio de Plasencia, fol. 107v.

83. Testimonio sobre cobranza de la mesada de los pueblos de Tisaleo, Patate, Pelileo, 1646, AMQ, Colección de cédulas reales dirigidas a la Audiencia de Quito, 1601–1660, fols. 397–99.

84. Parallels can be found here with studies of the Mexican clergy by Murdo J. MacLeod and Nancy Farriss. MacLeod, "The Social and Economic Roles of Indian Cofradías in Colonial Chiapas," in Cole, *Church and Society in Latin America*, 76–80; Farriss, *Crown and Clergy in Colonial Mexico, 1759–1821: The Crisis of Ecclesiastical Privilege* (London: Athlone Press, 1968).

85. Sobre forasteros y pago del estipendio al cura, ANQ, Tributos 3, fols. 10v–15v.

86. Ordenanzas para que los corregidores controlen los abusos de curas y de doctrinas, 1684, ANQ, Indígenas, caja 38.

7

The Limits of Religious Coercion
in Midcolonial Peru

Kenneth Mills

With the exception of the early years of the evangelization, and a few sporadic outbursts later, the conversion of the natives of Hispanic America to Christianity was achieved without recourse to that other famous Spanish institution, the Holy Inquisition. Nevertheless, from time to time, and in many disparate locations, Spanish ecclesiastical authorities worried about the purity of the Christianity practiced by the native peoples. In Peru, this concern manifested itself in a program that has come to be known as the Extirpation. In this program the secular clergy sought to eliminate, or extirpate, all traces of pre-Columbian religion among the natives. Kenneth Mills gives a detailed account of this process in his essay.

From the 1530s, natives had been excluded from the jurisdiction of the Inquisition; nevertheless, colonists feared that the natives were not fully embracing Christianity and, in fact, clung to their pre-Columbian religion. The Extirpation often succeeded in eliminating the outward and visible remnants of the old cults but proved unable to remove a deeper and more spiritual aspect. While native peoples in their religious practices utilized the stone images generically known as huacas, *the landscape itself also had spiritual meaning. While the images could be burned or destroyed, the landscape was always there. Moreover, Christianity in the process took on a distinctive Andean aspect, at least as it was practiced among the natives of the region.*

Kenneth Mills teaches history at Princeton University. He and William Taylor are the editors of Colonial Spanish America. *Mills is well known for his study of the Extirpation in seventeenth-century Peru,* Idolatry and Its Enemies.

From *Past and Present* 145 (1994): 84–121. Reprinted by permission of Oxford University Press.

Christ's injunction to go forth and teach all nations is forthright and clear. But the interpretation of his further instruction to compel them to enter the Christian fold is more problematic.[1] Does coercion lead to genuine conversion, or does it instead encourage dissimulation and feigned Christianity? Such questions deeply troubled many of the clergy and members of the religious orders who were involved in the evangelization of Spanish America in the sixteenth and seventeenth centuries.

Ideally (it was hoped) the conversion of indigenous peoples would come through their exposure to the natural appeal of Christian truths and teaching. While coercion was allowed, American conditions required that it be restricted. It was limited because Indians were regarded as new converts, deficient in intellectual capacity and especially vulnerable to the wiles of the Devil, but also because they were subjects of the Spanish crown. The great Dominican professor of theology at the University of Salamanca, Francisco de Vitoria (c. 1485–1546), developed lengthy arguments about the Spanish right to convert the native peoples of America and about the methods to be used to achieve this end.[2] In New Spain, the *junta eclesiástica* convened in 1539 by the bishop of Mexico, Juan de Zumárraga, recommended only "light punishments" in dealing with religious offenders and their sacred objects.[3]

But these and other theoretical restrictions on the use of force as an integral part of evangelization proved difficult to observe in the Indies. Churchmen grew impatient with their Indian charges as hopes for a New Jerusalem faded.[4] Faced early with religious resistance from powerful Indian opponents and also with more widespread cases of apparent subterfuge and duplicity among the newly converted, many regular and secular officials—including even Zumárraga himself—abandoned patience and restraint in favour of repression.[5] Accustomed as they were to the presence of an undercurrent of force in their efforts at evangelization, many churchmen saw no contradiction between means and end. The constitutions of the First Council of Lima (1551–52) simultaneously forbade and sanctioned the use of force in evangelization.[6] Moreover, the dividing line between instruction, moral regulation and outright coercion is far from clear in the response of evangelizers to the challenges they faced in the Indian parishes.[7]

A well-documented series of ecclesiastical investigations undertaken intermittently in the Indian parishes of the archdiocese of Lima between 1640 and 1750 provides extraordinary opportunities to explore further the relationship between religious coercion[8] and the transformation of an indigenous belief system. The first part of this essay introduces the forces in contention in this part of the seventeenth-century Andes: on the one hand, the "idolatry inspections" (*visitas de idolatría*) and their machinery of coercion, and on the other, post-evangelization Andean religion. The second part turns to the idolatry documentation for points of entry into this complex and often ambiguous world of confrontation and encounter, more than a century after the arrival of the Spanish in Peru. My particular concentration on the principal punitive and consecratory operations within a larger process of religious repression reveals much about both Spanish intentions and Andean responses. While it proves impossible to construct a simple model to explain exactly what different approaches to evangelization were achieving or what constituted "idolatry" in the midcolonial central Andes,[9] this religious information offers valuable insight into the minds of the extirpators and strongly suggests what some of the most important regional manifestations of Andean religion were becoming.

Religious change was occurring slowly, fitfully and, from the point of view of the agents of Christianization, sometimes "in reverse."[10] The Indian peoples of the Lima region, who were collectively to have been resettled and reoriented by generations of priests and administrators, were becoming parishioners. But they were doing so on their own terms, within the bounds of local relationships that included parish priests as well as "unofficial," Indian religious authorities. The Indians' accommodation to new, colonial pressures (and Christianity was but one of these) did not force the abandonment of trusted gods and practices.

By the end of the first decade of the seventeenth century, the confidence of the Catholic church in the success of its efforts to convert the peoples of the archdiocse of Lima, Peru, to a steadfast and orthodox Christian faith was severely shaken. The Indians' attachment to their own religious system had been, as the contemporary rhetoric put it, "discovered" or "unmasked": a secretive and vile "idolatry" had been revealed beneath the guise of proper Christian acceptance. The main thrust of efforts at evangelization in this part of the Andes was about to change. The predominantly missionary-style and parish-centered instruction of Indians was being superseded by a new obsession with the place of idolatry in the lives of baptized Indians. Official support grew quickly for a systematic and forceful initiative to solve the widespread problem of religious error and to continue the absorption of the Indians into Christendom.[11]

The process which developed to meet the new needs and express the change of will was "the Extirpation of idolatry."[12] The Extirpation amounted to a series of inquisitorial investigations held in a succession of parishes. Specially commissioned and empowered *visitadores de idolatría* invited individual confessions of guilt and denunciations of other religious offenders. Along with a range of punishments for the guilty, an idolatry visitation also meant a time of intense instruction for the Andean communities. In the eyes of its theoreticians and apologists, the Extirpation represented the perfect blend of the pedagogical, judicial, and penal measures needed to lead relapsed Christian Indians back into the fold. Depending largely on the inclinations of successive prelates in Lima and on the persuasiveness of the many provincial "enemies of idolatry," the

Extirpation was intermittently active in the seventeenth century. In some instances, its authority extended (though much more sporadically) into the first half of the eighteenth. Treatises on Indian religious error calling for the eradication of idolatry were written by contemporary churchmen in other parts of Spanish America (most notably New Spain), but unlike the manuals and other anti-idolatry material from seventeenth-century Peru, these were not accompanied by campaigns of investigation and punishment.[13] Despite the flaws in its organization and execution, its intermittent existence and its marked dependence on the patronage of certain archbishops and viceroys, the Peruvian Extirpation was the most systematic attempt ever made in colonial Spanish America to repress Indian religion and uproot its alleged perversions of Catholicism.[14]

The tenure of Archbishop Pedro de Villagómez of Lima (1641–71) represented a critical moment in the church's struggle with Andean religion. Villagómez revitalized the Extirpation in the middle of the seventeenth century after it had been out of favour for almost three decades.[15] Yet even though Villagómez's long archiepiscopate saw the most intense and prolonged persecution of the central practices of Andean religion that the region had ever known, not all churchmen supported him. The same period also saw the rise of some compelling doubts and fears.

There was opposition—both in the Lima region and beyond—to this return to systematic persecution.[16] Much of the disagreement hinged on what measure of force should accompany the continuing evangelization of Indians. The Society of Jesus went so far as to withdraw from official participation in the idolatry campaigns in the 1650s, citing, as one of their provincials put it, "reasons of some weight." Jesuit reservations can be seen as part of a constant fluctuation of opinion among contemporary churchmen on the difficult issue of the most effective means of eradicating persistent Andean religion.[17] The Jesuits had supervised the instruction and detention of the principal religious offenders since the beginning of campaigns in the second decade of the seventeenth century. Most importantly, they had always accompanied the idolatry inspections. Their refusal to do so came at a crucial moment, depriving Villagómez's renewed Extirpation of its most gifted teachers just when the Jesuits' unrivalled contemporary reputation for effective evangelization among the Indians was most needed. For the Indians, once the Jesuit presence was removed, the punitive aspects of the Extirpation came to the fore. Although a *visitador de idolatría* was meant to preach, hear confession, and direct the reformation of individuals, he could not escape the fact that he visited the Indian parishes primarily as a judge. Moreover, to a number of significant contemporary churchmen,[18] the Extirpation's commitment to forceful measures and a harsh rhetoric of dissuasion all but cancelled its reason for existence—namely, its reformative aims. Perhaps an excessive dose of juridical force was being administered at precisely the time when only more intensive and vigilant efforts at Christian instruction could save the Indians from perpetual error and the damnation that came with it.

More worrying still, from the point of view of the church in Lima, was the possibility that the *visitas de idolatría* might further frustrate the already uneven effects of the Catholic mission in this part of Spanish America. Tactics like those being employed by the Extirpation might be partly responsible for Indian religious survival. For, in spite of the triumphal tone of the official correspondence and of the anti-idolatry treatises, the effects of coercion, forceful dissuasion, and harsh punishment were unpredictable.[19]

The elaborate edifice of justification which Archbishop Villagómez and others had built upon the reformative elements in the idolatry investigations was clearly meant to disarm concern and criticism.[20] Yet the programmes of instruction were consistently overshadowed by coercive actions. The *visitadores'* punitive and destructive operations during the course of their idolatry investigations, usually known as *diligencias*, were central to the intended reform of the parishes of the midcolonial archdiocese of Lima. By means of such actions, religious offenders could be isolated by the Spanish authorities in order to be disciplined and ridiculed before their own people, and the so-called instruments of idolatry, the false gods, the ancestors' remains and the sacrificial materials, could be physically destroyed. Yet it was what the performance of the *diligencias* was meant to achieve which is most important. Nothing was thought to be more instructive for the Indians, or more symbolic of their spiritual fate, than the religious spectacles that featured the destruction of their forbidden cults. Accordingly, almost all idolatry trials featured *diligencias* of some description.

Often, these operations were the culmination of a *visita*'s stay in a parish, occurring after the judicial proceedings.[21] A whole range of public acts of punishment (usually floggings of persons who had been shorn, tied and stripped), penance and "processions of shame" (in which the guilty were dressed in conspicuous pointed headgear known as *corozas*, made to carry crosses in their hands and attended by criers to broadcast their religious crimes) were administered to those with the heaviest sentences.[22] Some of those deemed most dangerous and least likely to reform their ways—so-called sorcerers (*hechiceros*) and witches (*brujos*), the ministers of Andean gods and the ritual specialists[23] —would be publicly banished to a correctional prison, the Casa de Santa Cruz, in Lima, or to the care of some convent, in an effort to remove both their persons and their reputations from the places where they held spiritual sway. And there were *autos de fe* at which any object both idolatrous and transportable would be burned before the people who had been assembled in the local plazas.

The fact that memories of these destructive acts lingered so long is the greatest testimony to their brutal effect. Scholars have noted the power of similar recollections among indigenous peoples in New Spain.[24] Andean declarants before *visitadores* in the 1660s frequently recalled in vivid detail the deeds of extirpators almost a half century before; the visits seem to have become negative reference points in the people's recollection of the past, remembered in much the same way as particularly bad droughts or the outbreaks of a killing disease.[25]

The practices which characterized the *diligencias* were a direct result of the church's determination to get across its message to the Indians through intensive catechizing, instruction, and—above all—by preaching against "idolatry."[26] Their ostensible aim was to expound the basic tenets of the Catholic faith in such a way that the teaching (and the fear inspired by interrogation) would reawaken understanding and induce baptized Indians to return to the fold. But in practice this intense programme of instruction and preaching most often took second place to their efforts to refute and humiliate Andean spiritual leaders and to degrade what the churchmen took to be central aspects of Andean religion.[27] In their attempts to make a complex belief system comprehensible to themselves by resorting to the limited canon of European concepts and learned opinion,[28] Spanish commentators had consistently disparaged Indian views of the world. By using such words as "idolatry" and "superstition," and by imagining in terms of these categories, they devalued Indian efforts to manage the forces which were thought to permeate every aspect of life.[29]

Even as such simplifications and misperceptions persisted, the instruction employed by the Extirpation took the affront a step further. The Indians who ministered to the ancestral gods and who acted as repositories for ancient knowledge, together with those who were adept in divination, healing and magic,[30] were subjected to two kinds of misrepresentation. The Indian spiritual élite were portrayed as servants of the Christians' Devil (who either inspired or directed their "idolatry") or else as evil charlatans who exploited the credulity of the masses for their own prestige and profit. Andean gods, whose significance and functions were changing in the colonial years, were even more crudely portrayed. Even allowing for the adaptation of these gods to the concerns of their seventeenth-century devotees, and for the scepticism with which some Indians viewed Andean religious forces, such beings as the *huacas* maintained their relevance for most people in the highland Lima region. For many, *huacas* were ancestors who had turned to stone in a mythical past and who now represented eternal forces in the regional landscapes. The *huacas*' great deeds and contributions to society were a central part of local religion and of the festival cycle. Yet to the extirpator in his role as preacher, they became nothing more than "ugly rocks," regularly soiled by animals and little boys.[31] Similarly, the *conopas*, sculpted and natural forms, often of stone, were, to many Andeans, mobile, personal founts of energy, fertility and good fortune. But by the preachers they were likened, no more sympathetically, to children's playthings and rag dolls.[32] When it came to the teaching of the Christian faith, the elementary doctrine classes were frequently offered not so much as opportunities for improved understanding, but as penalties for error, dullwittedness and recalcitrance. The sentences decreed by the *visitadores* often included supervised terms in the children's daily *doctrina* classes for adult religious transgressors.[33]

Through public punishment, demolition of religious objects and places, and the attempted appropriation of immovable Andean *huacas* to Catholic purposes, the process of instruction through destruction and humiliation continued. Indeed, theatrical coercion became something of a constant even when the extirpating prelate Villagómez was no longer supporting a centralized initiative. There was, for instance, little difference between the methods of the idolatry inspector Felipe de Medina in Cajatambo in 1652 and those of Toribio de Mendizábel in Huarochirí in 1723 or of Pedro de Celis in Chancay in 1724.[34] Medina dealt harshly with "an obstinate backslider and idolater" who was found to have concealed entire families of *malquis* (mummified bodies of the dead) from earlier *visitas*. Don Jerónimo Julca was exiled to Lima and his home was burnt to the ground, "so that the others might see who had been a *hechicero*."[35] In eighteenth-century Carampoma (Huarochirí), Mendizábal confronted the backsliding indigenous minister Juan de Rojas in a similar manner. After all the "idols" had been burned before the villagers' eyes in an *auto de fe*, Rojas's house was then flattened and "a cross was erected in memory."[36] Similarly, in 1724 Pedro de Celis assembled four hundred Indians of all ages in the plaza of San Pedro de Pacho in Chancay to watch an *auto de fe* of cult objects, and in the course of the same investigation, Pedro Quiñones, the experienced minister of many Andean gods in neighbouring Pachangara, reported that on numerous occasions throughout his life he had been publicly whipped for his relapses into idolatry.[37] An approach toward the eradication of Andean religion which historians have long associated mostly with the seventeenth-century campaigns of the Extirpation proves to be alive and well in the more sporadic initiatives of the eighteenth century.

In spite of all their intended edification and solemnity, the midcolonial *diligencias* revealed the most vulnerable point of the Extirpation: the point where idealism came face to face with reality. The results of the exercises were very different from the hopes that attended them. Common assumptions about the influence of the Devil on Indian beliefs and practices, and preconceptions about Indian immorality and mental inferiority, proved serviceable to *visitadores* in the course of most idolatry trials. Enemies to the faith and to the advancement of Christianity in the Indian communities could be defined, interpreted on a familiar grid, and castigated accordingly. Theory and theological opinion supplied comfort to faith and

fired the ambitions of extirpators whose rewards were often slight payment for the rigours of their labours in remote regions. But the "enemies"
sometimes slipped through the interpretative grid, events did not always
proceed as planned and the effectiveness of punishments and coercive
actions was often uncertain. In the performance of their duties, extirpators of idolatry and their notaries, perhaps more than any other firsthand
observers and recorders of the midcolonial realities of the Andean world,
were pushed outside the regulated, prejudicially constructed environments
of the treatise or of a letter to a superior. In their operations the *visitadores*
confronted ambiguous physical manifestations of a changing Indian religiosity that they imperfectly understood, yet were bound to obliterate.
Granted, when their actions were complete, extirpators might retreat to
the familiar domain of the written word. Many, as they defined the Indians' sins and pronounced sentence, were clearly reviewing the sheaves of
Indian testimony from within the refuge offered by the established conceptual canon. But the notaries' accounts of the destructive excursions of
the *visitadores*, read with care, can provide less scripted sources for the
examination both of these events and of the information they contain.
This exercise also enables us to focus on the religious situations they may
have helped to create. Such an approach, while revealing the imperfec-
tions of the extirpating operations, also leads us beyond the machinery of
repression to a deeper consideration of the changing and emerging entities that constituted post-evangelization Andean religion.

For there were occasions when the discoveries made in the course of
extirpating operations or in their aftermath must have made the act of
orthodox interpretation distinctly uncomfortable. It is worth recalling at
this point that the Andean world had been much affected by over a century of Spanish domination. Disease, warfare, dislocation, the disruption
of reciprocal patterns of economic exchange and social order, greater
demands for labour and tribute being made from fewer people, occasional
abandonment by Hispanicized Indian élites had all taken their toll on Indian society.[38] Most importantly for our purposes, the imposition of a parish structure, the lure of a powerful new religion, and the uncertain results
of evangelizing efforts had drawn some Indians closer to, and often into,
the Christian fold. Their initial introduction to Christianity had usually
come through the teaching and example of mendicant friars and, after
about 1570, of the Jesuits. Even in the Andes, where missionary numbers
and enthusiasm were not those of early New Spain, many Indian communities had at least a fleeting contact during the sixteenth century with a
more heterodox and experimental Christianity than that of later times.
Moreover, as the crown's policy of racial segregation proved illusory, there
was plenty of unofficial Christianization accompanying general cultural
exchange. Increased opportunities for contact with Spaniards, mestizos
and Africans and, most significantly for our purposes, with the diverse

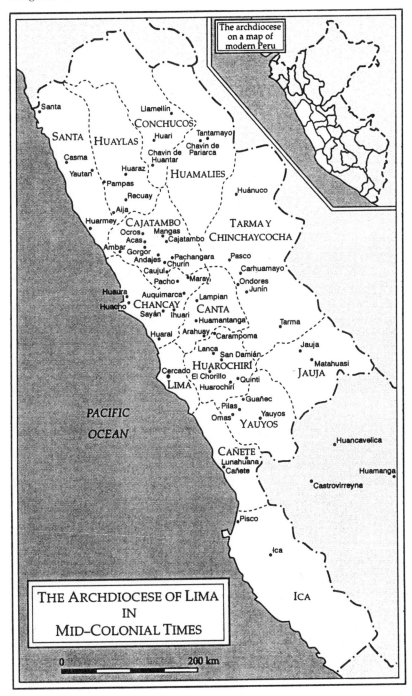

The archdiocese
on a map of
modern Peru

Santa

Llamellín

CONCHUCOS

SANTA HUAYLAS Huari Tantamayo

Casma Chavin de Chavin de Pariarca
Huantar

Yautan Huaraz HUAMALIES

Pampas

Recuay Huánuco

Aija

Huarmey CAJATAMBO TARMA Y

Ocros Mangas CHINCHAYCOCHA

Acas Cajatambo

Ambar Gorgor Pasco

Andajes Pachangara

Caujul Churin Carhuamayo

Pacho Maray Ondores

Junín

Huaura Auquimarca Lampian

Huacho CHANCAY CANTA

Sayán Ihuari Huamantanga Tarma

Huaral Arahuay Carampoma Jauja

Lanca

San Damián Matahuasi

Cercado HUAROCHIRÍ JAUJA

El Chorillo Quinti

LIMA Huarochirí

Guañec

Pilas

Omas Yauyos

PACIFIC YAUYOS

OCEAN

Huancavelica

CAÑETE

Lunahuana Huamanga

Cañete

Castrovirreyna

Pisco

Ica

THE ARCHDIOCESE OF LIMA
IN
MID-COLONIAL TIMES

0   200 km

ICA

Map prepared by Christopher Brest.

brands of Christianity they practised, offered Indians some inadvertent religious direction.[39]

Because of its capacity to absorb and make something of its new influences, the Andean religious system emerged a good deal less impoverished than might have been expected. The transformations of Andean religious ideas and practices, and the indisputable penetrations of Catholicism into an evolving Andean religious framework, seem, superficially, to have owed little to coercive tactics such as those of the Extirpation. Indeed, the institution pitted itself as much against alleged perversions of orthodoxy—what we might call popular Catholicism or emergent Andean Christianity—as against *huaca* worship and ritual "superstition." To employ an anachronistic image, at times the religiosity that was to be eradicated from the Indian parishes was, to its midcolonial extirpators, something like the creature of Frankenstein. What exactly the Indians believed was an unknown, and thus dangerous, monster—an inadvertent hybrid with recognizably Christian traits, for which the earlier mendicant orders and Jesuits, and ultimately the church itself, would find it difficult to deny at least part of the responsibility.

It is the uneasy encounter between the extirpators' orthodox idealism and the realities of an increasingly complex, postevangelization Andean religion that is so often revealed in the course of a *diligencia*, particularly the kind of *diligencia* that sent solemn excursions into the Andean hinterland to destroy and appropriate Andean *huacas* and other sacred places. For at few points were the agents of the Extirpation more exposed to the limits and realities of both Catholic efficacy and Indian religion than when its agents ventured away from the churches, plazas and grid-pattern streets of the resettled Indian *pueblos* in pursuit of their investigations.

The image of the extirpators leaving the familiar order of the resettled villages is an important one. Their excursions possessed a symbolic equivalence to the spate of church-building, resettlement and town foundation that had gripped Andean Peru about a century before.[40] The towns and cities were designed to do more than make Europeans feel at home. The ambitious urbanization, as well as assisting tribute collection and the organization of Indian labourers, sought to extend a Hispanic brand of civilization among the newly converted. The Indians were meant to be drawn in wonder to these designs, to fall upon their knees in pious awe beneath the arches of the churches they themselves had built for a new god. But the patterned Christian environments in the Andes, the ordered centres sweeping rectilineally outwards from the village plazas and church façades, began to dissipate at the edges. The organization into towns had wrought changes in Indian society which, however striking in their economic effects, are ultimately poor indicators of religious transformation. In the archdiocese of Lima at least, many Indians had been resettled not far from their ancestors' plots of land, their mythical places of origin (*pacarinas*),

their physical and spiritual homes. The ancient settlements which the notaries called *pueblos viejos* (old towns),[41] often near to the *huacas* and the
machayes or cave tombs of the *malquis*, remained well within reach.
Moreover, the resettlement of peoples into villages and towns (*reducciones
de indios*), especially by the viceroy Francisco de Toledo in the years after about 1570, had not always been successful. For example, the idolatry
inspector Juan Sarmiento de Vivero wrote from Guañec in the province of
Yauyos in 1660, complaining of Indians who had been absent from their
resettled communities for some twenty years, living instead in the ravines
and high plateaux of Paria Caca.[42]

The seventeenth-century extirpators learned much about the persistence of religious, social and economic connections between the people
and the surrounding landscape in the Lima region. Irrespective of how
much of this information could be appreciated by active extirpators, it
was clear—even to the crusading Christians—that in the postconquest
years the Indians' contact with their rich ancestral mythology and with
the fundamental dimensions of their religious system had been strained,
but not broken.[43] The aim of the Extirpation's *diligencias* was thus to fin-
ish a drawn-out task, to sever these roots—in some cases quite literally,
as we shall observe below. When *visitadores* penetrated the more remote
reaches and climbed to the *pueblos viejos*, their actions—at once destructive and consecratory—were attempts simultaneously to end the persistent spiritual hegemony of the Andean belief system and to extend the
appropriation of the Andean hinterland for the Catholic faith. A purpose
and an idealism that one century earlier would have prompted a pair of
friars to press for a local labour force to build an adobe church in a newly
founded village had come to require solemn forays into the countryside
to fell idols, peer into caves, dig up bones and erect tall crosses.

My attention to the shift in emphasis between the different kinds of
pastoral activity (evangelization and extirpation) is not meant to com-
press an intricate and uneven process into a tidy, dichotomous package.
Persuasion coexisted with force, both before and after some churchmen
grew disillusioned with the prospect of genuine Indian conversions.[44]
Destructive actions against indigenous shrines and the raising of crosses
had gone on since the first *entradas*—the rapid, surprise entries of the
Spanish conquerors into unknown lands. And efforts at peaceful conversion and sustained religious instruction were pursued in the seventeenth
and eighteenth centuries. My point is to emphasize the comparable spirit
of early colonial efforts at Christianization and the *diligencias* of the
middle colonial period. The analogy works in at least two ways, and spurs
us to think about how churchmen viewed both the towns they lived in and
the Andean countryside. Like the person who organized the building of a
first church or who rode in a conquering expedition, the seventeenth-
century extirpator on a *diligencia* participated in a new beginning, a

potential triumph in foreign territory. In his mind at least, a *visitador*'s acts of destruction and re-consecration in the mountains might be cause for a kind of optimism. Something was being started where nothing but evil and perhaps dormant potential were thought to exist. Yet in the *diligencia* there was often, at the same time, cause for pessimism. To varying degrees, indigenous gods and Andean religious organization had survived the attempted spiritual conquest; the need for idolatry investigations in general—and their destructive actions in particular—was evidence enough. The seventeenth-century *diligencia* was a rearguard action, an imperfect, late advance by churchmen into an "unconquered" countryside with the expectation of a retreat to the safety and order of their urban bases. Although many of them (as experienced parish priests) knew the realities of the midcolonial Andean world as well as any Spaniard in the viceroyalty, the *visitadores* frequently showed signs of feeling ill at ease outside the towns. In the *diligencia* they could recognize a desperation, perhaps even an admission of defeat.

Of all the officials conducting idolatry investigations in the Villagómez period, *visitador* Juan Sarmiento de Vivero may have been the most careful to ensure that an attending notary recorded his devotion to duty and the hardships he was forced to endure.[45] As a fortunate consequence, we possess descriptive accounts of a number of his *diligencias*, written on the spot while memories and excitement were fresh.[46] Features of a few of these operations provide us with a more vivid and solid basis for the present discussion.

A first example occurred in the highlands northeast of Lima, in the parish of Huamantanga, Canta, in 1664. Here, Sarmiento and a sizable entourage resolved to visit the old town of the Sigual kin group (*ayllu*) and a number of other places in the surrounding area. A declaration by the regional governor (*kuraka*), Don Rodrigo Rupay Chapa, and a denunciation by a woman named Ana María, had given the *visitador* reason to believe that his efforts would be rewarded.[47] On 1 June, Whitsunday (the "Pascua del Espíritu Santo"), the notary recorded that Sarmiento, mounted on a mule, set out for the ancient settlement of the Sigual accompanied by an interpreter, the ecclesiastical prosecutor, two local magistrates and "many other Indians."

The ancient settlement was perched high above Huamantanga, and by three in the afternoon the mules had passed as far as they might. Guided by the Indians, the party gained the summit on foot. They came upon some dilapidated homes and a small open area formed inside man-made walls of stone, from the edge of which Huamantanga could be seen far below. Inside this *plazuela* was an old and bountiful tree which produced coloured flowers.[48] The "roots" of this tree, Sarmiento discovered from the Indians, "were those of the people." While the *visitador* ordered the same people to pull up the tree and destroy its roots, he and the others spent the remaining daylight hours exploring a number of covered enclosures just below the open space,[49] which were found to contain numerous ancestors' remains. In due course, all were incinerated in a public *auto de fe*.[50] Three days later, the *visitador* returned with a work party to erect a large wooden cross (nearly three metres in height). In standard fashion, the place was renamed as that of the Holy Spirit, because "on that day the idolatry of the *pueblo* had been revealed." It was not, perhaps, the appropriate moment to recall that similar idolatrous revelations by previous investigators had chequered this parish's recent past; the notary recorded only the pious hope that the cross would become a place "where all might worship."[51]

Another example from the same *visita*, though presenting different challenges, confirms the general pattern of the operations. In the afternoon, Sarmiento set out with the *pueblo's* officials, a Mercedarian friar and some "sixteen Indians armed with spades, sticks and three large wooden crosses."[52] Before long they came upon a number of bountiful plots of land. Overlooking these was a great pinnacle of rock "in the form of a human head," the features of which the notary felt especially obliged to remark upon. When they were questioned the Indians explained that this was *Vicho Rinri* (the notary's rendering), a *huaca* ancestor who was much celebrated in dances and songs.[53] Three attempts to dislodge the *huaca* with sticks and levers—the last of which involved a new, thicker lever, an invocation of God and the addition of the exertions of the *visitador*—finally sent *Vicho Rinri* plummeting into the ravine below. Sarmiento ordered that a cross be fashioned out of the large lever, erected and shrouded in flowers. The place of *Vicho Rinri* was then renamed in honour of the Holy Sacrament. The *diligencia* ended only after the party had worshiped before the cross and the notary had made a record of the day's events.[54]

These are official outlines of what happened, meant to be repetitive, triumphantly repetitive, and carefully prepared in order to record zealous endeavour and to demonstrate a *visitador's* diligence in acting upon information that the Indians had supplied about Andean religion. The patterned coercive manoeuvres against Andean sacred places of course followed long-established Catholic practice in the struggle against "pagan" shrines. They resembled, for instance, the procedures recommended over one thousand years earlier by a man whom Archbishop Villagómez greatly admired and often quoted in his writings, Pope Gregory the Great.[55] Yet, in spite of the desires of Villagómez and some of his *visitadores* to assure themselves of a place in the grand sweep of Christian history, the documentation from the archdiocese of Lima offers us considerably more than a formulaic addition to the church's long struggle against paganism and the corrupting influence of the Devil. There were also moments of unease, times when what the extirpator encountered in the Andean landscape was intellectually and practically more cumbersome than the survival of purely Indian religious forms.

We may consider, for instance, what occurred just after the sacred tree above Huamantanga was uprooted and replaced with a cross. On this occasion, the denunciator, Ana María, interrupted the pious tenor of the moment to observe that the wall beside which they stood was very near to the recess where she and another witness had seen an accused "sorcerer," Cristóbal Chumbi Guaman (alias Llaguas), performing a suspicious act of worship. Cristóbal, who was also in the extirpator's company, protested that she lied, but Ana María proceeded to describe how she had seen him in that protected place, naked from the waist up, upon his knees, with his arms raised skyward, muttering to himself.[56] Viewing the recess for himself, the *visitador* discovered an upright piece of wood nearly three metres in height, with a horizontal groove in which a second piece of wood would have rested. The Indian magistrates informed Sarmiento that these were the remains of a cross that had been erected eight years earlier by another *visitador de idolatría*, Don Pedro de Quijano.[57] In this way, the triumphal and edifying story, the comprehensible, almost surgical act of desecration and re-consecration, are interrupted, not so much by persistent Andean religion, as by the traces of a more confusing kind of religious error. An extirpator's regional victory for Christianity over "idolatry" is complicated by the undecipherability of midcolonial Indian practice.

Yet if the discovery of the somewhat sorry traces of a predecessor's efforts at that site troubled the mind of Juan Sarmiento, we do not learn of it in the notary's record. The subsequent find of a quantity of human bones and skulls in the same recess, behind the remnants of the cross, concentrated his attention upon the alleged idolatry (that is, Andean religious practices) of Cristóbal Chumbi Guaman[58] and upon the numerous other tasks at hand. There was no return to the intriguing matter of what went on in the recess in the old town which was now flanked by two of the Extirpation's crosses. As is so often the case with the idolatry documentation, we must look to neighbouring regions for more information.

Two years earlier, in somewhat similar circumstances, the disquiet of *visitador* Juan Sarmiento is less elusive. In late August 1662, Sarmiento was guided on a seven-point tour of the environs of *el paraje de Cañas* in the parish of Sayan, Chancay, by the region's *kuraka*, Don Diego Pacha.[59] The *diligencia* followed the standard pattern of demolition, cross-erection and Catholic consecration, but at two of the *huacas* the *visitador's* party discovered the familiar traces of the previous extirpating and sanctifying efforts of a parish priest. In both cases old crosses stood a few paces away from *huacas* that were massive outcroppings of rock which could not be brought down or otherwise destroyed. The state of the first of these places evidently satisfied Sarmiento, for, as the notary recorded, "they did not find any signs that superstitions or sacrifices had been performed there in those [recent] times."[60]

But the second site was more disturbing to the *visitador*'s conscience. His concern over the fate of the religious ground which had been distinguished by a predecessor's cross was natural; after all, previous extirpating actions were among the few yardsticks he had to measure the effect of the actions he solemnly continued. A previous testimony taken in the village had revealed the belief that the *huaca* at this place had been "consuming" (or stealing the health of) the children of the *kuraka*, Don Diego Pacha,[61] because he had not been honouring the god in the proper way. Moreover, the great white rock with its accompanying cross stood in the midst of an ancient settlement (*pueblo viejo*) in which they also found, in the notary's words, a "large cave," the ceiling of which featured "a great number of different figures of demons in the form of animals with horns, painted in black." Although Sarmiento seemed to accept that this same *kuraka* who now guided him had reformed his thinking with respect to the devouring *huaca*, the investigator clearly wondered about what had been the effect on the minds of other Indians of the cross that stood at that place. Standing in the *pueblo viejo* staring at the central Christian symbol in the shadow of the immovable rock whose Andean significance and supposed divine outrage (at the *kuraka*'s ritual negligence) were only dimly perceived, surrounded by other *huacas* and painted figures that had been called demons, might possibly have led Sarmiento to a sobering contemplation of the efficacy both of the policy of repeated *visitas de idolatría*[62] and, more immediately, of his own *diligencias* among the Indians. The notary registered that the *visitador* became preoccupied with "a quantity of small stones which appeared to have been placed by hand" at a point on the rock-face which proved impossible to reach by climbing.[63] Because a cross had already been erected, Sarmiento could only ease his apparent dissatisfaction with what was being achieved by naming the place after "the glorious Saint John the Baptist."[64]

The actions of the extirpators in these instances from Canta and Chancay in the early 1660s suggest a number of questions. Although most of them defy certain answers, taken together they begin to penetrate to the heart of what was occurring in the midcolonial archdiocese of Lima. We can consider the *ayllu*'s ancient settlement perched above, but not out of reach of, the resettlement of Huamantanga. What did this place, and others like it, mean to Indians in the midcolonial era? Before this *visita* occurred, what had been the attitude of the Mercedarian friars—who were the people's priests, *doctrineros* and confessors—towards continued devotion and commitment to the place? What were the effects of the *visita*'s *diligencias* that physically uprooted that ancient flowering tree, the roots of which were said to be "those of the people," the incineration of the ancestors' bones, and innumerable acts like these throughout the archdiocese? And what of the successive efforts by the *visitadores* to erase and supplant the traditional significance of Andean sacred places through the erection of crosses and propitious christenings?

The huge stone presence, the ancestor *Vicho Rinri*, whose sanctuary does not appear to have been assaulted until Sarmiento's visit, offers another challenge for our analysis. Even the admittedly slim evidence that we have in this particular case indicates that *Vicho Rinri*, like so many other *huacas* in the Andes, was a religious survivor, a manifestation of the fact that Catholic domination in the community and region did not negate Andean religious affiliations. In 1664 the reference to dancing and singing in his name suggests that his benevolence, and probably even his mythical past, were regularly commemorated. Like others of his ilk from neighbouring regions where different and more abundant details survive in the documentary evidence, we can imagine that *Vicho Rinri* was given offerings and consulted by a faithful minister, and that he was attended by others who depended on his protection and favour.

But we must further explore the intricacies of the changing religous situation of which this Andean ancestor-being had increasingly become a part. *Vicho Rinri*, like so many other surviving *huacas*, would have transformed himself in colonial times, mirroring the needs of his people. He acquired an expanded range of functions, a meaning and a relationship with people who increasingly participated in both Christian and Andean religious frameworks. *Apullana Guara* and *Mama Guanca*, two similar beings from Churin, were approached by their people not only to bring agricultural and pastoral abundance, but also to prevent the abuses of a parish priest and *corregidor*.[65] *Guaman Cama*, a principal *huaca* of Acas in midseventeenth-century Cajatambo, was asked by his people (among many other entreaties) for permission to attend the Catholic festival of the village patron, Saint Peter.[66] Although some Andean religious forms would prove less adaptable to the exigencies of the seventeenth century, *Vicho Rinri* from Canta was a familiar force in the regional colonial world, both a traditional guardian of agricultural prosperity and a pragmatic, evolving protector. The image of a *huaca* retaining importance through transformation, demonstrating the capacity to absorb innovation and expand a spiritual repertoire, can be viewed as a regional expression of what was occurring in the midcolonial Andean religious system as a whole.

How did the methods of the Extirpation fare against so variable and elastic a rival? *Vicho Rinri*'s fall into the ravine, like the destruction of other gods, was meant by the extirpators to be a finalizing event, a resolution. But how would the act of destruction have been interpreted by the Indians who had assisted the deed, or those who heard of it later? And would recollection of the event have affected their conception of the destroying lever-cum-cross that was meant to be the *huaca's* symbolic substitute? These central questions persist, and are not merely rhetorical.

While we can readily appreciate what was meant to be achieved by the *diligencia* operations, there are considerable indications that these acts of destruction and re-consecration did not inspire as much real confidence in extirpating circles as was often claimed for official and justificatory purposes. At times, once the thin crust of triumphalism is broken through, there is a pervasive sense of futility before an insurmountable problem. There is a feeling of resignation, even of desperation. When little else could be done to advance the faith, the ceremony of fashioning and raising the supreme Christian symbol was made to suffice. Perhaps the ceremonial reconsecrations by the extirpators of Andean sacred sites were even some extirpators' expressions of ultimate failure—acts of giving in, but with some dignity.[67]

For their tasks were, more often than not, physically—if not religiously—impossible. Extirpators frequently lamented the fact that many *huacas* were "born of the hills themselves";[68] others, although detached from the mountainsides, were so large or impossibly placed that they also proved indestructible.[69] Moreover, although in theory most *diligencias* set out against specific deities and shrines, in practice the actions could take on a weary and wanton character (like an early *entrada*, as noted above), eager to crush whatever they could find. These ecclesiastical judges felt a need to justify the considerable effort involved in mounting the *visitas* by achieving some—and sometimes any—material result. For example, in the parish of Omas, Yauyos, in 1660, no person seemed willing to lead the *visitador* to the "stone . . . in the form of a person" in the Yanapati ravine, not even knowledgeable Pedro Chumbi who had confessed its existence; yet the investigation contented itself by ravaging an ancient burial site that had been found along the way.[70] As has been suggested from evidence even beyond the limits of the Lima region, Indians became practised at sating the extirpators' almost indiscriminate appetite for "idols" while at the same time guarding what was most important.[71]

The apparent physical results of those efforts that found their particular targets are equally contentious. The meaning and presence of a *huaca* which was taken away, smashed into pieces, burnt in a plaza or heaved into a ravine were not necessarily forgotten. In fact, the actions of contemporary churchmen betrayed their growing anxiety over Andean religious allegiances which seemed impossible to extinguish. It became established procedure to dispose secretly of all pieces, dust and ashes of the *huacas* and *malquis* which had been demolished, for fear of the Indians' continued worship of "relics." As Andrés Guaman Pilpi of San Pedro de Acas, Cajatambo, explained to Bernardo de Novoa in 1657, the survival of the local *huaca Marcayan* could be accounted for, because "although it had been burnt, the 'spirit' [a gloss on the Quechua concept *camaquen*] of the said idol lived."[72]

If the success of the destructive exercises against *huacas* was frequently in doubt, then equally so were efforts at re-consecration. We cannot say with certainty what roles were assumed by the seemingly innumerable crosses that were meant to extinguish old Andean loyalties and point the spiritual way forward. But we can, of course, readily state what a few of those roles were supposed to be. For the most Hispanicized and Christian members of Indian society the crosses were to be a gift of encouragement; here was God's most powerful sign, His holy brand upon another part of His world.[73] Even more than that, the crosses commemorated the great acts of destruction and resanctification. The symbols were to provide the extirpators with an assurance of permanent effect that they desperately needed, just as they were to provide the Indians with strong memories of their *huacas'* humiliation and defeat. The words of Sarmiento's notary confirm that the renaming of the places where crosses were erected was undertaken to turn the localities into perpetual reminders of the day when idolatry had been banished and Christianity had triumphed. The actions in the mountains and ancient settlements effectively made it seem possible for the extirpators, in Anthony Pagden's phrase, "to transform the un-possessable."[74]

But, of course, for most indigenous people it was hardly so simple. The triumphal outline, the show of assured mastery, is a screen obscuring a more ambiguous reality. Many early missionaries seem to have recognized the fluidity of Indian religious constructs; this reality inspired caution in some, while others clearly tried to manipulate it in the interest of Christian conversion. According to Bernal Díaz del Castillo, Fray Bartolomé de Olmedo, who accompanied Hernán Cortés in the early days of the Spanish presence in Mexico, was inclined to be more cautious than the conqueror about the erection of crosses as reminders of the Spaniards' early preaching and their efforts to extirpate Indian cults. "In my opinion," Olmedo is said to have told Cortés, "it is too early to leave a cross in these people's possession . . . What you have told them is enough until they are better acquainted with our holy religion."[75] Ramón Gutiérrez's interpretation of the "confabulation" of Christian crosses with indigenous prayer-sticks in the early contacts between Spaniards and Pueblos in New Mexico would seem to underline Olmedo's point.[76] According to Gutiérrez, some Franciscans in New Mexico proceeded as many of their earlier brethren had done in New Spain, salvaging aspects of the Indian religiosity which were already present and employing these supposed parallels for Christian ends. Indigenous peoples would come to recognize "the power of the men who brandished crosses," and from that point it would take little effort "to convince them to worship the cross."[77] Perhaps. But it is dangerous to look for, and to think in terms of, some of the

very parallels between European and Indian religions that colonial Spanish churchmen sought. Moreover, quite what the "worship" of the symbol
meant to a seventeenth-century Puebloan or, to return to present concern,
an Andean religious imagination in the midcolonial years, remains open
to question.

The idolatry trial evidence from midcolonial Peru reminds us that the
roles of crosses in the Indian religious world, the roles of elements of
Christianity in general, should inspire caution in historians. For there
were many "degrees" of what has commonly been called the process of
Christianization in the midcolonial Andean world. Among the many
possible variables, these degrees were affected by the nature of previous
evangelization, exposure to persuasive anti-idolatry preaching and the
rival messages of any Andean dogmatizers who might exist. As a result,
the roles of Christian symbols and concepts depended on the decisions—
and sometimes even the opportunistic whims—of a varied indigenous
society.[78]

In interpreting the religious allegiances of the Andeans we must be
careful not to be misguided by the religious assumptions of contemporary Spanish churchmen. For it was in terms of a clear-cut Augustinian
opposition between Christians and idolaters, between the camps of light
and darkness, between those who had been won over by the gospel and
those who wickedly resisted it, that many midcolonial missionaries and
extirpators preferred to interpret the religious reality in Indian areas.
Conceiving of a neat division between those who chose God and good
and those who chose idolatry and evil had its explanatory advantages. It
provided a time-honoured and convenient dualism with which to explain
the constitution of Andean parishes where religious recalcitrance seemed
a growing problem despite the people's long-standing relationship with
Catholicism.[79]

But what basis is there to think of midcolonial Andean society in
terms of a strict polarity of religious feeling, a factionalism along religious lines?[80] It is important to view the time of a *visita*'s presence in an
Indian parish as an abnormal time of fear and tension, a time of unreality
when an artificial dualism might be imposed. As historians of the Inquisition and of ecclesiastical law will not be surprised to discover, idolatry
denunciations in the Andean communities multiplied when they were encouraged, and when the climate of opinion was such that something might
easily be gained through them.[81] But religious boundary lines and the ec-
centricities of local belief structures which were being transformed during the colonial years were not usually policed so tirelessly. When the
visita moved on—depending, of course, on such crucial variables as the
views of a parish priest and the degree of Andean religious survival—
there could be a return to what might tentatively be called normal times.
Individual priests or friars, perhaps in the interests of village tranquility

or because of a tolerance bred by experience, might overlook certain kinds of Indian error. Indians, free from the pressure to conform absolutely, might actively seek the benefits and solace offered by a growing pool of spiritual opportunities. Andean religious life, the interaction between indigenous and Spanish religious conceptions and practices, could be less constrained and more harmonious than is often implied.

This is not to suggest that contestation between Spanish Catholic and Andean leaders over religious (and secular) power in the parishes was eliminated or lacked significance. In many communities there were clearly Indians who, through their testimonies, demonstrated that they were allies of the priests, and that as committed Christians they were opponents of Andean religion. And there were ardent practitioners of Andean religion who articulately countered the religious assimilations they could discern and who actively disputed the growing place for elements of Christianity in the Indian world. In Acas, Cajatambo, dogmatizers warned that if the *huacas* and *malquis* were not nourished by offerings the people would "lose their plots of land . . . and their irrigation canals and springs would dry up" and they would be condemned "to walk poor and desolate and . . . all waste away."[82] Such stark warnings were not made without reason, for few people faced Christianity with an attitude of either complete acceptance or steadfast opposition. Many, in effect, contravened the precise dictates of both their parish priests and their Andean dogmatizers, proving themselves more discerning and even experimental in their religious decisions. The possible examples are numerous, ranging from elaborate instances such as those noted above when *huacas* and saints were absorbed into each other's observances, to more mundane ones. In 1661, for instance, Magdalena Callao (alias Condoriana), a famous healer from Lanahuana, Cañete, consulted an unnamed outcropping of rock and employed largely Andean substances and massaging methods in the performance of her art; yet, by her own admission, she rubbed her patient "in the name of Our Father and Our Lady."[83]

It is this middle ground which is frequently labelled "syncretism." Yet the term is imprecise; its multiple associations with parallel religious systems, clean conceptual substitutions, cloaks and guises, tops and bottoms, and so on, hinder our understanding far more than they help it. While the entrance or incorporation of elements of Christianity into Andean religious thinking and practice are undeniable and are increasingly apparent in a number of spheres, these aspects of the Europeans' faith became elements in the Andean religious framework by a fluctuating agenda, varying from place to place, individual to individual, and usually without clearly eclipsing the existing religious connections. The crosses erected by the *visitadores*, near or on top of the regional *huacas*, take their place amidst these complicated realities in the midcolonial Andean religious world.

Once they had been stuck in the soil at the base of a cliff or propped up in a pile of stones in a *pueblo viejo*, and once the *visita* had moved on, the holy crosses became ambiguous monuments, supremely Christian symbols in deeply Andean contexts.[84] Their new meanings must have formed gradually, as part of a developing process.[85] The partially disfigured cross which Sarmiento found standing in the old town above Huamantanga may have meant nothing. More probably, however, it had a function and significance which remain unknown to us. In that case, ill will and procedural complications obscure any serious clues as to what the place with the cross had come to mean and what rites might have been observed there, if not by the accused, Cristóbal Chumbi Guaman, then perhaps by others. Comparable information from neighbouring regions provides some suggestive complements, even if the interpretative task remains a difficult one.

Many people who came before the *visitadores de idolatría* were conspicuously reticent about the fate of the *huacas* and of the important places that had come to the extirpators' attention and been "Christianized" by a cross and perhaps a name. Examples abound of midcolonial Indian witnesses who, having experienced previous idolatry investigations, had learned how to face an extirpator or a zealous priest. Veterans of the extirpation process grew adept at strategic silence, at concealing what would surely draw rebuke and punishment, and protecting what mattered. The meaning of the places would remain a mystery, were it not for the fact that the people's muteness and obfuscation in the face of persistent interrogation are not always as unhelpful as they might seem.

Juan Paria Vilca of Lanca in the parish of El Chorrillo, Huarochirí, for instance, was insistently questioned by Sarmiento in 1659 about a place in the Lanca ravine called *Acora* (or *Acoia*) where an earlier *visitador*, Dr. Ramírez,[86] had erected a cross. When Sarmiento asked, "Had the ancients worshiped (*mochado*) at it?," Juan answered obliquely that the Indians of El Chorrillo were angered with those of his village because the latter "spoke so freely and would confess to the Jesuits who then destroyed all the errors."[87] The man, not wishing to substantiate his neighbours' charges, remained evasive or completely silent. A year later María Chumbi Ticlla of Guancari in the parish of Quinti, Huarochirí, was denounced for her practices on a great hill named *Guaya Manco* where Francisco de Avila had raised a cross decades earlier. Although she denied it, the prosecutor, Don Diego Bartolomé, claimed that she "cried in voices in the custom of the elders and ancients," and that others, too, "cried out the ancient names on that hill." María said that she did not know if the hill had ever been a *mochadero* (a place for Andean offerings and worship). But she was conspicuously quick to deny another alarming allegation which came up against her, namely, that she and others prayed with rosaries and engaged in self-flagellation (*disciplinas*) on the hill. In her own defence, she claimed that she performed her acts of Christian penance only in her home or in the church.[88] María Casa Suyo of Quinti was similarly cryptic concerning her many visits to the place called *Guaychipan* where there was a *huaca* named *Raypa Nusca*. Although two Jesuits, Padres Salazar and Clavero, had erected crosses and consecrated the place with holy water, María disingenuously claimed not to know why the missionaries would have gone to that effort.[89] And when in 1696 Juan Saavedra y Osorio questioned the well-known ritual specialist Juan Baptista about a *huaca* marked by a cross on the road near the village of Marco in Canta, the notary recorded only "that he answered in the negative as he had done for the preceding question."[90]

The most intriguing characteristics which El Inca Garcilaso de la Vega attributed to *huacas*, as he struggled to define them for his readers and posterity, were their astonishing variety and versatility. The most illuminating single source for colonial Andean religion, the "Huarochirí Manuscript," concurs, even telling how the "visible forms" of some *huacas* might be rediscovered in colonial times.[91] Some of the crosses erected on or in place of *huacas* by the Extirpation's *diligencias* may have gradually become—if not *huacas* themselves—at least elements integrated into a religious system which was, according to place and specific conditions, deep in the process of creative change.

The reluctance of Andeans to tell of the histories and redefined significance of the Christianized shrines, springs and caves is eminently understandable. These things, like other indications of Andean religious change, were rewarded only with lashings, banishments and shame. The changes in the Indian religious world that we are documenting represent the beginnings of what we might call an Andean Christianity; but this complex entity was, by any definition, at variance with the demands of the purveyors of the official faith during the years of extirpation. The Extirpation sought to enforce a rupture with the past in the Indian communities, not only the pre-Hispanic past but also the past since the Spanish conquest, because years of religious mixture, contestation and reformulation had generated a host of new meanings in the Andean world. When Domingo García of Arahuay in Canta was imprisoned by an extirpator in the early 1740s, one of the charges against him was that he planned to smear llama's blood on the foundations and adobe walls of a new local church "to make it strong." The *provisor* in Lima asked him how a "Christian" could do such a thing; Domingo answered that it was standard procedure in constructing a church. He even noted that his forefathers had done the same when building the church at Pampacocha. Under pressure from his interrogator, Domingo eventually attempted to back down a little, claiming that this practice was only "a tradition he had acquired from his ancestors." Anyway, he assured his judge, when he had purchased a second llama for the purpose, he had been careful to offer its sacrificial blood only to the church floor.[92]

Holy crosses, patron saints, invocations, coexistent terminology and concepts, Christian penance and rites associated with feast days in both Andean and Catholic calendars—all these were becoming part of the religious activities and observances that continued at Andean religious places. This much Indian witnesses could only partially conceal, but this much most midcolonial extirpators proved unable to face. The physical excursions into the Andean hinterlands, and the destruction and strategic placement of crosses which were the material results, were meant to inspire in the Indians a final acceptance of prescribed Catholic devotions and a dread at the thought of the diabolically motivated errors of the past. The fact that, generally speaking, they did not—not even for Indian people who professed to be *cristianos*—is a reflection of the failure of the process of the Extirpation to be what its greatest proponent Pedro de Villagómez claimed it was: the ultimate antidote to suspect Andean religiosity.

The entry of Andean peoples into a deepening relationship with Catholicism began with the baptisms and teachings of the first missionaries in the sixteenth century. It continued in the day-to-day relations between priests and their Andean parishioners,[93] relations that were of little or no interest to the idolatry inspectors of the seventeenth and early eighteenth centuries. The progress of this relationship was slower in the Andes than, for example, in parts of central Mexico. The number of friars in New Spain was greater from the beginning, and—as many scholars have shown—many of their attitudes towards the evangelization of Indians had been formed in earlier, more optimistic times.[94] Moreover, in central Mexico such difficulties as the decades of civil war and immense geographical constraints, factors which were immediately present in the Andes, raised fewer obstacles to missionary endeavour. Finally, the Christianization of the Andeans was clearly not limited solely by self-imposed restraints, nor by the invincibility of Indian religious tradition, nor by a presumed recalcitrance. Andeans were active agents in the challenges that beset their world, but the particular face of the Christianity which was epitomized by the idolatry *visitas* and their *diligencias* contributed significantly to the religious outcomes. Extirpation campaigns bred a sort of natural resistance which allowed for myriad forms of religious intermixture;[95] extirpation encouraged an aversion to what was being trumpeted as official Christianity. The Extirpation's forms of coercion may also have fostered a need to withdraw and a deep distrust and hatred which would brew until an outlet was found in later rebellions.[96] And it is not so difficult to know how to interpret an indigenous response to religious investigation which is more common in the evidence from the eighteenth century, that of guarded silence. We know that in at least one region elders had learned a valuable lesson by 1725:[97] they instructed people to keep their true beliefs to themselves.

Notes

1. Matt. 28:19 and Luke 14:23 respectively. On the development of Augustine's position on punishment and restraint in the early fifth century, see P. Brown, "St. Augustine's Attitude to Religious Coercion," *Jl Roman Studies*, liv (1964), pp. 107–16; P. Brown, "Religious Coercion in the Later Roman Empire: The Case of North Africa," *History*, xlviii (1963), pp. 283–305. Pope Gregory the Great's authorization of severe measures against enemies of the faith and "false Christians" is to be found in his letter to bishop Januarius of Cagliari in July 599, quoted and discussed in W. D. McCready, *Signs of Sanctity: Miracles in the Thought of Gregory the Great* (Toronto, 1989), pp. 61–2. For the influential thoughts of Saint Thomas Aquinas on the subject of forcible conversion, see his *Summa theologiae*, Blackfriars edn, 61 vols. (London, 1963–81), xxxii, pp. 60–4 (2a.2æ. 10, 8); xxxii, pp. 74–8 (2a.2æ. 10, 12); lvii, pp. 110–14 (3a. 68, 10). On the methods and aims of the Catholic church against successive medieval heresies, see R. I. Moore, *The Birth of Popular Heresy* (London, 1975); R. I. Moore, *The Origins of European Dissent* (Oxford, 1977); M. D. Lambert, *Medieval Heresy* (London, 1977).

2. See Francisco de Vitoria, "On the American Indians (De Indis)" and "Lecture on the Evangelization of Unbelievers," in *Francisco de Vitoria, Political Writings*, ed. A. Pagden and J. Lawrance (Cambridge, 1991), pp. 233–392 and Appendix B, pp. 339–51, respectively.

3. "Capitulos de la junta eclesiástica de 1539," in J. Garcia Icazbalceta, *Don Fray Juan de Zumárraga,* 4 vols. (Colección de escritores mexicanos, xli–xliv, Mexico City, 1947), iii, pp. 149–84, cited in I. Clendinnen, "Disciplining the Indians: Franciscan Ideology and Missionary Violence in Sixteenth-Century Yucatan," *Past and Present*, no. 94 (Feb. 1982), pp. 27–48 (at p. 30). Ramón Gutiérrez has shown how, influenced by the course of evangelism in early colonial New Spain, Franciscans among the Pueblos in New Mexico employed the parental imagery of Aquinas in particular to rationalize the use of force and fear in their missions as "fatherly love": see R. Gutiérrez, *When Jesus Came, the Corn Mothers Went Away* (Stanford, 1991), pp. 74–5, also the words of Fray Antonio Margill de Jesús, quoted ibid., p. 107.

4. The progress of clerical disillusionment has been best studied in early colonial Mesoamerica: see J. L. Phelan, *The Millennial Kingdom of the Franciscans in the New World: A Study of the Writings of Gerónimo de Mendieta (1525–1604)* (Berkeley, 1956); J. A. Llaguno, *La personalidad juridica del indio y el III Concilio Provincial Mexicano 1585)* (Mexico City, 1983); I. Clendinnen, *Ambivalent Conquests: Maya and Spaniard on Yucatan, 1517–1570* (Cambridge, 1987); S. Poole, "The Declining Image of the Indian among Churchmen in Sixteenth-Century New Spain," in S. E. Ramirez (ed.), *Indian-Religious Relations in Colonial Spanish America* (Syracuse, 1989), pp. 11–19.

5. The investigations and punishments undertaken by Juan de Zumárraga (especially the condemnation of the *cacique* of Texcoco, Don Carlos Ometochtin, in 1539, but also those of his episcopal Inquisition which followed) and Diego de Landa (among the Maya of Yucatan, especially in the 1560s) are the best-documented cases in sixteenth-century Mesoamerica: see especially R. E. Greenleaf, *Zumárraga and the Mexican Inquisition, 1536–1543* (Washington, D.C., 1962); R. E. Greenleaf, *The Mexican Inquisition of the Sixteenth Century* (Albuquerque, 1969); Clendinnen, *Ambivalent Conquests*; Clendinnen, "Disci-

plining the Indians." In the south-central Andes in the mid-1560s, viceroy Francisco de Toledo dispatched Cristóbal de Albornoz to suppress an indigenous religious movement known as the *Taki Onqoy*: see L. Millones, "Un movimiento nativista del siglo XVI: el Taki Onqoy," *Revista Peruana de Cultura*, iii (1964), pp. 134–140, and Albornoz's *informaciones* in the collection of documents and articles compiled also by L. Millones, *El retorno de las huacas: estudios y documentos sobre el Taki Onqoy, siglo XVI* (Lima, 1990).

6. R. Vargas Ugarte (ed.), *Concilios Limeños (1551–1772)*, 3 vols. (Lima, 1951–4), i, pp. 11, 21–2 (Lima I, naturales 7, 26, 27), cited in S. MacCormack, "'The Heart Has its Reasons': Predicaments of Missionary Christianity in Early Colonial Peru," *Hispanic Amer. Hist. Rev.*, lxv (1985), p. 445 nn. 10, 11.

7. A number of scholars have begun exploring these themes in different regions, particularly from the angles of confession and the "interiorization" of Christian concepts and imagery: see especially Clendinnen, "Disciplining the Indians"; S. Gruzinski, "Aculturación e individualización: modalidades e impacto de la confesión entre los indios nahuas de México, siglos XVI–XVIII," *Cuadernos para la historia de la evangelización en América Latina*, i, (1986), pp. 9–33; S. Gruzinski, *The Conquest of Mexico: The Incorporation of Indian Societies into the Western World, 16th–18th Centuries*, trans. E. Corrigan (Oxford, 1993), esp. pp. 195–200 (orig. pubd. as *La colonisation de l'imaginaire: sociétés indigènes et occidentalisation dans la Mexique espagnol, XVIe–XVIIIe siécles*, Paris, 1988); J. J. Klor de Alva, "Colonizing Souls: The Failure of the Indian Inquisition and the Rise of Penitential Discipline," in M. E. Perry and A. J. Cruz (eds.), *Cultural Encounters: The Impact of the Inquisition in Spain and the New World* (Berkeley, 1991), pp. 3–22; J. J. Klor de Alva, "Sahagún and the Birth of Modern Ethnography: Representing, Confessing, and Inscribing the Native Other," in J. J. Klor de Alva, H. B. Nicholson and E. Quiñones Keber (eds.), *The Work of Bernardino de Sahagún* (Austin, 1988), pp. 31–52; M. Barnes, "Catechisms and *Confesionarios*: Distorting Mirrors of Andean Societies," in R. V. H. Dover, K. E. Seibold and J. H. McDowell (eds.), *Andean Cosmologies Through Time: Persistence and Emergence* (Bloomington, 1992), pp. 67–94; Gutiérrez, *When Jesus Came*, chs. 2, 3 (on Franciscan procedures among the Pueblos in New Mexico).

8. For more on the methodological debts of the Peruvian process to, and deviations from, the Holy Office of the Inquisition, see P. Duviols's long preface, "De la inquisición a la extirpación," to the compilation of documents *Cultura andina y represión: procesos y visitas de idolatría y hechicerías, Cajatambo, siglo XVII*, ed. P. Duviols (Archivos de historia andina, v, Cusco, 1986). On these themes, see also I. Gareis, "Extirpación de idolatrías e Inquisición en el virreinato del Perú," *Boletín del Instituto Riva-Agüero*, xvi (1989), pp. 55–74; A. Acosta Rodríguez, "Los doctrineros y la extirpación de la religión indígena en el arzobispado de Lima, 1600–1620," *Jahrbuch für Geschichte von Staat, Wirtschaft und Gesellschaft Lateinamerikas*, xix (1982), pp. 69–109 (arguing for less attention to be paid to European and Inquisitorial precedents); A. Acosta, "La extirpación de las idolatrías en el Perú: origen y desarollo de las campañas. A propósito de *Cultura andina y represión* de Pierre Duviols," *Revista Andina*, ix, no. 1 (July 1987) pp. 171–195. Most recently, Ana Sánchez offers a welcome realignment of opinions in her meandering introduction to *Amancebados, hechiceros y rebeldes (Chancay, siglo XVII)*, ed. A. Sánchez (Archivos de historia andina, xi, Cusco, 1991), a transcription of regional idolatry documentation which complements *Cultura andina y represión*, ed. Duviols.

9. This is not the place to survey the range of representations of "syncretism" in this part of colonial Spanish America or beyond. Some of the best work treats

the Mesoamerican setting. A useful synthesis and a way forward are offered in W. B. Taylor, *Magistrates of the Sacred: Priests and Parishioners in Eighteenth-Century Mexico* (Stanford, 1998), ch. 3. A complex process of religious "reconstruction, adaptation and fusion" in the context of indigenous response to diverse forms of Christianization is evocatively portrayed in Nancy Farriss, *Maya Society under Colonial Rule*, chs. 10, 11 (Princeton, 1984); see also the conclusions in Nancy Farriss, "Indians in Colonial Yucatan: Three Perspectives," in M. J. McLeod and R. Wasserstrom (eds.), *Spaniards and Indians in Southeastern Mesoamerica: Essays on the History of Ethnic Relations* (Lincoln, Neb., 1983), esp. pp. 33–4.

10. See the suggestive remarks of Elizabeth Wilder Weismann describing (and showing) a similarly fluid process of change in Mexico: E. Wilder Weismann, *Art and Time in Mexico: From the Conquest to the Revolution* (New York, 1985), esp. p. 10. I am indebted to Scott Sessions for the insights he has shared with me during our discussions of this book.

11. The most important Peruvian precedent was the investigation of Albornoz into the *Taki Onqoy* (see n. 5 above). On the influence of an ambitious parish priest from Huarochirí, Francisco de Avila, on the changing climate of opinion in official circles in early seventeenth-century Lima, see especially A. Acosta, "Francisco de Avila, Cusco 1573(?) - Lima 1647," in *Ritos y tradiciones de Huarochirí: manuscrito quechua de comienzos del siglo XVII*, ed. and trans. G. Taylor (Lima, 1987), pp. 551–616. More generally, see P. Duviols, *La lutte contre les réligions autochtones dans le Pérou colonial* (Lima, 1971), which I have used in Spanish translation: P. Duviols, *La destrucción de las religiones andinas*, trans. A. Maruenda (Mexico City, 1977).

12. I follow Pierre Duviols in capitalizing "Extirpation" in order to differentiate between the institutionalized seventeenth-century initiative and the more general act of extirpation: see Duviols, "De la inquisición a la extirpación."

13. An adequate study comparing New Spain and Peru in light of these differences remains to be written. The most important of the treatises and manuals to which I refer are: A. de Olmos, *Tratado de hechicerías y sortilegios*, ed. and trans. G. Baudot (Mexico City, 1979); H. Ruiz de Alarcón, "Tratado de las supersticiones y costumbres gentilicas que hoy viven entre los indios naturales desta Nueva España" (1629), in *Tratado de las idolatrías, supersticiones, dioses, ritos, hechicerías y otras costumbres, gentilicias de las razas aborígenes de México*, ed. F. del Paso y Troncoso, 2nd edn, 2 vols. (Mexico City, 1953), ii, pp. 17–180, or in the better of the two available English translations, *The Treatise of Ruiz de Alarcón*, ed. and trans. J. R. Andrews and R. Hassig (Norman, 1984); Pedro Ponce, "Breve relación de los dioses y ritos de la gentilidad," in *Tratado de las idolatrías*, ed. Paso y Troncoso, i, pp. 369–80; J. de la Serna, "Manual de ministros de indios para el conocimiento de sus idolatrías y extirpación de ellas" (1656), in *Colección de documentos inéditos para la historia de España*, 112 vols. (Madrid, 1842–95), civ, pp. 1–267. Fascinating, if differing, discussions of the religious information in the works of Ruiz de Alarcón and Serna especially are pursued by Taylor, *Magistrates of the Sacred*, ch. 3, and by Gruzinski, *Conquest of Mexico*, pp. 147–83.

14. I refer to a few earlier instances of sporadic persecution in n. 5 above.

15. Until recently, the midcentury period has been largely neglected, by comparison with the era of the Extirpation's beginnings under Archbishop Bartolomé Lobo Guerrero (1609–22). *Cultura andina y represión*, ed. Duviols, made accessible a number of fascinating midcentury trials from the province of Cajatambo, a trend continued by the collection from Chancay, *Amancebados, hechiceros y rebeldes*, ed. Sánchez. For interpretations of parts of the Cajatambo material, see

S. MacCormack, *Religion in the Andes: Vision and Imagination in Early Colonial Peru* (Princeton, 1991), ch. ix; K. R. Mills, *An Evil Lost to View? An Investigation of Post-Evangelization Andean Religion in Mid-Colonial Peru* (Univ. of Liverpool Monograph Ser., xviii, Liverpool, 1994); M. E. Doyle, "The Ancestor Cult and Burial Ritual in Seventeenth- and Eighteenth-Century Central Peru" (Univ. of California, Los Angeles, Ph.D. thesis, 1988).

16. I refer to the opinions and criticisms of the *alcalde del crimen*, Juan de Padilla; the priest and examiner in the languages of Quechua and Aymara from the Cusco region, Juan Pérez Bocanegra; the bishop of La Paz, Feliciano de Vega; the bishop of Quito, Alonso de la Peña Montenegro; and Villagómez's sceptical Creole predecessor in the see of Lima, Hernando Arias de Ugarte. See especially the treatises of J. Pérez Bocanegra, *Ritual formulario e institución de curas para administrar a los naturales de este reyno* (Lima, 1631); A. de la Peña Montenegro, *Itinerario para parochos de indios* (Madrid, 1668).

17. Some padres felt that their collaboration with the *visitadores'* punitive actions was undermining their position as trusted confessors and missionaries in the eyes of the Indians: see the interpretations of R. Vargas Ugarte, *Historia de la Iglesia en el Perú*, 5 vols. (Lima and Burgos, 1953–62), iii, pp. 9–11; Duviols, *Destrucción de las religiones andinas*, pp. 225–30. Although an equivalent of the Extirpation did not materialize in seventeenth-century New Spain, a similar oscillation and multiplicity of opinion can be detected there: see Gruzinski, *Conquest of Mexico*, ch. 4, esp. pp. 147–8.

18. See n. 16 above.

19. P. Duviols has suggested that the exemplary punishment and exile of "idolatrous" leaders by the Extirpation accomplished exactly the opposite of what was intended: Duviols, "De la inquisición a la extirpación," p. lxxvi.

20. P. de Villagómez, *Carta pastoral de exortación e instrucción acerca de las idolatrías de los indios del arzobispado de Lima* (1649), ed. H. H. Urteaga (Colección de libros y documentos referentes a la historia del Perú, 1st ser., xii, Lima, 1919), passim.

21. Most of the idolatry investigations conformed to a pattern. A Spaniard—or occasionally a Hispanicized Indian—prosecutor (*fiscal*) assisted the *visitador* in making the principal charges, apprehending offenders and gathering witnesses. Although many priest-*visitadores* understood (to varying degrees) the kind of Quechua spoken by most of the declarants, an interpreter was usually present. He was often a cooperative Indian assigned by the *visitador* to travel with the *visita* for a time, though he might instead be the *fiscal* performing double duty. A notary, familiar with the established pattern of procedure, completed the official entourage. It was not uncommon for a number of local officials to establish themselves as key informants and "friends of the *visita*." Their motives were potentially many, but their concern for self-protection is frequently easy to discern. Observing the lessons of Inquisition procedure, these latter figures were the very "opening wedges" that in 1621 the shrewd Arriaga had deemed essential for the Extirpation's success: J. de Arriaga, *La extirpación de la idolatría en el Perú*, ed. H. H Urteaga (Colección de libros y documentos referentes a la historia del Perú, 2nd ser., i, Lima, 1920), pp. 132–6. For more on the pattern of Extirpation procedure, Duviols, *Destrucción de las religiones andinas*, ch. 3, is still indispensable. The imitation of Inquisition methods, adjusted to suit Indian offenders, is clear: see H. C. Lea, *A History of the Inquisition in Spain*, 4 vols. (New York, 1906–7), iii, bk 7, esp. ch. 5, H. C. Lea, *A History of the Inquisition of the Middle Ages*, 3 vols. (New York, 1888), i, chs. 9, 12–14; H. Kamen, *Inquisition and Society in Spain in the Sixteenth and Seventeenth Centuries* (Bloomington, 1985), ch. 10. See also n. 8 above.

22. The public nature of the punishment of Andean rebels and religious offenders had roots, not only in Europe, but in symbolic castigations in sixteenth-century Peru. For a discussion of the execution of the last Inka rebel Tupac Amaru in 1572, and on the processions of shame used by Albornoz in his suppression of *Taki Onqoy*, see MacCormack, *Religion in the Andes*, pp. 249–54.

23. These practitioners were healers, diviners and workers of various kinds of "magic." The rites they performed might involve offerings to Andean gods; indeed, many of the specialists were also ministers.

24. S. Gruzinski, "Le filet déchiré: sociétés indigènes, occidentalisation et domination dans le Mexique central, XVIe–XVIIIe siècles" (Univ. of Paris, doctoral thesis, 1986), pp. 254, 289, cited and supported in F. Cervantes, "Christianity and the Indians in Early Modern Mexico: The Native Response to the Devil," *Hist. Research*, lxvi (1993), p. 181. A considerably shorter recent adaptation of Gruzinski's thesis is to be found in his *Conquest of Mexico*.

25. Such examples abound; see, for example, the recollections of Francisco de Avila as "he who destroyed and burnt everything," and who directed destructive missions from San Damián, in Quinti, Huarochirí in 1660: Archivo Arzobispal de Lima (hereafter A.A.L.), Legajo 2, Expediente 21, fo. 8^r; ibid., Leg. 4, Exp. 32, fo. 7^r; or the memory in Xapallanga, Jauja in 1665 of punishments meted out by Diego Barreto de Castro: A.A.L., Leg. 5, Exp. 11, fo. 1^r. (I use archival classifications in use in 1989–90, during the directorship of Mario Ormeño. The classification of the "Hechicerías e Idolatrías" section of the A.A.L. has recently been changed under the new director. See her published catalogue: Laura Guttiérrez Arbulú, "Indice de la sección hechicerías e idolatrías del Archivo Arzobispal de Lima," in G. Ramos and H. Urbano (comps.), *Catolicismo y extirpación de idolatrías, siglos XVI–XVII* (Cusco, 1993) pp. 105–36.) There is a sad similarity here to the way that contemporary Andean peoples in the Ayacucho region (and doubtless in many other areas) identify negative "epochs" in their recent past, so marred by both guerrilla and army violence. I was prompted to make this comparison by B. J. Isbell, "The Texts and Contexts of Terror in Peru," in R. Howard-Malverde and W. Rowe (eds.), *Textuality in Amerindian Cultures: Production, Reception, Strategies* (Oxford, forthcoming).

26. Arriaga, *Extirpación de idolatría en el Perú* (a detailed guide to an optimal *visita* procedure in 1621) was endorsed and added to by Villagómez in his *Carta pastoral de exortación e instrucción* of 1649.

27. See particularly the contemporary and widely disseminated sermons of H. de Avendaño: *Sermones de los misterios de nuestra santa fe católica en lengua castellana y en la general del Inca impugnanse los errores particulares que los indios han tenido* (Lima, 1649). A less well-known and more eccentric set of contemporary anti-idolatry texts is F. de Avila, *Tratado de los evangelios que nuestra Madre la Iglesia nos propone en todo el año* (Lima, 1648).

28. For a good discussion of the European "canon" in relation to the interpretations of Bartolomé de Las Casas, see A. R. Pagden, "*Ius et Factum*: Text and Experience in the writings of Bartolomé de Las Casas," *Representations*, no. 33 (Winter 1991), pp. 147–62; and for a development of this theme, see A. R. Pagden, *European Encounters with the New World* (New Haven, 1993). L. Burkhart, *The Slippery Earth: Nahua-Christian Moral Dialogue* (Tucson, 1989), is illuminating on the challenges of language and concepts in the evangelization of the Nahuas in New Spain.

29. For an interesting interpretation of "idolatry" and "superstition" in the Maya belief system of colonial Yucatan, see Farriss, *Maya Society under Colonial Rule*, esp. pp. 287–93, 317–18. Even the term "religion," which most mod-

ern historians apply—in one way or another—to the intellectual frameworks, expressions and practices of Indian peoples, can be misleading without careful definition; there is insightful discussion of all that might constitute "colonial Catholicism" in Taylor, *Magistrates of the Sacred*, esp. preface and ch. 3. In a provocative representation of "the Indian view of things" in colonial New Spain, S. Gruzinski defends "idolatry" as the least restrictive and problematic among the host of unsatisfactory terms: Gruzinski, *Conquest of Mexico*, esp. pp. 150–1, 170–2.

30. In the colonial era, at least, the ministers and the ritual practitioners were often the same people.

31. Avendaño, *Sermones de los misterios de nuestra santa fe católica*, sermon II, fo. 20[b]. Other common spellings of *huaca* include *wak'a* and *guaca*. On these beings, see F. Salomon, "Introductory Essay," in *The Huarochirí Manuscript: A Testament of Ancient and Colonial Andean Religion*, ed. and trans. F. Salomon and G. L. Urioste (Austin, 1991), esp. pp. 16–19.

32. Avendaño, *Sermones de los misterios de nuestra santa fe católica*, sermon V, fo. 62[a–b]. The more common name for similar modern figures in the southern Andes is *illa*: see the insightful essay by J. A. Flores Ochoa, "*Enqa, enqaychu, illa y khuyma rwill*," in J. A. Flores Ochoa (ed.), *Pastores de puna uywamichq punarunakuna* [Pastoralists of the High Andes] (Lima, 1977), pp. 211–37.

33. The elders were to be made all the more conspicuous by the wooden crosses hung round their necks: Villagómez, *Carta pastoral de exortación e instrucción*, chs. lxiii–lxiv (ed. Urteaga, pp. 250–2). The employment of instruction as punishment was common for the Inquisition among, for instance, Morisco religious offenders in sixteenth-century Spain: see H. C. Lea, *The Moriscos of Spain: Their Conversion and Expulsion* (New York, 1901), p. 115.

34. See the Map for the locations of these and other places discussed. I am grateful to C. Brest for its preparation.

35. A.A.L., Leg. 6, Exp. 9, Cajatambo, Cajatambo, 1652, fo. 2[r–v].

36. A.A.L., Leg. 3, Exp. 9, fos. 14 ff.

37. A.A.L., Leg. 3, Exp. 10, Santiago de Maray, Checras, 1724–5, fo. 12[r] and fos. 7[v]–8[v], 8[v] respectively. The man claimed to be 115 years old.

38. On the population decline, see N. D. Cook, *Demographic Collapse: Indian Peru, 1520–1620* (Cambridge, 1981), esp. chs. 9, 11, 12; Andean reciprocity and land use is described by J. V. Murra, *Formaciones económicas y politicas del mundo andino* (Lima, 1975), esp. ch. 3. On the Toledan resettlement programme, see A. Málaga Medina, "Las reducciones en el Perú," *Historia y cultura*, viii (1974), pp. 141–72; on the complicated roles of Andean *kurakas* as intermediaries, see especiallly Karen Spalding, "El kuraka en el sistema de producción andina," in S. Moreno Yañez and F. Salomon (eds.), *Reproducción y transformación de las sociedades andinas, siglos XVI–XX* (Quito, 1991), pp. 401–14; S. Stern, *Peru's Indian Peoples and the Challenge of Spanish Conquest: Huamanga to 1640* (Madison, 1982), ch. 2.

39. On the breakdown of the *república de indios* in different settings, see M. Mörner, "The Segregation Policy of the Colonial State," in M. Mörner, *Region and State in Latin America's Past* (Johns Hopkins Symposia in Comp. Hist., xxi, Baltimore, 1993), pp. 19–32. On the transfer of more diverse forms of Spanish Catholicism in the viceroyalty of New Spain, see the interpretations of Gruzinski, *Conquest of Mexico*, esp. pp. 197–200; Cervantes, "Christianity and the Indians"; and, more expansively, F. Cervantes, *The Devil in the New World: The Impact of Diabolism in New Spain* (New Haven, 1994), chs. 1, 2. Even further afield, Richard White, *The Middle Ground: Indians, Empires and Republics in the Great*

Lakes Region, 1650–1815 (Cambridge, 1991), though concerned principally with the very different context of Indian-French relations in the *pays d'en haut*, is an interesting exploration of cultural exchange and re-creation.

40. For an interesting contemplation of the meaning of architecture and town foundation for Spanish builders, friars and residents, see V. Fraser, *The Architecture of Conquest: Building in the Viceroyalty of Peru, 1535–1635* (Cambridge, 1990). Important connections between urbanization and evangelization were convincingly made almost fifty years ago by George Kubler, *Mexican Architecture of the Sixteenth Century*, 2 vols. (New Haven, 1948), esp. i, pp. 68–104. This work adds valuably to the discussion of missionary methods by R. Ricard, *La "conquête spirituelle" du Mexique* (Paris, 1933), available in English translation by L. B. Simpson, *The Spiritual Conquest of Mexico: An Essay on the Apostolate and the Evangelizing Methods of the Mendicant Orders in New Spain, 1523–1572* (Berkeley, 1966).

41. There is not space here to explain in sufficient detail the people's connections to these places. Many of them formed part of pre-Hispanic settlement patterns known as *llacta*. An admirable introduction to Andean landholding, kinship and reciprocity is to be found in Salomon, "Introductory Essay," esp. pp. 21–3.

42. A.A.L., Leg. 4, Exp. 26, fo. 1^{r-v}. Indian desertions of the seventeenth-century *reducciones* are emphasized in Irene Silverblatt, *Moon, Sun and Witches: Gender Ideologies and Class in Inca and Colonial Peru* (Princeton, 1987), esp. chs. 9, 10. On developments to the southeast, see A. M. Wightman, *Indigenous Migration and Social Change: The Forasteros of Cuzco, 1520–1720* (Durham, N.C., 1990). Similar situations are described in colonial Guatemala by W. G. Lovell, *Conquest and Survival in Colonial Guatemala: A Historical Geography of the Cuchumatán Highlands, 1500–1821*, rev. edn (Montreal and Kingston, 1992), esp. pp. 82–9.

43. This is becoming more evident as scholars digest both the collection of religious information from Huarochirí and the idolatry trial information from the Lima region as a whole. For the former, see *Ritos y tradiciones de Huarochirí*, ed. and trans. Taylor; *Huarochirí Manuscript*, ed. and trans. Salomon and Urioste.

44. See the works cited in n. 4 above. I am indebted to William Taylor for encouraging me to reflect on the comparison elaborated in this paragraph. A number of the ideas I express were spurred by our correspondence on the subject.

45. Sarmiento was fifty-six years old in 1664, the year in which the events to be described below occurred; his age was about average for an idolatry inspector active in the time of Archbishop Villagómez. Of noble Spanish stock in Lima (according to papers presented to the Council of the Indies by his brother Jerónimo, an ancestor had participated in the military conquest of Peru), he was educated by the Jesuits and ordained in 1637 at the age of twenty-nine. He want on to obtain a bachelor's degree in canon law from the Royal University of San Marcos in 1653. In addition to spending a number of years as chaplain to the Convent of the Incarnation in Lima, Sarmiento accepted from his prelate at least two commissions as *visitador general* (in 1649 to visit the diocese of Huamanga and in 1655 as inspector of the archdiocese of Lima). He was named *visitador de idolatría* in 1660. Sarmiento was atypical in not having served as a priest (*doctrinero*) in an Indian parish before his participation in the Extirpation. See Archivo General de Indias, Seville, Audiencia de Lima 303, Villagómez to king, Lima, 28 Aug. 1658, Villagómez to king, Lima, 8 June 1663; ibid., 304, Villagómez to king, Lima, 5 Dec. 1664.

46. Sarmiento de Vivero was Villagómez's busiest idolatry inspector. Of some fifty-four *visitas* which he conducted in the Lima region, seven (all from the

colonial district of Chancay) are transcribed in *Amancebados, hechiceros y rebeldes*, ed. Sánchez. Many accounts of other inspectors' *diligencias* come only from the more detached and self-congratulatory medium of letters and *informaciones de servicios* written after the fact. As with so many colonial officials, *visitadores* often filled these accounts with boasts of their zeal and of the beneficial results of their services; see, for example, the case of Bernardo de Novoa reported in the document in Archivo General de Indias, Audiencia de Lima 333 printed in *Cultura andina y represión*, ed. Duviols, pp. 423–35.

47. A.A.L., Leg. 1, Exp. 3, fol 11^v (the governor or *kuraka*); fos. 1^{r-v} (Ana María).

48. What the people called the flowers was rendered only in Castilian as "anto con las hojas": ibid., fo. 3^v.

49. Ibid., fos. 3^v–4^r.

50. This took place on 8 October 1664. The elaborate process is recorded in some detail at ibid., fos. 17^v–19^r.

51. Ibid., fo. 8^r.

52. Ibld., fo. 10^r.

53. They reportedly sang, "Vicho Rinri papa [potato], Vicho Rinri oca [another edible South American tuber, either *Oxalis O. crenata* or *O. tuberosa*]" ibid., fo. 10^{r-v}. "Rinri" means ear, and "Vicho" or "Vichu" could be what the lexicographer of Quechua, Diego González Holguin, calls "Vicçu," meaning "tuerto" in colonial Spanish, or "twisted (either inside out or back to front)" in English. It is possible that the notary, who, along with the *visitador*, had the features of this anthropormorphic god's "head" explained to him, may have taken a description of a distorted feature to be the name of the deity; or the *huaca* may simply have had an ear that was twisted. Yet the mention of the song that included the name, along with what we can know about other *huaca* names in the region, suggests otherwise. A possible—if crude—translation of the *huaca*'s name might thus be "Twisted Ear." See D. González Holguin, *Vocabulario de la lengua general de todo el Perú llamada lengua qquichua o del Inca*, 3rd edn, ed. R. Matos Mendieta (Lima, 1989), pp. 318, 351. (I am grateful to Frank Salomon for help in arriving at these suggestions.) A number of regional *huaca* histories (often called *tradiciones* in the documentation from the idolatry trials) about similar beings and places interlace *Huarochirí Manuscript*, ed. and trans. Salomon and Urioste.

54. A.A.L., Leg. 1, Exp. 3, fols. 10^v–11^r. On 24 June 1664, a similarly equipped party was led along the royal road towards Canta to yet another great stone embedded in a hill. Since this *huaca* proved impossible to topple, a cross was erected and the spot was appropriately named after Saint John the Baptist: ibid., fos. 11^r–12^r.

55. See especially R. A. Markus, "Gregory the Great and a Papal Missionary Strategy," in G. J. Cuming (ed.), *The Mission of the Church and the Propagation of the Faith* (Studies in Church Hist., vi, Cambridge, 1970), pp. 29–38.

56. The details of the confrontation are at A.A.L., Leg. 1, Exp. 3, fo. 8^r; see also ibid., fos. 6^r–7^r (Ana María's denunciation).

57. Pedro de Quijano Zevallos conducted an eventful *visita* in Huamantanga in 1656: see A.A.L., Leg. 2, Exp. 11.

58. A.A.L., Leg. 1, Exp. 3, fo. 8^{r-v}. This case is made even more interesting by the fact that both Ana María and Cristóbal escaped from Huamantanga and sought to influence the proceedings by appealing to Archbishop Villagómez in Lima. We learn that pre-existing enmity had motivated Ana María's denunciation to the *visitador*, thus increasing the possibility that Cristóbal had been wrongfully accused. See A.A.L., Leg. 1, Exp. 1, 1664.

59. A.A.L., Leg. 5. The main *diligencias* were conducted on 25 and 30 August. Each of the stops on this "tour" of the community's *huacas* can be examined in the transcription in *Amancebados, hechiceros y rebeldes*, ed. Sánchez, pp. 67–71.

60. A.A.L., Leg. 5, Exp. 5, fo. 4[v].

61. Ibid., fo. 1[v].

62. Following Arriaga's recommendations, Villagómez argues that the *visitas* in the Indian parishes, including whatever punishments and destruction of Andean *sacra* proved necessary, should be repeated: Villagómez, *Carta pastoral de exortación e instrucción*, ed. Urteaga, esp. pp. 25–33, 80–5, 105–26.

63. It was common for small, smooth stones to be included in offerings to mountain *huacas*: see, for example, A.A.L., Leg. 4, Exp. 8, Carhuamayo Junin, Felipe Nuna Vilca (at fo. 2[r]), transcribed in K. R. Mills, "Persistencia religiosa en Santiago de Carhuamayo (Junin), 1631," in Martin Lienhard (ed.), *Testimonios, cartas y manifiestos indígenas (época colonial y primer periódo republicano)* (Caracas, 1992), pp. 222–31 (at pp. 227–8).

64. A.A.L., Leg. 5, Exp. 5, fos. 4[v]–5[r]. The cross had been erected by the parish priest, Gregorio de Utrilla.

65. A.A.L., Leg. 3, Exp. 11, 1725, fo. 6[r].

66. On what ensued with the image, see Mills, *Evil Lost to View?*, pp. 61–83.

67. I am indebted to Peter Brown for sharing with me his knowledge of similar extirpation methods in late antique and early Christian Europe and stimulating me to explore this possibility further.

68. See A.A.L., Leg. 7, Exp. 1, Lunahuana, Cañete, fo. 4[r].

69. See, for instance, Sarmiento's recorded confrontation with a massive stone outside Andacoto in Canta: A.A.L., Leg. 4, Exp. 22, Atavillos, Canta, 1659, fos. 1[v]–2[r].

70. A.A.L., Leg. 2, Exp. 18, San Pedro de Pilas, Yauyos, fos. 24[r]–26[r].

71. See A. M. Wightman,"Diego Vasicuio: Native Priest," in D. G. Sweet and G. B Nash (eds.), *Struggle and Survival in Colonial America* (Berkeley, 1981), pp. 38–48; F. Salomon, "Ancestor Cults and Resistance to the State in Arequipa, ca. 1748–1754," in S. J. Stern (ed.), *Resistance, Rebellion and Consciousness in the Andean Peasant World, 18th to 20th Centuries* (Madison, 1987), pp. 148–65.

72. For accounts of careful Jesuit actions in Cajatambo and Huamanga, see Archivum Romanum Societatis Iesu, Rome, Carta annua de 1664, 1665 y 1666, Peru 16, T. V, fos. 108[r] and 138[r] respectively. For Guaman Pilpi's testimony, see *Cultura andina y represión*, ed. Duviols, p. 185. On the divine energy, *camaquen*, that extirpators frequently glossed as "soul" or "spirit," see especially P. Duviols, "*Camaquen upani*: un concept animiste des anciens peruviens," in R. Hartmann and U. Oberem (eds.), *Estudios americanistas: libro jubilar en homenaje Hermann Trimborn con motivo de su septuagesimoquinto aniversario*, 2 vols. (Collectanea Instituti Anthropos, xx–xxi, St. Augustin, 1978–9), i, pp. 132–44.

73. See H. de Avendaño, *Sermones de los misterios de nuestra santa fe católica*, sermon II, fos 20[a]–21[b]. For more on the intended symbol, the cross as Christ's victory, see G. Aulen, *Christus Victor: An Historical Study of the Three Main Types of the Idea of Atonement* (New York, 1969).

74. Pagden, *European Encounters with the New World*, pp. 17–49, esp. p. 27.

75. Bernal Diaz del Castillo, *The Conquest of New Spain*, trans. J. M. Cohen (Harmondsworth, 1963), p. 137.

76. Gutiérrez, *When Jesus Came*, pp. 82–3. For a more nuanced discussion of the possible meanings of crosses and crucifixes to sixteenth-century Mexican Indians, see I. Clendinnen, "Ways to the Sacred: Reconstructing 'Religion' in Sixteenth-Century Mexico," *Hist. and Anthropology*, v (1990), pp. 128–9.

77. Gutiérrez, *When Jesus Came*, p. 82. On methods in New Spain in general, see Ricard, *Spiritual Conquest of Mexico*. Gutiérrez, *When Jesus Came*, offers but one example of the common search for compatibility between Indian and European beliefs and practices to help in the explanation of gradual Christianization. An interesting, much earlier example of the approach is U. Lamb, "Religious Conflicts in the Conquest of Mexico," *Jl Hist. Ideas*, xvii (1956), pp. 526–39 (I owe this reference to David Johnson). For an emphasis on the "predisposition" of the Indians to convert, see also S. Cline, "The Spiritual Conquest Reexamined: Baptism and Christian Marriage in Early Sixteenth-Century Mexico," *Hispanic Amer. Hist. Rev.*, lxxiii (1993), esp. p. 477; J. Lockhart, *The Nahuas after the Conquest: A Social and Cultural History of the Indians of Central Mexico, Sixteenth through Eighteenth Centuries* (Stanford, 1992), pp. 203–4.

78. Similar "degrees" of religious change in colonial Mexico are discussed by Gruzinski, *Conquest of Mexico*, esp. ch. 4 passim and pp. 178–80.

79. On the diabolic aspect of contemporary European perceptions, see the brilliant (and remarkably concise) remarks by J. H. Elliott, "The Discovery of America and the Discovery of Man," in his *Spain and its World, 1500–1700: Selected Essays* (New Haven, 1989), pp. 42–64, esp. pp. 59–60 (first pubd as the 1972 Raleigh Lecture, *Proc. Brit. Acad.*, xlviii (1972), pp. 101-25). More generally, see J. H. Elliott, *The Old World and the New, 1492–1650* (Cambridge, 1970), chs. 1, 2, esp. pp. 14–27.

80. Factionalism is stressed in many studies of post-evangelization Indian societies; see, for example, R. A. Gutiérrez on the Pueblos of the 1660s and 1670s: Gutiérrez, *When Jesus Came*, pp. 123–4.

81. Idolatry accusations often became channels for ill will, self-interest and local political disputes. See the work of A. Acosta Rodríguez on an earlier period in the Extirpation's history, especially "Doctrineros y la extirpación."

82. Francisco Poma y Altas and Juan Raura, in *Cultura andina y represión*, ed. Duviols, pp. 189 and 192 respectively. For further discussion, see Mills, *Evil Lost to View?*, pp. 105–26.

83. The words came in response to the *visitador* Sarmiento de Vivero's query: "What words had she said when she was rubbing . . .?" Warm wine was the one non-Andean element used in her healing rituals. See A.A.L., Leg. 7 Exp. 1, fo. 26^{r-v}. For an interesting survey of the mixing medical traditions, and of the intellectual and practical world in which contemporary urban healers in Peru lived, see F. Iwasaki Cauti, "Fray Martín de Porras: santo, ensalmador y sacamuelas," *Colonial Latin Amer. Rev.*, iii (1994), pp. 159–84.

84. For a synthetic interpretation of the symbol's accumulated meanings in current Andean society, see J. L. González, *El huanca y la cruz: creatividad y autonomía en la religión popular* (Lima, 1989), esp. pp. 43–85.

85. S. Gruzinski's idea that post-conquest Indian painting in New Spain demonstrates an "identity in gestation" conceptualizes a similar state of flux: Gruzinski *Conquest of Mexico*, p. 26.

86. Diego Ramirez was commissioned at the same time as Hernando de Avendaño and was at his busiest in the second decade of the seventeenth century: see Duviols, *Destrucción de las religiones andinas*, pp. 187, 289–90, and the comments on his diligence in Arriaga, *Extirpación de la idolatría en el Perú*, ed. Urteaga, pp. 8–10.

87. A.A.L., Leg. 6, Exp. 14, fo. 4^r.

88. See A.A.L., Leg. 2, Exp. 22, one small loose folio, unnumbered, and fo. 2^r.

89. A.A.L., *legajo* and *expediente* unnumbered, San Lorenzo de Quinti, Huarochirí, 1660, fo. 9^v. The trial proceedings took place between 12 March and 23 May 1660.

90. A.A.L., Leg. 5, Exp. 25, fo. 14^{r-v}.

91. Garcilosa de la Vega, *Royal Commentaries of the Incas and General History of Peru* (1609), trans. H. V. Livermore, 2 vols. (Austin, 1966), bk 2, chs. 4, 5; *Huarochirí Manuscript*, ed. and trans. Salomon and Urioste, ch. 20. On the possibility of colonial *huacas* with localized, recent histories, see the arguments of Gary Urton, *The History of a Myth: Pacariqtambo and the Origin of the Inkas* (Austin, 1990).

92. A.A.L., Leg. 3, Exp. 17, 1741–2, fos. 2^{r-v}, 6^{v}, 7^{r}.

93. For a beginning, though with later emphases, see C. Hunefeldt, "Comunidad, curas y comuneros hacia fines del periódo colonial:ovejas y pastores indomados en el Perú," *Hisla*, no. 2 (1983), pp. 3–31; D. Cahill, "Curas and Social Conflict in the Doctrinas of Cuzco, 1780–1814," *Jl Latin Amer. Studies*, xvi (1984), pp. 241–76. For a particularly rich treatment of these relations in late colonial Mexico, see Taylor, *Magistrates of the Sacred*.

94. See especially Ricard, *Spiritual Conquest of Mexico*; Phelan, *Millennial Kingdom of the Franciscans in the New World*; E. Sylvest, *Motifs of Franciscan Mission Theory in Sixteenth-Century New Spain* (Washington, D.C. 1975); L. Gómez Canedo, *Evangelización y conquista: experiencia franciscana en Hispanoamérica* (Mexico City, 1977).

95. For S. J. Stern's reflections on resistance, see his essay, "New Approaches to the Study of Peasant Rebellion and Consciousness: Implications of the Andean Experience" in Stern (ed.), *Resistance, Rebellion and Consciousness*, pp. 3–25. J. Lockhart has also recommended a careful employment of categories like "resistance" and "conversion" in the case of the post-conquest central Mexico: Lockhart, *Nahuas after the Conquest*, p. 203. Many possible forms of insubordination are explored in a broad comparative context by J. C. Scott, *Domination and the Arts of Resistance: Hidden Transcripts* (New Haven, 1990).

96. Amid a growing literature, see Stern, "New Approaches to the Study of Peasant Rebellion and Consciousness"; J. Szeminski, "Why Kill a Spaniard? New Perspectives on the Andean Insurrectionary Ideology in the 18th Century," in Stern (ed.), *Resistance, Rebellion and Consciousness*, pp. 166–91. The work of Scarlett O'Phelan Godoy and David Cahill is particularly instructive: see especially S. O'Phelan Godoy, *Rebellions and Revolts in Eighteenth-Century Peru and Upper Peru* (Cologne, 1985); Cahill, "Curas and Social Conflict"; D. Cahill and S. O'Phelan Godoy, "Forging their Own History: Indian Insurgency in the Southern Peruvian Sierra, 1815," *Bull. Latin Amer. Research*, xi (1992), pp. 125–67.

97. See evidence from San Juan de Churin in A.A.L., Leg. 3, Exp. 11, 1725, fos. 4^{r}, 9^{v}, 10^{r}.

III

Cultural Issues

8

Native Icon to City Protectress to Royal Patroness: Ritual, Political Symbolism, and the Virgin of Remedies[1]

Linda A. Curcio-Nagy

Devotion to the Virgin Mary was an important aspect of Spanish popular religion. With the evangelization of the New World, Mary was implanted along with other aspects of Spanish Christianity. Linda Curcio-Nagy traces the history of the cult of the Virgen de los Remedios in early colonial Mexico—a cult intimately associated with the conqueror Hernán Cortés, who took the image of the Virgin as his personal standard. Nevertheless, as Curcio-Nagy points out, some of the earliest references occurred among natives.

In the second phase, Remedios became closely linked to the municipal council of Mexico. It was logical that this group of Spanish settlers would choose to identify with the image that had led the conquerors several decades earlier, although native themes still occupied an important place in the legends surrounding the image and in the paintings that were commissioned to decorate her shrine. The final stage occurred in the early seventeenth century, when the cult of the Virgin shifted from the Conquest to the city of Mexico itself. She became the patroness of the capital as well as a spiritual advocate called upon in times of great need, especially to protect the city from floods and other natural disasters. The development of the many aspects of the Virgen de los Remedios is a fascinating look not only into popular piety in colonial Mexico but also at the way in which a particular image came to be associated first with the Conquest, then with the natives, and eventually with the corporate identity of Mexico City.

Linda Curcio-Nagy is a member of the Department of History at the University of Nevada, Reno. A leading scholar in the study of cultural

From *The Americas* 52, no. 3 (January 1996): 367–91. Reprinted by permission of the Academy of American Franciscan History.

history in colonial Latin America, she served as guest editor of an issue of The Americas entitled "Spectacle in Colonial Mexico."

Kind, gentle, humble, mother to all. This is the traditional Catholic image of the Virgin Mary. Beginning in the fifth century A.D., the popular devotion to the mother of Christ increased rapidly in Europe.[2] Numerous apparitions and accompanying shrines during the late Medieval and early modern period demonstrated her new role in folk Catholicism. In Spain, as in other areas of Europe, the Virgin Mary became one of the major intercessional images, protecting believers from drought, floods, and sickness.[3] Considering her role in the popular belief system of the Iberian peninsulars, it was only logical that the sacred image of Mary would travel the Atlantic to New Spain and appear to Native American neophytes who years earlier had worshiped Tonantzin, Mother Earth, among other female deities. The image of the Virgin Mary could easily incorporate diverse groups under a single symbolic entity. Catholicism held that she was open to all, listened to all, aided all of pure heart. Mary was a force of integration; yet, depending upon the circumstances and the believers, such devotion could also fragment society.[4] This study analyzes the history of one such symbol; an integrating force that is best remembered as being one of the most divisive: the Virgin of Remedies of Mexico City.[5]

According to the traditional apparition histories of the colonial period, the Virgin of Remedies was the first manifestation of Mary in Mexico, and played a pivotal role in the Spanish success during the Battle of Tenochtitlán. Cortés apparently placed the statue of Remedios in the main Aztec temple; and, she caused it to rain, proving that she was more powerful than the indigenous gods. During the Noche Triste, native warriors attempted to remove the image from the altar and she fought against them. Amid the chaos of the retreat, Spaniards sought to retrieve the statue only to find it missing.[6] Later that night she reappeared and threw clumps of dirt into the eyes of the Mexica at a location then known as Otomcapulco.[7]

Twenty years later, she repeatedly appeared before Juan de Tovar, a Christianized cacique, who had been among the Natives during that fateful night in 1520. Tovar, unsure and fearful, sought the council of Franciscan friars residing in Tacuba. They warned him about having too vivid an imagination and doubted that the mother of God would appear before a lowly Indian. Committed to ignoring all further signs and visions of Remedies, Tovar avoided passing Tetoltepec hill, the location of the apparitions.[8] While aiding the construction of the church at Tacuba, Juan fell from the scaffolding and was seriously injured. Assumed to be near death, he received confession and was taken home. At midnight, the Virgin appeared and gave him a miraculous leather belt that instantly cured him. (Presumably, the waistband was Augustinian and was connected to friar Agustín de Coruña, a friend of Juan and a member of that religious order.)[9] The next day he returned to work on the church to the astonishment of all, including the Franciscan friars. One day while hunting for food, he was drawn into the ruins of a pre-Columbian temple (dedicated to Ehecatl, wind manifestation of Quetzalcoatl) on the hill where, guided by the Holy Spirit in the form of a white dove, he found, underneath a maguey plant, a small statue of the Virgin holding the Child Jesus.[10]

Tovar took the statue to his home and placed it in the santocalli (saint's house).[11] There Remedies, known as Cocotzin (Señora Niña), remained as the patron deity of the Tovar household for some ten to twelve years. Juan built an altar, decorated it with flowers, marigolds, garlands, and scented herbs, and gave offerings of tortilla, eggs and mole, fruit, water, and incense to the Virgin. She responded by emanating beautiful rays. However, as time progressed, she would disappear only to be found once again at the pre-Columbian ruins on the hill. The devoted cacique finally, after consulting with Alvaro de Tremiño (a member of the Cathedral chapter in Mexico City), gave the Virgin to the nearby community church of San Juan, where she continued to return to the destroyed Native temple. Finally, in 1553, realizing the true wishes of the Virgin, Tovar, again with Tremiño's aid, decided to construct a modest structure on the site to accommodate the increasing number of devotees and pilgrims seeking solace and miracles from the image.[12]

According to the official history sanctioned by the Mexico City Cabildo some 47 years later, the cult and shrine apparently declined after the death of Tovar and other indigenous individuals directly involved in the early devotion. Beginning in 1574, the city council took great interest in the image, becoming the official patron.[13] The city fathers erected a new church and, in 1579, formed a confraternity to promote and maintain devotion to Remedios. The accounts claim that the Virgin herself sanctified the Cabildo's involvement at the shrine through a vision first seen by a black slave named Julián. He stated that, while he was grazing sheep and during the feast of Saint Hippolytus (also known as the conquest festival), he saw lights and heard music; immediately following this, angels appeared and built a church. Later other individuals also saw the lights and the angels. According to these eyewitnesses, the church eventually constructed by the Cabildo was exactly the one in the visions.[14]

The various parts of the apparition history coincide with a number of European Catholic traditions concerning miraculous images during the late Medieval and Early Modern period. In part I, Remedies is a fighting image, appearing at just the exact moment needed by her devotees as they battle pagans or infidels. These actions are similar to other "militaristic" apparitions during the Spanish Reconquest. In these visions, the backdrop to the apparition is a perceived enemy, a non-Christian "other" such as the Moors, against whom the community can affirm its faith in its own god.[15] As if to further emphasize this parallel, Saint James, the Moorslayer, was seen at Remedios's side, attacking the Aztec.

In part II, the Juan de Tovar segment, the Virgin reappears and the history follows quite closely the "shepherd's cycle" that characterizes many apparitions in Europe, especially those in Spain. In this cycle, a miraculous image, usually Mary holding the Christ Child, appeared before shepherds, herdsmen, or farmers as they tended their livestock or fields. The category of individual was important as they apparently were considered "intermediaries," more sensitive to these supernatural and natural events than urban dwellers.[16] The Novohispanic apparition follows the pattern with an interesting twist—the cacique Juan is a Christianized and partially Hispanicized Native. The shepherd's cycle also emphasized individuals who were considered "marginals." The Remedios histories claim that Juan was Otomí, an ethnic group looked down upon by the Nahua majority. In the traditional European case, the statue was found at the location of the divine appearance. The "shepherd" doubted and vacillated regarding what he had seen; but, finally he attempted to carry off the statue and worship it privately. The image was eventually returned to the original site where it became accessible to all. A church was built on the site and it became a major religious shrine to nearby townspeople.[17] In general, the most powerful protector saints were located at shrines in the countryside and reaffirmed and explained the community's relationship to Nature and agriculture.[18] In this case, the church of the Virgin of Remedies was placed high on a hill with ravines and cliffs nearby, and, she would become the major intercessor regarding drought and famine.

Within the conquering image and shepherd cycle traditions, the apparition of the Virgin of Remedies is particularly interesting given the complexity of sixteenth-century New Spain. Although she first appeared as a Spanish fighting icon, Remedios was primarily seen by Native Americans, specifically Tovar, who later recognized her. In addition, she consistently returned to the ruins of a Native American temple. During the first twenty years of the cult to Remedies, she was primarily a miraculous icon to Natives; for instance, she cured Tovar of injuries due to a serious fall, and, as such she received offerings. In addition, even before the construction of the first *ermita* (shrine), she was the focal point for large numbers of pilgrims, presumably Native Americans, from the surrounding area. It is significant that the apparition histories mention the cult in connection with only one Spaniard, Tremiño, who after the erection of the first church returns to Spain, never to return to Mexico and never again to appear in the histories of Remedios. Neither the Franciscan nor the Augustinian friars associated with the story had any direct involvement in the cult. The devotion to the Virgin at this early point appears to have been spontaneous and indigenous.

Although the cult to the saints that characterized Native Christianity was a phenomenon of the seventeenth century, Remedios appears to have been a significant focus of devotion in the local area during the sixteenth century. Patron saints became a major point of community identity and unity and were associated, in some cases, with pre-Hispanic traditions and sociopolitical entities. By the 1600s, indigenous households had one or more images of saints as patrons. Therefore, it is not inconceivable that a local Native nobleman discovered an image in a pre-Columbian temple that became a major center of devotion to his constituent villagers and that through his aegis a small shrine was constructed.[19]

The first "official" entity to become clearly associated with the miraculous image was the Mexico City Cabildo. No doubt due to the popular nature of the devotion, the city fathers decided to appropriate the image, institutionalizing a local cult. Similar European apparition and pilgrimage traditions included a final stage when spontaneous devotion gave way to bureaucratic and centralized control by church and civil authorities.[20] In addition, it was not uncommon for cities to appropriate the devotions of nearby rural chapels, and, by doing so, alter the original meaning of the image.[21] At some point, the aldermen became convinced that the image was the same one carried by the Conquerors during the Battle of Tenochtitlan. In early petitions, municipal authorities always referred to Remedios as the conquering pro-Spanish image and connected her to Saint Hippolyptus.[22] In 1576, the Vatican granted the shrine the authority to distribute indulgences because of the Virgin's role in the Conquest of the territory for the Catholic Church.[23] Yet, the apparition histories all date from the early seventeenth century after the Cabildo was firmly in control of the image. All claim to have utilized the city council records as well as the testimony of "eyewitnesses."[24] Most importantly, all emphasized a dual perception or parallel devotion to Remedies.

Although Cisneros in his 1621 publication set the standard account (duplicated by all subsequent histories) and with it a definite dichotomy between Mary the Conquistadora and Mary the benevolent personal intercessor, the basic Remedios story already existed in some concrete form during the late sixteenth century. In 1595, José López, vicar at the shrine, commissioned Alonso de Villasana, prominent artist of the day, to paint special murals in the church. López believed that such an important devotional image required more sumptuous decor.[25] Ten large murals lined the interior walls of the building, all relating the miracles performed by Remedies. Three frescoes recounted the Conquest events: 1) Cortés placing the image in the temple of Huitzilopochtli; 2) the Aztecs attempting to remove the statue from that temple; and, 3) the Virgin throwing dirt into the eyes of Mexica warriors during the Noche Triste. The majority of the murals, however, related the story of Juan de Tovar and Mary's aid to

individuals in time of need. The indigenous leader was shown giving offerings to the Virgin in his home and being cured after his fall from the
scaffolding at the Tacuba church. A shipwreck at sea led to no fatalities
because the crew and captain, Alonso de Ribera, called on Mary to save
them. A cripple, brought to the shrine by concerned relatives, was cured
when the statue was placed on his forehead. On another wall, the Virgin
cured large numbers of sick Indians and saved Luís Mayo from sure death
as he was dragged towards a cliff by his runaway mule.[26] Thus, in the
murals, both Spaniards and Native Americans benefited from the intercession of the Virgin.

Nonetheless, special attention was focused upon indigenous worshipers and pilgrims to the church. Religious officials were certainly aware of
the usefulness of murals as didactic tools. Cisneros himself stated that
paintings were the "books of the uneducated."[27] For example, a large painting below the choir included the Virgin giving a caduceus or staff of office to an Indian as she stated in Latin, "Peace be with you. You are no
longer guests or strangers but citizens of the House of God."[28] The Virgin
welcomed Natives and defined their status as Christians. The lettering
was in Latin, a language unfamiliar in written form to the average Native
(or Spanish) worshiper, but not to clergymen or highly educated Spanish
colonists. Indigenous devotees most surely recognized the staff of governing authority. The mural was a powerful statement to both Spaniards
and Natives. Educated Spaniards, in particular the friars, saw evangelized
Natives elevated to a status on a par with Europeans. Natives saw the
mother of God bestowing special status, a leadership role, upon them; it
was an affirmation of their relationship to the spiritual world. It is important that the Virgin gave a caduceus to a Native American. From the point
of view of an indigenous leader, such as Juan de Tovar, it upheld the social and political hierarchy in the community and further legitimized the
native nobility's right to rule. The overall impact of this indigenous-
oriented mural was to emphasize a powerful Virgin as the Madonna.

Perhaps more important than this large mural was the constant utili-
zation of sun imagery throughout the wall decoration. It is true that as-
trology and celestial bodies were important metaphors and emblems in
Renaissance and Baroque painting, design, and literature; but the Virgin
Mary traditionally was associated with the moon and, by extension, water, hence her efficacy against drought and floods. This traditional perception had roots in Apocalypse 12, verse 1, in which a woman clothed
with the sun has the moon at her feet, and is crowned by twelve stars.
Seventeenth-century metaphors consistently posited the Virgin as the moon
and Christ as the sun. In three instances, emblems or portions of murals
connect Remedios to the moon and the stars.[29] Nonetheless, many of the
images that accented the murals associated the Virgin with the sun and
might have been utilized with pre-Columbian native religious beliefs in

mind. For example, above the painting showing the miraculous cure of Juan de Tovar was located a brightly shining sun. In other locations, sunflowers, an eagle and her chicks, and a phoenix about to rise again, all looked towards the sun. Apollo, the Greek sun god, appeared twice. On the large mural below the choir, Apollo stood larger than life, pointing to Remedios, while muses and nymphs showered "abundance" from an overflowing cornucopia onto the inhabitants of a city.[30] Apparition historian Mendoza wrote that Remedies was the sun, and that in her procession, she traveled west to east and then back again. He pointed out that originally the Virgin had duplicated the exact movement of the sun as she traveled from the temple of Huitzilopochtli to the site on the hill (i.e., east to west).[31] The images may have reflected tenets of the early evangelization program. Early missionaries manipulated the indigenous concepts of primordial darkness and chaos and posited Mary (and Christ) as bearers of light and a new celestial order.[32] Thus, through metaphors and painting, the pre-Hispanic and colonial belief systems were linked.

Only two of the murals referred to miracles loosely connected with the city council and included the construction of the second shrine by the angels accompanied by lights and music, and the first venida (or large-scale procession) to Mexico City in 1577 by which the Virgin ended an epidemic.[33] Cabildo efforts began in 1574 when the aldermen claimed that the building constructed by Juan de Tovar was in ruins.[34] Viceroy Manrique wanted to encourage Native worship to Remedies and, therefore, supported the city council's decision to build a new ermita. As the century progressed, the aldermen became increasingly more attentive to the nature of popular devotion at the church. For example, in 1586, they feared that indigenous devotion was dropping at the shrine because chaplain appointees were not multilingual.[35] The situation worsened and was so serious that the viceroy and the archbishop in 1589 moved to give jurisdiction of the ermita to the Franciscans, who were still located at nearby Tacuba. Reluctantly, the city fathers appeared to accept this change; nonetheless, they attacked the Franciscans for neglecting the cult in its early stages. In the meantime, the vicar Alonso Valdez, probably with the approval of the city council, created a major scandal when he took the statue from the shrine and hid it in the Cathedral. Refusing to reveal the location of the statue, he was duly arrested and remained in jail for 30 days until the arrival of a new viceroy, Luís de Velasco (II). Velasco released Valdez and reappointed the Cabildo as official patrons. The statue immediately reappeared at the shrine. In addition, the viceroy ordered all Natives who lived near the ermita to worship there rather than travel to Franciscan churches.[36] Henceforth, the city council made a concerted effort to hire bilingual chaplains and the issue does not arise again in the records. From this period forward, the Cabildo was on guard regarding any attempts to usurp its authority. By 1607, there were so many lawsuits connected to the shrine that councilmen ordered a special report on the status of each, so they could keep track of them all.[37]

The period from 1574 to 1621 (the publication of the first history) appears to have been particularly important in the development of devotion to Remedios. The city council gradually altered its perception of the Virgin from a strictly Conquest image to one that included significant popular and indigenous support for a benevolent Mary. The first apparition account clearly reflected this development. However, this does not eliminate, and perhaps even strengthens, the idea that the city council and ecclesiastical friends molded or embellished certain popular beliefs connected to the early devotion. Neither does this eliminate the possibility that they created a history, especially the segment regarding Juan de Tovar, to explain and/or promote popular indigenous devotion.

Nonetheless, by the seventeenth century, under the continued patronage of the Cabildo, Remedios lost all symbolic connection to the Conquest and completely took on the persona of the Madonna, or protectress of Mexico City and environs. She became the premiere urban image. It was logical that the primary devotional patroness of the Cabildo would bestow her benevolent intercession on the entire city. A number of devotions to manifestations of Mary existed at the parish, confraternity, and personal levels; over time a hierarchy of miraculous petition developed in which Remedies during the seventeenth century was the only image consistently utilized in large-scale spectacle to protect the entire city from epidemics, drought, and famine.[38] The venida of the Virgen de los Remedios was an ostentatious citywide event, the success of which was predicated upon popular multiethnic participation. Thus, by the early 1600s, a discourse of domination had shifted to one of integration; conquest now gave way to colonization. The symbolism of Remedies was altered to correspond to changing colonial reality. In the apparition histories, she appears before a Native American and an African slave, reflecting changing demographics and heterogeneity in Mexico City. Now popular devotion to Mary was utilized as an integrating social force in the capital.

From 1577 to 1696, the Cabildo brought the Virgin of Remedies to Mexico City on eighteen separate occasions.[39] A huge procession, increasing in number as it made its way from her shrine to Mexico City, accompanied the Virgin to the Cathedral. That Mary should have been chosen as a major intercessor for famine and water-related disaster was customary for the period. In addition, petitionary processions and novenas were a standard method of seeking Marian aid; for example, over 600 processions to Mary for drought occurred in Barcelona between 1515 and 1631.[40] Novohispanic author José de Noriega claimed that Mary had dominion over water from the very beginning of her life. Saint Albert the Great associated the following statement with Mary: "If men wait for me like rain, then as rain I shall appear to remedy their sins." In addition, the connection to water extended to Mary's suffering at Calvary. As she watched her son die, dark clouds appeared to share her grief.[41] In 1668, poet/author Alonso Ramírez de Vargas claimed that the Virgin brought forth an impregnated dark cloud that gave birth and rained all over the inhabitants of the city.[42] Furthermore, Remedios was particularly effective at sea; at least two miracles in the Pacific Ocean were attributed to her.[43] The moon was associated with water and the Virgin had connections to that celestial body, as mentioned previously, in the Book of Revelation.

Although epidemics, droughts, and poor harvests were at issue, the sinfulness of the inhabitants of the central valley was the cause of these natural disasters. Contemporary estimates claim that 20,000–40,000 people walked with Remedios, praying for her intercession and the forgiveness of their sins.[44] Ramírez de Vargas claimed that the sick starved while doctors and pharmacists ate well and profited. Pregnant women died giving birth in great numbers. Plants perished; even birds could not find food to steal.[45] For that same year (1668), Antonio de Robles stated that it was amazing that only 15–20 funerals took place per day.[46] All this was caused by vice. Each person was a flame (of sin) with a heart of ice.[47] One author pointed out that in the Book of Isaiah, people suffered drought because their sins were so numerous that God punished them. Therefore, flagellant processions were an essential part of the larger avenida.[48] Participants shed their blood in imitation of Christ and for the remission of their sins.[49]

The procession, however, articulated a contractual relationship between the Virgin and the faithful that could alleviate their pain and the drought. Through penance, contrition, suffering, and remorse, their prayers could reach the Virgin. A miracle could only take place if the devotee was pure of heart and true to the required rituals such as praying, confessing, walking in the procession, and attending the novena masses. Mary, in particular, understood their suffering because she had suffered so greatly as she watched her son die on the cross. If the processional participants could duplicate her posture, then she would intercede with her son who, in turn, would stop the drought, famine, or epidemic.[50] People shared similar hardships and "lived" the sorrows of Mary; and, consequently, they received absolution and a direct "material" benefit if the Virgin did indeed intercede. However, it was essential that everyone recognize and repent their sinful ways. This was considered a community affliction that had to be dealt with collectively. A procession of this kind, given the desperate circumstances, demanded emotive sincerity from all and probably reached a fever pitch. It allowed participants to deal with an otherwise overwhelming catastrophe in a special manner, outside of the normal mundane, sinful world.[51]

Native American perception of Catholic theological justification for the procession is presently unknown. Nonetheless, there were pre-Columbian precedents for the relationship of drought, rain, and human moral error. For example, Nahuas believed that Nappatecuhtli, one of the rain gods and patron of the mat-makers, bathed (or rained upon) individuals and pardoned their faults. During the festival to this deity, mat-makers swept the floor before the image and spread new mats before him.[52] During the venida to Remedios, Natives swept the route before the Virgin and scattered flowers in her path. Furthermore, Natives had a whole series of large-scale public festivals and rituals, during the months of Etzalcualiztli, Tecuilhuitontli and Uey tecuilhuitl (equivalent to late May to mid-July and milpa planting season) in which rain and fertility were the focal points.[53] Venidas usually occurred in June or July. Perhaps, most importantly, whether Spaniard or Indian, people believed that the Virgin of Remedies consistently answered their supplications and brought relief, attesting to her miraculous powers. She became an essential icon to an agriculturally based society always at the mercy of weather and disease.

The procession began in the early morning when Franciscan friars and Native Americans, all carrying candles, accompanied the image, which was placed on a carriage, to the church of Tacuba.[54] There Native Americans built flowered arches, shot off gunpowder, played music, and danced.[55] The Virgin was elaborately dressed in the finest silk, velvet, and lace embroidered with pearls, and wore a crown of silver and diamonds.[56] Then the procession slowly continued en route to Mexico City. At the entrance of the city, the viceroy, the archbishop, all the confraternities, the regular and secular clergy, and the city council joined the procession. It now measured 2,000 varas or one mile long. At this point, the Virgin was carried on the shoulders of Franciscan friars and the Cabildo carried the canopy that sheltered the sacred image from the sun. Bells clamored throughout the capital; it was so loud that individuals could not understand each other except by hand signals and motions. Everyone proceeded to the church of Santa Veracruz where more services took place and the Virgin remained until the next morning. The following day was the most important of all as the procession wound its way to the Cathedral where Remedios would remain for nine days of masses, prayers, penitential acts, and songs. Two hundred Native American and 100 Spanish confraternities participated. As they did for Corpus Christi, Indians constructed arches of flowers and scented herbs that covered the processional route; and confraternities erected ephemeral, yet sumptuous, altars where the procession stopped, prayed, sang hymns, and then continued on. A "disciplina de sangre" or parade of flagellants was an essential part of the venida, and both Spaniards and natives participated.[57] Merchants sold food, especially candy and drink, and people erected makeshift bleachers to better view the Virgin.[58] It was not uncommon for many people to actually touch the Virgin as she passed by, thus emphasizing the intimate personal relationship to the mother of God that existed within this highly ritualized religious event.[59] In some cases, the procession was specifically designed to coincide with Corpus Christi; and, in 1653, her venida took place during the entrance of a new viceroy, the Duke of Albuquerque, and coincided with such profane elements as bullfights, theatrical performances, and a masked parade.[60]

The Cabildo, as official sponsors and confraternity brothers, provided candles for the municipal officers and royal authorities such as the Audiencia and the viceroy. They hosted a meal for highly placed dignitaries who walked in the procession.[61] In addition, they were responsible for church and cathedral decorations, at least one high mass at the cathedral, and maintenance and repair of the processional route.[62] The central plaza was lit up each night and the public was encouraged to do the same with their houses. Although the procession was an expensive venture for the city council, they routinely collected large donations (over 1,000 pesos) from worshipers who attended the novena at the Cathedral.[63] This more than paid for expenditures. In fact, two aldermen stood by the door of the Cathedral to collect such donations.[64] In addition, indulgences could be purchased for attendance and participation in the procession, and the Cabildo/confraternity sold medallions and prayer cards to the faithful.[65] All proceeds went to the confraternity of the Virgin, which maintained the shrine and guest house for pilgrims, paid for clergymen to say masses at the ermita, and defrayed the cost of future venidas.

Patronized by the Cabildo, accessible to all the inhabitants of the city in time of need, the Virgin of Remedies retained her importance as intercessor for Native communities, especially those in the jurisdiction of Tacuba. Thus she had both a local and a citywide sacred devotion. Native American participation was great in the large city procession, a fact attested to by contemporaries, including the indigenous chronicler Chimalpahin, who wrote about the 1597 venida.[66] However, Natives celebrated the Virgin as their patroness right at the shrine. The Cabildo, aware of the devotion and limited resources of Natives, not only provided for a chaplain to say mass but donated money specifically to provide for regular services for indigenous devotees.[67] The local fiesta on August 28 marked a high point of Native devotion to "la Niña," as they sometimes called her.[68] The festival itself included a procession, arches of flowers and plants, music, dancing, singing, and fireworks. Special invitations were sent and the shrine was decorated. During the late seventeenth century, the average cost of the festival was 423 pesos, an amount that was more than covered by the donations collected from Natives during the festival.[69] Additional costs of the festival, for example, the elaborate meal prepared for Indian leaders, was actually paid for by donations from individuals from Mexico City and as far away as Michoacan who sent money to the shrine.[70]

Although ongoing research should shed light on the exact nature of popular devotion to Remedios during the seventeenth century, some characteristics have emerged. In 1668, Angel de Betancur claimed that the main altar was covered with small heads, legs, bodies, and eyes, all symbols of the cures that supplicants sought from the Virgin.[71] Personal vows and pilgrimages were connected to the shrine as was the case with the sailors saved at sea. In addition, oil from a lamp near the statue was thought to be miraculous and was requested as a remedy for all sorts of ailments, and probably accounted for the large number of donations to the shrine from all over the viceroyalty. It also apparently was common practice to allow pilgrims to touch the image.[72] Personal devotion at the shrine was such that the city council renovated and expanded the church and sought permission from the Vatican to establish an official romería (a vow to do an annual procession).[73]

A unique aspect of popular devotion to Remedios revolved around the Peregrina (the Traveler or Pilgrim), a second image of the Virgin, that was endowed with the powers of the original. This duplicate image made regular visits to nearby Native communities that greeted her with large processions. As the Peregrina, Remedios received the personal supplications of Indians, castas, and Spaniards who resided in those villages. The donations collected went for the upkeep of the shrine. The existence of a second statue probably explains the persistent miracle that Remedios could be in two places at one time, namely, at her shrine and at the Cathedral in Mexico City. Other processions took place at the ermita and were organized by Native farmers (with the permission of the aldermen), whenever they suffered natural disasters in the local area.[74] A precarious balance existed between the local Native patroness and the Cabildo urban protectress, a balance that occasionally went askew. The most long-standing difficulty between the Natives and the city council revolved around who had the right to police the Native festival. The dispute came to a head in the early eighteenth century as the municipal council ordered the priest who was in their employ to cancel the festival. In 1731, royal officials sided with the Native Americans who retained control of their celebration.[75] Plans to touch-up the statue also were abandoned because the Cabildo feared angering the Natives who most certainly would have objected. By 1775, so many Native groups celebrated the festival that no space existed in the shrine for Spanish/criollo elite visitors or priests. The city council, through diplomacy, sought to encourage Natives to make room for them.[76]

A festival of such importance did not just cause friction between the Cabildo and Natives but also among the Indians themselves. The indigenous populations of Tacuba and Tlalnepantla and various other districts claimed the Virgin as their patroness and sought to control her August festival. In this case, the city fathers attempted to serve as intermediaries by suggesting that Natives alternate years of patronage. Although unsatisfactory to all the Natives concerned, by 1751 the concept was still in operation when 30 pueblos from the central valley attended, including Natives from Guadalupe and Santiago Tlatelolco.[77]

Given the popular (and indigenous) and criollo devotion to the Virgin of Remedios through most of the colonial period, the question remains: How did she become the premiere icon of the royal forces during the wars of Mexican Independence? The revolt of 1692 appears to have played a pivotal role in this change in symbolism. The Virgin was brought to the capital due to famine, the same situation that had caused the grain shortage that, in turn, sparked the revolt.[78] One week after the riot of Natives and castas, the city council hosted a festival to the Virgin asking for rain in which these same ethnic groups participated.[79] Most significantly, however, the sacred image remained in the Cathedral until 1695, a situation that had previously been inconceivable. For the first time since the 1577 procession, the Virgin of Remedies did not protect the city from natural disasters, but rather protected the city and royal governments from further uprisings. Her next venida in 1696 would not be for the welfare of the general public, but for the safe arrival of the Spanish fleet, a tradition that would become law in a 1698 royal decree.[80] The 1699 procession was for the secure passage of the fleet, threatened by enemy vessels, and for a plague afflicting the city. In an interesting aside, the fleet, bound for Spain, apparently carried a dress of the Virgin and this sacred garment protected them.[81]

The eighteenth century marked further change for the Cabildo and Natives of Tacuba and Tlalnepantla. The Virgin of Remedies was increasingly appropriated for royal festivals, the fleet, and even the personal illnesses of viceroys.[82] From 1700 to 1810, the Cabildo or royal officials brought the Virgin from her shrine to Mexico City thirty-two times. Although she retained her association with weather calamities and epidemic diseases, almost one-half of the venidas were connected to royal events or the fleet.[83] Her intervention for the safety of the fleet built upon Mary's relationship to water and earlier miracles at sea. However, royal and fleet processions were mandated by the viceroy (and the monarch) and did not reflect any particular personal devotion or vow, and were not correlated to individual moral behavior on the part of the majority of the inhabitants of the capital. Most importantly, the Cabildo only brought the Virgin for traditional religious reasons as it had done the previous century; and, the viceroy only brought the Virgin for profane reasons. Symbolic import of the Virgin was further divided and now was shared by Mexico City, Native Americans, and the King.

The 1708 venida contrasted greatly with the penitential processions of the seventeenth century described earlier. In this year, an heir, Luís Felipe, was born to King Philip V. In the main sermon, it was claimed that Remedies specifically protected the royal family and was responsible for the good health of mother and child. A procession took place but the solemn novena became a massive nine-day festival that included bullfights, plays, and fireworks. The guilds were ordered to host a series of parades in which they presented allegorical carts. Fifteen guilds participated and showcased floats that depicted the joy of the major viceregal cities upon hearing the news of the birth. Puebla, Merida, Veracruz, Valladolid, Oaxaca and Xochimilco, Puebla, and Mexico City were represented.[84]

Theoretically the parallel interpretations of Remedies could have co-existed without incident for years. However, Bourbon administrators began to usurp the prerogatives of the city and the Natives. Royal festivals and rogations increasingly took place at her shrine, upsetting the regular schedule of services for Native Americans.[85] The case of the 1719 procession is particularly interesting: although a severe drought afflicted the central valley of Mexico, royal officials decided against a procession; yet, one month later, they brought Remedios for the welfare of the monarch.[86] In addition, and perhaps most importantly, the viceroy ordered a venida to the city for profane reasons and refused to return the Virgin to her sanctuary when the novena was over. In some instances, she remained for years at a time. The viceroys ignored the protests of the Cabildo even when Natives also began to complain.[87] As long as the Virgin remained at the Cathedral, they could not hold their festival. In 1720, the city council secretly fired off a letter to the King demanding that something be done about the situation. They were concerned that such a miraculous public image was not being respected; she should be returned to her shrine. To their chagrin, the governor learned of the letter and the city council was forced to visit the palace "to kiss the hands of the viceroy" (i.e., apologize). The conflict continued until 1750 when a royal decree clearly stated that she was the royal Virgin, naming her La Conquistadora. The king, in one respect, did side with the Cabildo and stipulated that the Virgin had to return to her shrine immediately after a novena at the Cathedral.[88]

Nonetheless, much damage had been done. The Cabildo continued to bring Remedios for traditional motives; yet, it increasingly claimed lack of funding to support the processions and her stay at the Cathedral. On some occasions, like in 1789, popular attempts to induce the city council to host a venida at the Cathedral were refused, and when others did sponsor it the Cabildo did not attend.[89] In what was perhaps a last-ditch attempt to exert some sort of control over the image, the aldermen attempted to foster patronage of the venidas for the fleet onto the Consulado of Cádiz.[90] The city council's disaffection with Remedios parallels increasing criollo devotion to the Virgin of Guadalupe. From the 1730s to the

1750s, just when the royal government began to usurp the Cabildo's authority over Remedios, the devotion to Guadalupe increased rapidly due to the dedicated efforts of many curates schooled in the city. In 1756 the city celebrated a huge festival to Guadalupe in honor of her designation as patroness of the viceroyalty.[91] Although Remedios was still an important miraculous image, the Cabildo began to shift allegiance to a Virgin that was particularly attractive to criollos and where there existed less competition over symbolic control. By the end of the eighteenth century, Remedios no longer epitomized the city and its inhabitants as she had 100 years earlier.

Napoleon's invasion and subsequent domination of the Iberian peninsula had an unequivocal impact on royal government appropriation of the Virgin of Remedios. The image of the Virgin was manipulated to consolidate popular and Native support for the Spanish monarch, Ferdinand VII, who was held prisoner by Napoleon. For example, one publication was supposedly written by a Native and attempted to duplicate popular speech. In it the indigenous author comforted Spaniards and assured them that the Virgin of Remedies, who had performed so many miracles for Natives, would surely protect Mexico from its enemies, and that Natives were willing to die for her, the symbol of royal government.[92] The 1810 procession sought the Virgin's aid against the French usurper; yet, the focal point of the event was actually the king and the Native Americans. The author describing the event remarked how the altar tradition along the route no longer included statues of saints and Mary. Inhabitants now decorated their houses with tapestries and statues of Ferdinand. The procession organizers also introduced an innovation—an allegorical cart. On this float sat a loyal Native American, waiting for the defeat of Napoleon due to the intervention of Remedios. Next to the Indian was an angel standing upon a defeated Bonaparte. An accompanying banner proclaimed: "Indian Loyalty Without Rival." Large numbers of Natives dressed in pre-Columbian costumes escorted the cart. Also in the procession were representations of Juan de Tovar. Just as the author of the description, Luís José Montaña, was about to publish his work, Miguel Hidalgo called for Mexican independence. Montaña, in the final pages of his manuscript, stated that a lack of respect and religious fervor had brought about the revolt.[93] Now sin caused rebellion, not weather calamities or illness.

In response to the Hidalgo revolt in 1810, Remedios was proclaimed publicly as the Conquest Virgin. New apparition histories and tracts were published resurrecting the events of the Noche Triste in 1520. She was called upon by royalists to once again fight against Natives, this time against those who made up Hidalgo's army. Poetry and broadsides intended for Natives lauded the benefits of Spanish empire. They stated that thanks to the Conquest, the Virgin of Remedies came to New Spain.[94] Other commentators resurrected the paintings at the shrine, but only those that represented the Conquest portion of the apparition histories. They placed special emphasis on the Virgin injuring Natives as they attempted to remove her from the Aztec temple. There was even a movement to celebrate her feast day on August 13, alluding to her essential role in the Conquest.[95]

Remedios was also named the *Generala* (General), the official head of the royalist forces. The nuns of San Jerónimo even dressed the statue in military garb.[96] Author Agustín Fernández de San Salvador wrote that the Virgin, at the Cathedral, brought clouds and a great wind to the city. Lightning struck near her shrine, a sign that she did not wish to leave the capital, but rather wanted to protect the inhabitants from Hidalgo, who sought "to vomit all the calamities of civil war onto New Spain." Consequently, the Virgin became responsible for the successes of the royal forces against Hidalgo. The author claimed that this was a lesson to all those who thought they could insult the Virgin with impunity.[97] The *Generala* had liberated the people from "demonical fanaticism" that had threatened religion and the Crown. The procession and novena of February 24, 1811, were in gratitude to Remedies for the defeat of the rebels.[98] Thus, by 1811, the symbol of integration, Mary benevolent to all regardless of ethnicity, once again had become the Conquistadora, patroness of the political heirs of Hernán Cortés.

Symbols are always extricably linked to the cultural context, to the society that imbues them with meaning. In addition, the significance of religious symbols, in particular, reflects changing relations between human beings and the divine. Saints gained or lost popularity according to their perceived efficacy, changing world views, and political climates, as appears to have been the case with the Virgin of Remedies in Mexico City. In this instance, government officials (first the Cabildo and then the Monarchy) capitalized on a popular devotion to an image renowned for her miraculous powers. Eventually, competing interests regarding control of the symbolism of the Virgin led to a gradual discrediting of the very image itself. In Europe, one Marian devotion typically was substituted with another.[99] In Mexico, Guadalupe, in a sense, "replaced" Remedios as the primary official Virgin and, eventually, as premiere personal intercessor as well. The success of a vow or devotion to a miraculous image was based upon the extent to which petitions were heard and answered. In this regard, the 1736 plague appears to have been a major turning point because the power of Remedios over epidemics and drought was questioned. The Virgin of Guadalupe eventually ended the plague. Increasingly, she, not Remedies, would be called upon to end drought, epidemics, and all manner of afflictions.[100] In the hierarchical devotional system in operation in the colonial capital, Remedios was overtaken.

Yet belief systems, in this case the legitimacy of a miraculous image and advocations to it, are not easily destroyed. After Independence, five more traditional venidas to end drought occurred; however, by the mid-nineteenth century, devotion to Remedios was confined to her parish. The Virgin of Remedies as a symbol had come full circle. To many she would forever be linked to the Spanish. The Virgin of Guadalupe, in turn, became the symbol of Mexico. Nonetheless, her role as personal intercessor continued and still exists today. Although few contemporary inhabitants of Mexico City are familiar with the Virgin of Remedies, her festival still takes place on top of Tetoltepec hill; among the main attractions of the festival are Native American dance performances, a living legacy of that original sixteenth- and seventeenth-century popular devotion.

Notes

1. All translations are my own except for the Latin text, for which I am indebted to Stafford Poole.

2. For a history and early devotion to Mary, see Michael P. Carroll, *The Cult of the Virgin Mary* (Princeton: Princeton University Press, 1986), chapter 3. For a detailed analysis of changing institutional perceptions of the Virgin, see Marina Warner, *Alone of All Her Sex: The Myth and the Cult of the Virgin Mary* (New York: Random House, 1976).

3. William A. Christian, *Apparitions in Late Medieval and Renaissance Spain* (Princeton: Princeton University Press, 1981), p. 14; also see his work, *Local Religion in Sixteenth-Century Spain* (Princeton: Princeton University Press, 1989), chapter 3. For further discussion of the popular religion and the devotion to the saints and to Mary in Spain, see Julio Caro Baroja, *Las formas complejas de la vida religiosa: Religión y sociedad y carácter en la España de los siglos XVI y XVII* (Madrid: Akal, 1978) and Carlos María Stalhin, *Apariciones* (Madrid: Razón y Fe, 1954).

4. James J. Preston, "Conclusion: New Perspectives on Mother Worship," in *Mother Worship, Themes and Variations* (Chapel Hill: University of North Carolina Press, 1982), p. 333.

5. Very few recent religious histories of the apparition and miracles of the Virgin of Remedies exist. See, for example, Miguel Flores Solís, *Nuestra Señora de los Remedios* (México: Jus, 1972). José Bravo Ugarte, *Historia de México* (México: Jus, 1947), vol. II and Joseph H. L. Schlarman, *México: Tierra de volcanes* (México: Jus, 1951), both discuss the apparition history. A number of Remedies manifestations of Mary are located in Spain and include the one in the Mercedarian convent in Madrid and the one at Fuensanta, Albacete. Other images of Remedios, sometimes referred to as Our Lady of Protection, are also found in Mexico and are usually connected to hospitals. See Victor and Edith Turner, *Image and Pilgrimage in Christian Culture: Anthropological Perspectives* (New York: Columbia University Press, 1978), p. 66–67. For the Remedies shrine at Cozumel, Yucatan, see Mariano Cuevas, *Historia de la iglesia en México* (México: Editorial Patria, 1946), vol. I, p. 334.

6. Lorenzo de Mendoza, *Orígen de la milagrosa imagén, y Santuario de Nuestra Señora de los Remedios de México, sus venidas a la ciudad y maravillas que á obrado* (México, 1685), f. 11v. Mendoza includes in his account the first work published on the Virgin of Remedies written by Fray Luís de Cisneros, *Historia de el principio y orígen, progresos, venidas á México, y milagros de la Santa Imagén de nuestra Señora de los Remedios, estramuros de México . . .* (México:

Emprenta de Bachiller Juan Blanco de Alcázar, 1621). In addition, Federico Gómez de Orozco reproduces a large segment of the Cisneros' text, in "Las pinturas de Alonso de Villasana en el Santuario de los Remedios," *Anales del Instituto de Investigaciones Estéticas* (UNAM) no. 15 (1946): 65–80. Francisco de Florencia reproduces the work of Cisneros and Mendoza in his *La milagrosa invención de un thesoro escondido en el campo, que hallo un venturoso cazique, y escondio en su casa, para gozarlo a sus solas: patente ya en el santuario de los Remedios en su admirable imagen de Nuestra Señora; señalada en milagros, invocada por patrona de las lluvias, y temporales; defensora de los españoles, avogada de los indios . . . noticias de sus orígin, y venidas a México . . .* (Sevilla: Siete Revueltas, 1745). Other apparition histories include Juan de Grijalva, *Crónica de la orden de NPS Agustín en la provincia de la Nueva España: en cuatro edades desde el año de 1533 hasta el de 1592* (México: Imprenta Victoria, 1926), p. 2, chapters 14 and 15; and, Capitán D. Angel de Betancur, "Historia de la milagrosa imagén de Nuestra Señora de Remedios cuyo Santuario está extramuros de México cuya conquista se toca, " located in the Archivo General de la Nación (henceforth AGN), *Ramo Historia*, vol. 1, exp. 17, f. 236–247. Also see Genaro García, *Historia incidental de Nuestra Señora de Remedios* (México: Jus, 1909) which provides a synthesis of Florencia and Cisneros. Also see Mariano Fernández de Echeverría y Veytia, "Baluartes de México (1775–1779)," in *Testimonios históricos guadalupanos* (México: Fondo de Cultura Económica, 1982), pp. 565–77.

    7. Mendoza, *Orígen*, A2, A2v. Saint James, the Moorslayer also appeared and aided the Spanish. Although it is unclear whether the Spaniards had the image of the Virgin with them at this point, Betancur claims that they did and that they dressed the statue in black as they mourned their defeat. He also states that Cortés ordered that his comrades hide the image. See AGN, *Ramo Historia*, vol. 1, exp. 17, f. 239v, p. 242.

    8. For the basic description of these events, see Mendoza, *Orígen*, A2–3. Juan's indigenous name was Ce Quauhtli or One Eagle. Mendoza claims that Tovar avoided the hill where the apparitions took place because he believed that the Virgin was too beautiful to look at. The friars, at one point, supposedly told Tovar ". . . que era poca persona para que la Madre de Dios se le apareciesse, y hablasse."

    9. Grijalva, *Crónica*, p. 2, chapter 14.

    10. Mendoza, *Orígen*, 3v. After the miraculous cure, the friars apparently believed Tovar, but no action was taken to investigate the appearances of Remedies on the hill. The apparition histories do not name the deity of the pre-Hispanic temple. For the reference to Ehecatl, see Betancur, AGN, *Ramo Historia*, vol. 1, exp. 17, f. 242. Mendoza and Cisneros date the actual apparition to 1540 or 1542. The provenience of the Remedios statue is unknown; how it arrived in New Spain is also a mystery. The accounts speculate that a soldier named Juan Rodríguez Villafuerte carried the statue in a tin box across the Atlantic. It supposedly had been given to him by his brother who had fought in Flanders. See Mendoza, *Orígen*, 9v; Florencia, *La milagrosa*, pp. 17, 18. The statue is approximately one foot high and is sometimes referred to as a saddle image as it was small enough to be carried into battle as a protectress. See Turner and Turner, *Image*, p. 63.

    11. The santocalli was a household shrine, usually located in the patio of a traditional house compound. The structure in the pre-Hispanic period housed pottery representations of Native deities, and, during the colonial era, served as a house for the statues of Catholic saints.

    12. See Mendoza, *Orígen*, pp. 4, 6–6v; Florencia, *La milagrosa*, pp. 8, 9; and, Betancur in AGN, *Ramo Historia*, vol. 1, exp. 17, f. 244. Florencia claims that the first sanctuary was built after consulting unnamed individuals in Mexico City. This first structure was called the Shrine at Apparition Hill (la Hermita del Monte

de la Aparición). See *La milagrosa*, pp. 10, 33. Bentacur claims that the first sanctuary was built by Cortés (f. 244v).

13. City councilmen García de Albornoz visited the shrine and spurred the Cabildo to take action. See Mendoza, *Orígen*, f. 18v–19.

14. For a description of these events, see Mendoza, *Orígen*, f. 17–17v. Cuauhtemoc surrendered to Cortés on August 13, 1521, which happened to be the feast day of Saint Hippolytus, a Roman priest martyred circa 235 AD. From that moment forward, the feast day of the saint celebrated the conquest.

15. See the examples of the apparitions of Santa Gadea in Burgos (1399) and Jaén (1430) in Christian, *Apparitions*, p. 55.

16. Ibid., p. 19.

17. It is called the shepherd's cycle because it refers to the journey of shepherds during the Nativity. They arrived at the manger, guided by angels and other supernatural phenomena, and found Mary and the Christ child. In Europe, these apparitions proliferated beginning in the ninth century. In almost all cases, the emphasis is on the Virgin Mary and not on the Christ child held by the statue. For further discussion of the shepherd's cycle, see Turner and Turner, *Image*, p. 42; Christian, *Apparitions*, pp. 34, 15, 186–87; Vicente de la Fuente, *Vida de la Virgen María con la historia de su culto en España* (Barcelona, 1879), vol. II; and, Steven Sharbrough, "El ciclo de los Pastores," *History of Religions at UCLA Newsletter* 3 (1975): 7–11.

18. For an interesting analysis of the relationship of ancient fertility goddesses and the Virgin Mary in Europe, see Pamela Berger, *The Goddess Obscured. Transformation of the Grain Protectress from Goddess to Saint* (Boston: Beacon Press, 1985), especially chapter 6.

19. For native devotion to the saints during this period, see James Lockhart, *The Nahuas after the Conquest: A Social and Cultural History of the Indians of Central Mexico, Sixteenth through Eighteenth Centuries* (Stanford: Stanford University Press, 1992), pp. 236–237, 243. As previously stated, it was a frequent feature of the cycle that the "shepherd" found a statue. It is also conceivable (and probably unprovable) that Juan de Tovar purchased an image from a Spaniard or from indigenous craftsmen who by the late sixteenth century had established quite a business in carving and selling incense burners in the form of saints to their fellow Natives. For this trade, see Ibid., p. 237.

20. Turner and Turner, *Image*, p. 26.

21. Christian, *Local Religion*, p. 152. For the city of Madrid and its appropriation of rural devotions, see Jerónimo Quintana, *Historia de Madrid* (Madrid: Artes Gráficas, 1954), pp. 148–49, 158, 173–74, 890, 911, 927, 995. For further discussion of the rural/urban relationship through religious shrines, see Peter Brown, *The Cult of the Saints: Its Rise and Function in Latin Christianity* (Chicago: University of Chicago Press, 1981), pp. 42–46.

22. *Archivo Histórico del Antiguo Ayuntamiento de la Ciudad de México* (hereafter AHA), vol. 339A, f. 177–79; *Actas del Cabildo de la ciudad de México* (henceforth *Actas*) (México: Aguilar e Hijos, 1889–1911), Libro 12, pp. 385–86. In addition to the appearance of the angels building the second church on the feast day of Saint Hippolytus, the city council, in the 1597 procession, brought the Virgin to the church of the conquest saint for a visit. See *Actas*, Libro 13, p. 45.

23. "Gregory XIII, Dum praecelsa meritorium, 20 octubre 1576," in *American Pontificia Primi Saeculi Evangelizationis, 1493–1592* (Vatican City: Libreria Editrice Vaticana, 1991), vol. II, no. 340.

24. The city council paid 1000 pesos to fund the publication of Cisneros' history. See *Actas*, Libro 22, pp. 115–116. Cisneros interviewed the daughter of

Juan de Tovar, the steward of the church of San Juan, and the steward of the 1553 shrine, as well as researching among the Cabildo documents. All three informants had to have been in their eighties or nineties. Subsequent apparition histories not only reproduced Cisneros' account but commented on his sources and their own. Although many volumes of documentation regarding the confraternity and the shrine exist in the Archivo Histórico del Antiguo Ayuntamiento de la Ciudad de México, the fire of 1692 destroyed almost all of the Remedios sixteenth-century records. No sixteenth-century apparition histories exist, a fact accepted by later apparition historians like Mendoza. He explains this omission by stating that the miracles were too profound and that the conquerors were too busy conquering to write down the details. See Mendoza, *Orígen*, Av. Yet, none can explain the apparent silence of Franciscan and Augustinian missionaries in regards to the miraculous events that occurred to Juan de Tovar.

25. Gómez de Orozco, "Las pinturas," p. 66. In 1629, the church was renovated and enlarged. The interior was gilded and, in the process, the poems and emblems that accompanied the murals were removed. See Florencia, *La milagrosa*, pp. 42–43.

26. The murals are described in Ibid., pp. 65, 69, 70, 71, 72, 78. In 1603, Remedies aided Lope de Ulloa and his crew who were also shipwrecked by a storm. In both cases, the ships were coming from the Philippines and were bound for Acapulco. The captains and sailors vowed to do a pilgrimage to the shrine of the Virgin if she would aid and save their lives. The cripple was Gabriel de Aguilar. Blas García de Palacios was also saved from a runaway horse episode by the Virgin. In 1612, Juan, a Native from Azcapotzalco who had been crippled for five years, was miraculously cured during the indigenous celebration at the shrine. See Florencia, *La milagrosa*, pp. 100–101, 103, 105–107. The poet, Betancur, was moved to pen his Remedios history in verse because his wife, afflicted with a debilitating leg injury, was cured by the Virgin. In addition, he sponsored and participated in a procession of flagellants to her. See his poem in AGN, *Ramo Historia*, vol. 1, exp. 17, f. 246v.

27. As quoted in Gómez de Orozco, "Las pinturas," p. 65.

28. Ibid., p. 79. "Pax vobis. Iam non estis hospites, aduenae sed ciues sanctorum domestici Dei." This passage comes from Saint Paul in Ephesians, chapter 2, verse 19.

29. See, for example, Juan de Narvaez y Saavedra, *Sermón en la solemnidad que se consagró a Cristo Señor Nuestro Sacramentado y a su Santíssima Madre en su Milagrosa Imagen de los Remedios por el feliz sucesso de la Flota en el viage de buelta a España* (México: Herederos de la Viuda de Francisco Rodríguez Lupercio, 1699), pp. 7, 8 and Florencia, *La milagrosa*, p. 92. For Mary as stars, see Gómez de Orozco, "Las pinturas," p. 70; as the moon (representing silence), and as sun, moon, and stars, see Ibid., p. 73.

30. Ibid., pp. 69, 71, 78, 79.

31. Mendoza, *Orígen*, 29v.

32. Louise M. Burkhart, *The Slippery Earth: Nahua-Christian Moral Dialogue in Sixteenth-Century Mexico* (Tucson: University of Arizona Press, 1989), pp. 83–85.

33. Gómez de Orozco, "Las pinturas," pp. 76, 77.

34. Future research may show what the actual status of the building was at this time. The city council may have judged the structure in ruins because it was not an appropriate church in their eyes, but rather a small rural chapel. They did make constant reference to the fact that no priest was attached to the shrine.

35. *Actas*, Libro 9, p. 143.

36. Mendoza, *Orígen*, pp. 19v, 28, 28v, 29.

37. *Actas*, Libro 16, 422 and Libro 17, p. 30.

38. For a similar pattern in Spain and Italy, see Christian, *Local Religion*, p. 64 and Richard Trexler, "Florentine Religious Experience: The Sacred Image," *Studies in the Renaissance* 19 (1972), 17. Flooding, however, created a gap in the supplication system. In this instance, the powers of Remedies appeared to have been in doubt. In 1607, city officials considered bringing her to the capital due to flood and canceled the procession, choosing instead to entreat aid from Saint Gregory the Wonder Worker (*Actas*, Libro 17, pp. 91–92). In 1611, the shrine itself was in danger of severe damage due to flooding (*Actas*, Libro 18, p. 224). The 1629 flood has often been cited as the first battle of the Virgins, i.e., Remedios and Guadalupe. Although the flooding continued for four years, Guadalupe has been credited with the miracle. See, for example, Jacque Lafaye, *Quetzalcoatl and Guadalupe: The Formation of Mexican National Consciousness, 1531–1813* (Chicago: University of Chicago Press, 1976), p. 254; and, the sonnet located in AGN, *Ramo Historia*, vol. 1, exp. 18, f. 247v. However, in actuality, the city evoked Remedios, Guadalupe, and Saint Gregory without any real amelioration. Part of the legend claims that a nun had a vision of Mary who then interceded. See Stafford Poole, *Our Lady of Guadalupe: The Origins and Sources of a Mexican National Symbol, 1531–1797* (Tucson: University of Arizona Press, 1995), pp. 97–98. The true challenge to Remedios concerned her power over plagues and drought and it would come in the eighteenth century.

39. The years and reasons for which Our Lady of the Remedies was brought to Mexico City were as follows: 1577: epidemic (*Actas*, Libro 3, p. 44); 1597: drought (Agustín de Vetancurt, *Teatro mexicano. Descripción breve de los sucesos ejemplares de la Nueva España en el Nuevo Mundo Occidental de las Indias* (Madrid: Porrúa Turanzas, 1960–61), vol. III, p. 358); 1616: drought (*Actas*, Libro 21, 5, 13, 342–44); 1618: drought (*Actas*, Libro 22, 137); 1638: drought and sickness (*Actas*, Libro 31, 347–48); 1639: drought and sickness (in conjunction with the Corpus Christi, *Actas*, Libro 31, 346); 1641: drought (Vetancurt, *Teatro*, vol. III, p. 359 and *Actas*, Libro 32, p. 226); 1642: epidemic (Vetancurt, *Teatro*, vol. III, p. 359 and *Actas*, Libro 32, 303); 1653: drought (Vetancurt, *Teatro*, vol. III, 359 and Gregorio M. de Guijo, *Diario 1648–1664* (México: Porrúa, 1952–53), vol. I, p. 208, 215); 1656: preserve the fleet against English pirates in the Caribbean (Vetancurt, *Teatro*, vol. III, p. 359); 1661: drought (Ibid.); 1663: drought (Ibid., p. 360); 1667: drought and disease (Antonio de Robles, *Diario de sucesos notables 1665–1703* [México: Editorial Porrúa, 1946], vol. I, pp. 36, 40); 1668: drought and epidemic (Ibid., 67–68); 1678: drought (Vetancurt, *Teatro*, vol.III, p. 360 and Robles, *Diario*, vol. I, 241–42); 1685: drought (Vetancurt, *Teatro*, vol. III, p. 360); 1692: drought then rebellion (Vetancurt, *Teatro*, vol. III, p. 360 and Robles, *Diario*, vol. III, p. 13); 1696: fleet (Vetancurt, *Teatro*, vol. III, 361 and Robles, *Diario*, vol. III, 49); and, 1699: epidemic and fleet (Narvaez, *Sermón en la solemnidad*, lv, 2). See Fray Balthasser de Medina, *Chrónica de la santa provincia de San Diego de México, de religiosos descalzos de NSPS Francisco en la Nueva España* (México: Juan de Ribera, 1682), 31, section 102–103, for a list of venidas from 1577 to 1678. Cisneros, Mendoza, and Florencia also list the processions up to their respective dates of publication.

40. Christian, *Local Religion*, p. 46. A similar number of processions took place in Nueva Castilla and Sevilla (Ibid., p. 47).

41. José de Noriega, O.M., *Sermón panegyrico en la Santa Cathedral en rogativa por agua, hecho a la miligrossima Imagen de Nuestra Señora de los Remedios* (México: Viuda de Bernardo Calderón, 1685), pp. 3, 5.

42. Alonso Ramírez de Vargas, *Descripción de la venida, y buelta de la milagrosa imagen de Nuestra Señora de los Remedios de esta ciudad de México en año 1668, por causa de la gran sequedad y epidemia de viruelas* (Cádiz, 1668), 5v.

43. Florencia, *La milagrosa*, pp. 100–101.

44. Mendoza, *Orígen*, 35v and Florencia, *La milagrosa*, p. 78.

45. Ramírez de Vargas, *Descripción*, A2v, A4.

46. Robles, *Diario*, vol. I, 67–68.

47. Ramírez de Vargas, *Descripción*, A4.

48. Noriega, *Sermón panegyrico*, 4v. See, for example, Isaiah, chapter 24, verses 4–7. Many clergymen did not approve of the popular custom of touching the Virgin as she passed by in procession because the faithful dishonored Mary with their stain of sin. See, for example, Medina, *Crónica*, p. 32.

49. Christian, *Local Religion*, p. 185.

50. Narvaez, *Sermón en la solemnidad*, 5). For example, in 1597, the Cabildo brought the Virgin to the capital ". . . para que sea yntercessora de nuestor Señor . . ." See *Actas*, Libro 13, p. 44. Eric Wolf comments that Latin Christianity eventually reached a stage in which God retreated into heaven and only special appeals could reach him. These supplications were most often successful when presented by a "super-saint" such as the Virgin Mary. See his work, "Society and Symbols in Latin Europe and in the Islamic near East: Some Comparisons," *Anthropological Quarterly* 42:3 (1969), 296.

51. For a discussion of the concept of sin, Marian intercession, and the unique space of processions, see Turner and Turner, *Image*, p. 15 and Christian, *Local Religion*, p. 97.

52. Burkhart, *The Slippery Earth*, pp. 111, 120.

53. Frances Berdan, *The Aztecs of Central Mexico. An Imperial Society* (New York: Holt, Rinehart, and Winston, 1982), p. 136.

54. Cisneros described the 1577, 1597, and 1616 venida. Mendoza and Florencia describe subsequent ones and claimed that the 1616 procession was considered the standard for later venidas in the seventeenth century. See Mendoza, *Orígen*, 34v. Also see Medina, *Crónica*, 32, Section 107. For a description of a standard procession at mid-eighteenth century, see *Ceremonial de la Nobilisima Ciudad de México por lo acaecido en el año 1755* (México, 1976), pp. 37–42.

55. Florencia, *La milagrosa*, p. 71.

56. AHA, vol. 3898, exp. 8, f.s.n.

57. For details of procession, see Florencia, *La milagrosa*, pp. 72–73. Natives did not erect the thatched arbor nor did they participate in the penitential procession in 1577 because of the severity of the epidemic in indigenous communities. See Mendoza, *Orígen*, 30v.

58. AHA, vol. 3712, exp. 6, f. 1; vol. 1066, exp. 3, April 28, 1809. During the eighteenth century, laws were promulgated to ban such profane aspects of the procession.

59. Medina, *Crónica*, p. 32.

60. See *Actas*, Libro 31, p. 346 and Guijo, *Diario*, vol. I, pp. 208, 215.

61. The meal for dignitaries could cost 190–200 pesos. See *Actas*, Libro 20, p. 344, Libro 21, p. 5. Candles at the shrine alone could cost 63 pesos. See *Actas*, Libro 21, p. 13.

62. For cost and preparations details, see the following years: 1597 (*Actas*, Libro 13, 45); 1616 (cost came to 1082 pesos; Mendoza, f. 34v, *Actas*, Libro 20, 342); 1639 (*Actas*, Libro 31, 347–48); 1716 (INAH, Fondo Lira, f. 4, 7); 1717 (*Actas*, Libro 48–50, tomo 2, 43); 1738 (cost came to 2030 pesos; AHA, vol.

3898, exp. 8, accounts of April 26, 1738); 1793 (cost came to 280 pesos; AHA, vol. 3901, exp. 37, account of July 15, 1793). Expenditures were higher in the 17th century, a reflection of the strong devotion of the city council at that time. For instance, in 1640, the viceroy decided to visit the shrine, an event that cost the Cabildo 1314 pesos. See *Actas*, Libro 32, p. 18.

63. Donations in 1616 came to 1430 pesos (Florencia, *La milagrosa*, p. 76). High ranking officials and wealthy citizens donated jewels, gold crosses, gold figurines of Mary and Jesus, clothing for the image, and poets composed special verses which were left at the shrine. See Ibid., p. 77. In 1736, 1346 pesos were collected from the faithful (AHA, vol. 3895, exp. 2, confraternity accounts for 1736–37). A year later, 2900 pesos were donated (AHA, vol. 3898, exp. 8, April 26, 1738, cuentas del novenario). In 1793, the confraternity collected 2569 pesos (AHA, vol. 3901, exp. 37, cuenta del novenario de July 15).

64. *Actas*, Libro 31, p. 347.

65. In 1694, the proceeds of such sales came to 5743 pesos. See AHA, vol. 3898, exp. 8, f.s.n. Thirty-seven years later (1731), the councilmen ordered 1700 "estampas finas y ordinarias" to sell to pilgrims at the shrine. See AHA, vol. 3989 exp. 8. For an 1812 list of items for sale, see AHA, vol. 3895, exp. 2, records of the August festival.

66. As quoted in Lockhart, *The Nahuas*, p. 244.

67. This was already an established practice before 1589, see *Actas* Libro 9, p. 143; also see, Libro 17. p. 259 and Libro 14, p. 191.

68. Burkhart in *Slippery Earth*, pp. 150–159 states that missionaries of the sixteenth century translated the term virgin (as in Mary) as ichpochtli in Nahuatl, meaning post-pubescent girl who has not taken on the status of adult, irregardless of her sexual condition. To express virginity, qualifiers were added that amounted to saying "still really a girl." This status of girl and the diminutive size of the statue of Remedies may account for the constant reference to her as la Niña.

69. In 1675, the festival cost 582 pesos (AHA, vol. 3895, exp. 5, f.s.n.). From 1679 to 1683, expenditures for the Native fiesta (all taken from AHA, vol. 3898, exp. 7) was as follows: 1683 = 1016 pesos (f. 62, 63, 64); 1680 = 462 pesos (f. 64, 65); 1681 = 422 pesos (f. 65, 66); 1682 = 277 pesos (f. 67, 68); 1679 = 291 pesos (f. 122, 123). Similar figures for 1688 to 1691 (all from AHA, vol. 3898, exp. 8, f.s.n.) include: 1688 = 376 pesos; 1689 = 300 pesos; 1690 = 330 pesos; and 1691 = 269 pesos. In 1790, the confraternity paid 336 pesos for the indigenous celebration. See AHA, vol. 3901, document dated June 30, 1791. In 1675, Natives contributed 589 pesos (AHA, vol. 3895, exp. 5, f.s.n.). From 1679 to 1683, the confraternity collected 1931 pesos total (AHA, vol. 3898, exp. 7, f. 57). For eighteenth century donations, see 1737 (148 pesos) and 1738 (74 pesos), both in AHA, vol. 3895, exp. 2, accounts of 1736–37; and, 1790 (429 pesos) in AHA, vol. 3901, document dated June 30, 1791.

70. In 1675, the dinner cost 90 pesos (AHA, vol. 3898, exp. 7, *Cuenta del mayordomo de la cofradía*). During the four year period from 1679 to 1683, the meal averaged 80 pesos annually (Ibid.). For the 1688–93 period, the shrine collected 16,336 pesos from all over the viceroyalty. See AHA, vol. 3898, exp. 8, f.s.n., listed under "gastos del santuario."

71. Betancur in AGN, *Ramo Historia*, vol. 1, exp. 17, f. 247.

72. For vows and donations, see Florencia, *La milagrosa*, pp. 100–10, 108–109. The Cabildo provided oil for the lamp on a continuous basis. See *Actas*, Libro 25, 114–15. The confraternity/Cabildo tried to stop the tradition of touching the image in the early eighteenth century. See AHA, vol. 58A, July 4, 1732.

73. The issue of popular devotion and a new shrine was raised in 1621 (*Actas*, Libro 24, 32); the new building was completed in 1629. The aldermen would grant indulgences and pardons to those who participated in the romería. They charged fray Pedro de Zamudio, an Augustinian, with the task of investigating the possibility in Rome. Apparently nothing came of it as no formal romería was hosted by the city council/confraternity. See *Actas*, Libro 23, p. 229.

74. For the description of this second image, see Florencia, *La milagrosa*, pp. 119, 123. It is quite possible that worshipers did not know that the Peregrina was a duplicate image of the original. Duplicate or pilgrim images of Guadalupe and Fatima travel today, attesting to the importance of such a traditional practice. I thank Stafford Poole for bringing this contemporary phenomena to my attention. For the case of Native farmers and their petition to the Cabildo in 1624, see *Actas*, Libro 25, p. 145.

75. The dispute first surfaced in the records in 1606 (*Actas*, Libro 16, 365) and was still ongoing in 1614 (*Actas*, Libro 19, 250). For 1731, see AHA, vol. 3898, exp. 12, f. 13. In 1735, it still was an issue. See AHA, vol. 60A, August 29, 1735.

76. For the issue of the statue, see AHA, vol. 86A, f. 35. Later documents from 1812 show that the confraternity did purchase another image and new clothing. See AHA, vol. 3895, exp. 2, 1812 accounts. For city council diplomacy, see AHA, vol. 3898, exp. 8, f.s.n., letter dated August 23, 1775 from Luís de Monero y Guerrero y Luiando.

77. See AHA, vol. 60A, August 29, 1735 and AHA, vol. 3900, exp. 22, f.s.n.

78. Robles, *Diario*, vol. II, 265.

79. AHA, vol. 35, June 22, 1692.

80. Robles, *Diario*, vol. III, 13, 49, 71.

81. Narvaez, *Sermón de la solemnidad*, 1v, 2, 9v. They first did a novena to Christ and then brought the Virgin to the city. However, she solely was held responsible for the miracle.

82. This was the case in 1717 when the procession occurred for the Duke of Linares who was fatally ill. See *Actas*, Libro 48–50, tomo 2, 39.

83. The venidas are as follows: 1702: fleet and drought (AHA, vol. 372A, June 2, 1702); 1704: drought (AHA, vol. 372A, April 18, 1704), possibly at the *ermita*); 1705: drought (AHA, vol. 372A, May 8, 1705, possibly at the *ermita*); 1706: for the monarchy (*Actas*, Libro 43–47, 55–56); 1708: birth of an heir to the throne (*Actas*, Libro 43–47, 103); 1710: unclear why brought to the cathedral (*Actas*, Libro 43–47, 34); 1711: drought and sickness (*Actas*, Libro 43–47, 86); 1712: birth of heir to the throne (*Actas*, Libro 43–47, 181–83); 1713: drought (*Actas*, Libro 43–47, 196); 1716: fleet (*Actas*, Libro 48–50, tomo 2, 162); 1717: drought and ex-viceroy's health (*Actas*, Libro 48–50, tomo 2, 39); 1719: the monarchy (*Actas*, Libro 48–50, tomo 2, 188); 1732: fleet (AHA, vol. 59A, tomo 1, f. 31–38); 1734: fleet (AHA, vol. 59A, tomo 1, f.s.n.); 1735: drought (AHA, vol. 60A, f. 43–44); 1761: fleet and drought (AHA, vol. 82A, May and June, 1761); 1762: wars in Europe (AHA, vol. 83A, July 22, 1762); 1766: fleet (AHA, vol. 86A, f. 68); 1784: epidemic (Manuel Antonio Valdes, *Gazetas de México, Compendio de noticias de Nueva España* (México: Zúñiga y Ontiveros, 1784–1809), vol. I, 150; henceforth *Gazetas*); 1785: drought (*Gazetas*, vol. I, 308); 1786: epidemic (*Gazetas*, vol. II, 106); 1790: drought (*Gazetas*, vol. IV, 122); 1793: wars against France (*Gazetas*, vol. V, 380–81); 1794 (twice): drought and war with France (*Gazetas*, vol. VI, 323, 707 respectively); 1797: drought (*Gazetas*, vol. VIII, 279); 1789: drought (*Gazetas*, vol. IX, 37); 1799: drought and sickness (AHA, vol. 3895, exp. 2, f.s.n.); 1800: drought and general happiness (Ibid.);

1802 (twice): health of Monarch, Charles IV and drought (*Gazetas*, vol. XI, 5, 85 respectively); 1804 (twice): epidemic and drought (*Gazetas*, vol. XII, 59, 111 respectively); 1808: epidemic and drought (*Gazetas*, vol. XV, 416); and, 1810: drought and general happiness (AHA, vol. 3895, exp. 2, f.s.n.).

84. For the sermon, see Blas de Pulgar, *Sermón que en acción de gracias ofrecido a Dios . . . en su imagen de los Remedios . . . por el parto de la Reyna . . .* (México: Viuda de Miguel de Rivera Calderón, 1708), 1–3. The Virgin had been asked in a formal petition to protect the queen, see Miguel González de Valdeosera, *Gentheliaco elogio, prognóstico felice, and la expectación del Real Agosto parto . . . que venera esta Nueva España con la advocación de los Remedios* (México: Juan Joseph G. Carrascoso, 1707). The floats are described in *Actas*, Libro 43–47, 103.

85. AHA, vol. 3895, exp. 2, f.s.n.; vol. 372A, September 13, 1700; *Actas*, Libro 48–50, 12, 176.

86. *Actas*, Libro 48–50, pp. 188, 220.

87. *Actas*, Libro 48–50, tomo 2, 118; AHA, vol. 376A, January 25, 1724; and, vol. 3898, exp 8, f.s.n.

88. The 1720 incidence was particularly troublesome. The Virgin had been brought to the cathedral for the health of the monarchy rather than for the drought plaguing the region. In addition, the Jesuits petitioned to have Remedies attend their patron holiday, thus extending her time in Mexico City even more (*Actas*, Libro 51–53, 53). Although the city council apologized to the governor for their duplicity, they instituted an investigation to determine who had leaked the information regarding the letter (Ibid., p. 83). In 1733, the Native festival was once again canceled because the viceroy would not allow the image to return to the shrine. See AHA, vol. 3898, exp. 8, f.s.n. For the 1750 royal decree, see AHA, vol. 3900, exp. 21, f.s.n.

89. For the case of 1754, see AHA, vol. 386, exp. 21, f. 1. The city claimed that it was busy dealing with damage caused by an earthquake. They further stated that they were doing their real job and did not have time to attend festivals. This marked a striking contrast to their sentiments of 100 years earlier. For 1789, see AHA, vol. 3895, exp. 2, f.s.n.

90. AHA, vol. 3898, exp. 8, f.s.n.

91. William B. Taylor, "The Virgin of Guadalupe in New Spain: An Inquiry into the Social History of a Marian Devotion," *American Ethnologist* 14:1 (February 1987), 14. According to Stafford Poole, it was a criollo devotion encouraged and spread by diocesan, Jesuit, and Franciscan clergy. See his *Our Lady*, p. 217.

92. *Clamor que un indio hizo a nuestra Señora de los Remedios en su santuario la mañana del 11 de agosto de 1810* (México, 1810), 1.

93. Luís José Montaña, *Rasgo épico. Peregrinación de la sagrada Imagen de la Santísima Virgen María. Nuestra Señora de advocación de los Remedios* (México: Arizpe, 1810), pp. 9, 13, 14.

94. *Desengaño a los indios haciendoles ver lo mucho que deben a los Españoles. Conversación que tuvieron en el campamento de esta ciudad un Dragón con una Tortillera y su marido Pasqual, y la precención A.V.* (México, 1810), p. 11.

95. AHA, vol. 3903, exp. 65, f. 1, 2.

96. Poole, *Our Lady*, p. 3.

97. Agustín Pomposo Fernández de San Salvador, *Acción de gracias a nuestra Generala María SS. de los Remedios, Disipiadora de las nubes fulminantes de la ira de Dios . . .* (México, 1810), pp. 2–3, 5.

98. *México a su Generala María Santísima de los Remedios en la procesión solemne del día 24 de febrero con que concluyó el novenario de acción de gracias por la prosperidad de las armas del Rey contra los rebeldes* (México: Arizpe, 1811), pp. 285, 283.

99. For a discussion of sacred images and their relationship to change, see Turner and Turner, *Image*, p. 29; Christian, *Apparitions*, p. 15 and *Local Religion*, p. 93.

100. Officials first invoked the Virgin of Loreto, Remedios, Guadalupe, and then other images. The epidemic apparently ceased after the Cabildo became the official patrons of Guadalupe; and, therefore, she is credited with the miracle. See Poole, *Our Lady*, pp. 175–76, 181.

9

The Woman of the Apocalypse

Stafford Poole

By far the most famous of the Virgins of Mexico is the Virgin of Guadalupe. In modern times she has come to be known as not only the patroness of Mexico but of the Americas as well. In Mexico today, and among Hispanic Americans, the cult of Guadalupe is preeminent. Stafford Poole focuses on the development of the devotion to Guadalupe as it came to flower in the early seventeenth century.

The traditions of the story of Guadalupe in Mexico begin within decades of the Conquest, although the legend as we know it today actually dates from the first few decades of the seventeenth century. Just as Linda Curcio-Nagy has indicated with the Remedios cult, the Guadalupe cult started among the natives and then later spread to Spanish residents of the colony. Poole takes a look at the major force behind the dissemination of the story, the parish priest Miguel Sánchez, who in 1648 published the first account of the Virgin's appearance. The Nahuatl version of the legend, the Huey tlamahuiçoltica, *was published by Luis Laso de la Vega, the vicar of the shrine of Guadalupe, in 1649. Poole gives an extensive analysis of this important source for Guadalupan studies.*

Stafford Poole has written several important works on sixteenth-century Mexico. Noted among them are a biography of Pedro Moya de Conteras, the third archbishop of Mexico, and a study of the development of the cult of the Virgin of Guadalupe, from which this selection is taken.

In 1648 and 1649 the silence that shrouded the apparitions [of the Virgin of Guadalupe] changed dramatically with the publication of the first accounts of them. These were the work of two criollo priests, Miguel Sánchez and Luis Laso de la Vega, who together opened up an abrupt new chapter in the history of Our Lady of Guadalupe. Sánchez, in particular, was responsible not just for first making the story known but also for bonding it to criollo identity.

From *Our Lady of Guadalupe* (Tucson: The University of Arizona Press, 1995), 100–26, 259–63. © 1995 by The Arizona Board of Regents. Reprinted by permission of the University of Arizona Press.

The appearance of the apparition story coincided with the flowering of criollismo. By the early seventeenth century the growing numbers of the criollos made them a force to be reckoned with. That and the failure of the dismal prophecies about their eventual physical and mental deterioration meant that they could no longer be disregarded. Though peninsular-criollo antagonisms still existed and broke out in open hostility, the snobbery and prejudice of the previous century generally assumed subtler forms. The criollos had come to dominate the ranks of the diocesan clergy, for the diocesan priesthood was more open to them than other avenues of social mobility, and the peninsular bishops, who needed the diocesans in their conflicts with the orders, were generally favorable to them. The Jesuits, whose educational work was primarily among the criollos, also tended to be sympathetic.

The eagerness and rapidity with which the criollos, especially the clergy, embraced the new devotion and used it as the basis for a myth of uniqueness and distinct identity show that criollismo had reached a critical mass by the mid-seventeenth century. It needed only the opportunity to express itself, and that opportunity was provided in a special way by Miguel Sánchez. New Spain was not just the homeland of the criollos, it was also the new homeland of the Virgin Mary, who, through the miracle of the image, had her second birth there. Though initially centered in Mexico City, the new devotion quickly spread outward. For half a century, the image/apparition devotion, which logically should have appealed to the Indians, was exclusively criollo. The fusion of Guadalupe and Mexican identity began not at Tepeyac in 1531 but in Mexico City in 1648. In the story of the apparitions, criollismo found its legitimacy.

This period also saw a flourishing of Nahuatl language studies. Whereas in the sixteenth century these studies had been mostly in the hands of the Franciscans, in the seventeenth century they came to be the domain of the Jesuits. Of these, Horacio Carochi, the author of a Nahuatl grammar, *Arte de la lengua mexicana*, is probably the most famous. In addition to grammars and dictionaries, the Franciscans of the sixteenth century had produced numerous *sermonarios* and *confesionarios*. In contrast, works in Nahuatl in the following century began to include those of a more secular culture, such as translations of Spanish plays. There also seems to have been a conscious attempt to revive the classical Nahuatl of pre-Hispanic and early postconquest times.

Miguel Sánchez

Miguel Sánchez was a learned and highly respected priest of the archdiocese of Mexico who in later life joined the Oratory.[1] He was born in Mexico City in 1594 and studied at the Royal and Pontifical University, where he received the degree of *licenciado* (licentiate, a degree intermediate between bachelor and doctor). As a young man he unsuccessfully sought a teaching position at the university. He was considered a great authority on the writings of Saint Augustine, although the claim that he knew them all by heart is implausible.[2] His reputation as a preacher was high, though on the basis of his extant writings his style must be judged baroque, meandering, and highly metaphorical. At unknown dates, he was chaplain to the nuns of San Jerónimo and later of the Hospital Real. At the time of his entry into the Oratory in 1662, he was the chaplain of the ermita of Remedios. He was noted for the simplicity and voluntary poverty of his life. In 1640 he published a sermon on San Felipe de Jesús in which he said, "I remain hopeful of another major writing: the second Eve in our sanctuary of Guadalupe."[3] At an unknown date he resigned his chaplaincy and retired to Guadalupe, where he died on 22 March 1674.

Sánchez was the author of the first published account of the appearance of the Virgin of Guadalupe to Juan Diego, the earliest one to which an indisputable date can be attached. This work was titled *Imagen de la Virgen María, Madre de Dios de Guadalupe, Milagrosamente aparecida en la ciudad de México* and was published in 1648.[4] In format, the book begins with the approval of the censors and then Sánchez's introduction. This is followed by a brief exegesis of the principal verses of Revelation 12, then a second exegesis applying these verses to the Virgin Mary, and then a narration of the apparitions. After this account, there is a third exegesis of Revelation 12, a word-by-word application to the Virgin of Guadalupe. There follow descriptions of the procession of 26 December 1531 and the sanctuary and a series of miracle stories. The book concludes with laudatory letters by Francisco de Siles and Luis Laso de la Vega.

Approval for the work was given by two censors.[5] The first was Juan de Poblete, the *chantre* (choirmaster) of the cathedral chapter. He spoke of the carelessness that had prevented the publication of the apparition account until such a late period after the events. "With special attention and more than human disposition, the great enterprise has been reserved after 116 [*sic*] years to the superior genius, sharp intelligence, eloquent speech, and delicate pen of the author."[6] The other approbation was by Fray Pedro de Rozas, professor of theology at the Augustinian convent in Mexico City. "Should this prodigy remain in silence? No, for such a singular favor was reserved to a careful preacher, the licenciado Miguel Sánchez, whose rare devotion has raised him up to understand the miracle and, profiting from it, to declare it to us to our profit. Let all New Spain thank him that after 116 [*sic*] years he took up his pen in order that what we knew only by tradition, we may understand without distinction, in its details and defined with authority and foundation."[7] Again, there is a reference to the lack of written sources.

Sánchez himself claimed to have studied the matter for more than half a century. In a sworn declaration before representatives of the cathedral chapter in 1666 he stated that "for more than fifty years in these parts he has had individual notices, both remote and proximate, of the tradition and apparition of the most holy Virgin of Guadalupe."[8] Yet in an introduction to his book entitled the "foundation of the history" [fundamento de la historia], he admitted that there were no authentic written records.

> With determination, eagerness, and diligence I looked for documents and writings that dealt with the holy image and its miracle. I did not find them, although I went through the archives where they could have been kept. I learned that through the accident of time and events those that there were had been lost. I appealed to the providential curiosity of the elderly, in which I found some sufficient for the truth. Not content, I examined them in all their circumstances, now confronting the chronicles of the conquest, now gathering information from the oldest and most trustworthy persons of the city, now looking for those who were said to have been the original owners of these papers. And I admit that even if everything would have been lacking to me, I would not have desisted from my purpose, when I had on my side the common, grave, and venerated law of tradition, ancient, uniform, and general about that miracle.[9]

Sánchez is maddeningly vague when referring to his sources. The phrase "some" (unos) may refer to the elderly, but more probably to documents. All Spanish-language authorities who have written on this point agree that he was referring to some sort of native documents. What were these? He did not say or even hint. He was clear about the fact that he was unable to find official records of the apparitions, but he also implied that his primary source was an oral tradition among the Indians. Significantly, however, he never named or specified any of his sources, other than what he called a reliable tradition.

The lack of documentary evidence would be noted by others and would present a difficulty even for the earliest proponents of the apparitions. In 1666, Sánchez gave the following explanation for this lack that he said he had heard from a rector of the sanctuary of Guadalupe. "The reason for not finding the original papers of this miraculous apparition that were written on that occasion had been and was because many papers were missing from the archbishop's archive of the administration of this archdiocese by reason of their being in the shops where every kind of spice was sold, a theft that originated and was caused by the shortage of paper in this kingdom in that year."[10] Aside from the fact that the assertion is secondhand and seems rather bizarre, it presents other difficulties. There was, indeed, a paper shortage in New Spain about the year 1621, but there is no record of the extremities that Sánchez mentioned.[11] Although many papers have been lost from Spanish and Mexican archives, as any researcher can attest with deep frustration, there was also a tendency for administrators and archivists to make multiple copies of significant documents. It seems improbable that a paper shortage would have led to the wholesale looting of all testimonies to the Guadalupe apparitions. Sánchez's explanation is too pat for a major problem—the total absence of corroborating documentation prior to 1648.

In his account of the apparitions, Sánchez followed what has become the standard chronology, though his wording was not always clear. The first apparition occurred on Saturday, followed by the first interview with Zumárraga and then the second apparition. On Sunday (though it was not specified as such), Juan Diego went to mass and instruction at Tlatelolco and after ten o'clock in the morning went to see Zumárraga. Sánchez did not describe that interview; rather, he had Juan Diego describe it to the Virgin in the third interview, when he also told her of the bishop-elect's request for a sign. Monday (which was referred to only as "the following day") was spent in trying to find medicine or a doctor for Juan Bernardino. The attempt to avoid the Virgin and the fourth apparition took place on "the third day, in reference to the one on which he was with the Virgin Mary,"[12] as did the gathering of the flowers and the fifth apparition, that to Juan Bernardino. Sánchez did not, however, assign any dates to these days.

Sánchez was the first person to describe the transferal of the image from the cathedral, where Zumárraga had taken it from his home, to the new chapel at Tepeyac. He wrote that after the bishop-elect had consulted both cabildos, that is, the city council and the cathedral chapter, Zumárraga set Tuesday, 26 December 1531, as the date for the procession, which Sánchez described in exuberant detail. He referred to the dances by the Indians, although Zumárraga was known to be opposed to these. Once arrived at the shrine, Zumárraga blessed it and celebrated a pontifical mass.[13] In the account of the transferal of the image to Guadalupe, he added that both Juan Diego and his uncle lived out their lives at the sanctuary. This, too, has become a constant tradition.

With regard to the ermita, Sánchez stated that "the principal [invocation] and title of the ermita is that of her [the Virgin's] nativity."[14] In his description of the sanctuary he addressed the question of why it was built at the foot of the hill, not on the top, on the actual site of the apparitions.

The wish to obey the mandate of the Virgin Mary and the experience of the favor that had been received, impelled the Most Illustrious Bishop don Juan de Zumárraga and the citizens of Mexico to build the first ermita in a short space of time. It was constructed at the base of the hill in order to protect it from the north winds, which blow strongly at that spot. It was established in sight of and along the royal highway, which, where the causeway ends on the bridge, divides into different highways for all New Spain. And since the first apparition of the Virgin was on the summit of the hill and in the sprouting of miraculous flowers, it was a grave matter that she permitted them to build her ermita at the base and on a site so frequently traveled. Perhaps the mystery of that permission is that of Genesis 31.[15]

He went on to draw a parallel from that biblical passage, actually Genesis 35:19-20, which describes how Jacob buried his wife, Rachel, by the roadside rather than in a nearby city, so that future generations would pass by her tomb.

In the interior of the sanctuary, according to Sánchez, there were more than sixty silver lamps hanging from the ceiling. The number is different from that given by Miles Philips, but the essential idea is the same. The description of the image states that it had a crown. Like Philips, he described the curative spring, which was at the base of the hill, on the side looking east. According to Sánchez, it was the spot where the Virgin stopped Juan Diego when he was trying to avoid her. He described the waters as being heavy and miraculously healing.

As was standard practice in hagiographical accounts, Sánchez related the various miracles that had occurred through the intercession of the Virgin of Guadalupe. These will be considered in detail in the next section, where they will be compared with similar accounts by Laso de la Vega. The greatest miracle, according to Sánchez, was the preservation of the image, on its fragile base, for so long. This, too, was to be a standard argument of other writers throughout that century in response to the lack of documentary sources.

The account was followed by two laudatory letters. The first was by Francisco de Siles, a member of the cathedral chapter, professor of theology at the university, a friend of Sánchez, and later an enthusiastic champion of Guadalupe. It reflected a strong criollo consciousness. The Virgin of Guadalupe was called "our criolla sovereign" and the image "the criolla image of Guadalupe, so that she may always intercede for her homeland," and at another point, "I speak and I write for the whole homeland, which receives this history, the letters patent of its greatness." He commended Sánchez for writing a book "for those born in this land."[16]

The second introductory letter by Luis Laso de la Vega, the vicar of the ermita at Guadalupe, had no such criollo emphasis. It has, however, been the subject of some dispute. For a clear understanding of the nature of this dispute, it will be necessary to quote the letter at length in all its baroque complexity.

And although I have always venerated, admired, and praised it [the image] as much as my thoughts have been capable of, after I read the history of her miracle, which with such living emotion you have written and published, I confess that there have grown in my heart the desire to be totally hers and the glory of having her as mine with the title of her priest-minister. I think that what happened to our father Adam has happened to me. God favored him by putting him in paradise, in the freshness of its woodland and its fertile plain by the river, where the trunks and branches were the bonds that embraced it. He slept in sweet abandon. God took one of his ribs, from which he formed Eve, that miraculous creation. He placed her before the eyes of Adam, who woke up. And seeing her, he first claims her as his own and then declares her to be his love in tender expressions. Hoc nunc os ex ossibus meis, et caro de carne mea: haec vocabitur virago . . . quamobrem relinquet homo patrem et matrem et adhaerebit uxori suae.[17] Now Eve is flesh of my flesh and bone of my bone. Ler her be called virile[18] and for her sake let father and mother be forgotten, preferring her love to all love. Here Adam was being notably mysterious because Eve had always been his; he had her as his own, as he declared. It seems that when he looks at her from a distance, well formed and distinct in parts and the perfection of beauty through God's care, then he says that she is his: hoc nunc. And because his heart could not endure that he merely proclaim it, it moves him to praise her sweetly, protesting in his love everlasting support. It was something great. If Adam was aware of it through contemplation, now that he is awake it is stated openly and in his very own pledge he shows special appreciation that she is his, dedicating his whole will to her.

I and all my predecessors have been sleeping Adams, possessing this second Eve in the paradise of her Mexican Guadalupe among the miraculous flowers that painted her, and amid their fragrance we were contemplating her in wonder. But now it falls to me to be the Adam who has awakened in order that he might see in print the account of her history: well formed, composed, and shared, in the prodigious fact of the miracle, in the event of her apparition, in the mysteries which her picture signifies, and in the brief map of her sanctuary, which now speaks, having decoded what previously it kept silent for so many years. I can say what Adam said, Hoc nunc os ex ossibus meis, because, although she was already mine by my title as her vicar, I now proclaim myself to be her glorious possessor.[19]

There is disagreement as to whether Laso de la Vega was speaking with baroque hyperbole, as Lafaye suggests, or whether he was stating categorically that the account of the apparitions was entirely new to him.[20] His words "we were contemplating her in wonder" can be taken to mean that he and his predecessors were aware of the marvel prior to Sánchez's book. On the other hand, the entire letter and its context clearly expresses wonderment and surprise—like Adam, he realized that he possessed the wonder only after he awoke. In addition, the comments made by Antonio de Lara, Francisco de Siles, and Antonio de Robles, which will be discussed below, reinforce the conclusion that the story of the apparitions was unknown to the Spaniards and criollos of Mexico City in 1648.

Sánchez's work contained some obvious historical errors, such as referring to Zumárraga as the consecrated bishop of Mexico or to the cathedral chapter as existing in 1531, five years before its establishment. These errors may reflect Sánchez's own views rather than his sources. They are not strong arguments against the veracity of his account. On the other hand, because Sánchez is so vague about his sources, it is impossible to say to what extent he embellished the story.

Sánchez's book is baroque in character, its style ornate and repetitious. Writing as a hagiographer, not a historian, he sought to link the Virgin of Guadalupe with the woman of the Apocalypse (Revelation 12). "[And] a great sign appeared in heaven, a woman clothed with the sun, and the moon under her feet, and on her head a crown of twelve stars. . . . She cried out in childbirth and was in pain until she gave birth. . . . There was a great battle. . . . The woman fled into the wilderness. . . . Two wings were given to the woman . . . and the serpent sent [a torrent] from his mouth. . . . The dragon was angered against the woman."[21] Consequently, his account of the apparitions was interrupted by lengthy commentaries, digressions, exegetical tangents, and theological excursuses. The narration itself seems like a paraphrase of the standard account as found later in the *Nican mopohua*, though he omits the doublets, terms of endearment, and poetry of the Nahuatl version.

Criollismo is the central theme of the book. His reason for writing it was that he was moved by "the homeland, my people, companions, citizens, those of this new world; I thought it better to reveal myself to be presumptuously ignorant for such an undertaking than to give a motive for presuming such a guilty ignorance on the part of all."[22] The story of the apparitions is little more than a framework on which Sánchez can build his criollo interpretations. He had a messianic view of Mexico City, which he sought to put on a par with the great religious centers of the Catholic world. He compared Zumárraga to Saint John the Evangelist and Mexico to Patmos (the island where the Evangelist was exiled), and he interpreted Revelation 12 in terms of Mexico and the Spanish empire. The woman clothed with the sun was the city of Mexico. Mary, he asserted, had aided the Spanish conquest; she was the "assistant conquistador."[23] New Spain was her homeland. His emphasis, which took up most of the first part of the work, was that Revelation 12 prefigured Mexico, Guadalupe, and the destiny of the sons of the land. Guadalupe was for him primarily a devotion for those "born in this land." They had an "intimate and special brotherhood of relationship with Mary in this her image, since she is reborn miraculously in the land where they are born."[24] His reasoning was often contrived, for example, when he pointed out that Juan Diego was called by Mary, and he was named for John and James, whose mother was named Mary, or when he formulated elaborate relationships based on the name John between Juan Diego, Zumárraga, and Saint John the Evangelist. The eagle whose wings were given to the woman fleeing the dragon was the eagle on the escutcheon of Mexico. The eagle in flight formed a cross and so the eagle that symbolized pre-Christian New Spain was to be Christianized by Mary, giving the gift of the cross.

He blamed the periodic floods in the city on the influence of the moon and made a bizarre observation about the climate, when discussing the fact that the woman of Revelation 12 was clothed with the sun: "We have learned, as something evident, that by nature this land and new world were a torrid zone and a region burned by the sun and presumed to be uninhabitable. Most holy Mary took control of the sun, moderated its rigors, reduced its heat, calmed its fire, tempered its rays, served as a cloud."[25]

What must strike the modern reader as strange is that the traditional account as given by Sánchez offers no objective basis for his unrestrained criollo interpretations. In itself the story is directed toward the Indians, not the Europeans, though it is cast in the classic European apparition genre. Although at times Sánchez included the Indians in the devotion and spoke of the apparitions as a special blessing to them, it is difficult to say what place he intended to give them. He did remark, however, on the strength of their devotion. In a very real sense Sánchez took a cult story that should have been exclusively Indian and appropriated it for the criollos. In this he was followed by the preachers and writers of the seventeenth and eighteenth centuries, especially the diocesan clergy and the Jesuits. It is impossible to trace the subsequent history of the Guadalupe devotion without the awareness that it was a criollo devotion in which the sons of the land saw their own special election. If the Indians had any share in it, it was apart from the criollos. This meant in turn that the Indian aspects of the story would have to be devalued or diluted.

The emphasis on criollismo and the downplaying of the Indian aspect of the story are clear in the differences between the dialogues in the *Imagen* and those in the *Nican mopohua*, which appeared six months later. As they are quoted by Sánchez, the native element is definitely attenuated. In the *Nican mopohua* the Virgin reveals to Juan Diego her wish for a church in tender words: "I ardently wish and I greatly desire that they build my temple for me here, where I will reveal, I will make known, and I will give to people all my love, my compassion, my aid, and my protection, for I am your compassionate mother. . . . There I will hear their weeping and their sorrows in order to remedy and to heal all their various afflictions, their miseries, and their torments." In Sánchez's wording the message is brief and generic. "I want a house and ermita built for me here, a temple in which to show myself a compassionate mother with you, with yours, with my devotees, with those who seek me in order to remedy their needs." Her words on Tuesday morning are even more tender and poignant in the *Nican mopohua*: "Know, rest very much assured, my youngest child, let nothing whatever frighten you or worry you. Do not be concerned. Do not fear [your uncle's] illness nor any illness or affliction. Am I, your mother, not here? Are you not under my shade and my shadow? Am I not your happiness? Are you not in my lap and in my carrying gear? Is there anything more you need? Do not let anything worry you further or upset you. Do not let your uncle's illness worry you. He will not die of what is now upon him. Rest assured, for he is already well." Sánchez's wording is in the third person and has all the poignancy of a government report. "He was [not] to fear dangers, fear illnesses, nor be afflicted in his tasks, taking her for his mother, for his health and protection, that the illness of his uncle, who was not to be in danger of death, would not hinder him, and she assured him that from that moment he was completely well."

Although Sánchez's book was printed in only a limited number of copies, it was quite influential. At the time of his death on 22 March 1674, his obituary, written by Antonio de Robles, testified both to the impact of his work and to the fact that the apparition account was new to the people of Mexico.

> [He lived retired] for some time in the sanctuary of Our Lady of Guadalupe, to whom he was very devoted. He wrote a learned book about her apparition, which seemingly has been the means by which devotion to this holy image has spread throughout all Christendom. It had been forgotten, even by the citizens of Mexico [City], until this venerable priest made it known, since there was in all Mexico [City] only one image of this sovereign lady, in the convent of Santo Domingo, and today there is not a convent or church where it is not venerated, and rare indeed is the religious house or cell where there is not a copy of it, universally in all New Spain, the kingdoms of Peru, and in almost all Europe.[26]

Robles may have been exaggerating, or speaking from limited knowledge, when he said that there was only one picture of Our Lady of Guadalupe in Mexico City. The Basque artist Baltasar Echave Orio made a copy in 1606, and Archbishop Juan Pérez de la Serna commissioned an engraving in 1615 which was put on sale to help fund the construction of a new chapel at Tepeyac. Stephanie Wood has found at least one example in the Toluca region of a household image of Guadalupe bequeathed in a will in 1632.[27] More important, it is antecedently improbable that a religious event as transcendently important as the Guadalupe apparitions could have been forgotten or lost, even in the course of a century.

In 1653, Sánchez published a sermon that he preached at the University of Mexico in honor of the Immaculate Conception. Although he made one reference to Revelation 12, there was no mention of Guadalupe.[28] In 1665 he published a devotional book called *Novenas de la Virgen Maria, Madre de Dios, para sus devotisimos Santuarios de los Remedios y Guadalupe*. The censor for the book was Doctor Antonio de Lara Mogrovejo, who wrote in his letter of approval, "Having brought to light the rare and mysterious apparition . . . it was a pledge of his obligation to arouse new fervor with this book in the devotion of the faithful, when he introduced it to their notice. . . . The history of the apparition of Guadalupe cost him much hard work. Traditions and fragments weakened by the for-getfulness of time and the scant curiosity of the ancients always put the truth at risk, even though his learning made it so clear that he achieved his purpose easily."[29] The fact that the apparitions were unknown in 1648 is confirmed by a second approbation by the same Francisco de Siles who had written one of the introductory letters to Sánchez's *Imagen*. The au-thor, he wrote, "made known the apparition, forgotten in the course of more than a century and rescued by his effort from the lack of care within a brief time; a book so profitable that I do not know if before he gave it to the press this miracle was well known, even in our America."[30] These state-ments show again that the tradition was unknown and that there was little or no evidence for it. It also opens up the possibility that Sánchez may have embellished the original account from which he worked. The exact extent to which the standard apparition account is an Indian tradition or the work of the Oratorian's imagination will never be known for sure.

Although Sánchez's work was influential in encouraging the Guadalupan devotion, its overall impact seems to have been blunted by the small number of volumes printed and his ornate, gongoristic style. It has rarely been reprinted.[31] In 1660, at a time when the devotion was be-ginning to spread, the Jesuit Mateo de la Cruz published anonymously an abbreviated and vastly improved version of Sánchez's work.[32] It enjoyed a great popularity and probably did as much to spread the devotion as Sánchez's original. Florencia, writing in 1688, considered it the best ac-count. De la Cruz excised the long digressions and scriptural exegeses of Sánchez's work and reduced it to a summary of the apparitions them-selves. In fact, his work is more rewrite than abridgement. It was the first published account to give dates for the apparitions, specifically 9 to 12 December. It follows Sánchez's chronology of the apparitions rather than that of Laso de la Vega.

De la Cruz omitted almost all the extravagant criollismo of Sánchez's account. He was, however, one of the first authors to note the growing rivalry between Guadalupe and Remedios and the first, so far as I can determine, to refer to them in print as La Criolla and La Conquistadora/ La Gachupina. He also cited their different invocations: Guadalupe against floods, Remedios against drought. He went to some pains to demonstrate that the image of Guadalupe was that of the Immaculate Conception. In one of his few nods to criollismo, he contrasted the Extremaduran Guadalupe with the Mexican.

> The former image was made by Saint Luke, the latter was painted either by God or the Virgin herself or at least by angels. Over there they sent it from Rome to an archbishop of Seville, over here from heaven to an archbishop of Mexico. Over there it was buried 600 years, like a seed, in order to come to its invocation 200 years after being discovered over there, to bloom as if born over here, more than 3,040 leagues away. In

both places it is called Guadalupe which . . . means "River of Wolves" . . . wolves being symbols of the demons . . . and she wanted this place to be called Guadalupe in order to show that by her presence she put to flight the hellish demons of this place . . . there, where they used to worship the demons in the idol Theotenantzin, with the title of the Mother of the gods.[33]

In 1662 this version was reprinted in Spain under the patronage of Pedro de Gálvez, former *visitador* of New Spain, a member of the Council of the Indies (1657–1662), and later bishop of Zamora, who was an ardent devotee of Guadalupe.[34]

Although Sánchez's work was the first published account of the apparitions, it has not become the standard account. That was to come from the vicar of Guadalupe.

Luis Laso de la Vega

In 1649, Luis Laso de la Vega, the vicar of the ermita of Guadalupe, published the *Huey tlamahuiçoltica*. Almost nothing is known about his life except that he was vicar of the ermita in 1648 and received the post of *medio racionero* of the cathedral chapter nine years later.[35] The publication of the new work followed very closely on that of Sánchez. Laso de la Vega's introduction to Sánchez's work was dated 2 July 1648, and Baltasar González's approbation of the *Huey tlamahuiçoltica* carried the date 9 January 1649, a time span of approximately six months. The book was poorly printed and contained a number of typographical errors, perhaps a sign of haste in preparation. It is also full of orthographic inconsistencies, especially in the use of diacritical marks. It is Laso de la Vega's only known publication.

The approval for the book was given by the Jesuit censor, Baltasar González, who wrote, "I find that it is in agreement with what is known of the event by tradition and annals."[36] Almost immediately, however, he seems to bear testimony to a degree of ignorance and disinterest, "because it will be very useful and profitable to enliven devotion in the lukewarm and engender it anew in those who live in ignorance of the mysterious origin of this heavenly portrait of the Queen of Heaven."[37] Again, there is a frustrating lack of precision about what the "tradition and annals" are.

Laso de la Vega's authorship of all parts of the *Huey tlamahuiçoltica* is open to question. The book is clearly a compilation of diverse elements, dating from different periods and written in varying styles. Both Stage 1 and Stage 2 Nahuatl are to be found in it. Hence, authorship in this context may be taken in the sense of compilation or perhaps sponsorship and supervision.[38] Even if he was the author in a more substantial sense, like many Spanish clerics of the day he undoubtedly gave it to native assistants for final polishing.

The *Huey tlamahuiçoltica* is divided into six distinct parts: (1) Laso de la Vega's introduction; (2) the account of the apparitions (the *Nican mopohua*); (3) a brief description of the image; (4) an account of the miracles worked at Guadalupe (the *Nican motecpana*); (5) a life of Juan Diego; and (6) an exhortation and prayer.

The Introduction

Laso de la Vega's introduction is phrased as a prayer to the Virgin. The introduction appears to have been written specifically for the book or close to its publication. The language is complex and seems almost consciously archaic. Garibay praised its "perfect Nahuatl," whereas Lockhart sees it as having the flavor of a translation from Spanish.[39] The introduction implies that not all Indians were aware of the miracle and needed instruction about it in order to make it known to others. "That fact has enticed and encouraged me to write in the Nahuatl language the very great miracle by which you revealed yourself to people and you have given them your image [which] is here in your precious home in Tepeyacac. May the Indians see there and know in their language all that you have done on their behalf and your love for people" [Ca ye yèhuatl in onechyoleuh, in onechyolchicauh inic nahuatlàtolcopa onoconìcuilo in çenca huei motlamahuiçoltzin inic otimoteittitìtzino, ihuan inic oticmotemaquilìtia in mixiptlatzin in nican motlaçòchantzinco Tepeyacac ma onc_ quittacan in maçehualtzitzintin, ma intlàtoltica quimatican in ixquich in impanpa oticmochihuili motetlaçòtlaliztzin]. "Therefore, may it be written in different languages in order that many people may be called in different languages to see and to know your wonder and your very great miracle that you have worked on their behalf" [Ipampa ma nepapan tlàtoltica mìcuilo inic mochintin in nepapan tlàtolica monotza quittazque, quimatizquè in momahuizçotzin, ihuan in çenca huei motlamahuiçoltzin in inpampa oticmochihuili].[40]

The *Nican mopohua*

Following the introduction is the most important part of the book, the actual account of the apparitions, called the *Nican mopohua* (Here is recounted), written in a smooth, standard Church Nahuatl that shows minimal Spanish influence. Because of its status in the history of Guadalupe it requires a detailed study.

The *Nican mopohua* does not appear to be directly dependent on Sánchez's book. It parallels Sánchez's in many ways, but it is not a translation or even a paraphrase of the earlier work. In fact, Laso de la Vega made no reference to Sánchez at all. The approach and style of the two accounts are strikingly different. The *Nican mopohua* follows a chronology of the apparitions that differs in details from that of Miguel Sánchez, specifically by omitting the third apparition, in which Juan Diego told the Virgin about his interview with Zumárraga.[41] Laso de la Vega, or his native aides, may have adapted Sánchez's account and given it the Nahuatl style that characterizes it. An equally likely hypothesis is that they both used an unwritten common source, perhaps a story in circulation among some local Nahuas.

Did Laso de la Vega write the *Nican mopohua*? He clearly stated four times in his introduction that he was the author of the apparition account and made no reference to either written documents or published works. "I who have traced and written your miracle in Nahuatl" [In onocontlilan onoconnìcuilo nahuatlàtolcopa in motlahuiçoltzin]. "That fact has enticed and encouraged me to write in the Nahuatl language the very great miracle by which you revealed yourself to people" [Ca ye yèhuatl in onechyoleuh, in onechyolchicauh inic nahuatlàtolcopa onoconìcuilo in cenca huei motlamahuiçoltzin inic otimoteittitzino]. "There is also one other item by which I took heart and was encouraged to write your miracle in the Nahuatl language" [Auh ca ocno centlamantli inic oniyoleuh inic oniyolchicauh nahuatlàtolcopa noconcuìloz in motlamahuiçoltzin]. "In order that I may trace in the Nahuatl language your altogether great miracle by which that you revealed yourself to the humble Indians" [Inic nocontlilanaz nahuatlàtolcopa in cenca huei in motlamahuiçoltzin inic otiquinmottititzino icnomacehualtzitzintin].[42] Despite these claims, Laso de la Vega's authorship of the *Nican mopohua* is questionable. Velázquez believed that the great difference in style between Laso de la Vega's gongoristic letter of introduction to Sánchez's book and the unadorned narration of the *Nican mopohua* made Laso de la Vega's authorship suspect. The same can be said about his rather florid introduction to the *Huey tlamahuiçoltica*. Lockhart also believes that "the story proper is in such fluent and idiomatic Nahuatl that Laso de la Vega would have had to possess very unusual language gifts to have written it himself unless he was guided by an already existing model; indeed, the tale itself is so smooth that it gives the impression of having been through the polishing process of frequent telling by various narrators." Lockhart adds, however, "since Spanish ecclesiastics had long been wont to ignore the fact that their indigenous aides actually put the texts they published into Nahuatl, there is nothing to prevent us from assuming the existence of a Nahua ghostwriter who could have had much latitude."[43] It can safely be presumed that Laso de la Vega entrusted his manuscript to native writers for final embellishment.

Laso de la Vega made no reference to sources for his account. He did mention that much had been lost during the passage of time and also testified to a lack of written sources. "Very much has been abandoned, which time has erased and which no one remembers any longer, because the ancients did not take care to have it written down at the time it happened"

[Auh ca çenca miec in omocauh, in oquipolò in cahuitl, in aoc mà aca quilnamiqui inic àmo oquimocuitlahuiq in huehuetq in ma quimìcuilhuiani niman in ìquac mochiuh].⁴⁴ People, he complained, tended to forget heavenly favors very quickly. In order that everything should not be forgotten or blotted out with time, he wrote, the Queen of Heaven wanted it written and published, "although it has been brought about with difficulty, because it happens that there is still need for other [sources] here and there" [maçihui ohuìtica in omoneltili, inic çen nohuian tepan àçitiuh motemachiltitinh].⁴⁵

Almost all commentators have praised the quality of the Nahuatl in the *Nican mopohua.* In his letter of approval, Baltasar González, a *nahuatlahto* (speaker or student of Nahuatl), spoke of the "correct and elegant Mexican language" of the account.⁴⁶ Andrews thinks that the author's use of directionals lies somewhat between that of Tezozomoc (which he considers quite skillful) and that of the *Historia Tolteca Chichimeca* (which, he says, "demonstrates a less felicitous use").⁴⁷ Ascensión H. de León-Portilla speaks of its "elegant language and full of metaphors in the style of classic Nahuatl literature, as it was transcribed in the alphabet of the sixteenth century."⁴⁸ Burkhart considers it "standard church Nahuatl, a linguistic variety developed by priests and literate Indians early in the colonial epoch and maintained with few changes throughout the colonial era. It is formal and archaizing, with a syntax simplified so that nonnative speakers could more easily understand it, and with relatively few Spanish loanwords."⁴⁹ Lockhart judges the entire work to be in excellent Nahuatl that could have been written at any time from 1550 or 1560 onward, "with overwhelmingly indigenous and traditional vocabulary and idiom, no obvious calques, and a few Spanish loan nouns."⁵⁰ Siller, who considers the account to be very ancient, calls the language classical Nahuatl, which he extravagantly describes as "a plain, direct, smooth, precise, elegant, sonorous, beautiful, profound, highly meaningful, and even sublime language."⁵¹ Its style may also reflect the cultural and linguistic renaissance of the mid-seventeenth century, one aspect of which was a move to restore a pristine, classical form of Nahuatl.

From style and language alone, however, it is impossible to date the *Nican mopohua* with exactitude. There are some expressions, such as *notecuiyoè* (O my lady, the female equivalent of lord), *tlacatlè* (O personage), *cihuapillè* (O noblewoman), *noxocoyohuè* (O my youngest child), and *nochpochtzinè* (O my daughter), that were typical of preconquest polite speech: the first three as terms of inferior to superior, the last two as polite inversions. On the other hand, the use of the Spanish rather than Nahuatl numbering system and the use of *omocac misa* (mass was heard) instead of the more common sixteenth-century *omottac misa* (mass was seen) argue for a provenance from the late sixteenth or early seventeenth century.

Bierhorst has pointed out similarities in vocabulary between Laso de la Vega's account and the *Cantares mexicanos*. The uses he specifies are *tzinitzcan* (the Mexican trogon, a species of bird), *manoce* (a common conjunction: nor, although), *nocuexanco nictemaz* (I will fill my lapfolds with them, for which Laso de la Vega has *quicuxanten*, "he filled his lapfolds with them"), *iuqui[n] tepetl quinnahnanquilia* (for which Laso de la Vega has *iuhquin quinananquilia Tepetl*, "as if the hill answers them"), *coyoltototl* (the bellbird), *in xochitlalpan in tonacatlalpan* (in the land of flowers, in the land of abundance), *xixochitetequi* (for which Laso de la Vega has *xochitl xictetequi*, "cut the flowers"). His conclusion is that "one suspects that Lasso [*sic*] de la Vega had access to our manuscript."[52] Granted that this is a possibility, still the differences between the two are so stark that, as has been mentioned before, it is impossible to consider any of the *Cantares* as a source for the *Nican mopohua*. On the other hand, many idioms and phrases used in it can also be found in the *Bancroft Dialogues* published by Karttunen and Lockhart. Thus both the *Dialogues* and the *Nican mopohua* use the identical phrase *nictequipachoz in mixtzin in moyollotzin* (I will disturb your spirit, an apology for importunity, often used at the beginning or end of a speech). Both use *mati* in the sense of to feel and *huelmati*, to feel well, in an inquiry. In the *Dialogues* the question is *quen ticmomachiltia in moteopixcanacayotzin* (literally, How do you feel your priestly flesh? or Father, how is your bodily health?), while the *Nican mopohua* has *cuix ticmohuelmachitia in motlaçònacayotzin*. Similarly, both use the preconquest descriptive terms for God, *ipalnemohuani, in tloque in nahuaque, ilhuicahua tlalticpaque,* and *teyocoyani* (the *Dialogues* twice use *ipalnemohuani teotl dios*, the same form used by the *Nican mopohua*), both use *macehual* as a possessive noun meaning "deserve," both use *-col, -achton* to mean "ancestors" and *coco teopouhqui* for "affliction." All these terms, however, were common in standard Church Nahuatl of the time. If, as is probable, Laso de la Vega entrusted his manuscript to Indian secretaries for final polishing, it is quite possible that they were responsible for the verbal similarities.

Because the *Nican mopohua* appeared in its first and final form in a printed work, it has no manuscript history as such. There are, however, handwritten copies in the New York Public Library and the Bibliothèque Nationale de France, Paris, that must be considered, though ultimately they provide no useful information.

There is a partial manuscript of the *Nican mopohua* in the New York Public Library, Monumentos Guadalupanos, series 1, volume 1, number 12.[53] It is written on European paper and consists of eight folios, torn at the edges and sometimes difficult to read. It goes only as far as Juan Diego's encounter with the Virgin after he has attempted to avoid her on Tuesday. The hand is semicursive, and the scribe was clearly copying from another document. Letters that were left out were inserted between the lines, incorrect copyings were smudged out, and there are occasional repeated words or phrases and in one instance an entire sentence.

On the basis of the hand and the use of *h* to indicate glottal stops, Burkhart dates it from the late sixteenth or very early seventeenth century.[54] While it is true that this manuscript frequently uses *h* to mark glottal stops, the usage is inconsistent. Sometimes the accent grave (`) is employed, sometimes the two together. There are other distinctive features. One is the carrying over of a final letter of one word to the beginning of the following one. Generally this occurs with *n* (*in nocan, in noc, in noquicac*), but it also occurs twice with *c* (*ic comonehlchiuh, oc quipan*). Such carryovers, which seemingly reflected speech patterns, were not unusual in early Nahuatl documents. There is a frequent doubling of letters, especially the *l* of the applicative but also in such forms as *innic, nopiltzinne, noxxocoyouh, oquimahuizzo, moquetztzinohtica*. The letter *z* replaces *s* in some Spanish loan words, while the reverse occurs in many Nahuatl words (*Dioz, obizpo, quinientoz, quesqui, metstli, yas*). On occasions the hard *k* sound is reduplicated (*monecqui*). There are also some simple orthographic errors, such as *moçuep*. Burrus believed that the manuscript dated from the mid-sixteenth century and that if not the original, it was at least a copy of it, thus making it the oldest existing copy of the *Nican mopohua*.

> The paper, the watermarks, the spelling of the words, the form of the individual letters, the expressions and the language—all are characteristic of mid-sixteenth-century Spanish American documents, as anyone can ascertain from a careful comparison with dated writings of the same period and in the same area. . . . Deserving particular notice are the letters "b," "h," "ç" (before "e" and "i") and the initial "rr" as in "rreal/religiose" [*sic*]. Father Mario Rojas . . . called my attention to the fact that not only are the spelling and writing characteristic of the mid-sixteenth century, but also the vocabulary and language, sentence structure, idioms, and style, etc. He observed a marked difference between the two oldest copies. The first, a mid-sixteenth-century production written in a much more popular style, reflects the way the Indians spoke at the time. The second copy, made about forty years after the first, toward the end of the sixteenth century, was written in a far more careful and literary style.[55]

These assertions are confusing. Burrus seems to be referring to the Spanish rather than the Nahuatl document. The letter *b*, which does not exist in Nahuatl, occurs in the manuscript only in Spanish loan words, and there is nothing distinctively old in the way it is written. The same is true of the letter *r*, which also does not occur in Nahuatl, and *rr* never appears in the document at all. Similarly, there is no notable difference in wording between this document and the second copy, which is considered in the next

paragraph. Attempts to date this document prior to Laso de la Vega's publication rest on frail evidence and are impossible to reconcile with the
total silence of authors and commentators prior to 1648.

In that same collection, series, and volume there is a manuscript of
the *Nican mopohua* and the *Nican motecpana*, the latter including the
exhortation and prayer. It is the "second copy" mentioned by Burrus and
consists of twenty-one folios. Though this copy of the *Nican mopohua* is
sometimes cited as having a sixteenth-century provenance (Burrus dated
it at the close of the century), the hand is clearly later.[56] Stylistically, in
contrast with Laso de la Vega's version, it consistently uses the *o-* prefix
for the preterit and modal suffixes for verbs (especially *-catca*) and frequently uses the verbal reverential (*-tzino*). The version from which this
copy was made contained several major omissions, all of them noted by
the copyist. The narrative is first interrupted when Juan Diego informs
the Virgin that he is going for a priest for his sick uncle and resumes with
her assurance that he will recover. The poignant questions the Virgin asks
on Tuesday concerning her protection of Juan Diego are omitted. The text
is interrupted again at the point at which the Virgin commands Juan Diego to go cut the flowers and resumes with her command to take them to
the bishop. It omits the attempts by the bishop's servants to look at the
flowers in Juan Diego's tilma. It also omits much of Juan Diego's final
dialogue with Zumárraga. Most remarkably, it omits the entire narrative
of the delivery of the roses and the appearance of the image. In the light
of all this, no special importance can be attached to this copy. Sánchez
Rojas's claim that it was written in a more literary and less popular style
than the partial manuscript discussed in the previous paragraph is impossible to accept.

In the Bibliothèque Nationale de France, Mexicains, 302, there is the
"Fragment d'une histoire de N. D. de Guadalupe écrite en langage nahuatl
par le Br. Luis Lazo de la Vega en 1649." It corresponds with Laso de la
Vega's version of the *Nican mopohua* from folio 1v to folio 23r and with
the *Nican motecpana* from folio 28v to folio 33r. The *Nican mopohua*
lacks Laso de la Vega's introduction and ends with the words "ca
onicneltilito in miîyotzin, in motlatoltzin" [I go to carry out your mes-
sage]. It resumes on folio 28v with the words "ihuan in ixquich
tlamahuiçolli ye quimochihuilia" [and all the miracles that she works].
The copy was made by the criollo priest José Pichardo (1748–1812) some
time in the late eighteenth or early nineteenth century.[57] Folio 24r and v
contains a written note, unsigned and undated, on the documentary history of the *Nican mopohua*. It specifically states that the first publication
in 1648, that is, Miguel Sánchez's book, was not based on any Nahuatl
sources. The note also surveys the copies of the *Nican mopohua* in
Botturini Benaduci's *museo*, none of which appears to have any special
significance in the history of the account.

De la Maza and Garibay mentioned a manuscript that they said had once belonged to the collection of the English engineer and amateur historian G. R. G. Conway.[58] This document was supposedly the handwritten original of the *Huey tlamahuiçoltica*, possibly a printer's copy, signed and dated 1646. Garibay claimed that he had seen it at the publishing house of Porrúa in Mexico City. After Conway's death his collection was broken up and sold. At the present time, the Archivo General de la Nación has photocopies of seventeen volumes of the collection, of which only the first seven have been inventoried. Much of Conway's collection covered the colonial period, but it is not clear whether it contained any Nahuatl manuscripts. Garibay's claim for the manuscript's authenticity is impossible to accept. Working copies of manuscripts used by printers were not usually saved or rarely survived. That a document of such surpassing importance should suddenly appear and then fade again into the unknown or that Garibay made no effort to secure a copy, if only to compare it with the standard version, goes beyond all credibility. This, however, conforms to a consistent pattern in Guadalupan history: authors such as Becerra Tanco, Florencia, Sigüenza y Góngora, and Garibay claim to have seen or used an authentic, corroborating document but without publishing it or, in most cases, even citing it.

In the twentieth century the *Nican mopohua* has been widely accepted as the foundational account of the apparitions because of the claim that in its original form it was almost contemporaneous with the events. Yet it appears to have had little or no impact on the Spanish or criollo population of New Spain. Botturini Benaduci commissioned a translation in the early eighteenth century. This translation, which is very literal, was published in 1895 by the Mexican scholar Fortino Hipólito Vera from an incomplete copy made by José Pichardo sometime in the late eighteenth or early nineteenth century.[59] Archbishop Francisco Antonio Lorenzana, who was very interested in everything that concerned Guadalupe, commissioned Carlos Tapia y Centeno to translate the *Nican mopohua* into Spanish from a "maguey document written in Mexican [Nahuatl] in the handwriting that the Indians used at the beginning of their conversion" that had been found in the *museo* of Botturini Benaduci at the Royal and Pontifical University.[60] The copy of Tapia y Centeno's translation that is presently in the Bibliothèque Nationale de France is more a paraphrase than a translation. It ends with Juan Diego's greeting to the Virgin on Tuesday after he tried to avoid her, suggesting that it may have been translated from document 1 in the New York Public Library mentioned above. The paraphrase was never published. *Nican mopohua* was not cited by preachers in Spanish in the seventeenth or eighteenth century and, as will be seen, seems to have influenced only one Nahuatl sermon. It was not translated in full until 1926, when Primo Feliciano Velázquez published a photographic reproduction of the entire *Huey tlamahuiçoltica* together with his translation of it. Only in this century, and specifically after the publication of Cuevas's *Historia* in 1921 to 1994, did the *Nican mopohua* become the *textus receptus*.

The documentary sources for the seventeenth century tell us nothing about the impact of the *Nican mopohua* on the Indians' devotion. There are no known Nahuatl sermons on Guadalupe for that century, as there are for the eighteenth century. On the other hand, there is evidence that the Indian devotion to the Dark Virgin, as it exists today, dates from the eighteenth century.

The Tilma Description

After the account of the apparitions comes a paragraph that describes the tilma and the image. This is written in a different, later style, with several Spanish loan words (*cruz, corona, ángel*) and the consistent use of the *-ticac* modal. It is clearly of a later date, for it presupposes that its readers were not familiar with Mexica dress in the pre- and immediate postconquest periods. "The cloak on which the image of the heavenly Lady appeared was the garment of Juan Diego. The maguey cloak was rather stiff and well woven because at that time the maguey cloak was the clothing and the covering of all the common people. Only those who were nobles, leaders, and valiant warriors adorned and dressed themselves with soft cotton thread cloaks" [In tilmàtzintli in colol (*sic* for eolol) catca in Iuan Diego in itech tlamahuiçoltica monexiti in ixiptlatzin ilhuicac çihuapilli ca Ayatzintli achi tilactic catca, ihuan tlayec ìquitilli yèica ca in iquac in, in maçehualtzitzintin mochtin ayatl in intlaquen in inNeololtzin catca, çan yèhuantin in Pipiltin in Teteuctin, yhuan in yaotiàcahuan in yamanqui in ichca tilmàtli ic mochìchihuaya, ic mololoayal.][61] Certainly, in the thirty or forty years after 1531 such an explanation would have been unnecessary. This description was clearly written for natives who had no recollection of preconquest society. It appears to belong to Stage 2 Nahuatl.

The Miracle Stories

The tilma description is followed by an account of miracles that were worked through the intercession of the Virgin of Guadalupe. Miracles were an integral part of apparition stories. They were a divine seal of approval on the validity of an apparition, a devotion, or the sanctity of a person's life. Even today they are a standard element in the procedure for the canonization of saints. Sánchez and Laso de la Vega included miracle accounts to show both the authenticity of the apparition account and the devotion based on it and also to encourage fervor in those who were not yet devotees of the shrine. Hence, the miracles centered on dramatic rescues from danger and cures from life-threatening illnesses.

Laso de la Vega's collection of miracle stories, known from its opening words as the *Nican motecpana*, is often attributed to the native historian Fernando de Alva Ixtlilxochitl, thus dating it toward the beginning of the seventeenth century. The style of this section is so different from that of the *Nican mopohua* that it can safely be said that they are the works of different authors. Velázquez considered the *Nican motecpana* to be both later than and stylistically inferior to the *Nican mopohua*.[62] In support of this he cited the large number of Hispanicisms (*testamento, ánima, aceite, candela, sacristán, altar, misa, lámpara, freno, caballo*) and various ungrammatical expressions. His arguments are persuasive but raise the troubling question of whether Alva Ixtlilxochitl would have written in such highly Hispanicized Nahuatl. The most likely hypothesis is that the *Nican motecpana* is a compilation of miracle stories associated with the shrine but with diverse origins. Sánchez and Laso de la Vega joined them to the *Nican mopohua* and edited some of them to give them a Guadalupan significance.

There are similarities and differences in the stories given by Sánchez and Laso de la Vega. The former has seven miracles, while the latter has fourteen. In general, Laso de la Vega gives more details than Sánchez, and his accounts tend to be more vivid. Sánchez concluded the narration of each miracle with a complex and often esoteric biblical parallel, relating each one to some event in Scripture and then drawing conclusions for the edification of his readers. Laso de la Vega's few commentaries tended to stress the Virgin Mary's love and concern for the Indians. The following are the miracles related, with an indication of the differences between the two authors.

The first one given by Sánchez involved an Indian accidentally killed by an arrow in the neck during a mock skirmish that was part of the celebration of the dedication of the first ermita at Tepeyac on 26 December 1531. His body was carried before the image, and when the arrow was removed, the Indian was immediately restored to full health. Laso de la Vega added some details, including the fact that the resurrected Indian remained at Tepeyac as a custodian for the shrine. Both Sánchez and Laso de la Vega saw this as a sign of the Virgin's special care for the Indians.

The second occurred during the epidemic of 1544, one of the worst to strike the Indians of New Spain in the sixteenth century. Because of the vagueness of symptomatic descriptions, it is impossible to identify the sickness with certainty. It was characterized by bleeding from the nose and high fever and, according to Sánchez, was killing a hundred Indians each day.[63] Mendieta wrote that 150,000 Indians died in Tlaxcala and another 100,000 in Cholula.[64] According to tradition, Juan Bernardino died during this epidemic. Sánchez wrote that the Franciscans organized a procession of boys and girls, age six to seven, from Santiago Tlatelolco to Guadalupe to pray for its end. According to Sánchez, the epidemic began to abate the next day. Laso de la Vega gives a longer description and adds that the children took the discipline (*momacahuitectaque*) during the course of the procession. These two are the only sources for the story of the procession.[65]

The third concerned don Juan Tovar, the Indian who was credited with finding the image of the Virgin of Remedios. Laso de la Vega, whose account is much more detailed than that of Sánchez, emphasizes the priority of Guadalupe. He says that don Juan found the image of Remedios on the hill called Totoltepec and took it to his home, where he kept it for some years. Later he built a small chapel in front of his home and placed the image within it. Both Sánchez and Laso de la Vega say that some time after that Tovar fell ill during an epidemic. Seeing himself very ill and remembering how the Virgin had cured Juan Bernardino, he begged his neighbors to take him to Guadalupe. There the Virgin smiled at him and cured him. She also directed him to build a chapel on the summit of Totoltepec for her image. More so than Sánchez, Laso de la Vega sought to subordinate Remedios (which later became the peninsular devotion) to Guadalupe (the criollo and Indian devotion). On the other hand, Sánchez preached both devotions, and in the mid-seventeenth century there were few signs of the rivalry that would emerge later.

On another occasion a gentleman named Antonio de Carvajal left Mexico City for Tulancingo on horseback, accompanied by a young relative. On the way out of the city the party stopped and prayed at Guadalupe in the manner described by Miles Philips. Having resumed their journey, they discussed the wondrous image and the miracles it had wrought. The young relative's horse bolted and carried him precipitously through ravines and rocky territory. His companions followed after him, expecting to find him dead. Instead he was alive and unharmed, with the horse in a bowed and reverential position. He explained that during his danger he had invoked the Virgin of Guadalupe. The Virgin, exactly as painted on the image, appeared and grabbed the horse's reins. The horse stopped and knelt before her. Again, Laso de la Vega's account is more detailed. This became one of the most popular miracle stories associated with Guadalupe.

Sánchez tells of a man who was praying before the image of the Virgin when a cord supporting a ceiling lamp broke and it fell on his head. Neither the man nor the lamp was harmed in any way. The glass was not broken, the oil was not spilled, and the flame continued to burn. Laso de la Vega's account is almost the same, except that he identifies the man as a Spaniard.

Once, when the licenciado Juan Vázquez de Acuña, at that time the vicar of Guadalupe, went to the main altar to say mass, all the candles had been blown out by the strong winds prevalent in the area. As his acolyte went out to relight them, the priest and others in the chapel saw two rays of light that miraculously lighted the candles. Laso de la Vega's version is almost exactly the same.

In relating the miracles worked at the shrine or by the image, Sánchez includes the flood of 1629 to 1634, of which he was an eyewitness. He writes that the flood began on Tuesday, 25 September (he does not mention the year). At the direction of Archbishop Francisco Manso y Zúñiga, the image was brought to Mexico City and kept for the night in the archbishop's palace. The next morning it was taken to the cathedral, where it remained through the entire period of the flood. The flood subsided little by little, and the credit was given to the Virgin. After the flood had subsided, the archbishop returned the image to Guadalupe. The procession took place on Sunday, 14 May 1634. Laso de la Vega does not give this story, which is the last of the miracles related by Sánchez.

Laso de la Vega added seven other miracles, six of them accounts of cures. A Spanish woman suffered from distension of the stomach because of dropsy. The physician's effort to help her only made matters worse. After ten months of suffering she had herself brought to Guadalupe. After she had drunk some water from the spring her body felt better, and she fell asleep. An Indian saw a large, frightful snake emerge from under her, and his cries for help awakened her. Both their cries brought help, the snake was killed, and the woman's swelling disappeared.

A Spanish nobleman suffered severe headaches and earaches. On the way to Guadalupe, he made a vow that if he was cured he would make an offering of a head made of silver. He was cured as soon as he arrived.

A young woman named Catalina suffered from dropsy and asked to be taken to Guadalupe. On drinking water from the spring she was instantly healed. This appears to be a doublet of the first miracle.

A Discalced Franciscan named Pedro de Valderrama had cancer of the toe and was instantly cured when he showed it to the Virgin of Guadalupe.[66]

A Spanish nobleman named Luis de Castilla suffered from a swollen foot, which turned gangrenous. Valderrama, it was said, recommended that he go to Guadalupe. He had a silver foot made, the same size as his, which he sent ahead of him to the ermita. When the delivery was made, the nobleman was cured.[67]

The son of the sacristan Juan Pavón had a swelling in the neck that threatened to kill him. He was taken to Guadalupe, where he was anointed with oil from one of the lamps. He was immediately cured.

The seventh miracle was not a cure but the Blessed Virgin's intervention to bring religious peace to Teotihuacan at the time that the Augustinians were attempting to establish a house there. Laso de la Vega's account is an almost verbatim version of the one attributed by Cuevas to Alva

Ixtlilxochitl and is probably the source of the one published by Vera and quoted by Cuevas.

These miracle accounts obviously belong to a more credulous age. Viewed from today's standpoint, they are fanciful, legendary, and even frivolous or grotesque. No serious credence can be given to any of them. They are, however, significant for other reasons. The majority of the miracles narrated by Sánchez and Laso de la Vega involve Spaniards, not Indians. This lack of Indian emphasis or orientation is a clear difference between the *Nican mopohua* and the *Nican motecpana*. In addition, five of the six cures in the *Nican motecpana* were brought about by actions that were associated with the shrine and its spring rather than with the image as such. The two cures of dropsical women were brought about by drinking water from the spring at Guadalupe. The son of Juan Pavón was healed by anointing with oil from one of the lamps. Two Spaniards were healed because of their ex-voto offerings, a common occurrence in the genre of miracle stories. Only Pedro de Valderrama made a direct appeal to the image.

The language and style of the miracle stories in the *Nican motecpana* indicate that they did not have a common origin. Of the fourteen miracles only three benefit natives; the rest are worked on behalf of Spaniards. Most of the latter appear to have a later origin than the former. The story of the Indian miraculouly restored to life at the time of the dedication parade contains no Spanish loan words and uses the older term *nican tlaca* for natives. The account of Juan de Tovar, the Indian discoverer of Remedios, has only one Spanish loan word (*leguas*). The story of the governors of Teotihuacan has Spanish loan words only for technical terms and refers to the viceroy Luis de Velasco as the Virgin's "beloved son." It also uses the older form *yolia anima* for soul. As has been noted earlier, this event dates back to the time of its actual occurrence in the sixteenth century, though without the intercession of Guadalupe. It would not be rash to say that in its original form it may date from the sixteenth century and may be Stage 1 Nahuatl.

In general, with certain exceptions, such as the story of the rescue of Antonio de Carvajal's young relative, the narration of the miracles performed for Spaniards is less rhetorical, ornate, and elaborate. They are brief, simple, and at times almost stark, perhaps because they were translated from Spanish originals. This, too, permits us to surmise an earlier origin for the Indian stories. The briefer stories, such as the cure of the son of the sacristan Juan Pavón, also contain the largest number of Spanish loan words and seem to belong to Stage 2.

Important testimony concerning these miracles is found in one of the earliest known reproductions of the image of Our Lady of Guadalupe in its present form, an engraving by the Flemish artist Samuel Stradanus that probably dates from 1615.[68] Stradanus (the Latinized form of van der

Straet) was a native of Antwerp who came to New Spain early in the seventeenth century. The engraving was commissioned by Archbishop de la Serna, who intended to sell copies to raise funds for the new chapel at Tepeyac. The copy consulted for this study belonged to the collection of H. H. Behrens, who donated it to the Metropolitan Museum of Art in New York City in 1948.[69] In the center is the image as it is known today, except that it has a crown and is surrounded by the cherubim mentioned at a later date by Florencia. Above the image are some miscellaneous ex-voto, and on each side are two lamps. On the right and left sides of the engraving are eight panels depicting various miracles worked at the shrine with captions that narrate the miracles. Because of the deteriorated condition of the original copper plate, the captions are difficult or even impossible to read.

Viewed clockwise from the top right-hand side these include (1) Antonio de Carvajal's relative's horse accident; the young man is shown dangling from the stirrup; at the very top is a view of Tulancingo (of which the caption says that the elder Carvajal was mayor) and in the upper left-hand corner is the image of Guadalupe; (2) the fall of the lamp on a Spaniard while he was praying in the shrine; the lamp is shown striking his head; the image of Guadalupe is above and behind the altar; another Spaniard and a nun witness the accident; the caption says that the lamp was heavy and that no oil was spilled and the glass was not broken; (3) the cure of the son of the sacristan Juan Pavón, who is shown being presented to the image, which is behind the altar, by his father, while a woman, perhaps the boy's mother, kneels before the altar; the caption says that the child was cured as soon as he was anointed with oil from the lamp; outside the church is a group of buildings labeled "the great city of Mexico"; (4) the miraculous lighting of the candles when Vázquez de Acuña was preparing to say mass; a man in Spanish dress and a woman (perhaps a nun) are in the foreground, while another man in Spanish dress is kneeling at the communion rail; the image is above and behind the altar; the caption says that "the candles were miraculously lighted by Our Lady"; (5) the cure of Luis de Castilla, who is shown lying in bed with one bare leg outside the covers; a friar (Valderrama?) holds the silver foot that Castilla offered; in the foreground a woman, perhaps a nun or Castilla's wife, kneels before a table that holds a crucifix and an inkstand; in the upper left-hand corner is a church labeled Guadalupe; there is no image in this picture; the caption states that as soon as the silver head was hung in the church Castilla was cured; (6) Pedro de Valderrama, the Discalced Franciscan cured of a tumorous toe, who is shown displaying it to the image, which is above and behind the altar; Valderrama is sitting and praying with the foot exposed; another friar is kneeling and praying; on the ground are a friar's hat and walking staff; a man in Spanish dress is walking through the door, through which can be seen a group of buildings labeled Pachuca; the caption is one of the most difficult to read but appears to say that after the cure Valderrama walked to Pachuca from Guadalupe; (7) the cure of Catarina de Monta, who was suffering from incurable hydropsy and was cured by drinking water from the spring; she is shown lying before the image and also lying outside the door of the shrine, where the spring is also clearly visible and identified; the image is above and behind the altar; a man in Spanish dress with arms extended is in the foreground with his back to the viewer, apparently pointing to the image; in the upper right-hand corner can be seen a group of buildings labeled Mexico-Tenochtitlan; this panel is significant because it makes a clear allusion to the spring as the place where the Virgin appeared ("Mexico-Tenochtitlan: Catarina de Monta . . . hydropic for eleven years, without hope of health, attended novenas and drank from the water of the spring where Our Lady of Guadalupe appeared and she was immediately cured"); (8) the Spaniard cured of headaches when he offered a silver head; he sits on the edge of his bed fully clothed with his left hand to his head; a man in Spanish dress, apparently a servant, stands holding the silver head; through the door a friar or nun can be seen kneeling in prayer; there is no image; the caption gives the sick man's name as Bartholomé Grandía (the last name is almost illegible) and says that he was cured as soon as the head was hung in the church.[70]

The Stradanus engraving shows that by 1615 at least eight of the miracle stories had reached a stage close to their final form and were well known. This does not mean, however, that they had yet been gathered together in the *Nican motecpana*. The miracle panels offer some tantalizing insights into the development of the Guadalupe tradition. There are variations from the accounts given by Sánchez, Laso de la Vega, and later Francisco de Florencia. Five of them were used by Laso de la Vega but not by Sánchez. The engraving gives the full names, not always intelligible, of the Spaniard cured of headaches and the young lady cured of hydropsy. Two sets of miracles appear to be developments of a common source: the cures of the two hydropsical women and the cures of the two Spaniards, one of a disease of the foot, the other of headaches. Though six of the eight panels show the image, not all the miracles were directly attributed to it. One was the result of drinking water from the spring, one from anointing with oil from the sanctuary lamp, and two to the presentation of ex-voto offerings. All the persons involved were Spaniards; no miracle benefits an Indian. Two of the most important of those related by Sánchez and Laso de la Vega which dealt with natives, the cure of the wounded Indian in the mock battle and the apparition to Juan de Tovar, are absent from this engraving. It is particularly interesting that the cure of the young hydropsical woman, Catarina, refers to the Virgin's having appeared at the spring. This may well represent an early stage in the development of the apparition story. Most significant of all, of course, is that the greatest miracles of all – the apparition to Juan Diego and the cure of Juan Bernardino – are not shown. There is nothing in the engraving that refers in any way to the traditional apparition account.

The Life of Juan Diego

After relating the miracle accounts, Laso de la Vega added information about the later life of Juan Diego. This included his moving to Guadalupe, where he lived a life of work and penance. "He was a widower. Two years before the Virgin ever appeared to him, his wife died. She was named María Lucía. They both lived chastely, they kept themselves [chaste]. She died a virgin. He also lived as a virgin. He never knew a woman" [Icnoquichtli catca, oc yuh òxihuitl quimottititzinoz iz çenquizca Ichpochtzintli in omomiquilì in içihuahuàtzin catca itoca Maria Lucia; auh in ehuan chipahuaca nenque, mopixque mochpochmiquilì in içihuah, no yèhuatl telpochnen, aic quixtimà Çihuatl].[71] The reason given for this was the sermon by Motolinía that caused the couple to resolve to live in celibacy, though this is inconsistent with the assertion of lifelong celibacy.

The story of the celibate marriage has become an accepted part of the tradition, although it involves chronological difficulties. If, as this account asserts, Juan Diego died in 1548 at the age of seventy-four, he would have been born about the year 1474 and would have been approximately fifty at the time of Motolinia's arrival in 1524 and approximately fifty-seven at the time of the apparitions. The marriage, then, would clearly have been preconquest, a time when the concept of a celibate marriage, or celibacy itself outside the Mexica priesthood, would have been all but incomprehensible. If María Lucía died in 1529, there would have been five years of celibacy at the most. Becerra Tanco, writing in 1666, and Francisco Javier Clavigero, writing in 1782, seem to have been the only writers of the colonial period to have noticed the discrepancies, for they wrote that the couple refrained from the use of marriage after the sermon.[72] In the seventeenth century, virginity and celibacy were viewed as a primary sign of virtue that also validated the seer's message. Combining, as it did, asceticism with renunciation of one of life's strongest forces, it added credibility to the visionary's message. Clearly this is the intrusion of a postconquest Catholic outlook into the story of Juan Diego.

This brief biography belongs to the category of European hagiography, especially in its emphasis on the celibacy of Juan Diego. It also shows signs of Spanish borrowings, such as the calque "he never knew a woman" (*aic quixtimà Çihuatl*), which is ultimately derived from biblical Hebrew. Significantly, it is totally separate from the *Nican mopohua* and shows signs of later composition. In all probability it had a later and distinct origin from the apparition account.

The Conclusion

The book concludes with an exhortation to devotion to Guadalupe and a prayer. Like the introduction, these were probably written by Laso de la Vega or his native assistants in a complex and archaic style at some time close to the publication of the book. The exhortation contrasts Guadalupe, which is seen primarily as an Indian devotion, and Remedios, which belongs to the Castilians. It also strongly implies that the account had fallen into oblivion and was now being revived.

> And that is what the people of the world were like formerly. Only at that very moment did they wonder at and give thanks for the favor of the heavenly sovereign noble lady. If they have obtained what they want, from that time onward they go casting it into their forgetfulness, so that those who come here afterward will no longer have the good fortune of obtaining the light, the sun of Our Lord. And that is how it is, because of this the favor of the heavenly noble lady by which she appeared very miraculously here in her home of Tepeyaca has perished somewhat and has been abandoned, because not to the extent that was necessary did her commoners [Indians] make it known nor did they have it acknowledged, that she built her house there for their sakes in order that there she might hear their afflictions, their grief, their tears, and their entreaties, and she might give them and bestow on them the favor of her help.[73]

Unlike Sánchez, Laso de la Vega did not identify the Virgin of Guadalupe with criollismo; rather, he pictured her as the mother and protectress of the Indians, toward whom she shows a special love. As a result, he claimed, the Indians turned away from idolatry and destroyed the images they had hidden in their homes. This claim later became part of the Guadalupe tradition, that is, that the apparitions were followed by a mass conversion of the Indians to Christianity. Laso de la Vega also saw the apparition and image as the crowning work of the Virgin in New Spain, together with Remedios and other devotions.

The years 1648 and 1649 are the crucial ones in the history of the Guadalupe apparitions. Miguel Sánchez made known to the criollos of New Spain a story that until that time was unknown or forgotten. Suddenly, as if out of nowhere, he gave them a story that he and they appropriated as divine witness to the legitimacy of criollismo. In the years that followed, the predominantly criollo secular clergy would embrace the story wholeheartedly and spread it among the criollos. With Sánchez began the long process whereby Guadalupe was fused with Mexican identity. Laso de la Vega, in contrast, sought to bring the message of compassion and consolation to the Indians. If he had any success, it was limited, because it was not until the eighteenth century that the Indians began to seek refuge under the shadow of the Virgin of Tepeyac.

Notes

1. For information on Sánchez, see López Beltrán, *La primera historia*, 9–16. A brief biography, heavily dependent on earlier sources, can be found in Gutiérrez Dávila, *Memorias historicas*, part 1, book 4, par. 619, 253–55. The oratory was not a religious order, like the mendicants or the Jesuits, but a union of diocesan clergy.

2. This claim was made in an obituary of Sánchez by Robles, *Diario*, 1:144–46. It was repeated by Gutiérrez Dávila, *Memorias historicas*, 254.

3. Quoted by de la Maza but without further details (*El guadalupanismo mexicano*, 49).

4. The work is reprinted in *Testimonios historicos guadalupanos*, 153–267, and, with some omissions, in López Beltrán, *La primera historia*, 39–190. It is very difficult to find copies of the first edition today. The one used for this chapter is in the John Carter Brown Library, Providence, Rhode Island. The first edition contains a well-executed engraving of Juan Diego opening the tilma before a kneeling Zumárraga, an engraving later used also by Laso de la Vega. To my knowledge this is the first known illustration of the apparition account.

5. López Beltrán makes references to these approbations but does not include them in *La primera historia*.

6. Sánchez, *Imagen de la Virgen María*, unpaginated; THG, 153.

7. Sánchez, *Imagen de la Virgen María*, unpaginated; THG, 155.

8. Sada Lambretón, *Las informaciones jurísdicas*, facsimile 112.

9. Sánchez, *Imagen de la Virgen María*, unpaginated; THG, 158. López Beltrán does not include this in the prologue in his reprint of Sánchez's work, nor can this sentence be found anywhere in that reprint. López Beltrán asserts categorically that he scrupulously reprinted the original, "word by word and line by line without adding or removing even a tittle" (*La primera historia*, 19). The conclusion seems inescapable that López Beltrán deliberately omitted the *fundamento*. De la Maza refers to this as "mala fe" (*El guadalupanismo mexicano*, 56). Actually, López Beltrán took a number of liberties with the text.

10. Sada Lambretón, *Las informaciones jurísdicas*, facsimile 115.

11. The scarcity of paper was mentioned in the viceregal approval for Luis de Cisneros's history of Remedios. See Beristáin de Sousa, *Biblioteca*, 2:116.

12. Sánchez, *Imagen de la Virgen María*, f. 26r; THG, 186.

13. It is unclear whether a bishop-elect, with special faculties, could celebrate such a mass.

14. Sánchez, *Imagen de la Virgen María*, fol. 92r; THG, 255.

15. Sánchez, *Imagen de la Virgen María*, fols. 77v–78r; THG, 240.

16. Sánchez, *Imagen de la Virgen María*, unpaginated; THG, 261. López Beltrán places these two letters at the beginning of his version of Sánchez's book.

17. Genesis 2:23–24.

18. Laso de la Vega has a confused translation here. *Virago* in classical Latin means a manlike woman but in this context in the Vulgate simply means woman. "She shall be called woman because she has been taken from a man (haec vocabitur virago quoniam de viro sumpta est)." This was an attempt to translate the original pun and popular etymology of the Hebrew into Latin. Laso de la Vega seems to have taken it literally and translates *virago* as *varonil*.

238 The Church in Colonial Latin America

19. Sánchez, *Imagen de la Virgen María*, unpaginated; THG, 263–64.
20. Lafaye, *Quetzalcoatl and Guadalupe*, 246.
21. Revelation [Apocalypse] 12:1, 2, 7, 6, 14, 15, 17. The arrangement of verses given by Sánchez is out of order with the original.
22. Sánchez, *Imagen de la Virgen María*, fol. 93r; THG, 257.
23. Sánchez, *Imagen de la Virgen María*, fol. 19r; THG, 179.
24. Sánchez, *Imagen de la Virgen María*, fol. 69r; THG, 231.
25. Sánchez, *Imagen de la Virgen María*, 57v; THG, 219.
26. Robles, *Diario*, 1:145. Writing in the following century, Gutiérrez Dávila, who borrowed much of his material verbatim from Robles, was surprised that such a great event could have been forgotten. "The forgetting of such a great benefit that the Empress of Heaven did for our America, and especially for Mexico, was certainly something worthy to be pondered" (*Memorias historicas*, 254).
27. Wood, "Christian Images," 275. Since it is Nahua wills that are dealt with, there is little doubt that the Mexican image, not the Extremaduran one, was bequeathed.
28. Sánchez, *El David seraphico*, 26v.
29. Quoted in García Icazbalceta, "Carta," 112, n. 5.
30. Ibid.
31. The only reprints that I have been able to verify personally are those in THG, 153–267, and López Beltrán, *La Primera historia*.
32. De la Cruz, *Relación*, 267–81.
33. Ibid., 281.
34. Gálvez was fiscal of the council from 1654 until 1657 and a *consejero* (councillor) from 1657 until 1662. See Schäfer, *El real y supremo consejo*, 1:361, 368.
35. A *racionero* was a member of the chapter who received a salary for his participation in the liturgy but did not have a specific administrative function. A *medio racionero* received half the salary of a racionero. Ascensión H. de León-Portilla says that Laso de la Vega had studied at the University of Mexico and that he was fluent in Nahuatl, in which he preached (*Tepuztlahcuilolli*, 93). Unfortunately, she does not give a source for these statements, which I have been unable to verify.
36. Laso de la Vega, *Hvei tlamahviçoltica*, unpaginated; *Hvei tlamahvicoltiça* [*sic*], 20; also, in THG, 288. González was a devotee of the Guadalupan devotion and supposedly composed a history of the apparitions in Nahuatl. See Velásquez, *La aparición*, 100; Beristáin de Sousa, *Biblioteca*, 2:372. For a discussion as to whether this was the same as the *Nican mopohua* or whether González had helped Laso de la Vega in its composition, see Zambrano and Gutiérrez Casillas, *Diccionario*, 7:324–26.
37. Laso de la Vega, *Hvei tlamahviçoltica*, unpaginated; *Hvei tlamahvicoltiça* [*sic*], 20.
38. Garibay considered Laso de la Vega to be the author of the introduction, the description of the image, the concluding section (*Nican tlantica*), and the final version of the *Nican motepana* (*Historia de la literatura náhuatl*, 2:258).
39. Ibid., 2:257; Lockhart, *The Nahuas after the Conquest*, 250.
40. Laso de la Vega, *Hvei tlamahviçoltica*, unpaginated.
41. Velásquez's translation of the *Nican mopohua* includes the third apparition in a Spanish version but not in a Nahuatl one. He does not identify its source, saying only that it came from "a translation from a torn and very old piece of paper, written in Mexican," made by licenciado D. Joseph Julián Ramírez. Velásquez included it because it filled the vacuum of the third apparition (*Hvei tlamahvicoltiça* [*sic*], 100–1, n. 94). Ortiz de Montellano says that this transla-

tion comes from the beginning of the nineteenth century and that the full title was "Translation from a very old and torn piece of paper, written in Mexican, which was found among the books, maps, and other writings from the antiquities of the Indians, and which the lord archbishop of Toledo, don Franco [*sic* for Fran.co] Antonio Lorenzana gave to the archive of this royal university and they belonged to the knight don Lorenzo Boturini Benaduci, inventario 8, n. 7, made by the licenciado don Joseph Julián Ramírez, catedrático and synodal examiner of the said language in this royal university and archdiocese." A copy of Ramírez's translation, with this note included, can be found in the Bibliothèque Nationale de France (BNF), Mexicains, 317. The Nahuatl version that is occasionally found was a retranslation by Mario Rojas Sánchez. See Ortiz de Montellano, *Nic mopohua*, 101–2.

42. Laso de la Vega, *Hvei tlamahviçoltica*, unpaginated.
43. Lockhart, *The Nahuas after the Conquest*, 250.
44. Laso de la Vega, *Hvei tlamahviçoltica*, unpaginated.
45. Ibid., unpaginated.
46. Ibid., unpaginated.
47. Andrews, "Directionals in Classical Nahuatl," 2.
48. León-Portilla, *Tepuztlahcuilolli*, 93.
49. Burkhart, "The Cult of the Virgin of Guadalupe in Mexico," 204.
50. Lockhart, *The Nahuas after the Conquest*, 250.
51. Siller, *La evangelización guadalupana*, 5. He also says that it is written in different styles but does not specify them.
52. *Cantares Mexicanos*, 430.
53. Monumentos Guadalupanos, Rare Books and Manuscripts Division, New York Public Library, Astor, Lenox, and Tilden Foundations, all quotations with permission.
54. "It features the frequent but haphazard usage of the letter *h* to represent glottal stops, an orthographic convention typical of Franciscan and Jesuit texts of the late sixteenth and very early seventeenth centuries, later superseded by the Jesuit convention of using diacritics for that function" (Burkhart, "The Cult of the Virgin," 223, n. 18).
55. Burrus, *The Oldest Copy*, 3–4. Burrus believed that Antonio Valeriano wrote the *Nican mopohua* between 1540 and 1545.
56. Ibid., 5. In addition to the manuscripts noted in this section, there is a third copy in volume 1 of the second series, but it is clearly from the eighteenth century or even later.
57. Pichardo was pastor of San Felipe Neri church in Mexico City for twenty-three years and famed as a linguist.
58. De la Maza, *El guadalupanismo mexicano*, 74; Garibay, *Historia de la literatura náhuatl*, 2:257.
59. *El milagro de la Virgen del Tepeyac*, cited by Pompa y Pompa, "El gran acontecimiento," 286–87.
60. BNF, Mexicans, 317. Quoted with permission. The introductory note speaks of Lorenzana as archbishop of Toledo, thus dating the copy after 1772.
61. Laso de la Vega, *Hvei tlamahviçoltica*, fol. 8r.
62. Velázquez, *La aparición*, 134–35.
63. Prem, *Disease Outbreaks*, 31–34.
64. Mendieta, *Historia*, book 4, chap. 36, 515.
65. Processions of children who flagellated themselves as a means of averting epidemics were rather common in the apparition folklore of Spain. According to Christian, "In the fifteenth and sixteenth centuries, Barcelona children were prominently situated in penitential processions. In 1427 boys and girls . . . flagellated

themselves in a penitential procession because of an earthquake. . . . The Augustinian friars organized a procession in which 'small boys . . . barefoot in shirts
walked whipping themselves between men who carried lighted candles' " (*Apparitions*, 217–18). The miracle related here seems to belong very much to that
genre.

66. This miracle was also related by Baltasar de Medina in a biographical note
on Valderrama. Threatened with the amputation of his foot, he asked to be taken
to Guadalupe, where he was cured. Medina mentions that there was no documentary evidence for the miracle, but that it was well attested in a *lienzo* (picture on
a canvas) that was still conserved at the ermita. That may possibly refer to the
Stradanus engraving of 1615. Medina did not give a date for the cure but said that
Valderrama was professed in Mexico in 1601 and had been in religion for twenty-
nine years at the time of his death (*Chronica*, 121r-22v).

67. Florencia mentioned a Luis de Castilla, a regidor of Mexico and a knight of
Santiago, who made donations to the first Jesuits who came to New Spain (*Historia
de la provincia*, 117). He made no mention of a miraculous cure, however.

68. The earliest reproduction of the present image that I know of is a painting
by the Basque artist Baltasar de Echave Orio. See Ortiz Vaquero, "Notas sobre la
pintura," 29–30. The picture is reproduced on p. 31. The original is in a private
collection.

69. "Samuel Stradanus (1523–1605), Indulgence for Donation of alms towards
building a church to the Virgin of Guadalupe, the Metropolitan Museum of Art,
New York City, Gift of H. H. Behrens, 1948." The dates given are incorrect and
are based on a confusion of this Stradanus with another member of the famed
family of engravers. On Stradanus and this engraving, see Conde-Cervantes de
Conde, "Nuestra Señora de Guadalupe en el arte," 124–26; Peterson, "The Virgin
of Guadalupe," 40. Peterson's article also has a full-page reproduction of the engraving on page 41.

70. Florencia gave the man's name as Granado (*Estrella del norte*, chap. 25,
par. 279, fol. 143v).

71. Laso de la Vega, *Hvei tlamahviçoltica*, fol. 14v.

72. Becerra Tanco, "Origen milagrosos," in THG, 330; Clavigero, "Breve
noticia," in ibid., 581.

73. "Auh ca yeppa yuhque in tlalticpac tlaca, iz çan huel iquac, quimahuiztilia,
quitlaçòcamati in iteicneliltzin TlatòcaÇihuapilli, intla oquimomàçehuìque, auh
in moztla, in huiptla ca ye intlalcahualizpan contlaztihui inic aocmo inpan hual
àçi, iz çatepan hualhui, quihualmomàçehuia in itlanextzin, in itonatiuhtzin
Totecuiyo Auh ca huel ye yèhuatl in, in ipampa achi opoliuhca, omocauhca in
iteicneliltzin ilhuicac Çihuapilli, inic çenca huei tlamahuiçoltica omonexiti in
nican ichantzino Tepeyacac; inic àmo çenca in iuh monequia quihualmomachiltia,
quihualmocuitìtzinoa in imaçehualtzitzinhu_ in huel inpampa oncan omocaltìtzino
inic oncan quinmocaquililiz in innetoliniliz in inpatzmiquiliz, in inchoquiz, in
intlaìtlaniliz, auh quinmomaquiliz, quimocneliliz in itepalehuiliztzin" (Laso de
la Vega, *Hvei tlamahviçoltica*, fols. 15v-16r).

Bibliography

Andrews, J. Richard. *Directionals in Classical Nahuatl*. Texas Linguistic
    Forum 18 (1981): 1–16.
Becerra Tanco, Luis. Origen milagroso del santuario de Nuestra Señora
    de Guadalupe (1666). In *Testimonios históricos guadalupanos*. Ed.

Ernesto de la Torre Villar and Ramiro Navarro de Anda. Mexico City: Fondo de Cultura Económica, 1982, 309–33.

Beristáin de Sousa, José Mariano. *Biblioteca hispanoamericana septentrional.* 5 vols. Mexico City: Ediciones Fuente Cultural, 1883.

Burkhart, Louise. The Cult of the Virgin of Guadalupe in Mexico. In *South and Meso-American Native Spirituality: From the Cult of the Feathered Serpent to the Theology of Liberation.* Ed. Gary H. Gossen in collaboration with Miguel León-Portilla. Vol. 4 of *World Spirituality: An Encyclopedic History of the Religious Quest,* 198–227. New York: Crossroad Publishing Company, 1993.

Burrus, Ernest J., S.J. *The Oldest Copy of the Nican Mopohua.* CARA Studies on Popular Devotion, 4. Guadalupan Studies, 4. Washington, D.C.: N.p., 1981.

Cantares Mexicanos: Songs of the Aztecs. Translated from the Nahuatl with an introduction and commentary by John Bierhorst. Stanford, Calif.: Stanford University Press, 1985.

Christian, William. *Apparitions in Late Medieval and Renaissance Spain.* Princeton, N.J.: Princeton University Press, 1981.

Clavigero, Francisco Javier. Breve noticia sobre la prodigiosa y renombrada imagen de Nuestra Señora de Guadalupe (1782). In *Testimonios históricos guadalupanos.* Ed. Ernesto de la Torre Villar and Ramiro Navarro de Anda. Mexico City: Fondo de Cultura Económica, 1982, 578–96.

Conde, José Ignacio, and María Teresa Cervantes de Conde. Nuestra Señora de Guadalupe en el arte. In *Album conmemorativo del 450 aniversario de las apariciones de Nuestra Señora de Guadalupe.* Mexico City: Ediciones Buena Nueva, 1981, 124–26.

Florencia, Francisco de, S.J. *La estrella del norte de Mexico aparecida al rayar el dia de luz Evangelica en este Nuevo Mundo, en la cumbre del cerro de Tepeyacac, orilla del mar Tezcucano, à un Natural recien convertido; pintada tres dias despues milagrosamente en su tilma ò capa de lienzo delante del Obispo y de su familia, en su casa Obispal, para luz en la fé à los Indios; para rumbo cierto à los Españoles en la virtud, para serenidad de las tempestuosas inundancias de la Laguna. En la historia de la milagrosa imagen de Nuestra Señora de Guadalupe de Mexico Que es apareció en la manta de Juan Diego Compusola el Padre Francisco de Florencia de la Compañia de Jesus.* Mexico City: Viuda de Juan de Ribera, 1688.

———. *Historia de la provincia de la Compañia de Jesus de Nueva España.* 2d ed. Prologue by Francisco Gonzalez de Cossio. Mexico City: Editorial Academia Literaria, 1955.

García Icazbalceta, Joaquín. Carta acerca del origen de la imagen de Nuestra Señora de Guadalupe de México. In *Investigación histórica y documental sobre la aparición de la Virgen de Guadalupe de Mexico.* Mexico City: Ediciones Fuente Cultural, n.d., 21–70.

Garibay K., Angel María. *Historia de la literatura náhuatl.* 2 vols. Mexico City: Editorial Porrúa S.A., 1961.

Gutiérrez Dávila, Julián. *Memorias historicas de la Congregacion de el Oratorio de la Ciudad de Mexico . . . recojidas, y publicadas por el P. Julian Gutierrez Davila, Presbytero Preposito, que fue, de dicha Congregacion del Oratorio de Mexico.* Mexico City: En la Imprenta Real del Superior Govierno, y del Nuevo Rezado, de doña Maria de Rivera, 1736.

Lafaye, Jaques. *Quetzalcoatl and Guadalupe: The Formation of Mexican National Consciousness, 1531–1813.* Trans. Benjamin Keen. Chicago: University of Chicago Press, 1976. [Original French ed.: *Quetzalcóatl et Guadalupe: la formation de la conscience nationale au Mexique (1531–1813).* Paris: Editions Gallimard, 1974.]

León-Portilla, Ascensión H. de. *Tepuztlahcuilolli: Impresos en náhuatl, historia y bibliografía.* Vol. 1. Mexico City: Universidad Nacional Autónoma de México, 1988.

Lockhart, James. *The Nahuas after the Conquest: A Social and Cultural History of the Indians of Central Mexico, Sixteenth through Eighteenth Centuries.* Stanford, Calif.: Stanford University Press, 1992.

López Beltrán, Lauro. *La primera historia guadalupana impresa.* Obras guadalupanos de Lauro López Beltrán, 4. Mexico City: Editorial Tradición, 1991.

Maza, Francisco de la. *El guadalupanismo mexicano.* Mexico City: Fondo de Cultura Económica, 1981.

Medina, Baltasar de. *Chronica de la Santa Provincia de San Diego de Mexico, de Religiosos Descalços de N. S. P. S. Francisco en la Nueva-España. Vida de ilvstres, y venerables Varones, que la han edificado con excelentes virtudes. Escrivelas, y consagralas al glorioso San diego de alcalá Patron, y Tutelar de la Misma Provincia, F. Balthassar de Medina.* Mexico City: Por Juan de Ribera, Impressor, 1682.

Mendieta, Gerónimo de. *Historia eclesiástica indiana: obra escrita a fines del siglo XVI.* 3d facsimile ed. Mexico City: Editorial Porrua, S.A., 1971.

Ortiz Vaquero, Manuel. Notas sobre la pintura: guadalupana de 1606 de Baltazar de Echave Orio. *Imágenes Guadalupanas Cuatro Siglos* (Mexico City) (November 1987–March 1988): 29–31.

Peterson, Jeannette Favrot. The Virgin of Guadalupe: Symbol of Conquest or Liberation? *Art Journal* (Winter 1992): 39–47.

Pompa y Pompa, Antonio. *El Gran Acontecimiento Guadalupano.* Colección México Heroîco, no. 68. Mexico City: Editorial Jus, 1967.

Prem, Hanns J. Disease Outbreaks in Central Mexico during the Sixteenth Century. In *"Secret Judgments of God": Old World Disease in Colonial Spanish America.* Ed. Noble David Cook and W. George Lovell. Norman and London: University of Oklahoma Press, 1992, 20–48.

Robles, Antonio de. *Diario de sucesos notables (1665–1703).* Ed. and prologue by Antonio Castro Leal. 2 vols. Mexico City: Editorial Porrua, 1964.

Sada Lambretón, Ana Maria. *Las informaciones jurísdicas de 1666 y el beato indio Juan Diego.* Mexico City: N.p., 1991.

Sánchez, Miguel. *Imagen de la Virgen Maria, Madre de Dios de Guadalupe. Milagosamente aparecida en la ciudad de Mexico. Celebrada en su historia, con la profecia del capitulo doce del Apocalipsis.* Mexico City: Imprenta de la Viuda de Bernardo Calderón, 1648.

————. *El David seraphico, de la solemne fiesta, que la Real universidad de Mexico celebro a la Immacvlada Concepcion de la Virgen Maria, Madre de Dios: en que ratifico el juramento de Sv defensa: a deuocion del Bachiller Miguel Sanchez presbytero.* Mexico City: Biuda de B. Calderon, 1653.

Siller a., Clodomiro I. *La evangelización guadalupana: Cuadernos de Estudios Indígenas n. l.* Mexico City: CENAMI, December 1984.

Velázquez, Primo Feliciano. *La aparición de Santa María de Guadalupe.* Facsimile reproduction of the 1st ed. of 1931. Introduction and bibliography by J. Jesús Jiménez López. Mexico City: Editorial Jus, 1981.

Wood, Stephanie. Christian Images in Nahua Testaments. *Americas* 47, no. 3 (January 1991): 259–93.

Zambrano, Francisco, S.J., and José Gutiérrez Casillas, S.J. *Diccionario Bio-Bibliográfico de la Compañía de Jesús en México.* 16 vols. Mexico City: Editorial Jus, S.A., 1961–1977.

Suggested Readings

There is an extensive bibliography on the history of the Catholic Church in Hispanic America. Most of the books and articles are in Spanish, and many date from before 1800 and thus on several accounts are beyond the reach of interested readers. As a result, this essay will focus largely on those books written in English in recent years.

The history of the Church in Hispanic America begins with its development in early modern Spain. While the Spanish have written extensively about local churches and religious orders, there is little easily available in English. A good place to start is with William A. Christian, *Local Religion in Sixteenth-Century Spain* (Princeton, NJ, 1981). Thereafter one becomes involved in the religious dimensions of the early years of discovery. The best overview of the period, in terms of the theological implications, is Luis N. Rivera, *A Violent Evangelism: The Political and Religious Conquest of the Americas* (Louisville, KY, 1992). His work, which generally praises the mission of Fr. Bartolomé de las Casas, also includes important insights into imperial policy. The ground-breaking research on Las Casas has come from the pen of Lewis Hanke; those interested in the controversy generated by the Dominican in his day should consult Hanke's *The Spanish Struggle for Justice in the Conquest of America* (Philadelphia, 1949); *The First Social Experiments in America: A Study in the Development of Spanish Indian Policy in the Sixteenth Century* (Cambridge, MA, 1935); and *Aristotle and the American Indians: A Study of Race Prejudice in the Modern World* (Chicago, 1959). There are two scholars currently working on reappraising the life and career of Las Casas: Helen Rand Parish and Lawrence Clayton. Parish has already produced, in collaboration with Harold E. Weidman, *Las Casas en México: Historia y obra desconocidas* (Mexico City, 1992).

The evangelization of Mexico has received more scholarly attention than any other area. The pioneer work in the field was Robert Ricard, *La "conquête spirituelle" du Mexique: Essai sur l'apostolat et les méthodes missionaires des ordres mendicants en Nouvelle Espagne de 1523–24 à 1572* (Paris, 1933), edited and translated into English by Lesley B. Simpson and published as *The Spiritual Conquest of Mexico* (Berkeley, CA, 1966). The role of the Franciscans in the missionary activity, with their peculiar millenarian perspective, is studied by John L. Phelan, *The Millenial Kingdom of the Franciscans in the New World* (Berkeley, CA, 1970). The first

Bishop of Mexico and his development of the episcopal Inquisition are detailed in Richard E. Greenleaf, *Zumárraga and the Mexican Inquisition, 1536– 1543* (Washington, DC, 1961). Further study of the missionary activity of the Franciscans, and especially their interest in ethnography, comes from the pen of Georges Baudot, *Utopia and History in Mexico: The First Chronicles of Mexican Civilization, 1520–1569* (Boulder, CO, 1995). In my books, I have studied the organization of the financial life of the secular clergy, *Origins of Church Wealth in Mexico: Ecclesiastical Revenues and Church Finances, 1523–1600* (Albuquerque, NM, 1985), and the structure and social composition of the secular clergy, *Church and Clergy in Sixteenth-Century Mexico* (Albuquerque, NM, 1987).

Recent research has focused on the means whereby the missionaries sought to explain Christian ideas in an alien language. The most important thus far has been Louise M. Burkhart, *The Slippery Earth: Nahua-Christian Moral Dialogue in Sixteenth-Century Mexico* (Tucson, AZ, 1989). Further elaborating on the theme of two cultures not clearly understanding one another, Jill L. M. Furst has written on Nahua notions of the soul and how they differ from the Christian view in *The Natural History of the Soul in Ancient Mexico* (New Haven, CT, 1995), while Fernando Cervantes has analyzed Europeans' perceptions of diabolism in pre-Columbian Mexican society in *The Devil in the New World: The Impact of Diabolism in New Spain* (New Haven, CT, 1994). Similarly, scholars have begun to question the dramatic accounts of mass conversions of central Mexican natives. In *The Book of Tributes: Early Sixteenth-Century Nahuatl Censuses from Morelos* (Los Angeles, 1993), Sarah Cline has gone a long way in examining the reality of the early Mexican Church. By far the finest general works on Mexican colonial society and institutions are Charles Gibson, *Aztecs under Spanish Rule* (Stanford, CA, 1964), and James Lockhart, *The Nahuas after the Conquest* (Stanford, CA, 1992). While Gibson's work was extremely important, his research extensive, and his interpretations formed an entire generation, Lockhart studied the Nahua-Spanish relationship using native language texts, which Gibson did not, thus leading Lockhart to a whole different set of conclusions. One of the most important recent studies on cultural exchange in the colonial period is Serge Gruzinski, *The Conquest of Mexico: The Incorporation of Indian Societies into the Western World, 16th-18th Centuries* (Cambridge, UK, 1993).

The sacrament of marriage has received significant analysis. It was clearly important in distinguishing pre-Columbian customs from Spanish traditions; moreover, in marriage, modern scholars can most easily see gender roles outlined. A useful collection of essays on the subject has been compiled by Asunción Lavrin, *Sexuality and Marriage in Colonial Latin America* (Lincoln, NE, 1989), followed by Patricia Seed's analysis of the changing role of the Church with regard to marriage choice during the colonial period, *To Love, Honor, and Obey in Colonial Mexico: Conflicts over Marriage Choice, 1574–1821* (Stanford, CA, 1988). Richard Boyer approaches the issue slightly differently, looking at cases of bigamy, tried before the court of the Inquisition, in *The Lives of the Bigamists: Marriage, Family, and Community in Colonial Mexico* (Albuquerque, NM, 1995). Related to these works, but taking on experiences of Franciscan friars in the northern colony of New Mexico, Ramón Gutiérrez wrote a controversial study on the impact of Christian morality in the pueblos culture, *When Jesus Came, the Corn Mothers Went Away: Marriage, Sexuality, and Power in New Mexico, 1500–1846* (Stanford, CA, 1991).

The Church in the late colonial period in Mexico has been examined by several scholars. One of the first modern studies was Nancy Farriss, *Crown and Clergy in Colonial Mexico, 1759–1821* (London, UK, 1968). More recently, William Taylor has completed a mammoth analysis of the role of the Church and clergy in the late colonial period in *Magistrates of the Sacred: Priests and Parishioners in Eighteenth Century Mexico* (Stanford, CA, 1996). Dealing with Guatemala, Adriaan van Oss has attempted to create a Church history from the parish level upward, *Catholic Colonialism: A Parish History of Guatemala, 1524–1821* (New York, 1986). Perhaps one of the best-known features of Mexican Catholicism is the veneration of the Virgin of Guadalupe, and Stafford Poole has produced a thorough study of the history and development of the cult of the Virgin in *Our Lady of Guadalupe: The Origins of a Mexican National Symbol, 1531–1797* (Tucson, AZ, 1995).

The Yucatan peninsula has been an area of great interest for scholars in recent years. Although it currently is part of Mexico, it had a far different historical development. The presence of the Maya civilization created unique features in the evangelization of the region. One of the first modern studies to take a close look at the missionary activities there was Inga Clendinnen, *Ambivalent Conquests: Maya and Spaniard in Yucatan, 1517–1570* (Cambridge, UK, 1987). Nancy Farriss, who had already studied the clergy of central Mexico on the eve of Independence, then turned her attention to the unique circumstances of Yucatan in *Maya Society under Colonial Rule: The Collective Enterprise of Survival* (Princeton, 1984). While based on extensive archival investigation, Farriss did not utilize the existing documentation in Maya. Recently, Matthew Restall has published an analysis of the Maya under Spanish domination, drawing on native language texts and making comparisons with similar situations in central Mexico and in the Mixteca, *The Maya World: Yucatec Culture and Society, 1550–1850* (Stanford, CA, 1997)

Scholars writing in English have not studied the Hispanic experience in South America as much as in Mexico. As a result there are far fewer works on the evangelization of Peru than for Mexico. One of the earliest modern works was that of Antonine Tibesar, which studied the development of the Franciscan Order, *Franciscan Beginnings in Colonial Peru* (Washington, DC, 1953). In recent years, scholars have focused on the implications of the partial acculturation of Andean native peoples as well as the efforts by Spanish authorities to annihilate all traces of the pre-Columbian religious beliefs. One of the essential works for understanding the imperfect evangelization is that of Sabine MacCormack, *Religion in the Andes: Vision and Imagination in Early Colonial Peru* (Princeton, 1991), a comparison of European beliefs and the Andean response to them. Pierre Duviols wrote on the "Extirpation," the effort on the part of the Spaniards in the seventeenth century to eradicate all traces of the pre-Columbian religion, *La lutte contre les autochtones dans le Pérou colonial: L'extirpation de l'idolâtrie entre 1532 et 1660* (Lima, 1971). This work has been followed recently by two studies in English that look at the same issue but carry it into the eighteenth century: Nicholas Griffiths, *The Cross and the Serpent: Religious Repression and Resurgence in Colonial Peru* (Norman, OK, 1996), and Kenneth Mills, *Idolatry and Its Enemies: Colonial Andean Religion and Extirpation, 1640–1750* (Princeton, 1997).

Three books deal in a more tangential way with the Christianization process in the Andes by looking at specific instances of anti-European uprisings and the outbreak of pre-Columbian cults. Steve J. Stern focuses on the *taki onqoy* uprisings in Huamanga in *Peru's Indian Peoples and the Challenge of Spanish Conquest: Huamanga to 1640* (Madison, WI, 1982). Karen Spaulding studies the village of Huarochiri, the site of some of the most famous efforts at extirpation, in *Huarochiri: An Andean Society under Inca and Spanish Rule* (Stanford, CA, 1984). Finally, Irene M. Silverblatt focuses on issues of gender in the wake of the Conquest and settlement of the Andean region by the Spaniards in *Moon, Sun, and Witches: Gender, Ideologies, and Class in Inca and Colonial Peru* (Princeton, 1987).

Much can be learned about the Church from studying the architecture of its buildings as well as its artistic legacy. Some of the books central to the study of art and architecture in the missionary period are available in English. One of the earliest, and still useful, is the two-volume work by George Kubler, *Mexican Architecture of the Sixteenth Century* (New Haven, CT, 1948). John McAndrew has produced a fascinating examination of the relationship between church architecture and the evangelization in Mexico in *The Open-Air Churches in Sixteenth-Century Mexico* (Cambridge, MA, 1965). While no similar work exists for Peru, there are two solid contributions to the topic. The older of the two, which encompasses more material both topically and chronologically, is Harold Wethey, *Colonial Architecture and Sculpture in Peru* (Cambridge, MA, 1949). More recently, Valerie Fraser has taken a more concise view of the first century of Spanish occupation in *The Architecture of*

Conquest: Building in the Viceroyalty of Peru, 1535–1635 (New York, 1990). And Pal Keleman has analyzed the development of the baroque style in Latin America in his two-volume *Baroque and Rococo in Latin America* (New York, 1951). The baroque became extremely popular in Latin America and is closely associated with the unique nature of Latin American Catholicism.

Bibliography

Baudot, Georges. *Utopia and History in Mexico: The First Chronicles of Mexican Civilization, 1520–1569*. Boulder: University of Colorado Press, 1995.

Boyer, Richard. *The Lives of the Bigamists: Marriage, Family, and Community in Colonial Mexico*. Albuquerque: University of New Mexico Press, 1995.

Burkhart, Louise M. *The Slippery Earth: Nahua-Christian Moral Dialogue in Sixteenth-Century Mexico*. Tucson: University of Arizona Press, 1989.

Cervantes, Fernando. *The Devil in the New World: The Impact of Diabolism in New Spain*. New Haven, CT: Yale University Press, 1994.

Clendinnen, Inga. *Ambivalent Conquests: Maya and Spaniard in Yucatan, 1517–1570*. Cambridge, UK: Cambridge University Press, 1987.

Cline, S. L. , ed. and trans. *The Book of Tributes: Early Sixteenth-Century Nahuatl Censuses from Morelos*. Los Angeles: UCLA Latin American Center, 1993.

Farriss, Nancy M. *Crown and Clergy in Colonial Mexico, 1759–1821*. London: Oxford University Press, 1968.

———. *Maya Society under Colonial Rule: The Collective Enterprise of Survival*. Princeton, NJ: Princeton University Press, 1984.

Fraser, Valerie. *The Architecture of Conquest: Building in the Viceroyalty of Peru, 1535–1635*. New York: Cambridge University Press, 1990.

Furst, Jill Leslie McKeever. *The Natural History of the Soul in Ancient Mexico*. New Haven, CT: Yale University Press, 1995.

Gibson, Charles. *Aztecs under Spanish Rule*. Stanford, CA: Stanford University Press, 1964.

Greenleaf, Richard E. *Zumárraga and the Mexican Inquisition, 1536–1543*. Washington, DC: Academy of American Franciscan History, 1961.

Griffiths, Nicholas. *The Cross and the Serpent: Religious Repression and Resurgence in Colonial Peru*. Norman: University of Oklahoma Press, 1996.

Gruzinski, Serge. *The Conquest of Mexico: The Incorporation of Indian Societies into the Western World, 16th–18th Centuries*. Cambridge, UK: Polity Press, 1993.

Gutiérrez, Ramón A. *When Jesus Came, the Corn Mothers Went Away: Marriage, Sexuality, and Power in New Mexico, 1500–1846*. Stanford, CA: Stanford University Press, 1991.

Hanke, Lewis. *The Spanish Struggle for Justice in the Conquest of America*. Philadelphia: University of Pennsylvania Press, 1949.

.ubler, George. *Mexican Architecture of the Sixteenth Century*. 2 vols. New Haven, CT: Yale University Press, 1948.

Lavrin, Asunción, ed. *Sexuality and Marriage in Colonial Latin America*. Lincoln: University of Nebraska Press, 1989.

Lockhart, James. *The Nahuas after the Conquest*. Stanford, CA: Stanford University Press, 1992.

MacCormack, Sabine. *Religion in the Andes: Vision and Imagination in Early Colonial Peru*. Princeton, NJ: Princeton University Press, 1991.

Mathes, W. Michael. *Santa Cruz de Tlatelolco: La primera biblioteca académica de las Américas*. México: Secretaría de Relaciones Exteriores, 1982.

McAndrew, John. *The Open-Air Churches in Sixteenth-Century Mexico*. Cambridge, MA: Harvard University Press, 1965.

Mills, Kenneth. *Idolatry and Its Enemies: Colonial Andean Religion and Extirpation, 1640–1750*. Princeton, NJ: Princeton University Press, 1997.

Pagden, Anthony. *Spanish Imperialism and the Political Imagination*. New Haven, CT: Yale University Press, 1990.

Phelan, John L. *The Millenial Kingdom of the Franciscans in the New World*. Berkeley: University of California Press, 1970.

Poole, Stafford. *Our Lady of Guadalupe: The Origins of a Mexican National Symbol, 1531–1797*. Tucson: University of Arizona Press, 1995.

Restall, Matthew. *The Maya World: Yucatec Culture and Society, 1550–1850*. Stanford, CA: Stanford University Press, 1997.

Ricard, Robert. *The Spiritual Conquest of Mexico*. Translated by Lesley B. Simpson. Berkeley: University of California Press, 1966.

Rivera, Luis N. *A Violent Evangelism: The Political and Religious Conquest of the Americas*. Louisville, KY: Westminster/John Knox Press, 1992.

Ruiz de Alarcón, Hernando. *Treatise on the Heathen Superstitions*. Translated and edited by J. Richard Andrews and Ross Hassig. Norman: University of Oklahoma Press, 1984.

Schwaller, John F. *Origins of Church Wealth in Mexico: Ecclesiastical Revenues and Church Finances, 1523–1600*. Albuquerque: University of New Mexico Press, 1985.

———. *Church and Clergy in Sixteenth-Century Mexico*. Albuquerque: University of New Mexico Press, 1987.

Seed, Patricia. *To Love, Honor, and Obey in Colonial Mexico: Conflicts over Marriage Choice, 1574–1821*. Stanford, CA: Stanford University Press, 1988.

Shiels, W. Eugene. *King and Church: The Rise and Fall of the Patronato Real*. Chicago: Loyola University Press, 1961.

Taylor, William B. *Magistrates of the Sacred: Priests and Parishioners in Eighteenth Century Mexico*. Stanford, CA: Stanford University Press, 1996.

Tibesar, Antonine. *Franciscan Beginnings in Colonial Peru*. Washington, DC: Academy of American Franciscan History, 1953.

van Oss, Adriaan C. *Catholic Colonialism: A Parish History of Guatemala, 1524–1821*. New York: Cambridge University Press, 1986.